Machete Woman

Judy Lemon

Machete Woman

My Life Changing Journey From Aspiring Rock
Star to Shaman's Apprentice

1. Shamanism—Peru—Maynas Region. 2. Healing—Peru-Maynas Region. 3. Ayahuasca ceremony—Peru—Maynas Region. 4. Social life and customs—Peru—Maynas Region.

ISBN-13: 979-8-218-36564-6 (paperback)

Cover design by Milan Jovanovich

Photos courtesy of the author

Dedicated to Olaff Ribeyro Shult

28 January 1981 – 12 January 2015

CONTENTS

FOREWORD

I met Judy Lemon some years ago and we immediately struck up a friendship that has continued to this day. I found her to be quite engaging with a subtle but powerful presence. As we got to know each other, she shared some of the fascinating stories of the adventures she had while living in the heart of the South American jungles, including apprenticeships with three different shamans as well as her participation in the shamanic ceremonies that employed the traditional sacred plant medicine ayahuasca. Along with other friends I urged her to put together a book about her experiences in the jungle, and thus, *Machete Woman* was born.

Prior to these experiences in the jungle, she had moved to London with the dream of becoming a rock star and followed that path for a number of years. Though she has never actually given up on that quest, Life took her in a different direction when she walked into a magic shop in London.

Little did she know at the time, this would be the start of what would become an entirely different journey unlike anything you've heard before. Like Alice following the white rabbit into Wonderland, it would take her down the rabbit hole into a world to discover a different type of magic.

While at the pub one evening after class, one of her classmates mentioned he'd gone to the jungle to do ayahuasca. The discussion that ensued piqued her interest about this odd sounding substance. There, the seed was planted for what was to come, yet the voice of her Higher Self told her not to worry about it for now, that it would all make sense later.

It wasn't until she moved back to the States for a few years that she got the nudge to go to the jungle for the first time to participate in a retreat. It was then that she vigorously researched and devoured everything she could on the topic. At the initial retreat she met her first teacher who asked her to become his apprentice. Since then, she has made many visits to the jungle, during which she has apprenticed with three different master shamans. She has lived for months at a time under conditions that most of us would struggle with, yet with her steadfast determination and her machete at her side, she continued her journey for over twenty years and continues to do so today.

When you read this book, be prepared because you will be inspired, entertained, and deeply moved by the courage, clarity, and determination it took for her to follow this path into what was completely unknown territory. It will encourage you to follow your soul's path with even greater conviction and be willing to view life as one grand adventure.

Now as a Shamanic Practitioner and a certified Somatic Experiencing© practitioner she offers private healing and spiritual development sessions.

Dr. Steven Farmer

Psychotherapist, Shamanic Practitioner, and best-selling author

INTRODUCTION

This is the true story of an intrepid woman who likes to roam through the Amazon jungles of Peru and whack things with a machete: me. Over the years, I've regaled people with my stories of using this simple one-sided blade to build shelters and fend off poisonous snakes, all the while trying to look cool while being completely out of my element. My listeners usually respond with an incredulous look, shaking their heads and muttering something about how I should write a book about it someday. Well, someday finally came, and I'm proud to introduce you to *Machete Woman – My Life-Changing Journey From Aspiring Rock Star To Shaman's Apprentice.*

To give you an idea of how far back my desire to be a rock star went, I began taking guitar lessons at the tender age of seven and formed my first band with my sister, who started out playing a set of metal trashcan drums before embarking on her own keyboard lessons, much to my parents' relief. We called ourselves The Psychedelic Screwdrivers, named after an old hand tool of my dad's that had several different colors of paint on its handle. It was an apt name for a band in the 1960s, and perhaps a very early premonition of what was to come for its guitarist. Dad made a stage for us in front of the garage, and we put on concerts for the neighbors with songs that we'd written ourselves.

As I entered my teens and became more proficient with the guitar, I'd spend hours copying the riffs of my guitar heroes from their recordings. I would also sing at the top of my lungs, creating quite a cacophony in the house. I'm sure my poor folks were relieved when I eventually joined professional bands that had their own practice studios. We gigged in clubs and wherever else we could find work, and even had a few of our original songs played on local radio stations. After losing my voice on a tour of crummy clubs in the southwest, I started taking singing lessons and realized that I was a much better singer than guitarist, so I moved over to being a lead singer and secondary guitarist. I was in my early twenties and began to dream of rock stardom. This dream took me from Southern California to London, England, where it shifted from recording studios to shamanism.

Machete Woman is not a story about just taking plant spirit medicines in a jungle lodge or retreat center, nor about the many scientific studies that look at its chemical components and how they act on the human body. There are already plenty of those out there to choose from. While these amazing teacher plants are not the main stars of the story, they do have important supporting roles in my training as a jungle shaman's apprentice.

At the start, my intent was not so much to write a story about an amazing spiritual journey, but to simply share my ridiculous adventures for the sake of entertainment and a few chuckles. While some of my tales may seem hard to believe, I can assure the reader that this is indeed a true account drawn from a sequential five-year period in my life. It was only many years later that I was able to look back and recognize the common threads that ran through my experiences. I'm very grateful that I was able to endure all of the hardships and still come out on the other end with my sense of humor intact.

Yet as I wrote, I found it difficult to completely separate the travails from the teachings. My entire life had to fall apart in a dramatic and very painful shamanic death in order for me to see how possible it is to transcend one's self-imposed limits and boundaries. Along the way, I began to share with others the teachings that I'd received and experienced myself. These teachings—both from fellow humans and helping spirits--have had an incredible impact on my life, so I've included them where they appear in context to my experiences.

In addition to the student-teacher interactions, I also wanted to share about the culture that my *ayahuasquera* path comes from. While one can now find medicine ceremonies all around the world these days, many of those have been taken out of context and have no reference to the rich traditions from which this amazing plant healer originates. There are magical beings and ancient beliefs that I feel add a great depth to the ceremonies. The medicine does not simply stand on its own in its jungle culture: there is an entire way of life around it. These are the things I want to share with those who read *Machete Woman*.

The road to personal transformation is not always easy to walk, but the important thing is to begin the journey. I started out as a bumbling aspirant who makes just about every mistake in the book, but by the end of this first phase of my training, I became transformed through sheer determination to succeed. I also had a lot of help from those both in body and in spirit, for whom I'm eternally grateful. It is my hope that after reading my tale, some of you may feel called to make the first step in your own transformation, whatever that may be for you.

Because this is a true story, I've changed the names of people and places where necessary in order to protect their privacy. I have also not included specifics about certain rituals or procedures because these things are sacred and only meant to be shared between a teacher and their student.

And since this is also *my* true story, written about my own real-life experiences, some of the traditions and practices others may experience will likely have some similarities and differences to my own. I don't proclaim to be an expert or to have all the answers. I just continue to put one foot in front of the other and keep walking forward no matter how difficult the path may be. There is no one true way to the Self.

So now, I invite you to walk along with me through the mud and mosquito swarms, whacking a few vines out of the way with our machetes as we make our way deeper into the intense heat and humidity of the mysterious labyrinth of the Amazon jungle.

Watch out for the snakes!

PROLOGUE

London, England

I walk down the old narrow street just off the main square of London's Covent Garden. It's a little before six o'clock on a cold winter evening in 1999, so the streets are crowded with people leaving work, walking quickly and trying to stay warm as they hurry to wherever it is they are headed.

My own destination is just up ahead to my left: a very atmospheric shop that offers all things magical and esoterical. On pushing open the heavy dark red door, a small bell tinkles--not one of those annoying electronic types that seem to be everywhere nowadays, but a real metal bell. I think it's fitting for a shop that deals in such otherworldly subjects. This place sells every manner of magical tools you might be looking for: wands, ceremonial items, Tarot cards, candles, incense; you name it. For me, it's like being in Harry Potter's world, and I almost expect to see the boy wizard and his friends perusing the magical tomes and trying out wands.

I greet the employee behind the counter, a sweet young man with close-cropped bleached blond hair and gold hoop earrings, then make my way towards the staircase that leads to the upper floors where classes are held after the shop closes for the evening at six. To get to the classroom, after passing the front counter, I must wind around cabinets and shelves and pass into the smaller room to the left, head for another counter along the far wall and then ease through the narrow, almost invisible doorway in the corner. The passage beyond this door leads upwards to a steep, rickety flight of stairs. As I climb, I have to reach out and put my hands on the walls in order to keep my balance. The air around me begins to thicken, and it feels like I can't be sure where I might end up.

If the ground floor seems like a doorway into another world, the upper floor is that other world. The space itself is unremarkable, with a few crystals placed here, a candle there, and perhaps a batik-print cloth hanging in a doorway. Despite the room's plain physical appearance, I can feel a tangible presence around me. Years of spiritual work and rituals have left their impressions, and I can feel variations in the energy even as I walk from corner to corner.

Tonight's event is part of a series of classes I'm taking on advanced ceremonial magic, sometimes called high magick, and for some reason it feels right that it's being held in this nondescript, dimly lit room.

If the room itself is unexceptional, the teacher most definitely is not. Liam is in is forties, rail thin, and towering above me at six foot six. His gaunt face is framed with shoulder length, iron grey hair. His eyes have a piercing gaze as they linger on you. Or maybe through you. His feet are shod in large, clompy, worn out black leather boots, and his clothes…well…those clothes! He seems to favor ensembles of matching trousers and tops flaunting the most outrageous designs and colors that he can find. His favorite outfit is a pair of black knit flared trousers with colorful designs from the knees down to where the fabric ends at mid-calf, making them into capris. I suspect the garment was made for someone much shorter, but Liam doesn't seem to mind. These odd trousers are combined with a long-sleeved black T-shirt with the same designs on the front and sleeves, all framing a huge eye painted on the shirt at mid-chest. I feel that all he needs is a long, swishing silk cape to finish off the look.

Despite his appearance, Liam is easy to talk to and doesn't try to exude that egotistical air of superiority that is often found within the ranks of magical practitioners. He certainly has quite a pedigree: Witch, ceremonial magician, clairvoyant, Tarot reader, and Egyptian magic expert. Although I've been interested in all things esoterical from a very early age, from the moment he starts to speak I realize how little I actually know, and I've become a sponge for his teachings.

I've made friends with several of the other students, and we like to go out after class, wandering the streets of Central London in search of a good pub where we can dissect the night's lessons and discuss everything that we've learned. Jim is a graphic designer in his late thirties; tall, solid, ruggedly handsome, and very sweet. He seems rather normal and grounded to me compared to some of the other students, and I enjoy talking to him. David, another of my pub pals, is fascinated by the large medicine bag that Jim wears under his shirt and asks him about as we wait for our drinks during one of these excursions. The talk eventually turns to Jim's travels in the Peruvian Amazon with a man named Harold.

Harold is part of a local group that teaches courses in shamanism. He also leads trips to Peru to experience ayahuasca rituals with shamans in the jungle lodge he owns with a partner. I have no idea what a shaman is, and I'd never heard of this aya thing, but something is happening to me as Jim tells us about his fantastic experiences. I feel an energetic twist inside my gut and wonder what is going on.

"Don't worry about this right now—it's not time. We're just planting the seeds, and one day this will all make sense."

I hear this very clearly from within. It is the voice of my divine higher self, the one who came through when I learned to meditate many years before. It is a voice I've learned to trust very well as it guides me through my life. I have no idea that one word--ayahuasca--would have such a profound effect on my life in the years to come. But I do know without any doubt that one day I, too, will go to Peru to encounter the magic of the jungle.

PART ONE

The Beginning

CHAPTER 1

Out of the Frying Pan

"Tienes que sufrir, Judita."
You must suffer, Judita.

Argh! How many times have I heard this from my spiritual teachers? Okay, guys, I'm suffering! It's insanely hot, one hundred per cent humidity, and my entire body is covered in the itchiest bug bites I have ever experienced. My skin is on fire, and I'm sure that some of them are dancing the tango under my skin. I feel like I'm the main course in a gourmet restaurant for hundreds of jungle bugs, while I'm slowly starving to death with this infernal plant diet. I thought my life's destiny was to be a famous rock star, traveling the world in comfort and style. This is not what I had in mind! How did I get here? What the hell happened?

Okay, let's back up a bit so I can explain. What happened was that my dream of becoming a famous musician in London had turned into a nightmare before the whole house of cards came tumbling down traumatically in the space of about one year when I found out that my trusted husband had been cheating on me and threw me to the curb-- that's what happened! I'd worked so hard to create my life there, and after nearly twenty years it had all came to a horrible, jagged end.

I had always been enamored with two aspects of the British Isles: its myths and legends and its rock music. I swooned over the adventures of King Arthur and his Knights of the Round Table dashing about on their noble quests. When I was about fifteen, I found an older version of Sir Thomas Malory's *Le Morte D'Arthur* in the local library and traveled back through the mists of time. I believe that particular version of the book was written in Middle English, which only added to the tale's mystique for me. I went back to check it out it again years later, only to find that it had been replaced with a more modern version. I do remember it was a bit challenging to read as I had to keep looking up all the words I didn't recognize. Guinevere was wroth? What did that mean?

And then there was the music! Beatles or Stones? Led Zeppelin or the Who? Yes or Emerson, Lake, and Palmer? Their musicianship was incredible to my adolescent brain. I not only wanted to listen to them; I wanted to be them!

Growing up in Southern California with the rock of the 70s had a profound influence on me, so I followed my heroes into the world of gigging and recording as a singer and guitarist with various bands. In my early twenties, I started harboring the crazy idea of actually moving to England to see if closer proximity to the monsters of rock would rub off on me, so I started plotting to make this happen.

In the early 80s, I was working in the export department of a now defunct electronics company. It was such a fun company to work for in those days; the likes of which are long gone. I'd go to work by day and gig with my bands at night, coming in the next morning with wildly colored hair in the days long before it was trendy.

Working in the export department had the added advantage of giving me access to company representatives from all over the world. For someone who was wondering how to get a one-way ticket to the country of her dreams, I was particularly interested in the reps from our associate companies in the U.K. When we'd take them out to lunch, I would tell them how much I wanted to visit England, and they would tell me I had a place to stay if I ever made this happen.

I also became a member of various pen pal clubs, choosing potential contacts in a variety of cities that I thought might be interesting to visit. Remember, these were the days before the internet and social media, so writing letters was pretty much the only way to communicate with people from all over the world.

I continued to dream until one day in 1983, one of my pen pals invited me to spend Christmas with him and his family. Suddenly, all the wishing and hoping took on a solid form. I said yes, applied for my first passport, and contacted my other pen pals and work associates to see who might also be willing to put me up during my visit.

To make the countdown more exciting I took a stack of eight-by-ten sheets of paper, and on each one I wrote a number that corresponded to how many days remained until I was on my way. I taped them together in a vertical sequence, with the numeral one at the top, and the number of days until departure at the bottom. I tacked this long, ridiculous string of papers to the ceiling of my apartment, and each morning when I woke up, I removed the bottom one, ever more excited that there was one day fewer to go until I boarded the plane for my first foray across the Atlantic.

That trip alone could fill many pages of another ridiculous story in itself, including such foolish adventures as lumbering through the green fields of Glastonbury in an oversized, heavy raincoat that my mother insisted I needed to bring, all the while trying to avoid the killer sheep that I was sure were going to turn from their grazing and come charging after me.

As soon as I got home, I started planning my next visit. Just seven months later found me back in England once more, now looking seriously at how I might make this a more permanent situation. One of my pen pals, a Welshman who wrote enthusiastically about his "fifty pence record collection," told me that if I ever wanted to come back and try my luck with the British music scene, I could stay with him to get started. Within a year, I was back in the Isles, this time on a one-way ticket.

It was not an auspicious start to my future in the British music business. Not having made an international trip as an adult before, I was rather naïve about how to present myself when going through Customs and Immigration with a lot of stuff. I was on my own, yet I had two extra-large suitcases, two smaller bags, and various other items with me. As I was passing through the inspection hall where greying fold-up tables lined the walls, an officer called me over to ask about the extraordinary amount of luggage that I was pushing in front of me on the cart. I guess I seemed like a rather suspicious character to them, so they opened up my bags. There, nestled among all the clothes, were my music business essentials: things like microphones, demo tapes, and promo photos. What innocent tourist carries things like these? There were also questions about my one-way ticket, so I waffled on about how I was going to be travelling around and visiting other countries, making up my trip as I went along.

To make matters even worse, there was an old, forgotten roach clip that one of the officers discovered buried in the bowels of the extremely large purse I was carrying. The clip was something that was a fairly common item to have on one's person in Southern California in those days; so common that it was easy to forget to remove it from one's baggage when packing for a trip across international borders. The officer pounced on it and whisked it away to a lab for immediate testing to see if it contained any incriminating evidence. It did. Although it hadn't been used in many months, there was enough of "something" that still remained in its jaws to register a positive in their tests. Suddenly, all hell broke loose as more officers were called over to help process the now suspected drug smuggler. I was led into a small room lit with a stark fluorescent light and strip searched to see if I was indeed carrying anything illegal that might be stuffed into some body crevice.

I think they were rather disappointed that all they found when I took off my pants was my money belt and nothing more. Even though I was obviously a rather suspicious traveler, they eventually decided to let me go and enter the country as if nothing had ever happened. My future roommate was waiting for me, letting me know that he had almost given up and gone home. I told him all that happened and we both decided to head down to the pub for a couple of pints to celebrate my successful arrival. It wasn't exactly the welcome I'd expected for the first day of a trip I'd been dreaming about for years!

I stayed with him for several months in the western town of Reading before moving east to join a jazz rock group in Slough. For once, I had to find my own lodging, and I discovered the great British bedsit, which is usually a small room in a converted building with shared bathrooms and kitchens. I'm sure my tiny room had been a storage closet before the owner had divided the large house into separate living quarters. I had a child's twin bed, small dresser, an old, clunky wooden wardrobe, and a sink; the latter of which I found very helpful as it seemed like there was always someone else in the one bathroom we all shared.

I wasn't the only dodgy character in the house. Several of the double rooms were let to young couples who always seemed to be fighting and trying to kill each other, usually after a night out with too many pints at the nearby Pale Horse pub. Patrick dumped a pan of mashed potatoes over Julie's head, and she emerged staggering into the hall, potatoes and butter dripping down one side of her face onto the dull carpet. Robbie, an angry Liverpudlian, smashed a mirror over Joanne's head, leaving her lying on the floor between shards of broken glass. The noise from these fights inevitably would carry out into the rest of the house and the rest of us would arrive at their doors in time to witness the carnage.

The band I'd joined lived in a house a short distance away, so I'd hang out there to stay away from all this nonsense. It was your typical house full of young male musicians who were geniuses at wiring a studio but couldn't figure out how to use a broom or a dish brush.

The band members were all very talented, but like so many I'd worked with in California, they didn't seem to be able to function without copious amounts of marijuana and beer. For me, the problem with the constant need to be high was that no one had any ambition. While I would occasionally join in, I eventually became frustrated with the lack of progress. We had a great set list and people loved us, but when it came to the business side it literally went up in smoke. I decided it was time to make the big move uptown to London.

It was right around this time that I met my future husband-to-be. Anthony was with his friends, and I thought he was rather cute, so I had a drink sent over to him. He came over to say thank you, and we ended up getting married in October of 1986. We had many good years together, traveling through Europe and other places, eating in the finest restaurants run by London's celebrity chefs, and drinking expensive premier cru wine from Bordeaux.

In hindsight, I believe we had different goals for our shared future. I was never the stay-at-home wife and mother type, and I did talk to him about this before we even got engaged. He knew about my deep desire to be a rock star above all else, and he seemed supportive of it at the time.

For a good four years or so, I went to countless auditions, worked with some talented musicians, and also recorded on my own in my home studio, but nothing ever took hold. The scene in London during those years was based on what you looked like rather than what you sounded like. This meant that no matter how talented you were, if you didn't have a very particular look, you didn't get work. Trying to break into the entertainment business can be frustrating, and there were times that I needed to walk away from it all to refresh my creativity and energy.

During these breaks, I gave the more mundane life a try, and this usually served me well as inspiration to get back to the mixing desk. One long stint included a high-powered job with a multinational company, combined with studying for an engineering degree while working on my private pilot's license. Not surprisingly, this all led to a sense of overload and burnout. With our combined incomes, we were well off and had everything we could ever want, but the material side of life began to seem ever more hollow.

If I had to pin down the day that eventually changed the course of my life, it'd have to be the one in 1993 when I saw an ad for Transcendental Meditation in the local London newspaper. I felt called to attend the introductory presentation and was impressed enough to sign up to learn its meditation technique. As I faithfully engaged in the daily practices, it not only helped to reduce my stress levels but I also began to notice something else: an emerging voice that seemed to come from inside me. It was somewhat subtle and seemed to be wise and sensible. What was this voice? Who was speaking to me?

I asked my meditation teacher, but oddly, she didn't seem to know what I was talking about. Perhaps she thought I was a little freaked out and it was her way of trying to keep me calm and balanced, but I thought it was really cool!

What I do know was that the voice started to make me feel like I was on the right track with my life. The more I opened up, the more I began to realize the world was not just as it seems on the surface. I'd flirted with looking for fairies as a child, then casting spells as a rebellious teenager, so this view of the world didn't seem at all strange to me.

Six years later, an ad in that same *London Evening Standard* newspaper for a class on high ceremonial magic caught my eye, and apart from just sounding like an unusual thing to do, I signed up for the series and allowed myself to be drawn into the worlds beyond the physical. By this time, my marriage was unraveling and I needed something to cling onto, so the classes served as a distraction from my ever-deteriorating home life.

Feeling like an esoterical explorer, I followed the magic work down the rabbit hole to Wicca, then to secular witchcraft, and then finally to shamanism.

Liam, the magical genius I mentioned in the Prologue, and I had become good friends and would wander around Central London together. One day we were looking around the shops in London's Neal's Yard, an interesting little area not far from the magic store where he worked. Posted on the outside wall of one shop was a notice about an upcoming, week-long workshop at a camp in North Wales. I started to walk past it, but something forced me to stop and read it. The workshop was called "An Introduction to Shamanism," and was being put on by a well-respected group of shamanic teachers. I had not heard of them, but Liam had. He told me that if I was going to learn about shamanism, they were the ones to go to. I noticed the name for the contact information was Harold, and something again shifted inside me. I had forgotten about what Jim, my classmate who'd gone to the Amazon with Harold had said, but my subconscious had not. I didn't know how I was going to get there, but I knew I was going.

My week in that camp opened a door into the extraordinary, stunning realms that parallel our physical world. Of all the various spiritual paths I had walked and sampled, I knew this one was mine. I was home.

Throughout all of this, the rich life I'd built in London continued to painfully disintegrate. My long-time marriage crashed onto the rocks like a ship made of glass, when the man I trusted enough to marry ran off with another woman. As with me, he met her in a bar. Probably not a good sign, huh? We'd gone to Stockholm for the weekend to see a concert, and the second night there he decided to go hang out in the hotel bar instead of elsewhere with me. I knew there had been some niggles between us, but they didn't seem serious enough that an honest conversation or two couldn't resolve.

I think part of the problem had to do with alcohol. Anthony loved to drink, and many of our activities had to include pubs and bars, but we could never just nip in for a quick one and be on our way again. Now, I'm not averse to a drink myself when it's appropriate, but we could never leave until he'd had at least three pints. I tried various ways to identify with him: matching him drink for drink, total abstinence, one to his two, that kind of thing. But over the years I could see that rather than deal with a simmering, but solvable issue, he'd reach for the bottle and just check out. I couldn't help but wonder how a man who would tell me he loved me several times a day, every day, could suddenly change into such a completely different character. We had shared everything, but he pulled the rug out from under me and literally made my life hell. It was almost as if he wanted to get revenge for my announcing that I didn't think we should be married anymore once I'd felt that things had become irreparable. I'd felt us growing apart beyond where counseling or intervention may have helped, but I was not aware that he had been carrying on an affair with the girl from the bar.

The day that I discovered Anthony was cheating on me hit me like a thunderbolt through my heart. I'd dated a lot of rats before I'd met him, but I married him because he wasn't like all the others. I trusted him! It took many years for this shadow side to reveal itself, and when it did it really blindsided me. The revelation in itself is worthy of another story, combining intuition, spying and detective work, and a lot of womanly sneakiness in order to get to the truth. Let's just say I used some vodka to my advantage, and we'll leave that tale for another day.

I did learn one very deep lesson from all this that I will carry with me for the rest of my life, and it had to do with money. I had been laid off from my job at the multinational company several years prior and tried to get one related to my electronics degree. I was very good with computers and programming yet encountered the same problem over and over of needing on the job experience in order to get a job. No one wanted a novice.

London was also not the best city for electrical engineers, especially young female engineers. When I would get the occasional interview, I was asked questions like how old I was, when I was planning to have children and how many, when I would leave work, and things that were completely unrelated to designing circuits. Sometimes there was a job mentioned way up north or in the west of the country, but only one. What if we relocated and it didn't work out? Anthony had a good job in computers and it seemed risky to move away for a not very sure thing.

We did talk about moving to the States where jobs in our fields were more plentiful and paid well, but we did love London with its wonderful international culture.

I thought that perhaps it was time to renew my rock star campaign, and since Anthony made a good salary, he agreed that we did not need me to work. I would be free to work in my studio and produce music and see where it went, then we'd review things and decide what to do. It might sound like a fantasy come true to not have to work while you're pursuing your dreams, but it had a definite downside in that I became dependent on him for support. This may be fine when the relationship is going well, but when it isn't, being dependent is not a good place to be. It was this superior card that he played when he decided to concentrate on his girlfriend. Anyone who holds the purse strings also holds the power, and I vowed that I would never allow myself to be put in this position ever again. I chose to take back that power for myself.

In the meantime, I lost everything I'd spent years creating: my beautiful flat in the west of London, my music studio, my affluent material life, my security, my husband. Looking back now I can see why I had to be pulled from that life, but at the time it was very traumatic. Having nowhere else to go, I moved in with Liam for a year, mainly to avoid being alone in our flat after my husband left. We'd lived there for over ten years together, and it would have been too sad for me to remain there on my own after he'd moved out to live with his girlfriend in Sweden. Boy, did I jump out of the frying pan into the fire!

My life with the temperamental magical genius was hardly the refuge that I'd been seeking, but it gave me valuable experience with some of the basic shamanic principals such as not-doing, erasing personal history, petty tyrants, and most of all, being in the moment. *Now* is all that matters. I went from living an affluent, fairly materialistic lifestyle in a picturesque village in west London to an insecure life in a rough area in the southeastern part of the city where people fought outside my bedroom window and glass crashed in the night. Liam lived in a hideous council flat on a run-down estate, and it was the exact opposite of what I was used to. There were no curtains, no phone, no heating, no basic amenities, and certainly none of the luxuries I had been accustomed to. How had I sunk so low?

What it did have was the most fabulous collection of books on every mystical subject that I have ever seen in such a small space, including some rare and unusual volumes. Just about every area of magic from around the world was represented in his chaotic living room.

Being very cerebral, he paid no attention to such matters as cleaning and organization. It took me months to get that flat habitable before I could move in, and I had to continue to expend a lot of energy to keep it that way. As long as he had his chair and his little TV, with a table for a desk and enough space to work, keeping the flat and himself clean never seemed to enter his mind.

It got worse after I moved in with my much nicer television and video player, the latter of which he didn't have. What he did have was a huge collection of 1960s British science fiction videos that he hadn't been able to watch in years, so that infernal set was on all the time. He would grinningly excuse himself by telling me he hadn't been able to catch up with Doctor Who for a long time, so he just *had* to sit and watch one episode after the other, one video after the other. Over and over and over.

I didn't know it at the time, but my experience in that council flat paved the way for my future life in the jungle. To be sure, they are quite different settings, but it was more of the process that I went through, rather than the actual events themselves. I learned over time that feeling sorry for myself in a difficult situation is just a waste of personal power. If there are cockroaches in your council flat or rats next to your bed in the jungle hut, you just deal with them.

Despite all the character-building experiences and lessons, my life there was not really very pleasant. My eccentric flatmate, having grown up with a mother who doted on him and catered to his every whim, would become quite petulant if I had other things I wanted to do. One night, after telling him I preferred to read upstairs instead of watching yet another stupid TV show with him, he declared he was taking back his space and started hauling my stuff from the flat to the outside corridor where it wouldn't have remained for very long in that neighborhood. Of course, I had to drop what I was doing to engage in a tug of war with my things and his fragile ego, and then chase down one of my cats that had escaped.

My divorce continued to drag on interminably and eventually I hit the bottom of the barrel. I engaged in all sorts of destructive behaviors in order to anesthetize myself from the horrible reality that my life had become. It was now my turn to make friends with the spirit that lived in the bottle. As soon as I would wake up, I would start drinking whatever I had to hand—usually tequila-- then later on I would hit the local pub. I gained a lot of weight and looked like hell. I guess I was really hoping I would just pass out and never wake up, but I always did.

No matter what I was going through, my three precious cats would be right there with me, giving me the kind of unconditional love that only animals can seem to give. I made a vow to them that as long as they were with me, I would stay with them. They literally saved my life. In one of my interminable hazes, I had the classic shamanic vision of being taken to the underworld where I was torn apart by skeletons until I was one myself, then even my bones turned to dust and blew away in the wind. This was my first experience with shamanic death and rebirth.

I can see now that it was all part of a master plan to get me to where I needed to be, and I decided that as much as I had loved London it no longer loved me, and I needed to return to my roots in order to heal. In August of 2001, my three cats and I took a one-way flight from Gatwick back to California where my family still lived, and I began the long, painful process of putting myself back together again.

It took three more years for my divorce to become final. My ex had moved to Sweden, I was back in California, and the two sets of lawyers duked it out in London. It was probably the worst period in my life, yet

I believe the battle for survival instilled a resilience that I could draw from in the years to come, even though at that time I had no idea of what was just around the corner.

Then one day it was all over. I suddenly received a generous settlement and all the energetic ties were cut. I sat looking at my newly filled bank account in wonder, and then heard my inner voice again.

"And now *you* are going to the jungle!"

"What? Seriously? All right. Where do I sign up?"

I recalled the shamanic group I'd worked with in England and Wales and contacted them. By coincidence, a trip to their new jungle lodge was scheduled in three months, so I jumped in despite my not having a clue what a plant spirit medicine retreat was.

In case you're wondering, no, I don't just jump into things impulsively. My scientific training has led me to question everything and think things through logically. As anyone who has done any kind of magical work knows, trying to get away from the rigid walls of logic is probably one of the hardest battles you will ever fight. But to balance this, we have our inner voices, our gut instincts and intuition. Over time, my connection to this wise self strengthened, and I learned to live my life from following its advice. I trusted my inner vision because it had never led me wrong. So, I signed up for an experience I knew nothing about, once again jetting off to a country that I'd never been to before.

My life was about to change in a big way.

CHAPTER 2

Into the Fire

So there it was that I found myself on my very first morning in Lima not having a clue as to what was going on. Flights from the United States and other origins like Europe usually arrive in Lima very late at night, with several jumbo-sized jets disgorging their passengers at the same time. This results in the immigration hall being inundated with disoriented and irritated arrivals. It took over an hour to have my passport inspected and stamped, and then I had to smile sweetly while my bag was selected for manual inspection by a man who wanted to practice his English. Argh! Just get on with it!

By the time he zipped up my now slightly messed up bag, I was delirious and wondering how I was going to find my way to the hotel in the Miraflores area of Lima that Harold had reserved for our group. Emerging into the arrivals hall I found a taxi driver holding up a sign with my name on it slightly misspelled as Judi Limon. I wanted to shout, "O glory hallelujah!" but settled for a long exhale instead.

After the long, completely packed flight, I was hoping for at least the luxury of a double bed to stretch out in, but my room only offered two singles. The mattress was rock hard, reflecting the low cost of this budget hotel, but at least the sheets were clean.

On awakening, I assured my rumbling midsection that it would soon be getting a nice, solid breakfast after not having had anything filling for at least a half a day. The meal we'd had about an hour before landing was so typical of what is thrown together for those passengers seated behind business class. I was given a soft white bread roll of the cheapest kind. It looked like a shaped lump of refined flour and pretty much tasted the same way. A lone, nearly frozen pat of butter awaited the inevitable battle of the plastic knife, the frozen spread, and the super soft roll. I had to squeeze the foil-covered packet and hold it in my hand for a few minutes to warm it up a bit.

If the outside of the snack was unexciting, the inside was scary. There was one thin slice of some very processed meat-like substance. Was it turkey or ham, or some weird combination of both? A few red grapes accompanied this breakfast offering, and that had been it.

I was now ready for something more substantial. After a hot shower, I ventured downstairs into the dining room to take advantage of the included breakfast, foolishly assuming that this meant a small buffet with an assortment of both healthy and unhealthy food items. In fact, to my horror, the miserly meal turned out to be several slices of white toast, which might have been related to the airline's dull bread roll, a cold pat of butter wrapped up in foil that still had pieces of ice clinging to it, and an unfamiliar presentation of coffee.

The serving of this drink had me somewhat confused. I was presented with a jug of what the smiling waiter called *concentrado*, and another silver metal jug of hot water. He pointed first to the one containing the water, then to the one with the *concentrado*, which I assumed to just be regular coffee. Thinking the water must be for tea or another hot beverage, I poured myself a full cup of the *concentrado*. Taking the first tentative sip, I felt the top of my head begin to detach in preparation for lift off. The waiter, watching me in amusement from a nearby service station, approached me with a grin and indicated that I was supposed to pour some of the thick coffee concentrate into my cup first and then add hot water until I found a taste to my liking. So much for all of my Spanish classes!

As I nibbled on my under-toasted toast, desperately wishing for even a simple buffet with some kind of protein offering, I surreptitiously glanced around at the other diners, many of whom were like me, enjoying their simple morning repast in solitude. Were any of them on my tour?

In keeping with the feel of venturing into the unknown, there were no messages left for our group from Harold or Patrick, the other retreat organizer. I stood alone in the lobby after eating and felt like I was on some kind of mystery tour. Harold had provided us with a list of all the names of those who would be in the group, so I decided to head for the front desk to see if any of the others had arrived yet.

I found Barbara, a petite red head from Ireland, in a room around the corner from mine, and after introducing myself, we decided to go out and explore the city for a few hours. Her friend, Greta, would not be arriving until the evening, so she was glad to have the company. It was nice to be able to stretch our flight-weary legs as we wandered up and down the main streets, admiring all the beautiful leather goods and sexy clothes. We stopped for a bite to eat, sitting outside at a curbside café to enjoy the view. Unfortunately, this view also included an endless stream of beggars. The waiter told us that many of them, particularly the attractive children and teens, are actually hired to see if unsuspecting tourists would open their wallets, thus marking them for robbery targets shortly after they left the restaurant. I'd been advised to be watchful in Lima and was glad to see a strong police presence all around the city.

Harold finally made an appearance when we arrived back at the hotel, and he informed us that a bus would be coming the following day to take us back to the airport for our flight to Piura in the northwest part of the country, where our retreat experiences would officially begin. Barbara and I hung out together, talking about our different shamanic backgrounds and experiences. She worked with crystals, and I told her about some training I'd had with a local group where I felt like I was the only one who couldn't get the expected results.

"Do you know what it is that is preventing you from going into the shamanic realms?" she asked me.

"Yeah. Myself," I replied with a sigh.

Getting in one's own way has to be one of the major obstacles that students of any magical system will encounter. I felt like I was the master obstaculator.

The next morning, we began our journey to the site of our first adventure using various forms of transportation. One minibus collected us from the hotel and took us back to the Lima airport, where we boarded a cramped flight to Piura. Then another minibus transported us from that airport and delivered us to our final destination in the early evening. Tired and a bit cranky, we arrived at a somewhat loosely monikered "resort" near the small village of Colán on Peru's northwest coast.

To call the ramshackle assortment of old bungalows a resort was a bit ambitious. Each of us had our own little cabin that contained very unresortlike furnishings. The floor was unpolished hard wood scarred by nicks and stains of dubious origins. I had a basic double bed whose mattress had definitely seen better days. You know the kind I'm talking about where the middle of the mattress is sunken in like a crater, so no matter how you try to sleep around the firmer edges you always roll down into the center and end up twisting your back or neck. On top of this sat two flat pillows, which even if stacked together didn't provide enough cushioning for my head. A small chair and table completed the decor. The bathroom was also extremely basic. Cracked and chipped white tiles lined the walls and floor, and a single exposed bulb dangled overhead from a fraying ceiling cord. The only window was high up on the wall above the showerhead. It looked like it had been open for years judging from the condition of its filthy screen.

One nice feature that each bungalow could boast about was a front deck that faced the long, featureless beach. An outdoor restaurant with a bar was only a short walk away, and that was pretty much it. You even had to be careful if you ventured out in the water. We'd been told to look out for the many sting rays that buried themselves in the sand of the shallow waters. No worries! Just shuffle your feet a lot and that'll scare 'em off. You hope. While a tourist may have found the place severely lacking in amenities, it was an excellent location for our work.

We had come here to work with the spirit of the San Pedro cactus in two all-night ceremonies, so there seemed to be a lot of free time. The place was indeed peaceful, but I'd come for an adventure and found myself getting somewhat restless as the hours without any planned activities stretched out as long as the shoreline.

There was one sweet diversion, however: the animals who could loosely be called pets that called the property home. First, there was Aurora, the bright green parrot, who sat forlornly in a dirty cage made of rusty chain link fencing. I wondered if she was also bored because it looked like she had pecked the feathers off several areas of her body. On first meeting her, I saw that her water bowl was dry and there was no food in the cage. I poured some water out of my bottle into the bowl for the poor, parched parrot. There had been some corn on the cob, but it looked like the corn had been eaten off days ago. Aurora would peck at the empty cob and then look at me expectantly. I told her I understood about the food, and that I'd be back with something later.

For the rest of our stay, I would sneak parrot-pleasing food out of the restaurant at every meal. She seemed to greatly appreciate the attention and would make very funny noises at me. Her speaking abilities were still in the early stages, but every now and then she'd shout "Hola!" and go off into some really funny noises that sounded like laughing. I had the strong feeling that she enjoyed the company.

Shortly after I'd brought Aurora her first stolen snack, a hungry rooster got in on the handouts. He wandered freely around the property, but once he associated me with food, he'd somehow always manage to be present when I approached the parrot's cage with a little treat. He'd venture up close to me, so he, too, started getting some handouts.

Next up was a sweet little grey kitten, who at only nine months old was already visibly pregnant. She sat on the host's table but would happily come over for a belly rub, especially after receiving a tasty little tidbit from the meal leftovers. My scrap scavenging became rather complicated over the next few days as I had to grab things for the parrot, the rooster, the kitten, and the dogs.

Three black dogs completed the resort's menagerie. They were very obviously high-level nature spirits disguised as the cutest dogs on earth to fool those who stayed at this remote place. Like many street dogs allowed to run wild, it was hard to tell exactly what breed they were. There was a mother and her two puppies, the latter of which were about a year old at the most. In contrast to their jet-black fur, they all had these amazing, amber-colored eyes that seemed to glow. Just to watch them all together made me happy. They would charge into the surf, chase each other down the beach, and play hide and seek on the dunes. Sometimes they would sit with me until with an unspoken word, they'd all leap up together and go dashing away in delight.

We finally had a meeting with the entire group – the nine of us participants, plus Harold and Patrick, the two organizers. It was only a short meeting, lasting just a half hour before lunch to check in with everyone. There really hadn't been enough time for the questions and answers that would have facilitated greater understanding of what we were about to experience, especially for those like me who had no prior experience with this kind of work.

As a student progresses through a shamanic apprenticeship, they are eventually weaned away from depending on their teacher for information and discouraged from asking a lot of questions. While eventually they will get the answers from their own helping spirits, at the start they do need more interactions with their human teachers. We were all in that beginner's phase and would have benefitted from a more detailed discussion about the work instead of having some disconcerting surprises suddenly sprung on us.

The ceremonies were to take place on a wooden deck behind the restaurant near the kitchen area, so that is where our group assembled on the second evening to await don Juan and his two sons, Humberto, and Sergio. As I looked around at the small group, I felt like the only one who wasn't nervous.

The master and his apprentice sons seemed to melt into the scene. None of us had seen them coming; they were suddenly there among us. The boys, who were in their twenties, started setting up while their father went around to meet each of us. He had a palpable presence, and I had the strong feeling he was looking into me and seeing my story.

Maestro Juan and his older son, Humberto, who was the senior apprentice, were built like tanks. They were both about 5'8" but they had wide, strong bodies. You could almost draw a perfect square around their silhouettes. They were both wearing white *cushmas*--a long piece of fabric or woven cloth draped vertically from front to back and sewn at the sides to create openings for the head and arms--over jeans and dark shoes. This voluminous garment had the effect of making them look even wider. The younger son, Sergio, who acted more as an assistant, was more slightly built. He wore dark colored trousers and a black long-sleeved T-shirt, and the same black shoes. All of them had jet black hair and eyes and caramel-colored skin. And all three of them seemed very, *very* serious, never allowing a smile to crack even for a nanosecond. We were told this was due to constant exposure to the cold waters of the Las Huaringas lakes.

Juan's lineage was from this Las Huaringas region, where he began his shamanic apprenticeship at a very early age. The shamans of this area, *los curanderos*, believe the waters of the lakes have magical properties, so they must return frequently to recharge their own personal power.

Shamans around the world each have their own set of traditional tools. Maestro Juan's was the *mesa*, or table, His table was unlike anything I had ever seen before: it was more of a sacred altar. A large white cloth measuring about four by five feet was laid on the ground, and then an assortment of strange-looking objects was arranged just so on this cloth. There were swords and statues, stones, crucifixes, bottles of unfamiliar liquids, and sections of the cactus standing on end as if they were still growing in the earth. Each of these items was placed in its own designated spot. These *artes* were his power objects. We were told that the purpose of this sacred altar was to bring the power of the lakes to the ceremony and give everyone a place to focus. In that, I certainly felt it did its job even before the ceremony began. The carefully placed objects seemed to draw my attention in and invite me to examine them closer.

Since our group meeting earlier in the day had been so short, Harold had only given us the scantiest rundown of the various parts of the ceremony, and my own lack of experience led me to picture scenes that turned out quite differently in reality. No, the cactus brew itself doesn't make you sick; there's an optional something to clear out any hexing, and something else called *singado* that is supposed to be snorted up the nose. I and the rest of the unseasoned participants assumed that this third substance must be some kind of powder that we'd dip our fingers into and quickly inhale, one nostril at a time like snuff. Between my own expectations and these explanations I felt thoroughly confused about the different forms of the three plant medicines we were to work with that night.

We were arranged in a somewhat loosely formed U-shape around the mesa altar and given a particular seating order. As soon as we had settled into our assigned spaces, a large clay pot and serving gourd appeared. Although this was the optional offering, the *contrachisa*, we all decided to partake, so one at time, each of us approached Juan's *mesa* to receive our portion. Dipping the gourd into the mysterious liquid, he told us to drink it quickly. I found it to be warm, somewhat watery, and kind of herbal tasting, although I could not identify any particular plant or taste.

Once everyone had consumed their own gourdful, we all sat in silence for about fifteen minutes. The *contrachisa* was a potion made from the outer skins of the San Pedro cactus. Its purpose was to clear everyone present from the effects of any hexing or witchcraft that we may have been carrying by purging our bodies and spirits of toxins and hexes. As we sat in silence after imbibing, I awaited the vomiting that I was sure to come. In fact, I wanted it to come! I'd been through so much poison in my life that I just wanted to hurl it out all the way to the sea, but nothing happened.

Next, we were instructed to stand up. Sergio came around and presented each of us with a beautiful white conch shell that exactly fit into our right hands.

Humberto then came around with a vessel containing a thin, dark brown liquid, and he ladled about one ounce of this into the conch shells we held. We all exchanged side looks in puzzlement. What was this stuff? What were we supposed to do with this? Drink it? You could feel the low levels of alarm run from person to person.

This was the *singado*, a potion made with a base of *aguardiente*, an alcoholic drink made from sugarcane with roughly the strength of a brandy. To this white spirit was added a sweetener like honey, and the smushed up leaves of local tobacco. It looked really strong!

Patrick, the only one in the group besides me who spoke Spanish, translated the instructions to us from the maestro. Apparently, we were to actually snort this stuff up not one, but both nostrils! Each side had its own purpose. The left projective side, which was to be done first, is for extracting pain and bad influences, while the right receptive side was to call in the positive things that were desired. During each snort, the participant was to strongly visualize the desired results. See them, feel them!

Don Juan led the group in prayer. "With this tobacco I remove nightmares. With this tobacco, I receive luck in my home..." And so on.

Feet shifted nervously. Eyes darted from person to person. Why had no one told us that we'd be inhaling a strong liquid up our *noses*?

The maestro could see that we were uncertain about this part, so he told Humberto to demonstrate the technique for us. First, we'd have to tilt our heads back slightly. Then we'd hold the shell above our faces at an angle so that the pointed end would lead the juice into our upraised nostril, and as it started to dribble, we'd have to snort it fast! *Rapido!* It was important to do this with great energy so as to magnify the effectiveness of the *singado*. We not only had to suddenly tip up the end of the conch and inhale its contents, but we'd then have to dance and stomp around furiously on the wooden deck as the alcohol burned into the delicate nasal tissues and seared its way into our brains.

Since none of us had had any experience with this before, let's just say our techniques left a lot to be desired. Some had the brown liquid running all over their faces, then dripping off their chins as it splattered everywhere. The vile tasting infusion dripped down into the backs of throats or came out through our mouths. We were collectively stomping and spraying and gagging; and the energy was tremendous.

Next, Humberto had moved to the back railing of the deck, where he was holding one of the long, thin, silvery swords. As each of us finished our medicine portions, we were to run over to him, where he'd demonstrate a vigorous self-patting all over our bodies, followed by jumping jacks! Yes, jumping jacks! As we furiously patted and leapt,

Humberto would whack us with the flat side of the metal blade on our backs and sides to help knock out any negative energy. Imagine this scene: the moon is rising over the southwestern Pacific shoreline, the air is dampening, and all of us are flailing around as if we were possessed by some crazy demon, all while that magical sword flashed and sliced among us.

Once we had finished that round of aerobics and had expunged our collective negativity, we were called back for a second offering of the *singado*. Having already done it once, this round was a bit easier to ingest. But I now had three strong doses of liquids accumulating in my stomach, and none of them were settling peacefully. All the that running and leaping and being mercilessly whacked took its toll. I knew I had a lot to get rid of between the end of my marriage and reigniting the age-long battles with my mother, so when the urge to purge hit, it came with a violent reaction. Although the air around us was cold and damp, I felt hot and sweaty, dizzy, and just plain awful! I had to run back and forth to the railing, heaving the contents of my tortured stomach onto the sand. In between rounds of hurling, I would quickly scuttle to the primitive bathroom and purge from the other end. Sergio was dispatched to watch over me at the railing. Unlike his older brother, I found him to be a bit more sympathetic towards the total lack of grace I was displaying with their sacred medicines. I felt horrible!

Finally, it was time to imbibe the main teacher plant, known in Spanish as San Pedro and in Quechua, *huachuma*. I must've missed the announcement that this third offering was the main course, because I still wasn't sure what we were now drinking. The liquid was thick and bitter, and once again we were told to drink it quickly. Adding this heavy weight to my already convoluted guts resulted in another wave of nausea. I was not feeling any kind of psychedelic time warping, but I didn't know which end was up. I felt like a stupid klutz who was way out of her element, and the Neil Innes penned song immortalized by my comedic idols, Month Python, flowed into my head.

"How sweet to be an idiot…"

Eventually, my stomach settled and allowed me to sit in peace to observe the ceremony. I had no idea of how I was supposed to be feeling because I didn't feel anything at all. I looked around and watched as my companions sank into a lethargic, dream state, while I sat there wondering when we'd be taking this magical cactus thing.

Sometime later, it was time for the divination part. This was when each person would be called up to stand in front of the altar while the maestro read our stories through our energy. Juan started with our tour leader, whose main concern seemed to be trying to get close to some woman in Lima.

I was the third person to be called up and reeled over to the designated standing spot. I felt truly awful, still very nauseated, and ready to heave onto the rough wooden deck.

Each reading took about fifteen to twenty minutes. Patrick spoke Spanish fluently, so he had the unenviable job of acting as the group's interpreter. This can be enough of a challenge to do in ordinary reality, but now being heavily under the influence of the cactus, I felt kind of sorry that he couldn't enjoy his own journey. Although his command of the language was better than my own, I was glad to be able to communicate directly with the shaman, and thus give him a short break.

The maestro and his sons had also taken the three medicines, so they were also feeling the effects. Although I was sure that I was completely sober, everything else around me seemed to be happening in slow motion. I felt really irritated, wondering when we were going to be drinking the main potion that would give us beautiful visions. Why did it look like everyone was falling asleep?

I resonated with some of the reading. Yes, there sure had been long periods of suffering and disappointments in my life. He kept seeing *malas sombras*--dark shadows--around me, caused by someone half my lifetime ago that were still affecting me now in a negative way. Since by this time I had studied a lot of magic and energy work, it was hard to get my head around the idea of a spell with such an enduring influence.

I wasn't surprised, however, that he saw the discord between my mother and me. He also picked up on my previous professional musical background. When I was allowed to ask questions, I asked him what he saw for me as a career or life path. He said he'd discuss this with me at the next ceremony. While the two ceremonies were separated by a day of rest, they were to be considered as one event. This first one was for clearing out the negative influences, and the next one would be for bringing luck and goodness into the cleared spaces.

Once he finished the reading, he sprayed me with *agua florida* using his mouth. Agua florida is a totally synthetic, bottled cologne that has somehow become one of the main, go-to tools in Latin American shamanism, particularly for clearing away unclean energy. For this method, the healer drinks a small quantity of the perfume, and as he holds it in his mouth, he adds his own intent and prayers to the liquid. Using the lips to spray is a technique that definitely requires practice. Maestro Juan's extremely fine and measured mist certainly impressed me!

But they were not done with me yet! I was in for yet another surprise. After being sprayed, I was instructed to return to the back railing where Humberto was waiting to do a *limpia,* a more energetic clearing, on me. I was instructed to take off my shirt. To my dismay, that night I'd chosen to go braless, so there I was standing half naked in front of some strange man with long swords and bamboo rods. I also had to remove my trousers and shoes, so I stood before him in only my underwear and socks. By this time, the cold marine air had rolled in so it was pretty chilly without even one layer of clothing for warmth.

Since Humberto had also taken the medicines, he was able to see which area around my energy field needed to be pounded out. The swords and rods are not used as weapons, but rather to whip out the negativity. It's done with enough force that you feel the strength, but not so strong that it really hurts you. Although I am not really shy or self-conscious about my body, I must admit I felt very vulnerable standing there so exposed while this man I'd just met whacked me all over with the sword and rod while I hopped around in skivvies and socks. I began to question what I signed up for.

When Humberto was satisfied with his work, he also sprayed me with the cologne. I was then allowed to put my clothes back on and return to my seat.

The night was a long one as he passed from one participant to another. I went through all sorts of emotions as I sat there in what I believed to be a sober state, while the divinations seemed to carry on interminably. My ego was on overdrive telling me how hungry and tired I was, that this ceremony was kind of boring, and when were we going to get to drink the magical cactus elixir? I didn't expect it to be like this! I felt like the only one who didn't feel a thing, not realizing this is a common occurrence for those who work with plant spirit medicines, particularly in the early stages.

I leaned over and asked the guy next to me, Niall, what time it was.

"3:50," came his reply.

"Oh. I guess we're not going to get to drink the San Pedro now that it's so late, huh?"

Niall looked at me through his own dream state in confusion. "But we did already drink it! Don't you remember? That was the third one offered. We took it after the *singado*."

So now, realizing that I had already drunk the cup of visions that had given me no visions, I felt very let down. I was ready for the ceremony to end so I could go back to my lumpy bed and get some sleep.

Boy, did I have a lot to learn!

Scratch, scratch, scratch. Day by day, more bug bites appeared on my body. Hey, come on! We're at the beach with no vegetation around us! What the hell is causing this? No see 'ums, indeed! I'd brought Benadryl with me to use in the case of allergic reactions. While I wouldn't say I was especially sensitive, a number of weird things have set me off over the years, so when I travel, I am well equipped with whatever medications I feel I may need.

Quick aside here before I go any further. I want to point out that I had brought this antihistamine in ignorance. It's very important to note that many pharmaceutical medications cannot be safely combined with these strong teacher plants. If you're going to work with any consciousness-altering substances, make sure you know about any potentially troublesome reactions between those and any medications or supplements you are taking. This knowledge may not only prevent you from having a very undesirable medical emergency while in an altered state, but it could even save your life.

On top of this, let's politely say I was purging from the lower end of my alimentary canal. I think I was finally beginning to be grateful for all the non-scheduled downtime as my total being started to shed the many years of abuse and trauma I'd lived through.

We had another pre-lunch check in, and I asked Harold about the potency of spells. Having been immersed in the Harry Potteresque magical scene of the late 90s London pagan community, I understood full well what went into crafting spells. One of Liam's best friends, a very senior Witch named Elizabeth, who was quite an authority on Egyptian magic and general witchcraft, had talked to me one day about energetic intentions. She owned a country cottage in Norfolk, and it had recently been broken into with many items stolen. I asked her why she had not set up an energetic guardian to look over the place to deter intruders. My question kicked off an interesting conversation of various past guardians and their forms, but she said the one thing that was crucial in ongoing spells was to keep the intent alive. This is a lot harder than it sounds. Everyday life can get in the way, and the focus one sends out can get diluted over time unless it's accompanied by strong feelings that will keep it empowered.

Harold led us into an interesting discussion of linear versus shamanic time perception. Those who enter into the study and experience of shamanism will be familiar with what is called ordinary reality (OR) and non-ordinary reality (NOR). The former is how most of us perceive things in our daily lives. The sun rises in the morning and the events of the day occur in a logical progression. Our bodies age as time passes. The latter is usually considered to be the alternate dimensions that exist in parallel to the physical one. The shaman enters this world of NOR where everything is energy and all events exist at the same time.

So, in considering a years-long hex or spell, if you tried to imagine how someone could keep it up without wavering, this can seem like a herculean task. But if you looked at the issue from a shamanic standpoint where everything is happening all at once, then it would indeed be possible to keep up that energy through extended periods of time. I thought of a young man I'd lived with for a few months when I was in my early twenties. He was into ceremonial magic and I ultimately left him because he was manipulative and just not very nice. Was it he who had hexed me with the dark shadows? What a waste of energy!

It was now the night of our second ceremony with the sacred cactus. As my fellow travelers slowly filtered onto the wooden deck, I could feel that the group's energy was somehow different than that of the previous ceremony. I put this down to our now knowing the general order and what was expected of us. We resumed the same positions that we'd had the other night. Because this work was focused on bringing in good vibes after all the clearing we'd done, there was no need for the *contrachisa*. This time, however, we started off with the *huachuma*. The brew had been made a lot stronger, so there was no mistaking it for anything else.

There was, however, the *singado* to be dealt with again. I think that Harold and Patrick had conferred with the maestro and told him that we'd had a lot of trouble with the initial ingestion, so this time we were allowed to take it slowly. While this may have reduced the energetic component somewhat, if did greatly ensure that more of the aguardiente-based medicine ended up inside of us instead of all over our faces and clothing.

I watched in fascination as the maestro and his sons took their medicine with way more grace and ease than our group did. Don Juan consumed two very large cups of the cactus brew, then did his *singado* at the end of that round. Humberto, the very image of his father, was fierce. He stamped and grunted like a bull ready to charge, while his younger brother was quieter and more reserved.

As in the previous ceremony, we headed over to the back rail for more aerobics and sword whacking under the bright light of the full moon.

The second round of interviews began this time in reverse order, so I was third to the last. There was no purging this time, and I was happy to be able to sit peacefully feeling the effects of the magic. When my time came to approach the *mesa*, I was surprised that the questions seemed to be a repeat of the previous ceremony's. Once again, we looked at who may have hexed me, and while I did not have a close relationship with my mother, I just couldn't see her doing any kind of magic or spell work! At the time this just didn't make sense to me, but in all these ensuing years with my work as a trauma therapist, I now know that you don't have to wear robes and utter incantations over steaming potions in order to affect someone's energy in a negative way.

Then suddenly, he sat forward and peered at me across the multitude of sacred objects on his altar. This time, he saw me walking down a path covered in vegetation. One interpretation of this was that I was going to be able to flourish and take care of myself. He saw me having great adventures and asked what I'd planned to do with my life. I mentioned my great love for singing and performing, but that I'd not had any enduring success with it, so I wasn't sure I should keep trying to go down that road.

I'd had a growing sense that I was going to be led in another direction, to some kind of healing profession, but I didn't have any details or specifics. I told him I wanted to be able to see more clearly and to see the connection between all things, and he said he could help with this so my light could shine more brightly in the world.

He handed me a horn full of *singado*, and Humberto came to stand directly in front of me. We locked eyes and he did that full measure of *singado* for me, stamping and grunting, first in front of me, then behind me. I was frozen in awe at this extremely powerful sight and felt a great gratitude for this experience.

In fact, Humberto took the *singado* for several others that night, so by the end of the ceremony he had ingested an incredible amount of the burning liquid in order to help us achieve our goals.

After this, I was requested once again to remove my shirt so I stood there in front of the entire group with nothing to cover me from the waist up. Somehow, neither I nor anyone else seemed to care. Maestro Juan once again took the agua florida into his mouth and gave me quite a spraying.

Once we all had gone through our interviews, it was time for the floral baths. This consisted of stripping all the way off and having extremely cold, perfumed lake water poured over us. This was quite a challenge since it was late in the night and the cold, damp marine air provided a chill along with a breeze. Being new to these uncomfortable shamanic practices, I made more noise than the others who followed me, taking their baths far more graciously than I had. It was quite humbling knowing I had so much to learn.

More perfume followed, and we had to drink something that also contained the agua florida. I felt an allergic reaction coming on and all the bug bites that now completely covered my body began to flare and itch horribly. This seem to agitate my nervous system and I wasn't able to sit still afterwards. I had a lot of energy running through me, so I wasn't able to really sink down as deeply as the I would have liked. Once again, I began to feel that familiar sense of disappointment creeping in. We all get what we need on the night, and sometimes it is simply to recognize the battles we have with ourselves.

The following day was one of rest, but I couldn't relax. I took my frustration out on the beach crabs instead. Hundreds of the red, fist-sized crabs would come out of the water, and I found it hilarious to chase them around, watching them scuttle sideways, trying to get away from the two-legged lunatic who was harassing them.

We had our last pre-lunch meeting and Harold asked how I felt. I opened up and told the group how annoyed I was, particularly with my mother issues arising here so much. This is a tale that could take up an entire chapter on its own, so suffice it to say that my mom and I had battled each other from the day I was born. Although I understood my parents' desires that I get a good education and find a high-paying job with good benefits like they'd had, I just wasn't cut from the same pattern. My dad seemed happy to let me try out new things, but Mom was constantly criticizing and trying to control me so that I'd do what she felt I should be doing. I had been so relieved to leave those heavy weights behind when I'd left for the airport, only to find that I was still carrying them with me. Here I was thousands of miles away from home, yet I felt that they'd interfered with my ceremonies. Harold told me this was part of the healing process, then he told me something so profound that it has stayed with me clearly through all these years.

"You want beautiful visions and to be able to *see*, but you will not be able to get to that place while you're in a state of anger."

He explained how strong emotions act like clouds across a clear sky, blocking our vision. I think my mouth must've dropped open in shock because deep down, something inside of me felt this was the truth. It just seemed so darned simple. But still, argh!

I had arrived at this desolate, beachy place only a few days before, but it felt like I'd been turned inside out in that short time. I'd love to say that the intense spiritual work settled over me like a golden light, leaving me to float back to Lima in an enlightened bliss, but it felt like quite the opposite. I was really annoyed and pissed off, even though I had to admit I couldn't be completely sure what it was I was so burned up about.

I decided to drown my strong feelings in a pisco sour in the late afternoon before we met up for dinner. Before leaving my room, I once again set up the mosquito coil that I'd bought on a short outing to the nearby village a day or so earlier. Like the source of my irritation, I hadn't been able to see what had been attacking me. I eventually discovered an opening around the bathroom window where the seal had worn away, thus allowing the local mosquitos to have unfettered access to my sweet foreigner's blood. Before leaving for the ceremony the previous night, I had placed the lit mosquito coil on a piece of newspaper that I'd spread out on the wooden floor so as to catch the ash as it slowly burned away. I felt smug that at least I was doing something about the problem, and it seemed to do the job.

This time, since I'd seen that the main point of entry was in the bathroom, I put the paper and coil down on the tiled floor. Confident that there was nothing nearby that might come into contact with the burning spiral, I locked up my room and headed to the bar.

It's said that misery loves company, and it transpired that a couple of the other participants were also feeling raw. As we sipped our drinks, we shared our suffering and emotional purges. By the time we sat down to our final dinner together, we were feeling calmer and happier.

Harold informed us that we'd have one last meeting around 7 pm, so I returned to my bungalow to finish packing up. Walking the short distance in the sand, I saw a strange light flickering inside my room. Thinking I'd left the light on, I opened the door to find lots of small black things flying around. "Hah! Gotcha little bastards!" I said to what I thought were my annoying roommates trying to escape the deadly coil fragrance.

Except that the black things weren't mosquitos. I opened the bathroom door to find that the newspaper I'd placed under the coil was on fire, incinerating the insecticide soaked spiral, and a dark smoke was starting to fill the space. I quickly grabbed one of the cheap towels that was hanging on a nearby rack, moistened it, and smothered the fire. The burned newspaper and coil left an oily, dark residue on the white tile, and I knew it was my duty to clean up the mess. Niall, who had the bungalow next to mine, had also seen the flickering light and wondered what was going on. I ruefully showed him the remnants of the fried coil, and he very kindly offered to run to the dining area to get a broom and some rags.

"Just as a heads up on these things," he indicated the dead coil as he handed me the broom, "they're really meant for outdoor use."

"First time for everything, just like this trip. Lesson learned," I acknowledged ruefully.

It didn't take long to sort out the mini-disaster, and I told him that somehow it seemed fitting that this should happen on the last night. Perhaps I could consider it to be symbolic of burning away some of my old toxicity. I also realized how lucky I was. Had this happened the night before, we'd've been in ceremony and I wouldn't have returned to the room until nearly dawn. This time, I happened to return to my room just in time to prevent what would likely have become something more difficult to deal with and caused a lot more damage. Once I finished cleaning up and saw that there was no visual evidence of the potential disaster, I thanked the spirits of the place and vowed never to do anything so foolish again.

But the mosquitos did get the last laugh. Despite all the heavy smoke and the chemicals that had permeated the place, all my efforts had been in vain. I awakened in the night and heard the maddening whine of the cursed little flying bloodsuckers around my face. I was hot and itchy and sweaty and fed up. In a few hours we'd be on our way to Iquitos via Lima again, and I couldn't wait to get out of here. It hadn't occurred to me that there might be a lot more bugs in the jungle.

What I didn't know was that I was about to climb out of this frying pan of experience straight into the fire of Spirit.

CHAPTER 3

Welcome to the Jungle, Baby

We finally got to Iquitos the following day around 5 pm, all of us hot, tired, and really annoyed from the long day of travel. In Peru, all flights have to go through Lima with only a few exceptions. Ours was not one of those. Had we been able to go directly from Piura to Iquitos, we would have been able to get settled into our hotel and spend the rest of the day being completely overwhelmed by the sheer volume of noise and sensory overload of this city. Instead, we were completely underwhelmed with wasting an entire day of our trip traveling through three airports. Harold had no sympathy for us and our petty whining. He just shrugged his shoulders and responded that this is just how it's done here, so we just had to accept it.

Anyone who studies any form of shamanism, Eastern religions, spiritual practices, or even many self-help systems, will at some point be presented with the important concept of simply experiencing what is occurring right now, at this very moment. When we allow ourselves to be totally present and focused on what we are currently experiencing, we tend to find that everything seems to glide more smoothly because our reactions are far less likely to involve annoyance, stomping around angrily and ranting about things we can't change. Our group wasted a lot of energy reacting to situations instead of responding appropriately to them.

Our tour leaders had reserved rooms for each of us at a decent hotel not far off the Plaza de Armas, the central square of Iquitos. This landmark is usually crowded with people on all different kinds of missions: lovers, friends, families, scammers, tourists, and whoever just wanted to take a shortcut between Prospero and Fitzcarrald Avenues. From the square, it was only a short walk to the malecon, a somewhat rough-around-the-edges boardwalk where one could gaze out onto the mighty Itaya and Amazon Rivers.

One of the things that I really appreciated on this adventure was not being forced to share close quarters with someone else just because the hotel charges less for double occupancy like so many retreat centers do. Being new to this kind of work, I truly did not understand that the whole concept of a plant medicine retreat was to retreat into oneself and not to engage in a lot of external distractions. This entire journey had been designed to allow us a lot of solo downtime in order to be able to feel the subtle presences of the plant spirits.

I soon learned that another important reason to have this solitude is because our stuff is going to come up big time, and it's not going to be pretty. Most of us who go on sacred retreats do so for a specific reason. Perhaps we need healing of deep emotional wounds that clinical therapies haven't been able to address. Maybe we want to have a traditional healer examine a difficult medical condition. Or it could be that we want to go deeper into the spiritual realms. Any of these kinds of things can take us out of our comfort zones--sometimes quite far out--depending on our own personal stories and resilience. The resulting shakeup is what allows for some kind of transformation to take place, even if it's just a small shift. These kinds of energetic movements are often uncomfortable, especially if the issues have been in place for a long time. When the wave hits, it's not uncommon to be on the receiving end as the emotional domino chain collapses against us.

I was feeling a bit out of sorts and wondered if it was due to the anti-malaria tablets I'd just started taking, so I was very grateful to have my own quiet room. It was such a treat to take a hot shower without a bunch of mosquitos flying around. And the air conditioning! I could feel the cold air soothing the flaming bug bites I had all over my body. I laid down on the comfy bed and settled in for a short nap.

We'd all agreed to meet downstairs at 8 pm to wander up Avenida Prospero, the main street that ran parallel to the malecon. I didn't really feel like going out, but I told myself that I hadn't come all this way to miss out on some interesting local experiences. I found the others downstairs in the lobby, exchanging nervous grins, shifting back and forth on anxious feet. What a bunch of intrepid travelers we were! All huddled together in the lobby, fearing for our lives to venture out through the glass doors because we'd been warned to be careful in Iquitos, that it could be a dangerous town for the unwary. None of us had been in a place like this crazy jungle city before, and at times the energy was quite overpowering.

If it hadn't been for Gary, we might still be quivering on the safe side of the hotel's front door. Gary was a young Londoner from the East End, who'd been in Iquitos for several months already. He'd also been here on a previous trip, so he knew his way around well. We were in awe of the fact that he had a local girlfriend and shared an apartment with her not far from our hotel. He was one of us, but then again, he wasn't. *He was experienced! He was brave!*

Moving cautiously in a pack up the noisy road like a herd of animals trying to protect themselves against predators, we found ourselves at the center of the Iquitos universe: Ari's Burger.

If the streets of Iquitos were the veins and arteries of the city through which its incredible noise flowed, Ari's for me was the heart of the chaos. Ari's Burger is a large restaurant on a corner that is open on the two street sides from dawn to far into the evening. Those who sit within are sandwiched between the thousands of racing motos that fill the streets just a few yards away and the cacophony within the place itself. Given the way I was feeling, it probably wasn't the best place for me to be.

Ari's had a huge menu, and all I could do in my malaise was to stare at the photos of so many new dishes. But it was the list of energy drinks that really caught our attention. These concoctions contained local ingredients such as guarana, various roots and seeds, and luscious tropical fruits. They all had had rude names with sexual connotations like the Super Erectus or the *Insaciable*, meaning insatiable. My favorite, the *Infiel*, unfaithful, included luscious ingredients such as fresh coconut milk, guarana, honey, and a few other items I was unfamiliar with. I was beginning to get my first view of the very sexual nature of this exotic town, and these delicious drinks that gave a knowing wink to infidelity or extraordinary male prowess made us giggle like schoolchildren when we ordered them.

Being a little queasy, I ordered a simple spit-roasted chicken and plain rice. As I put my fork down to chew the mouth-wateringly seasoned meat, a bright blue and green insect suddenly appeared to the side of my plate. It looked like a grasshopper, but it turned out to be one of the multitude species of crickets that sings so sweetly in the night. I was immediately smitten with its amazing colors.

I waited for the six-legged work of art to leap off the table, but it did not. Upon closer inspection, I saw that it only had one leg. How had it gotten onto my table with only one leg? I recognized this as an unusual situation, one that would be called a sign or an omen in shamanism. Focusing my attention on the barely moving creature next to my plate, I got the message that like it, I too, was handicapped. I couldn't move forward into a new life because I didn't have enough energy or resources to boldly leap forward into my future.

Although I was glad to be with my companions, the increasing dizziness made it difficult for me to feel comfortable. At any moment, the delicious *pollo a la brasa* might decide to make a run for it back up from my mid-section, although there was nothing wrong with the food itself.

Two members of our group, Barbara and Greta, were not happy with the unruliness of the surroundings, so they decided to high-tail it back to the hotel as soon as they could. Not feeling up to trying to engage in lively conversation through the loud music and TV shows that were playing on three of the four walls, I decided to join them. As we walked back towards our hotel, I listened to their complaints about how primitive everything had been so far. Greta had arrived with four full-sized suitcases, all crammed with a change of clothes for different times a day and innumerable beauty tools that required electricity. She lived an affluent lifestyle in South London but was having an affair with her personal trainer at the gym, who she assured us treasured her far more than her husband did. She was a very pretty woman in her early fifties, with close-cropped, bleached blonde hair and a face full of makeup. She obviously cared a great deal about the image she presented to the world, so as her strategically applied face began to melt with the jungle heat and humidity, this was a great concern for her. My head was still circling the universe, and I just couldn't relate to what she was focused on. Why come to the jungle then? Weren't we here for the inside rather than the outside? I let myself into my room and took a deep breath. All I needed was a just little peace, quiet, and air conditioning to sort myself out.

We had some free time in the morning to investigate the local open-air Belen market. Harold told us that you could buy literally anything you could imagine there. The smell was overwhelming in the area where all the meats were sold. Coming from a culture where we buy judiciously inspected portions of meat offered in clean Styrofoam trays overwrapped in cellophane, to see the many carcasses dangling in the heat and attracting flies was quite an assault on our senses. The bodies of monkeys and turtles were offered along with those of pigs and chickens, the latter of which could be purchased either alive or dead.

Given the nature of our retreat, we were particularly interested in the small *paseo* that sold all manner of plant medicines, herbs, and amulets. Vendors beckoned us over to inspect their exotic wares, while we continued to cling together *en masse* to shield ourselves from the pickpockets we were sure had marked us out as vulnerable targets.

Do you want to change your life? Attract a lover? Make millions? All you have to do is buy one of these magical elixirs and boom! All of your desires will manifest. Many of the bottled offerings seemed to guarantee an amazing sex life. A very popular aphrodisiac, the amusingly named Rompe Calzones, or RC, was said to instill so much passion that one couldn't wait to rip off those pesky undergarments that were getting in the way, hence its name that literally means to break underwear.

Our Amazon odyssey began to take form later in the day with the arrival of the two shamans who would be conducting our night ceremonies and staying with us at the lodge. Once we'd all been assigned to our hotel rooms, Harold and Patrick had vanished without a word, leaving us to fend for ourselves. While I'm sure our leaders needed to take a break, we felt they shouldn't have just disappeared without giving us some way to contact them if necessary.

There was an air of excited anticipation as we gathered in one of the hotel's small meeting rooms. In addition to Javier and Atilio, the indigenous healers, there was also a sweet Shipibo woman, Teresa, who would teach us about their incredibly beautiful and complex crafts. The quartet was completed by a very thin young man with a hungry look in his late twenties named Geraldo. Geraldo spoke decent English, so he had been hired as an all-around helper and bridge between us participants and the shamans.

Not knowing how to honor the medicine men in their tradition, I'd brought along some high-quality cigars to gift to them. In many of the indigenous practices I'd studied from the Americas, pure tobacco seemed to play an important part in various aspects of the healing rituals. Both shamans graciously accepted the humble offering, and I was glad I'd brought them a little something.

Javier was about my height, but quite stocky. Jav was young, in his early thirties, with a full head of jet-black hair and an amazing mouthful of teeth. His wide smile showed a grand piano's worth of ivories, which could sometimes be a bit disconcerting. He was an indigenous Kichwa healer from a small village on the Napo River which flowed down from Ecuador. In the local traditions of that area, healing practices were passed down through a lineage: grandfather to father, father to son and perhaps occasionally a daughter, and so Javier had begun his training at an early age. With his wide smile and youthful energy, Javier was extremely charismatic and seemed to genuinely care about us.

The other shaman, Atilio, was in his fifties, and not much taller than Javier, but somewhat leaner. He exuded a quiet sweetness that I could feel across the room.

The encounter only lasted about an hour, with Harold explaining that we'd be meeting up with four other women the next day enroute to the lodge. For some reason, I felt a twinge of alarm at this announcement. The nine of us who had begun this journey together had already formed a very noticeable group synergy. Was it a good idea to add new personalities into the mix at this point? I kept my feelings to myself.

We met the four new women at the Iquitos airport, and I immediately noticed that same nagging feeling seep into my consciousness. The first to join us was a fat, pushy woman with a loud, whiney voice from the East Coast of the United States. A tiny yoga instructor from Scotland came next, followed by two middle-aged British housewives from the southeast part of England. Javier and Geraldo were also there. While friendly and helpful, I had the feeling that the latter was there for other, perhaps more self-serving reasons. I noticed that he looked each of us over very carefully as if he was memorizing every detail and filing it away for some unknown purpose. The others just seemed extremely happy to have someone who spoke English to interpret for the group.

We all piled into yet another minibus and headed to Nina Rumi, an embarkation spot on the Nanay River whose name in Quechua means fire stone. There, Javier sailed away with all of our luggage on one slower boat, while the rest of us piled into a faster motorboat. It was a bit crowded, and I found myself wishing that I could have taken the slow boat with the young shaman. This was my first experience on the river in the Amazon region, and I loved the feel of the air on my face. I sat at the front of the little boat and was grateful for the delicious breeze that provided some relief to the hot tropical air.

Watching the scenery on either side of the river slide by, we were getting closer to the camp where we'd be spending the next two weeks: Sacha Wasi, a Quechua term meaning jungle house. As we glided around a shallow bend in the Nanay River, we all suddenly fell silent. With the exception of Gary, none of us had worked with ayahuasca before, and we didn't know what to was going to happen. I'd started experimenting with mind altering substances around the age of fourteen, so I wasn't particularly concerned. I had a feeling that this part of our retreat was going to be very different from the fun and trippy voyages of my youth, and I looked forward to experiencing ayahuasca's extraordinary healing properties.

Our little motorboat slowed as it finally approached the camp, then our driver cut the engine and we drifted towards the shore. Just as we made contact with the muddy river bottom, a group of young boys suddenly appeared running down the steep slope towards us. Several of them grabbed long planks that were stacked nearby. These were placed carefully against the front of the boat as a makeshift ramp. Some of the boys positioned themselves around the planks to keep them in place as we each exited the little craft. Others held out their hands to help us somewhat wobbly travelers keep our balance so as to not begin our journey in the water or mud.

As I gazed up at the large main building that loomed over us, the *maloca*, which is where the ceremonies and other gatherings would take place, I felt a strong run of emotions. All those years ago, back in London, I had first heard of places like this. In the cold winter of that large Western European city, one man's description of his jungle journey had seemed almost unreal to me. I was suddenly transported back in time to that night after my magic class, when my first hearing of the word ayahuasca produced something like a jolt of recognition in me.

Then the words: "Don't worry about this right now—it's not time. We're just planting the seeds, and one day this will all make sense."

Ah, I get it. The circle has now been completed. Somewhere in the recesses of my mind, I heard a soft click, and then a little celestial bell chimed.

While the rest of the party flopped into chairs set out to overlook the Nanay River, I decided to do a little reconnaissance. I had read about the dieting huts called *tambos*, so I wanted to see what they really looked

MACHETE WOMAN

like. Tambos can take many forms, but they are basically a simple wooden platform set up several feet off the ground. Some are more like tree houses where you have to climb up a ladder to get onto the platform. There are no sides, leaving you wide open to the jungle--bugs, wind, rain, and whatever else might decide to climb down out of the trees to investigate the large pink stranger in its midst. A beautiful, steep, woven palm leaf roof completes the structure. There is usually a bed with a mosquito net, a hammock, and perhaps a small table, and that's it!

I wandered along the narrow path that led away from the maloca towards these sleeping platforms. Like Little Red Riding Hood, I tried them all out to see how they felt and chose a few that I would like to stay in for this part of the retreat. Each one was different. There were several that were set to look out over the river, with others hiding around a bend in the path in more leafy settings.

As I examined each little house, I wondered about these plant diets that we were going to be doing. Harold had sent out an information packet, but I didn't quite understand what a *dieta* was. Weren't we already doing one for the ayahuasca? Towards the end of our beach stay, we had started cutting out salt, sugars and spices, animal fats, and other things that are traditionally taken out of one's daily consumption in order to prepare the body and spirit to receive the amazing teachings of the plant spirits. I had so many questions that bounced around in my head and hoped I'd be able to get the answers to them soon before they started driving me crazy. Harold told us that after dinner, we'd be meeting with Javier to talk about which plants we wanted to diet, so I figured that'd be my chance.

I returned to the maloca to find the slow boat with our bags had just arrived. Leaning over the railing, I watched as it glided to a stop. Once again, the group of slender young jungle boys came running from all directions, racing each other to see who could arrive at the boat first. Most of them were barefoot, but a few of them wore simple rubber flip flops. They didn't pause for one moment as they jumped right into the mud and water.

Helping to unload passengers' luggage and anything else that may have been sent along the waterways was a way for the local youth to earn a few coins. They often could be seen hanging around not far from where the boats would come in. While it looked like they were just being typical cool teenagers, listening to loud music and jiving around, they were actually very aware of what was going on around them. When a boat was spotted angling towards the landing area, you could see that the energy within the group had suddenly sharpened. There were often more boys than bags, so the competition to get to the boat before everyone else could be fierce.

The attractive boys formed a line that went from the boat, up the slope of the riverbank and then to the stairs that led to the maloca entrance. Suitcases and supplies were passed along quickly like hot potatoes. I knew that some of our bags were quite heavy, yet they handled them all as if they weighed only a few pounds. Delighted laughter accompanied the unloading as if it were a game. The boys laughed and danced as each piece was sent up the human chain. Seeing this innate joy in even the most mundane of tasks surprised me, a citizen of the stressed-out, supposedly more civilized world. What did they know that I did not?

Our bags were now reunited with their owners, so it was time to choose which dieting hut each of us wanted. We were instructed to go out and carefully examine each one. There was a tambo for each member of the group, but if more than one person wanted the same one, they would have to draw straws.

Having already made my tour around the little houses on stilts, I had secretly decided on which one I wanted, and it turned out that no one else challenged me for it. Mine was just a plain rectangular living space without any of the special features that some of the others had, such as being perched high up in a tree and reached by a long ladder. I had considered those with the more interesting designs but weighed their access against convenience. I knew that we would be returning to our tambos in the dark after ceremonies, perhaps on wobbly, disoriented legs, so I chose mine based on proximity to the main buildings, as well as the larger size of its floor. There were only a few rungs from the dirt path to the tambo floor, never mind that I had a nice view of the river. Welcome to the Sacha Wasi Hilton!

Mercifully, no one fought over any of the other tambos, and soon our bags were being brought to each of us from the main hall. It didn't take long to settle in, and shortly afterwards, my traveling partners began wandering around to visit each other and inspect the surroundings.

Most of my companions seemed happy, but not all of them. Two of the women who had just joined us, Carol and Vanni, absolutely refused to sleep in an open-sided dieting hut, where they believed that anything could just crawl out of the trees and get under their bed nets, never mind the lack of privacy. When they found out there were a couple of cubbyholes within the main building that were usually reserved for staff or people with limited mobility, they made a huge fuss and insisted on being given one of these inner rooms. Then Greta, she of the four suitcases, expressed displeasure at the fact that there was no electricity. She had wanted to freshen up before dinner and use her curling iron to fluff up her humidity-flattened hair but had been thwarted by the lack of electrical outlets. I saw Harold and Patrick exchange glances, and I imagined they were thinking that it might be a blessing if something did crawl out of the foliage to carry these whiners off. I silently agreed: we were in the jungle, not some five-star luxury resort!

As we sat in the deck chairs after dinner, the jungle gave us a most stunning welcome in the form of an utterly spectacular lightning storm. There was no rain, and indeed not a cloud in the sky, so I was fascinated with how there could be such a light show without any sign of a storm. I asked Harold about this, and he told me that it had to do with a combination of heat and high pressure. At times, it made me think of my favorite science fiction TV show, the original *Outer Limits* series that had made its debut in the 1960s. Back then, there were no dazzling special effects or computer graphics, so you'd see some of the same cleverly designed scenes used in different episodes. One of these effects was swirling, flashing clouds that would alternately switch back and forth like seeing a printed photograph and its film negative. Jagged bolts of electricity inevitably would emit from these clouds as the latter would pulse back and forth between dimensions. Somehow, it seemed fitting to think of the *Outer Limits* on this journey as the sky continued to impress us with Mother Nature's special effects.

I'd never slept under a mosquito net before and I thought it was quite cozy at first, like slipping into a one-man tent. The bed was a simple wooden platform with a thin foam mattress and a funny hard pillow. There was a fitted bottom sheet and a thin blanket, but nothing else. I thought it was weird to not have a top sheet, especially since it was so warm. The type of nets we had in Sacha Wasi could hardly be called nets: they were more like muslin sheets sewn into the familiar hanging boxlike shape. You couldn't really see through them, but they were designed to keep out even the tiniest of biting bugs. Other *mosquiteros* are indeed more netlike and allow for better air flow, but miniscule blood suckers can then crawl through the net holes to find the sleeping banquet that is you. I couldn't decide if it would be better to keep out those no see 'ums all together or to be able to breathe fresh air and risk itchy, red bites.

Sometime in the middle of the night, I realized I had to go to the bathroom, so I carefully lifted up the bed net and crawled out. An important thing to consider when you are sleeping out in the wild is how to deal with your bodily functions., especially at night. It's not a good idea to be wandering around the jungle in the dark when you can't see what might be hiding in the bushes preparing to pounce. Here at the camp, there were two toilet cubicles in the main lodge, but these were not convenient for those of us in the tambos, particularly when nature called during the off hours. We were each given a small plastic basin with a handle and a roll of toilet paper for this purpose.

Once I completed my task, I realized we hadn't been told what to do with the contents of our chamber pots, so I decided to fling mine into the greenery outside the railing, figuring that any rain would wash away the evidence. Satisfied, I quickly got back under the net before any nearby mosquitos could zero in on me.

Our first morning in the jungle dawned peacefully after a cacophonous night. Millions of crickets, frogs, night birds and other creatures had started to sing loudly around dusk and kept up their concert until daybreak. While some of my companions found this noise to be disturbing, I grew to love this unique night song and the sense of serenity it brought me.

As I walked around to stretch, I looked out to where I'd flung the contents of my chamber pot in the night and was rather horrified to see bits of toilet paper clinging to the nearby leaves. I felt really guilty and apologized to the jungle spirits, wondering how I was going to clean up the mess I'd made.

But wait! Were my eyes deceiving me? It looked like the damp pieces were moving. I grabbed my binoculars and focused on a few of the larger pieces. Zooming in closely, I saw that the used TP was indeed being moved by an army of very large black ants. I estimated that they were about three-quarters of an inch long. As I watched, they would grab a piece of the fragile material and carry it down the leaves and branches off to some hidden ant lair. I was fascinated to watch my flung debris being broken down even farther and carted off in an orderly fashion through the foliage. When I checked again after returning from breakfast, there was not one speck of my crime that remained. I felt a bit better that these insect clean-up crews had erased my careless act, so I thanked the jungle spirits and promised never to pollute their home again.

This morning's event was learning about some of the traditional jungle medicines that were used by the locals. Aside from the plant-based remedies, the two that caused the most consternation among some members of the group were the toad venom and the dolphin oil.

For the first, an infusion is made with parts of the *sapohuasca* plant. *Sapo*, Spanish for toad; and *huasca*, Quechua for vine. Several drops of fresh toad venom were added to this infusion. Javier had brought along several of the large, squat, brown amphibians and began to demonstrate the technique of very gently squeezing the sides of the large toad. This slight pressure fooled it into believing that a predator had clamped its jaws around it in preparation for a meaty meal. The toad then fired a salvo against its hungry enemy by leaking a poisonous liquid through the skin close to where the fingers or teeth made contact.

Javier used a toothpick to carefully direct the venom into the bowl of sapohuasca, counting out a precise number of drops. He handed a warty toad to me and indicated that I was to mimic his technique. The large amphibian squirmed as it tried to escape from my gentle grasp, so he told me to apply just a bit more pressure.

"The toad will try to get away from the predator first, but if it feels trapped, only then will it start producing the venom," the young shaman told us.

Attempting to mimic the pressure of a bite from a larger animal, I was able to see small drops of liquid oozing through the toad's skin. Following Javier's example, I grabbed a toothpick and managed to get some of the venom into the sapohuasca liquid. Javier smiled at me and gave me a thumbs up. I was learning my first jungle medicine lesson!

Gillian, the petite yoga instructor from Scotland, had hung back during the first demo with a look of distaste on her face. Once she could see that absolutely no harm had come to the toad, she refrained from expressing her disapproval of the use of living beings for show and tell. Not so with the dolphin oil. As soon as she heard the word *cut*, she began shrieking about cruelty to animals and how unfair it was to the poor dolphin to be so abused.

The young shaman looked a bit confused, not understanding English, but realizing from her tone and actions that something wasn't acceptable. With Geraldo interpreting, he then explained that only a small cut was made in the aquatic animal's side to allow a little oil to be collected, then herbs are applied to speed the healing process. Javier explained that care and ritual are observed in this process, and the dolphin is then carefully released back into the water.

Gillian continued to throw a fit and eventually stomped back to her tambo. I silently considered that while we as foreigners may not frequently think about collecting substances from living beings to use as ingredients in our products, is it our right to condemn the practices of other cultures without having spent a lot of time experiencing their ways? After all, we do use cochineal insects to produce red dyes, and castoreum, a secretion from glands in a beaver's backside to add to perfumes and food, labelling these as natural scents or flavorings. So really, what's the difference?

Next up were the plant medicines. Javier indicated the line-up of recycled two-liter plastic soda bottles on a nearby table. Each was labelled with their contents, whose shades were in variations of a weird greenish-brown color.

The young healer told us that while it is most common just to diet one plant at a time for longer periods, we could choose up to three for this introduction to jungle plant spirit medicine.

I selected three of the plants. First up was *ajo sacha,* a plant with the scent of garlic that hunters use to help them sharpen their senses. Next was *guayusa* to aid in having more vivid dreams. And lastly, there was *chiricsanango*. We were told that this last plant was helpful for treating things like fever and inflammation, but I was more curious to experience its physical effects such as tingling and numbing in the body, in addition to making one feel really cold in the middle of the sweltering jungle.

We were instructed to come to the maloca first thing in the morning and drink small cups of our chosen plants, allowing plenty of time for absorption before consuming anything solid. We should then go back to our tambos and climb into our hammocks. Swaying gently within the thick striped cotton swings, we'd attempt to enter into a meditative state where'd we'd have a better chance of receiving communication from the plant spirits.

Javier had told us that the main purpose of restricting what we consume and also how we withdraw from the outside world is to aid us in preparing our physical and energetic bodies to receive what can at times be very subtle information. It acts to shift our attention from the earthly desires that are mostly centered around our physical feelings and needs, to the lighter, higher energy of the spirit realms.

This second part of the plant spirit medicine retreat had been designed to loosely follow the stricter and more traditional indigenous plant diets, which meant allowing us to have a lot of solitary time to be with the spirits. Perhaps because of Harold's increasing tendency to avoid us and not explain how things worked, the message hadn't been driven home far enough to our group. Harold had secluded himself in his own tambo, and our interactions with him had diminished to hardly anything. I had the feeling he no longer wanted anything to do with us, and this led to sentiments of resentment among certain members of our group. While some of us tried to diligently focus and remain in contemplation, the majority of the participants found all the solo time boring and would congregate in the ceremonial space to chat. This was not a respectful start to the retreat and proved to be a harbinger of things to come.

CHAPTER 4

Opening the Big Door

This was to be our first night with Madre, the spirit of the sacred ayahuasca vine, so dinner was not served. When working with these precious teachers you want to be able to give them every chance to be easily absorbed, so it's common to not eat anything for up to eight hours before the start of the ceremony. As someone who grew up in a family that believed you would surely starve to death if you didn't eat every few hours, I found this mini-fast to be challenging.

The concept of giving something to get something is an old one, and it is fully applicable in any kind of sacred ceremony. What do you want? How badly do you want it? How much are you willing to suffer in exchange for life-changing experiences?

Javier had suggested that we all come early to the maloca to take part in a ritual of light. He said that this was not something that was commonly done before an ayahuasca ceremony, but he had seen darkness and anger arise in some members of our group. He told us that if not cleared away, this negative energy would seep into the work and the healing experience would be negated because the compassionate, helping spirits will not come if there is no harmony present. This short rite included visualizations and Javier whacking us with his leaf rattle, called a *shacapa*, to cleanse our tainted energy fields, as well as having the ubiquitous agua florida poured on our crowns. I felt it was a nice way to begin what I hoped would be an epic journey. He then left briefly after telling us to find our spots for the night's work and to wait quietly for his return.

When Javier reappeared in the ceremonial room a short time later he was dressed very differently. Over his regular T-shirt and trousers was a sleeveless, flowered garment that looked like a dress. It was also a cushma like Maestro Juan and his son, Humberto, had worn, but this one looked less like their shorter poncho style coverings and more like a plain housedress. Several of the red and black huayuaro seed necklaces hung around his neck, and there were bracelets and anklets that rattled and clacked when he moved. A crown of leaves sat on his head. I found the look very attractive.

Since this was the first time that any of us beside Gary had worked with ayahuasca, we all got a small, introductory portion called a *poco*. It was served in a little round gourd shell called a *pate* that had been cut in half and hollowed out to make a cup. I wish I could say it tasted like the sweetest nectar to me, but it didn't. At first, there was a fruity chocolate taste, but this was quickly overshadowed by a strong bitterness that made me shudder. I found it was very difficult to drink and swallow. The thin dark liquid provoked instant retching in some of us, although we all managed to keep it down because the alternative was not very palatable: we would have to drink another cup!

The maestro suggested that we remain sitting up for about an hour to allow the medicine to work. He told us that it was not the actual drink itself that produced the effects, which we found confusing at first. He explained further that it merely acts as a vehicle for the spirit, who is called Madre or Mother, and it is she who decides what kind of journey you're going to have on any given night.

I sat up as advised but I needn't have worried about the effects. Apart from a few colored geometrical figures that disappeared quickly, there simply wasn't anything else that happened for me. Javier had indicated that this would be a gentle ceremony, but I felt restless and uncomfortable. There weren't enough of the wider, more comfortable chairs for each person, so I perched on a low hard stool for as long as I could. As with my first San Pedro experience, I just felt annoyed and wondered what all the fuss was about.

We had not been told beforehand about ceremonial etiquette, so I didn't know what to do. I was tired, hot, cranky, and still dizzy from the malaria pills I was taking. All I wanted to do was to get off that danged wooden stool and go to bed! I finally couldn't stand it any longer, so I quietly stood up and edged my way towards the rear of the maloca. My plan was to pass through into the room behind the ceremonial hall where the bathrooms were, and then make my way down another set of wooden stairs to freedom. I managed to achieve a stealthy exit and find my way back to my tambo without any problems. Gratefully crawling under the muslin net, I laid down and sighed in relief. Closing my eyes, a few greyish, obscure scenes floated across my field of vision, but I couldn't make out anything recognizable. I figured they were some latent effects from the brew and was happy to just lie back and watch the jungle TV scenes.

"That was very rude, you know."

What? Who was that? I sat up quickly in the darkness and peered around. Peeking out from under the net, I expected to see someone standing by my bed, but there was no one there.

Figuring I must have imagined the voice out of guilt, I laid back down.

"Leaving early like that is considered to be very disrespectful to the shaman."

This time I didn't move. I knew the voice was not coming from anyone near me, yet I knew I wasn't imagining it either. What came next was not so much hearing specific words, but rather a feeling that while I had been ignorant to leave a sacred ceremony without telling anyone. I would be granted a beginner's excuse this time and this time *only*. Even though I didn't know who had spoken to me, I apologized for being an idiot, determining that I would ask someone about my crime in the morning.

Although I had been a bit petulant because I thought nothing notable had happened, I was now beginning to wonder if something had indeed happened after all. In truth, I'd just had my initial encounter with Madre Ayahuasca, and she taught me the first of the many lessons I was to have with her.

While it turned out that I had not been the only one to disappear into the night, I still felt guilty. I sought out Geraldo to engage in a chat about ceremonial etiquette. He confirmed what Madre had told me about showing disrespect to Javier. The correct thing to do is to remain in your spot as long as the shaman is present. They will formally close the ceremony, and only after they leave the room is it considered polite to follow suit.

I took the opportunity to apologize to Javier when we went to the stream before lunch for our floral baths. These had begun yesterday, and I really liked having the fragrant, plant filled water poured over me, bestowing its sweet blessings as it flowed back to the earth. Jav was very forgiving and told me he understood, flashing that wide mouthful of teeth at me. Once again, I couldn't help feeling that had our retreat leaders sat us all down beforehand and had a discussion about ceremonial process and what to do when the various issues might arise, then perhaps these kinds of things wouldn't have happened. But as in the city, they had made themselves scarce and seemed to have as little interaction with us as possible.

To be honest, I can't say I really blamed them. After lunch, I was relaxing in my brightly striped hammock, when I heard female voices coming up the path. It was the two British housewives, Carol and Vanni, who had decided to venture away from the safety of the main building to see what our digs looked like. They didn't see me enveloped in the hanging cloth, but as they paused in front of my tambo, one said with emphasis,

"I'm so glad I'm not staying out here! I need a little bit of civilization."

I began to wonder what exactly was considered civilized, and if we were the uncouth savages after all. No wonder Harold and Patrick kept to themselves as much as possible!

We were given a choice between two different ceremonies that were being held later that night. We could do another ayahuasca one or go for the sapohuasca. I had to laugh when Niall asked me if I was going to do the vine of death or the poisonous frog. Because I knew we had several more ayahuasca ceremonies planned I decided to try the less common sapohuasca. Because of potentially dangerous interactions between the two we could not do both on the same night.

Since Atilio was not due to join us until tomorrow, the toad ceremony would be after dinner, followed by the work with Madre, both overseen by Javier. My chosen experience was only supposed to last for about an hour, but I was still keen to feel the soporific effects wash over me and relax all my tight muscles.

Plant spirit medicines create entirely different experiences for each person who partakes of them. One person may fly off into the night sky with just a small amount, while others may need a second cup in order to feel any effects. We were offered an additional serving on the toad medicine if necessary, but I didn't take it. Perhaps I should have as the experience was quite mild, but I wanted to gauge the effects of a single dose of the very horrible tasting concoction. After downing the drink, I chose a hammock to journey in. The experience was very pleasant and dreamy, and I could feel a lot of my tensions melting away.

There is a well-known problem that can arise with taking more medicine after your first cup. This is jokingly referred to as the "oh shit dose." Plant medicines, having an intelligence that you can communicate with, have their own agendas. Using ayahuasca as an example, on some nights it can take what seems like only minutes for the effects to begin, and other nights it can take over an hour or even longer. It is also not uncommon to sit there through the entire night and not feel a thing, then when the shaman announces that the ceremony is finished, only then do the big visions blast through. It can be tricky to know what to do. You could go up for that second dose, take it, go sit back down and suddenly the effects of the first dose kick in. That's when you say, "oh shit." Often, that second dose goes straight into the bucket or over the railing.

I heard from those who'd sat with Madre again that the effects were stronger. They'd been encouraged to take a higher dose called a *medio*, and several of the women didn't like the experience. Glenda reported that all sorts of very strong emotions had come up and she had trouble dealing with them. Given her current domestic situation carrying on with her personal trainer behind her husband's back, this is not surprising. We may be able to hide our thoughts and acts from other humans, but we cannot hide from the celestial spirit crews.

I remained in my tambo until nearly 4 pm, then I started to feel a bit restless again. Needing a short break, I wandered over to the main lodge to refill my water bottle. We were now referring to the maloca as our headquarters, and I found almost the entire group seated on the floor in a circle with Javier and Geraldo holding court. Geraldo was recounting previous medicine adventures he'd had with other tourists, some of them quite gross and disgusting. He was hilarious as a storyteller and everyone was rolling on the floor laughing, even Javier. Jav was happy to do an extensive Q and A session with us and fill in the gaps where we felt our leaders had been evasive or didn't feel like answering.

Atilio had arrived earlier, and he popped in briefly to greet us. It was his turn to lead the ceremony tonight and I was looking forward to sitting with him. Harold had told us he had a beautiful voice and amazing *icaros*. The icaros are the sacred songs that drive the ceremony. They have their own purposes, such as putting out protection for the participants and the ceremony, clearing fright or hexing out of the body, or bringing in love and blessings. It is not a concert where one is selected at random and performed like a pop song. The ceremonial leader acts as a channel for his guiding spirits and indeed, Madre herself, who is the one that calls the songs.

Most of us had gathered in the maloca a short while before the ceremony. It was dark, so sitting in the candlelit communal area was far more pleasant than sitting alone in our tambos, even if that is what we were supposed to be doing. Like the previous day, we were talking and laughing and cracking jokes, and generally making a lot of noise. We were a happy lot, but one of our leaders was not. The racket had carried over to Harold's tambo and was disturbing his introspection, so he came over to tell us to keep it down. We were told that our behavior was inappropriate since we were supposed to be preparing for a sacred ceremony. We acknowledged this, and the mood instantly had become quiet and reflective. Again, it would have been a lot more helpful if he or Patrick would have had regular check ins to discuss protocols. It seemed more like he'd wait until we committed some kind of infraction, then he'd confront us. And that was only when he decided to be in the same space as the group, which wasn't very often.

Atilio's ceremony was quite different. Not feeling quite ready for the much larger dose, I opted for a halfway measure between the *poco* and *medio*. The scientist in me likes to experiment with boundaries and measures. "So, if the smallest dose is hardly noticeable, what would happen with a dose and a half?" There were still plenty of nights to increase my intake all the way up to the maximum offering, the *grande* or *completo*.

I felt my fear and resistance melt away, but this being an ayahuasca ceremony, it had to go somewhere. Let's just say I spent a lot of time in the back room where the bathrooms were and leave it at that. Once the purging was done, I returned to my chair and allowed a feeling of great peace come over me. A bit later, I decided to walk out to the front deck to look at the river and the stars. It was so incredibly beautiful that it took my breath away. Deep beneath the sheer ecstasy, I felt a contact with a presence.

"It's not about the visions. It's about the universal connection and the wisdom within."

This one sentence has guided me for many years through hundreds of inner starlit nights.

The bomb dropped right after breakfast the next morning. Harold had come into the dining area and pointedly ignored every one of us. He was in a real snit about something, and you could almost see the top of the pressure cooker about ready to blow sky high. Once we'd finished eating, he very gruffly called a meeting and then got very angry at us, his paying customers. He ranted on about how he thought we weren't serious, and that we were nothing but a bunch of ayahuasca tourists who didn't know what we wanted. Several of the guys responded by pointing out that by his making himself so scarce and not speaking to us we didn't know what to do. They told him that we felt he was being evasive, difficult to approach, and was not clear when he did speak to us. No one had ever bothered to run us through the etiquette and protocols of these experiences that were new for all of us. How were we supposed to know?

After disagreeing that he was so unavailable to us, he wanted us to all state our intent for coming, but I felt that should have been done when applying for the retreat. Others tried to explain that we meant no disrespect, but he was in such a rage that he wouldn't listen. I decided to mention the long periods where at times we might feel a little bored. It was risky with him in that mood, but I got a response that I've continued to carry and apply whenever I work with plant diets.

"If you were taking your dietas seriously you would never be bored! You'd be living in this fabulous, multidimensional world." He continued by telling us to stop hanging around the maloca and socializing. The whole point of this retreat was to stay in our tambos to be with the spirits. He summed up by saying that yes, he was angry, but if he didn't care, he'd just let it all slide, and then this would not be giving us the true retreat that we had signed up for.

I had to agree. He was right. From that moment on, I cleaned up my act and stopped hanging around to socialize. I spent my time in my hammock waiting to hear the subtle voices of the plant spirits.

In the world of magic, we are told to be careful what we wish for because we may just get it. We were about halfway through our two-week jungle retreat, and it was now the day after my second ayahuasca ceremony. We were scheduled for another one tonight with larger doses. My body had been warning me all day long about the upcoming evening's session. I felt anxious and noticed an unusual tightness in my abdomen. So, I had a choice: I could call off the ceremony and have a peaceful night under the net, or I could face whatever was waiting for me out there in the dark. My cozy hammock surrounded me like a soon-to-be butterfly's cocoon. It swayed gently as I stuck my leg over the side and found the ground. Rising, I knew I really did not have a choice after all. I had made my decision years before when I made my commitment to follow the way of Spirit, to seek out who I really was and help others do the same. I looked off into the dense foliage and let my gaze become unfocused as I set my intent for the night's ritual.

"Madre, I know the path I must walk is not an easy one. Please remove all the obstacles that are in my way so that I may walk more surely on this road. Thank you."

My third ceremony did not get off on the right foot. We had all come to the maloca for an 8 pm start, but the nearby village was also holding some kind of ceremony of their own. There was loud, insistent drumming that would have been very disruptive to our more introspective work. It was Javier's turn to lead again, and after a brief consultation between Harold and Patrick, we were told we'd start an hour later to allow the neighboring session to wrap up.

I had climbed into one of the hammocks to await the delayed start to the ceremony and was about to drift off when an argument started between the British housewives and Joan, the tall, plump woman from Boston. She was one of those types that has to be involved in every transaction or conversation to the point where she was getting obnoxious. If we were seated at the picnic-style table eating a meal and she came in late, she refused to go sit at the second table when there was no room left at the first one. Instead, holding her plate, she would literally shove her way in between two people and immediately want to know what we were talking about.

Since we were waiting for the ceremony, most of the rest of us were doing our best to remain quiet and respectful. Carol and Vanni weren't having any of it. The rules obviously did not apply to them, and they continued to talk and occasionally let rip with something crude, shrieking loudly at their hilarity. Joan politely asked them to pipe down, but instead of doing so, they both turned on her and started yelling for her to go back to her own tambo if she wanted quiet. She responded that she hadn't come all this way to be attacked, and the two friends left in a huff. Don, a tall, fun guy from London who'd been enjoying his retreat so far, also left, saying he didn't want to sit with the fragile energy. Part of me also wanted to escape. I wasn't sure why, but I stayed put. This left eight of us to drink the medicine, which I felt was a better size anyway.

Tonight, I would be moving up to the larger dose that was called the *medio*, or medium. It was served in an empty brown gourd shell that resembled a cut avocado. I never knew the exact quantity that each gourd held, but I'd say this was one and a half to twice as much as the first night's dose, although it did not completely fill the shell. It still tasted horrible and was difficult to get down, especially with the larger quantity. I had a strong feeling that tonight was going to be very different than the previous two gentle ceremonies.

As I've previously described, the bathrooms were not in the main room where we held the ceremonies. The ceremonial room was a long rectangle with a balcony overlooking the river at one end and the kitchen and dining area at the opposite, inner end. If you can imagine the entire building shaped like a capital T with the right part of the horizontal line erased, or like a reversed, inverted L, the bathrooms were at the rearmost part of the top left. To get to them entailed crossing the length of the ceremonial hall to the back, then turning left through a doorway that led down a couple of rickety wooden steps.

Once you had stepped down carefully you would be in a large, nearly empty back room. The two toilet cubicles were located at the far end of this room to the right. This may not sound like a long walk in waking consciousness, but when you've lost your body and what used to be your legs now bounces like rubber, it suddenly becomes a real challenge. One of Geraldo's jobs was to help someone to the back room if they were unable to wobble there on their own.

Since this camp was not used year round, it was unfortunately not stocked with everything that was needed to support over ten people, such as having enough comfortable chairs for everyone to sit in. The owners had also forgotten to supply us with purge containers. I suppose we could've used the chamber pots in our tambos, but that thought was not really considered. Even rinsed out, the idea of carrying them back and forth was not very appealing. If the urge to purge hit, all you had to do was try to get up as quickly as you could and make a beeline for the railing. *If you could* being the key phrase here.

The first few of these railing runs was manageable until I started realizing that it was time to make the longer walk down the little wooden steps to the back room. Once there, I had a feeling that it might be a good idea for me to just stay near the convenient facilities instead of trying to walk back and forth to my chair.

I soon found myself in an almost unrecognizable world. The vine of the soul is well known for its purging qualities, and I was being purged in a way I never could have imagined. I vomited so violently that I was sure the far end of my intestines would come hurtling out of my mouth. What did come out were not the contents of my stomach, nor for that matter, anything physical at all, thanks to the strict diet I was following. Sickly purplish-black pellets fell into my cupped hands and then vanished when I tried to look at them closely. Electric red lightning bolts would suddenly appear all around me, and I staggered, trying to keep my balance until I would finally collapse on the ground like a rag doll. I laid there praying for rest, but the earth underneath me rippled as if some giant subterranean monster was about to emerge. Madre Ayahuasca very kindly warned me to get up before the next round of purging was about to begin in order to allow me to position myself for the best effect.

The vomiting was easier to prepare for than the purging from my back end. For this, I had to get to my feet and try to hold on to something fixed while maintaining a crouch position. Although most of what came out was not material, I wasn't going to take any chances when this urge came! To get to my feet, I had to roll over onto my front and very slowly rise to a stand. This is normally a simple task, but in the non-ordinary reality of this night it was very difficult. If I paused for even a moment, the ground would start rolling again, and then when I was halfway up, the view in front of me would rock back and forth as if the horizon was tilting. Trees would seem to lean in, beckoning me to come out and join them. I would put my hand on something solid like a tree or post, and then it would turn to Jell-O.

When I finally made it into the toilet cubicle, I would place my hands against the walls to steady myself. They moved in and out, breathing like a pair of lungs. The red lightning continued to flash around me. Turning to face the toilet, I heard it command,

"Feed me!"

"Oh yeah? You want me to feed you? Well, take THIS!"

Huuuuuuuurk!

After I cleared out whatever was needed at that moment, I'd stagger back and collapse onto the floor. Up and down, up and down. I was exhausted. I thought how wonderful it would be to die, and then I realized I was dying. Ayahuasca was ripping away the old parts of me that no longer served. Visions flew past me rapidly and I saw the DNA double helix. I tried to slow down the scenes so I could see them more clearly, but I was told that I could not, that the nature of energy was to be ever-changing. I was watching the true form of the universe, and it was exciting. Despite my physical discomfort, I knew I was not having a bad trip: I was in awe. I sank down once again to the ground, and this time it didn't undulate.

"Your mother loves you."

I rolled over and sat up, wondering who had spoken to m this time. I watched as the ground beneath me became transparent and I saw *Madre Tierra*, the Earth Mother. She reached up through the earth to me and I reached down through the floorboards to her. I cried happily as our palms touched. I knew I was going to be alright. There was a radiance around her, and such love! I laid back down and felt the greatest peace and love that I had ever felt in my life. Geraldo would pop in from time to time to check on me, whether to bathe my forehead in perfumed water or carefully spread the blanket from his own bed over me.

One of the fascinating aspects of this teacher plant is that you can experience such things as telepathy, being out of body, and occasional time travel. There is a noticeable difference between the somewhat cartoonish visions and these extraordinary states. At one point, I heard that night's ceremonial leader, Javier, shaking his leaf rattle and moving around to sing over each person. Since I was lying on the floor in a separate area of the building, I felt a little sad that I would miss his blessing.

I was stretched out on my left side, facing towards the back wall when I heard and felt footsteps on the wooden floor behind me. There was the unmistakable sound of dried leaves being shaken, and I could feel the leaf rattle moving the air around me. Sweet! He'd come into the back room to bless me after all. When it finished, I rolled over to say thank you, but *there was no one there!* I sat up in shock and amazement, wondering how this was possible.

Perhaps about an hour later when the journey had ended, the others all gathered around me to see how I was doing. I was so worn out I couldn't move and wanted to just sleep on the floor instead of trying to get back to the simple wooden structure I was staying in. Edwin, a very young man who had adopted his own version of the jungle man's attire, shorts, and a T-shirt if he felt like it, but nothing on his feet, knelt down gently and listened as I told him what I had set for my intention that night: to have all of my obstacles removed. He smiled and nodded in understanding.

"Well, you certainly got what you asked for, didn't you?"

Hoo boy, did I! I will be very careful what I ask for from now on.

Irene, the oldest member of our group at nearly seventy years old, knelt down and said it was too bad I'd missed Javier's blessing. "He came around to each of us and rattled his shacapa all around to give us an energetic cleansing," she told me softly.

At first, I felt a little confused, and then the light dawned. Without realizing it, Irene had just validated my telepathic experience. Javier *had* come into this back room in his spirit body to include me in his blessing while continuing to work with those who were still in the main room of the maloca. I just smiled, nodded, and kept the secret to myself.

I slowly peeled myself up from the ground and started to make my way back to my sleeping platform. I was not able to walk unaided, so Geraldo very kindly allowed me to drape myself over him while he sort of dragged and walked me back to my tambo. During this jaunt, he suddenly stopped short and shined his light on a colorful snake in our path. Its three colors, red, yellow, and black, alternated in a pattern that called to mind the one version of the old rhyme: Red and yellow, kill a fellow. Red touches black, you're all right, Jack.

"Is *naka naka*. Very poisonous!"

I caught a brief glimpse of the coral snake before it slithered into the bushes, and then suddenly felt that touch that I had come to know was my spirit guides sending me a message. There were no words, but I had a strange feeling that I'd be seeing the *naka naka* again for some reason.

Geraldo made sure I was able to climb up the short ladder to reach the platform where my bed beckoned, then he continued back towards the now silent maloca. I was sure I was going to wake up with the hangover from hell. The thought of doing this again the very next night rumbled in me and I shuffled over to the railing just in case. Nope, all done! I crawled under the net and heaved a large sigh of relief. As I tucked the edge of the tightly woven muslin mosquito net under my mattress, I reviewed how my pre-ceremony intent actually had driven the entire experience. What magic! Yes, I had indeed gotten what I'd asked for!

I opened my eyes cautiously the next morning, expecting my head to feel twice its normal size and throbbing painfully. Sitting up very slowly, I realized I actually felt good, maybe even great. I crawled out from under the oppressive cocoon I slept in and moved tentatively around the floor of my tambo. My body buzzed with a delicious lightness, and there was no nausea at all. How could this be?

We had our customary morning meeting to discuss the previous night's ceremony. Harold announced we'd be getting a larger dose tonight, the *completo*, a local word for the gourd cup filled to the brim. Although I felt surprisingly well after my ordeal, the idea of drinking even more of that vile tasting brew made me shudder. I felt like I needed a break between ceremonies and asked about taking the night off. Harold gave me a searching look. An accident many years prior had awakened his inner vision and I wondered what he was seeing in me. He shook his head slightly.

"You are very strong. You should face your fears or there will always be a shadow looming over you. Besides, we only have a limited number of ceremonies here. Did you come all this way to sit in a hammock?"

Yeah, he was right. Nodding, I said I would not make any decisions until the evening.

The day's feature was dubbed the shamans' clinic. This was where both Jav and Atilio would sit down with us individually and answer questions, perhaps do divinations, give advice, discuss what *preparado*--an herbal concoction usually made with an alcohol base--we might want to take home with us, or whatever else might be needed. Geraldo was also present to aid in the interpretation.

To my surprise, I didn't feel I had any big problems like many of the others did. I wasn't looking for a lover or a husband or how to make a million dollars. I'd finally passed through a ridiculously long divorce, and now I was free and felt fabulously wealthy.

"So why did you want all your obstacles removed?" Madre was back, guiding me.

"I want to be a healer!" I suddenly blurted out to the two shamans.

The three jungle men looked at me, an overweight wreck who was still recovering from a soul-destroying battle. I imagined they must have been thinking something along the lines of "This one wants to be a healer? Seriously?" But instead, they looked at me kindly.

I found unrehearsed words flowing from my mouth. "I come from one of the world's richest countries, yet it seems like most people I meet are not happy. There's this constant pressure to buy more, be more, work harder until your blood pressure soars and you drop dead of a heart attack, all so you can buy a bigger yacht than your neighbor's. We have everything, but we're not happy! Yet in the few days I've been here, I've seen the light in the lovely inhabitants of this jungle. Little kids using a rolled up piece of paper as a ball, pretending a large leaf is a boat to float on the water; everyone glows. It's not all about the stuff: it's about the people. I want to bring that light back to my country somehow."

Where did that come from?

The two shamans had a brief discussion and said something to Geraldo, who then turned to me.

"They are going to make *camalonga* for you to take with you. You'll get it once we get back to the hotel."

Camalonga? The pungent liquid that could knock out an army of vampires with its garlic and onion scent? I wondered why they had prescribed that for me but didn't ask. If they thought that's what I needed, I'd go along with it. Why not? I could always ask about this later.

Javier told me to write my name on a piece of paper and hand it to him before the ceremony started in the evening, adding that this was to aid in intercession with the spirits. I agreed to do this as I got up, lost in my own thoughts as the next person sat down at the table.

Atilio was leading this night's work, my fourth ayahuasca ceremony, with Jav sitting off to the side. I duly gave him my name and sat down in one of the chairs. Those of us present were able to take the big jump up to the *completo*—the full gourd! It was hard not to gag at even the thought of drinking so much of the extremely bitter brew. The *poco* had been bad enough, and this was probably about three times as much to get down.

It took about a half hour for the effects to kick in, but when they did, I received a reward for my bravery and persistence of the previous night, for not running away despite the discomfort and challenges. After two brief runs over to the railing, I selected a hammock and arranged myself happily inside its embrace. For the rest of the night, I flew among the stars and felt waves and waves of ecstasy wash over me.

And the love! Wow! We all have heard of near death experiences where the person is guided to a beautiful light, and feels the intense, unconditional love of a higher power, making them not want to return to their physical body.

"You came here seeking reality. What is real? This love is all there is. You are it, and it is you. This is your inherent nature, and you will never lose this feeling. It may become buried over time with the debris of everyday life, but it is still there, nonetheless. Can you now understand that you had to let go of all that hell before you could feel heaven?"

I nodded and acknowledged Madre's words and sighed deeply into the walls of the hammock that enclosed me. To think I had seriously considered missing this sacred revelation just because last night was a challenge! I silently thanked Harold for encouraging me to not only face my fear, but to go even bigger.

The next morning after breakfast, we had our follow up meetings with the shamans to get the results of what they had worked on during the previous night's ceremony. Javier confided that he had given me the power of two strong spirit beings. While this was normally done by tracing the figures on the skin, I had received mine energetically. He explained the gifts these spirits would give me, and how they would be useful to me as a healer.

Since part of our retreat package was for every participant to receive a custom-made plant medicine, the *preparado*, to bring home, the camalonga he'd prescribed for me left me a little puzzled. We'd used this strong smelling spirit protection before the ceremonies, rubbing it on the four corners of our bodies: the lower legs, arms, face, and back. Of the five or six ingredients in the camalonga formula what assails the nose on unscrewing the bottle cap is the sheer volume of chopped onion and garlic. No wonder the evil spirits stayed away! It began to dawn on me that maybe this would be a good thing when I'd be working with future clients.

Harold was obviously still plotting ways to get closer to the beautiful woman in Lima who seemed to be eluding him. He was now strutting around shirtless, with what looked like a large penis on a cord that hung around his neck. Somewhat aghast, I had to lean in for a closer look. Here was our elusive guide, the one who recently had read us his riot act and had hardly cracked a smile, now cavorting around like a rooster looking for his favorite hen.

"Um, Hal," I decided to go in with a direct approach. "Why are you wearing a penis around your neck?"

Looking at me in mock surprise as if I should have recognized the item dangling down the middle of his chest, he replied "It's from the *capinuri* tree. It's supposed to endow the wearer with great charisma and prowess."

All the men giggled like schoolboys, while we women looked at each other and rolled our eyes. Someone explained to us about this particular tree and how when the small appendages on the branches break off, they look like the male organ. I sure hope he removed the tree talisman if he was hoping to impress the lady in Lima.

As if to emphasize that his after-retreat plan was to score, his *preparado* was the popular *pusanga*. A *pusanga* is a sweet-smelling mixture of herbs and other ingredients, and it's formulated according to what the customer wants to bring into their life. Some people want to attract money or good luck, but perhaps the most requested *pusanga* is one that will attract a lover. The idea is to splash some of the magic potion on yourself while visualizing what you want to have happen. The combination of the shaman's skillful blending and the customer's visualization is said to lead to the manifestation of the desire. Somehow, after being on the receiving end of his earful of rage, I couldn't imagine him getting close to anyone. No wonder he needed those things!

We had another couple of days to transition back to our regular diets. This was made official with a potent mixture of salt, lemon juice, chopped onions and garlic. One sip was all that was needed to break the dieta. I was surprised at how much I had gotten used to the lack of salt. Even the small amount in the mix seemed overpowering. At once, I could see the reason that we remove such strong substances from our diets as we prepare for this special work. Now reintroducing the things we'd taken out showed me how their strong energetics can interfere with the transmissions from the more subtle plant spirits.

Our three and a half week plant spirit medicine retreat was now at an end. Leaving day had us up early so we could get the baggage boat loaded. We had to give it a two-hour head start before our own passenger boat took us back to the embarkation point upriver at Nina Rumi.

It's always a bit bittersweet at the end of a transformational experience. For me, it felt like it had taken up until the last two or three days here to settle down and really get into the groove. I thought I was just beginning to grasp the edges of understanding what was going on in these ceremonies. It was like when, as a child, I'd reached out to touch the waves in the ocean as they slid onto the sand, only to have them pull back and not leave any traces. I'd done a lot of reading and research about ayahuasca, but no book or video can make you understand what the sacred journey is really like. The only way to experience it is to experience it.

I also had been starting to feel that there was a lot more to this ancient practice than just handing out a bitter tea and singing special songs. Who were the spirits that were mentioned in the songs? What were their stories? Although I had to admit that I'd not been a perfect retreat guest, it was as if the jungle was showing me that there was another universe behind the ceremonies. It's a hard thing to describe, but it's as if the spirit of the jungle itself flowed through the ayahuasca and the ceremonies and then into me.

PART TWO

Destiny Calls

CHAPTER 5

Geraldo

Have you ever done something that you knew wasn't really good for you, but you did it anyway because you wanted to see what it would feel like or how it would turn out? This is how I got involved with Geraldo.

Our helpful jungle guide was in his late twenties, probably about 5'7"or 5'8" and fairly lean. He was Peruvian, but not indigenous like Javier, Atilio, and the villagers who lived around the Sacha Wasi camp. He had an interesting face, not bad looking at all, but not exactly handsome either. There was also a kind of defeated hungry look about him too.

During our stay at the camp, he had seemed to be very solicitous of all of us, tending to our needs even when we hadn't asked for anything. His capable skills with our language allowed him to befriend those who came to the retreat, but most people weren't around him long enough to see what an opportunist he really was. Still, there was some kind of weird attraction I felt towards him, just like the proverbial moth to the flame.

The baggage boat had already departed, so I had some time to kill before we too would return to the city. I meandered slowly through the camp, taking my time to notice how different I felt from when we'd arrived. The spring-loaded anger and frustration I'd brought with me seemed to have been replaced by an overall sense of calm and wholeness. As I passed by my tambo for the last time, I patted one of the structure's supports and expressed deep gratitude for all that had taken place, not just in these past two weeks in camp, but also the earlier work on the northwest coast.

Returning to the main building to await the speedboat, I sat at the top of the stairs that led downward from the maloca. Gazing out across the river, I was suddenly startled by someone plopping down next to me.

"Are you sad to be leaving now?" our young guide asked me.

"Yes. I feel like I need more time here. It's too soon to leave."

"Going back to Iquitos?"

"Yes, and then I'm planning on visiting Cusco and wandering around the Andes. I need to get some information about the best places to visit and where to stay."

He nodded thoughtfully and looked very, very serious.

Just then, someone announced the arrival of our motorboat. As I made my way to the landing, I turned around and gave Sacha Wasi a long searching look, then a silent thank you and goodbye. Something big had happened here–I could feel it—but I couldn't quite put my finger on it.

Geraldo sat next to me in the small motorboat, and we continued to chat as we followed our bags back up the river. He painted a picture of someone who was determined to succeed despite enduring many hardships, and I liked his positive attitude. He told me he would get up early to study English using any medium possible that was available: TV, radio, magazines, and books. Realizing that he'd have more job opportunities if he spoke English, he taught himself to a level of proficiency that would allow him to get work with tourists in jungle lodges. He'd known Javier for about four years, and the young shaman was teaching him about how plants heal, which ones were good for certain ailments, and other traditional practices.

He asked if I was married, so I told him I was divorced. "Free and single!" Hint, hint, hint.

Back at the hotel, he and the other guys helped bring in all the bags. I watched him put his backpack down, and what I thought was a clever plan began to form in my heat-addled head. I set my bag down right next to his so it wouldn't look strange to be seen to be fishing around looking for something. I didn't have any paper or a pen to hand, but spied a little stack of flyers on the reception desk that displayed a large *te amo* on the front: Spanish for I love you. They were advertising an event for Valentine's Day, which was less than a week away. I surreptitiously took one and folded it over so this message was the only thing that was seen on the top half. As I pretended to rustle around in my bag, I managed to put the paper in an outside pocket of his backpack.

Before we'd left Sacha Wasi, several people exchanged contact information. One of the girls, Sandra, had passed around a book to sign. When it got to me, I saw Geraldo's email on a blank page, so I memorized it. I don't always know why I do certain things, but I was sure that the big reveal would eventually appear. I just hoped it wouldn't blow up in my face!

We all still had a few days left on our tour, so various sightseeing activities were now finally being offered. Perhaps Harold, who seemed much sunnier now that he had his *capinuri* penis necklace and extra-strong pusanga order on the way, felt a little guilty for being so evasive. Even so, he turned over the tour guiding duties to Geraldo while he continued to disappear for long periods of time.

While Iquitos can be quite bone-jarring at times, for me it was preferable to return back to this jungle town and reacclimate slowly to city energy, rather than having to head straight back out into real life, whatever that may be. Being able to integrate the stunning experiences that had taken place while still being under the Amazon jungle's umbrella was quite profound for me. Something had gotten under my skin besides bugs. I wasn't able to identify it yet, but it itched all the same.

When I was in high school, my best friend and I ran what we called a spy service; the objects of our pursuit were always cute guys. We were masters of the stake-out, the reconnaissance mission, and peeking around corners. We fancied ourselves as clever detectives as we surreptitiously followed some poor classmate after school to find out where he lived. Despite all the years that had passed, I remained a practitioner of the stealthy arts and was always amazed at how unaware people can be at times.

I used Geraldo's purloined email address and simply sent him a test message. Nothing fancy; just plain and neutral. I had no idea how often he checked his email, how or where, so I didn't expect anything back. In the meantime, I knew time was running out. I felt I had to nudge the process along, so I needed to put on my spy cloak again and question certain people who might be able to help me.

That person turned out to be Gary's local girlfriend, Maria. After returning from Sacha Wasi, Gary had not come to the hotel with the rest of us; he went back to the apartment he was sharing with Maria, but he stayed in touch with us so they could join any outings. He also knew that we'd all soon be scattering in different directions.

The following day, Gary and Maria showed up as a bunch of us gathered once more in the lobby. I suddenly had a wild thought pop into my head and pulled Maria aside. I asked her if she knew Geraldo well, and on hearing her positive reply I impulsively told her I liked him. She agreed to help me, so phoned him to tell him to come to the hotel to talk to me. He wasn't able to come until the next day, but the seed was planted.

In the meantime, something else eased its way into my consciousness. While we had been waiting for our passenger boat to arrive at the lodge, I'd run into Edwin. He told me that Harold had warned him to expect Geraldo to try and hit us up for money or goods even though he'd already been paid well. Edwin, now looking full on like a denizen of the leafy deep in his cargo shorts, bare feet, and red huayuro seed necklaces, said that he'd had a vision of Geraldo caught in a sort of battle between his good heart and seeing us as walking wallets. I digested this for a moment and it felt right. Yes, I'd be on the lookout for this.

As travelers who journey to places where there are not many jobs or legitimate ways for the locals to earn money, we will at times find ourselves as the targets of various ploys designed to tug at our sympathy strings and get us to hand over some quick cash. While there are innumerable of these extraction attempts around the globe and many variations on the same themes, I found two in particular to be used quite frequently in Iquitos.

The first one is where you may be sitting in a café or on a park bench taking in the scenery, when someone will approach you in a non-threatening way. If you greet them in a friendly manner, they will take this as an invitation to sit down. You will soon be on the receiving end of the saddest sob stories you've ever heard, none of which are even remotely true, but each one crafted based on the situation. If these tales of woe were indeed for real, then half the city's population must surely be dying in the hospital from some horrible malady that could undoubtedly be cured with expensive medical care. It will then transpire that the afflicted person also happens to be the only breadwinner in the family. I had wondered throughout the trip why Harold and Patrick had restricted our movements at times, or otherwise took over some business transaction on behalf of the group instead of having us do it ourselves. But now that we were left alone without our guardians, I started to see what they were protecting us from.

As my dear, old dad used to say, "Fool me once, shame on you. Fool me twice, shame on me!"

The second way for the young people to earn money or goods was to become your girlfriend or boyfriend for however long this could be milked. All the guys in our group had already been solicited by beautiful young girls as we walked down the streets. They'd approach with different tactics, and after a while I found it amusing to guess which gambit the current one would use.

"Hi! Are you American?" For some reason they always started with this country first, referring to the United States. Any type of reply was met with batting eyelashes and chests thrust out of revealing halter tops. "Would you like to buy me a drink?" While some of these were simply working girls, others were hoping for longer term relationships where the flattered male would end up giving them lots of gifts and paying their bills.

Of course, the girls weren't the only ones hustling the game. It was a lot harder for the men to entice a visiting female, just as it is in pretty much any country around the world. One safe opening they could use was to sidle up to you as you were minding your own business and ask you if they could practice their English. You could be certain that a request for something else would be coming down the line soon enough.

So, while I was rather enjoying my own game, I went into the situation with open eyes. I wanted to watch the moves like a chess player. What piece was Geraldo going to move next? The scientist in me wanted to live a real-life experiment to see what it felt like. And of course, I'd be listening to my inner guidance.

Not wanting anyone else in the group to know what I was up to at this stage, I resorted to sending Geraldo emails. Most of these were fairly neutral, such as telling him that I thought he was interesting. I purposely didn't want to be too suggestive, but very quickly his messages became somewhat over the top. "Kiss! Baby, baby! I love you, baby." I couldn't help but think of Barry White.

Let's just say that through a combination of clever maneuvering and a very short miniskirt, hastily purchased at a women's clothing ship on Prospero, the following night we found ourselves at Noa Noa, a nightclub not far from the hotel. Despite the initial reaction at seeing me all fixed up, Geraldo turned out not to be such a pushover. He didn't really want to drink anything with alcohol, claiming that he had to get up early so he could guide us on the last two sightseeing expeditions early next morning. He seemed to be kind of distracted and suggested we move on to another club. Flying between the two clubs in the back of a motocab in an exotic location, the wind blowing through my hair, I felt like I truly was the heroine of a romantic novel. Finally, after all I'd gone through in the past few years, maybe tonight would be different.

But Geraldo wasn't doing his best to play his part in this tryst. I may have felt like the star of my own movie, but this younger man was fizzling out and considering heading home to get some sleep. When I tried to point out that it was still early, he said he'd have to get up early so he could get back to our hotel for 8 am. In desperation, I finally had to be very plain with my intent. "Well, you don't have to go back to your place, you know. If you have to be at our hotel so early, you could just stay with me and be already there!"

So much for ploy number two. He didn't seem like he was exactly going out of his way to be my boyfriend either, was he?

"Are you sure this would be okay?"

"Sure! I have plenty of room. No problem."

I thought most guys on the receiving end of an invitation like this would be prepared to drop everything to go back to inspect the furniture. Geraldo? He suggested that we stay at the second nightclub for a bit. Although I'd been told he was a shameless opportunist, I certainly wasn't seeing any evidence of this now. I had the feeling that it wasn't so much of his not wanting to take me up on my blatant invitation, but rather he couldn't believe what he was hearing. It was almost as if at any moment he expected me to yell out, "Ha ha! Just kidding!"

"Do you want to sleep with me?" he asked for clarification.

"Yes."

I guess all my sneakiness and subtlety hadn't translated very well, but this story had a funny twist. Despite the supposed convenience of not having to get up early to get to our hotel, he still wanted to go back to his boarding house to change and pick up a few things he'd need for the day. As he was telling me this, he let slip that he'd told the landlords that he might not be coming home for the night. So, who turned out to be the sneakier one?

My reluctant Latin lover returned as we were all waiting in the lobby, and the smirking began between us. One of the drivers who had been hired to take us to the port turned out to be a friend of his. I saw them talking, then the driver looked over at me. Thinking that Geraldo was telling him about last night and pointing me out as the goddess-like seductress, I boldly arranged myself on the sofa and returned the strong gaze. "Yeah? Heh heh heh," my body language transmitted across the room and through our milling group, none of whom had any idea of the almost imperceptible communication going back and forth. It was just so much fun! I felt so alive!

Harold had made arrangements with one of the men from the Sacha Wasi village who had a boat to take us to see the Bora Indians and a few other sights. Like so many other tourists who come to the Peruvian Amazon, we also wanted to see the famous pink dolphins. Marcio skillfully navigated the watercraft into the confluence, the junction where the Nanay and Amazon Rivers meet. And suddenly, there they were! They weren't exactly pink, but rather more greyish pink with a few brighter pink spots, but we were still thrilled at the sight of these legendary creatures.

Our first destination of the day turned out to be not much more than a marketing ploy before a hard sell of indigenous crafts, or *artesanía*. We were led to a structure that looked like a ceremonial room or meeting place. The high peaked ceiling was made out of the now recognizable, woven irapay palm panels, and there was a dirt floor. There were no solid walls around the building; several of the openings were filled with simple barriers made of young tree trunks nailed to two horizontal cross pieces.

The Bora were dressed up like something out of a Hollywood set. While both the men and women were clad only in short skirts made from tree bark with painted designs, the topless women were obviously a big draw. They'd developed quite a show for the tourists that involved their first doing a few dances on their own, then inviting us to join the circle and whirl around the room with them. The dancers all looked quite bored until it was time to stop the act.

As soon as we separated back out of the dance line and moved to the other side of the room, they suddenly turned and swooped in on us, shoving all sorts of their handicrafts in our faces. Our small group was completely surrounded and being hit with purses, bags, and carved items, along with the ubiquitous red and black huayuro seed jewelry that is so common in this area. It was almost like a small riot, and several of the women in our group were quite alarmed at the perceived attack. I asked Geraldo to have the overzealous sales crew back off a bit and explained that we'd prefer to be able to peruse their offerings at our leisure. They didn't seem very happy to hear this and continued to bombard us with so many goods that it was impossible to even consider anything.

Geraldo, having a few sly moves of his own, decided to try another tactic to distract them. "This one here," he indicated me, "is my wife."

Some of them paused and peered at me in disbelief. We assured them that I was indeed his wife, putting his arm around me to appear more convincing. I, of course, played along with the deception because I thought it was hilarious.

The diversion worked to shift their focus long enough to allow the members of our party to escape through the ring of natives that enclosed them. Once they were allowed a little breathing space, the Bora craftspeople were able to close a few sales. Their main sales pitch now completed, the natives lost interest in us and vanished through a side door while we made our way back to where Marcio was waiting with the boat.

The next stop was Pilpintuwasi, the butterfly farm. Once we all entered the beautiful complex, Geraldo pulled me by the arm back into a covered arbor where no one could see us. He handed me an exotic flower and said, "Let's get married."

At first, I thought he was joking and gave a little laugh, but then I realized he was serious. He knew I was leaving the area the next day so he pulled out all his lines.

"I really loved being with you last night. I like you a lot. I don't want you to go."

For once, I was speechless. Marriage, already?

Just then, someone from our group up ahead called his name.

"You go first," I instructed. "I'll follow in a moment." I figured I'd just sneak in and rejoin the group after he distracted them, so they wouldn't realize that something was going on between us.

I was enjoying the butterfly farm and the sheer variety of the gorgeous insects. Some of the patterns on their wings were incredibly intricate, and I had to remind myself that this was Mother Nature's artwork in its finest form. There were also a few mischievous little monkeys and a sad-looking spotted jaguar in a cage. While Geraldo had been contracted to interpret for the entire group, he dutifully carried out his tasks in between making soppy faces and doe eyes at me.

Because Marcio's boat couldn't fit our entire traveling party in one trip, he had to return us to our hotel so he could pick up the second group. I took my exotic flower and went up to my room to pack.

Later that day, we had a final meeting with our tour leaders and the two shamans, who had brought all of our prescribed *preparados* for us to carry back with us. My camalonga had been presented in an old one liter plastic soda bottle that looked like it had already been used several times before. It seemed like almost half the contents was made up of chopped onion. I twisted open the cap and took a whiff. The strong smell nearly knocked me out of my chair.

"Be careful with that; it's very potent," warned Atilio.

"Remember to use it for protection against the negative energies you may encounter," added Javier.

I must have looked puzzled because he added, "In your work as a healer."

I nodded, still not having any idea of how I was going to manifest this great transformation into a *curandera*, or healer.

Sitting in the clean hotel meeting room with Jav and Atilio, it felt to me as if the jungle lodge experience had never really happened. I looked around at my companions, particularly those who'd been present since we'd first met up in Lima and felt a little sad that our retreat was finally ending. We were planning to have one last meal together, and I wondered if Geraldo had been invited. Patrick's and Gary's local girlfriends were invited, so I thought as our group interpreter that my new beau should also join us.

As it turned out, Harold decided that none of the partners were to dine on his dime, so I made the decision that I would rather spend the last night with my potential jungle husband. I'd spent the last three and a half weeks with this group and was ready to move on to the next phase of my adventure. With this being my last night, I also had to figure out what to do about Geraldo.

The evening then took an unexpected turn. Joan, the annoying East Coaster who had tried to shove her way into everyone's business, decided that she, too, would make a play for Geraldo. After joining us for the second part of the trip, she had spent the entire time braying about being married and wanting a child, so what was all this about? By now, she knew that he and I had hooked up, but that didn't stop her. After unsuccessfully trying to pump me for information about what we'd been doing, she'd even told me that she was living vicariously through me. I found that pretty creepy. Whenever she would see us together, she'd make a beeline straight over and insert herself between us, sometimes actually shoving me aside. Then, looking at me with a false grin, would declare her apologies.

"I am *so* sorry! Oops! Clumsy of me! Hee hee hee." Grrr.

Inevitably, she would have some little present for Geraldo, like a snack or flower.

"Are you going to dinner with us tonight, Geraldo?" she gushed.

"I see you later, maybe," he promised.

I'd told him that since he wasn't invited to join the farewell dinner that I was not going either so we could spend the last night together. We agreed to make ourselves scarce until the group left to avoid any more interference.

In retrospect, I should have gone to the dinner. My plans for a romantic evening in my room with dinner brought up from room service turned out to not be all that romantic after all. Geraldo had returned to the boarding house to pack up his room and fix himself up for me. He returned in fresh clothing and wearing cologne. I ordered room service: a large T-bone with rice and mashed potatoes for him, and orange chicken with rice for me. So far, so good.

The problems started while we were waiting for the food to arrive. Geraldo spotted the television sitting on a chest of drawers against the far wall, and I saw his attention shift across the room.

"Do you mind if I watch a football game while we eat? One of my favorite teams is playing."

Sure," I replied. What would one game hurt?

Like many men in Latin American countries, he was an ardent football player. The game that is called soccer in the United States has a huge, fanatical following all over the world, and my companion was no exception. No sooner had one matched ended, then he'd flip through the channels to find another. I might as well have been alone in the room, although he kept me assuaged by occasionally turning around and giving me a squeeze and calling me honey.

There was something familiar about his behavior. He appeared like a man who'd crawled through the desert for days, dying of thirst, only to come upon a pool of pure well water from which he could slake his dry throat. Suddenly I saw it: Liam, the male Witch I'd moved in with who was also a TV addict. A sudden thought came to me.

"I'll bet you don't have a TV at home, do you?"

"No, I don't. I hope you don't mind."

I sighed. Sure, there was a part of me that wanted to chuck him back out on the street. But there was also a part of me that could see how much was lacking in his life. Was it so bad to allow him to eat a huge, expensive steak and watch his beloved footie, knowing that he may never get a chance to do this again? I took this all in. I'd gone into this liaison knowing full well it could never be lasting, but I was beginning to see how he might be milking me along to get what he wanted without having to pay for anything.

As I looked back on the past few weeks, I considered that what was supposed to have been a peaceful plant spirit medicine retreat had been anything but this thanks to many of our group members. By the last couple of days in the lodge, four of the women had already broken their dietas and refused to cooperate with Harold and Patrick any longer. The last straw for them apparently had been what I'll call the Great Drinking Water Deception.

In many jungle villages and camps, a well is dug to provide clean water for drinking and making up medicines. Sacha Wasi was no exception. While the source of this water comes from the nearby rivers, there are certain locations where it filters up through many layers of minerals, leaving it purified and safe to drink, even for non-locals. We'd been told to bring refillable water bottles and had been happily consuming this natural liquid without experiencing any negative health issues.

Unfortunately, a problem was created when Carol and Vanni suspected that Harold was hiding a case of bottled commercial drinking water in his tambo. I don't know how they discovered this, but they were mad as hell at the idea that he had instructed us to drink the purified ground water, while he himself was sipping on well-known local brands of quality bottled *agua.* Of course, Harold vehemently denied this, so they insisted on an immediate search of his living quarters. Possibly wanting to avert any more accusations or simply exonerate himself, Harold had agreed to their demand and led anyone who was even remotely interested over to his wooden platform. A quick search of his sparse tambo turned up nothing--not even one empty plastic bottle that could be used as evidence.

Harold and Patrick remained smiling innocently at the base of the ladder while the four women stomped off in a huff. Although Carol and Vanni had been the most dissatisfied and critical members of our group,

Barbara and Greta, who had also signed up for this adventure together, soon joined in with their incessant grumbling. While the rest of us had done our best to atone for our naïve sin of socializing too much, these four had gone the other way and planted themselves in the maloca as much as possible, talking and howling non-stop. They were done! Fed up and so outta here!

Any kind of introspective work can shake a person to their core. But when you have a large group of people, many for whom this was their first foray into self-reflection, that instability can radiate out from those shaken cores and negatively affect the entire group's energy. It's hard enough to feel so raw and vulnerable, but to do so in front of a bunch of strangers can result in feelings of insecurity and the need to lash out to protect one's personal space. When tempers simmered and flared or fights and disagreements had broken out within our group, there was usually no one in authority who was close enough to put an immediate stop to the nonsense.

I was glad to be getting away from all that drama. Even though I, myself, hadn't been a perfect participant, I felt a deep reverence for the traditions and knowledge I had been introduced to. I rued my ignorance and errors and was determined to be more attentive and aware as I continued on my journey.

I had hoped that we'd have a smooth sendoff to the airport, so I wasn't counting on big Joanie's final hideous hurl at Geraldo. Smirking horribly through curled lips that she obviously thought were seductive, she tried to drag him over to the other side of the lobby to whisper in his ear. Just to be obnoxious, I followed and looked at her expectantly. Somehow, this made her nervous, and she suddenly started braying loudly about how since her husband had lost interest in sex, she had a little surprise in store for him. The large woman announced that she was bringing back a number of magical potions that the shamans had assured her would make him fall hopelessly back under her spell. She gazed meaningfully at Geraldo.

Recalling the trip through the Belen market and seeing all the *preparados* with suggestive names, I had been amused at how many of them, like the Rompe Calzones were formulated for explosions, super libido, and non-stop action. The jungle was indeed a hot, steamy place!

I wondered if any of these medicines she'd obtained from Jav and Atilio had been specifically made for her, or if they had been obtained from one of those vendors in the Pasaje Paquito. I then wondered if her bizarre behavior might have been caused by her possibly cracking open the bottles to sample her potions ahead of time.

I must've drifted more deeply into my horrified musings than I had realized, because it felt like I was suddenly pulled out of my reverie, causing me to shake my head several times to clear away the awful images. Her voice had gone up in volume and pitch, and she now announced to the entire lobby that once her husband drank what was in those innocent looking bottles, we'd be hearing her scream all the way from Boston.

Geraldo and I exchanged looks of nausea and disbelief, while the others presented a varying range of reactions such as amusement, puzzled looks, and disgust. It wasn't difficult to see why her husband had lost interest in her.

Geraldo came into the airport with us to help with the check in. His mood became increasingly heavier.

"So, what are you going to do after we're gone?" I asked him.

"My mother lives nearby, so I'm going to visit with her."

I could understand his sadness, or at least this is the story I put to the feelings. From the pieces of his life that he'd shared with me in our short time together, I gathered that it was a life of want and unfulfillment. His biological father had disappeared after his birth, and his stepfather was a mean drunk who treated his mother badly and didn't contribute anything to the household. When Geraldo was able to get work, he would give her a portion of his wages so she could take care of herself and other members of the household. He never told me any of this upfront. He would simply answer my questions with those sad doe eyes as I tried to tease it all out of him a little at a time.

He'd had a little oasis of fun and interactions with us--he even got lucky--and now it was all vanishing through the security checkpoint.

I felt he was genuinely sorry to see me and the others go. He hadn't asked me for any money, so I discretely took out a fifty sol note, rolled it up, and put it in his jacket pocket. The nuevo sol is the Peruvian unit of currency, made up of one hundred centavos. It is written as S/n, where n is the amount. Thus S/50 is fifty soles.

"What are you doing?" he protested.

"It's for your mother, okay?"

While he didn't really protest too hard, neither did he try to return it. One could buy a lot of food with S/50 in Iquitos. Fifty soles were roughly equal to $15 USD at the time, so it didn't really hurt my budget.

After such a long time in the deep freeze, he'd made me feel good about myself again even if only for a little while. I didn't try to analyze how sincere he might have been because it didn't matter. I knew how I felt. I still didn't know what my plans were, but I did know that I would be back, and I let this slip.

"Please make it soon! I love you, Baby."

The minibus picked us up at the Lima airport for the short ride back to our hotel in Miraflores. I sat next to Gillian and realized that she'd mellowed out a lot over the last few weeks. When I told her I noticed that she seemed happier than when she'd arrived, she agreed. "I had just broken up with my fiancé and was a real mess. The ceremonies really helped me feel more centered."

Since she had gone shopping with me for the disco mini skirt, she'd known what I was up to. Because she wasn't all creepy and voyeuristic like Joan, I was happy to share a bit of the excitement with someone who was supportive.

"When did you start scheming on him?"

"I think it was that wild third ceremony where I laid on the back floor alone all night. He took the blanket off his bed and covered me with it so I wouldn't be cold."

"You should really come back and see him before you return to the States."

"Yes, I believe I will."

We agreed to meet up after getting settled in our rooms. Wandering down to the Larcomar promenade we found a restaurant that offered fresh local fish and allowed ourselves a leisurely lunch.

After buying some ice cream cones from a small stall as an after lunch treat, we found a travel agency in the mall and arranged our flights to Cusco for the next morning. Since I had never to that ancient city before, I decided to book a hotel package with an airport transfer and an included tour of Machu Picchu.

My mind wandered back to Geraldo. What was he doing right now? Did he miss me already? Did he miss me at all? I wondered if I could plan the rest of my remaining days so I could make a last pass back through Iquitos. Yes, it was possible. I was supposed to call him later.

We were told to return in two hours to pick up our tickets and documentation, so we walked back to the hotel. We found members of our retreat group gathered in the lobby discussing where to go for dinner. I'd had enough of wandering around streets all bunched up like fearful tourists, so I politely declined their invitation to join them. Gillian and I returned to Larcomar to get our tickets.

Enroute, we ran into another member of our group who was also ditching the pack. Niall had had lodgings next to me for both phases of our trip and I found him to be a grounding presence in the midst of all the feminine chaos. The only time I saw him lose his temper was during one of the night ceremonies when he wanted a chair to sit in but there weren't enough to go around. He'd gotten really annoyed, shouting at Patrick for not providing enough chairs for each person. Like I said before, when you dive deep into the psyche, your stuff comes up, and sometimes it's pretty ridiculous. Later on, when he could laugh about his outburst, he made up a name for himself: Singado Chairless.

After leaving the travel agency, we found a tobacco shop with a humidor and a bar, so he and I treated ourselves to snifters of Courvoisier and Cuban cigars, while Gillian kept trying to lean away from our smoke paths. In keeping with the Cuban theme, we found a restaurant serving that island's cuisine. The food was delicious, but the service was a bit ditzy and slow.

To make up for it, there was a small band playing in the corner of the room. By this time, the three of us were the only ones left in the restaurant, so we shouted back and forth good-naturedly to the musicians. They seemed happy to interact with us instead of playing to empty chairs.

"Are you *Americanos*?" asked the bass player.

"Are we not all *Americanos*?" I asked in reply with a wink.

That called for cheering and another round of whatever we were drinking by then.

It was after midnight when I got back to the hotel and began the frustrating process of trying to call Geraldo as I'd promised. I tried several times from my room phone but was unsuccessful at completing the call. I finally phoned reception, only to be told the room phones were blocked for all non-local calls. The operator put the call through for me, for an extra charge of course, and I heard Geraldo's voice on the other end. Unfortunately, the connection was very bad and I could hardly hear or understand him. He was out drinking beer with his friend, probably with the money I'd slipped into his pocket for his mother. He did sound very happy to hear my voice and a few garbled sentences made their ways over the crackly connection.

"Check your email. I sent you something."

"As soon as I get to Cusco." I wrote back.

As I put down the phone, I wondered why I was so attracted to this skinny jungle man who was so full of problems and almost young enough to be my son. I repeatedly felt that something was guiding me onto a path that I could not yet see. I considered that perhaps the big goal in my life wouldn't be reached by going directly in a straight line, but instead by taking detours off to the side at times. I felt that getting involved with Geraldo was one of these side trips, and that somehow, he would ultimately lead me back on to the main road.

CHAPTER 6

The Air Up There

The Andes Mountains started to come into view after our plane left the coastal city of Lima and headed southwest towards Cusco. I was glad I'd booked a window seat so I could have a condor's eye view of this magnificent mountain range that I'd read so much about over the years. I marveled at the ruggedness of its peaks, some of which were so high that they pierced the light cloud layer below. While I didn't know the exact altitude of these particular mountains that we were flying over, I was somewhat surprised, but also delighted to observe what looked to be small villages nestled far below in some of the valleys between the peaks. I wondered how their inhabitants were able to access such remote outposts without any obvious roads.

My plane touched down in the old Inca city, and I confidently made my way down the steps to the tarmac. I'd read about Cusco's high altitude, but never having been too far above sea level before, I figured that I was healthy enough to deal with some thin air. It couldn't be that bad, could it?

Yes, it could. It suddenly felt as if a plastic bag had been whipped over my head and tied firmly around my neck. Little spots of light danced before my eyes and I couldn't catch my breath. Did I eat something bad? Am I sick? Is someone trying to kill me? Did I breathe some dirty air?

Air?

It was the air, or rather, the lack of it. Or to be more precise, it was the lower amount of oxygen in this air high in the Andes Mountains. I'd been told about the effects of oxygen deprivation, especially when one arrived here quickly from an airport at 113 feet above sea level to one with an elevation of 10,860 feet.

As I entered through the airport's arrivals door, a heavy cloud of fog descended into my brain and I couldn't figure out where to go. Fortunately, I'd chosen that comprehensive travel package from the agent in Lima that included airport transfers. Just as I was about to walk into a wall I saw a smiling woman in a crisp, businesslike uniform holding up a sign with my name on it: Judi Limon. Name looks familiar. Is that me?

The hotel rep who was there to collect me from the flight easily recognized what was wrong with me. "Don't worry. We've got something back at the hotel that'll help with this. It's not far. Just take it very easy."

On arrival at the hotel, my uniformed angel sat me straight down on a couch in the lobby. "Wait here while I check you in. Here's some tea that'll should help you deal with the altitude."

I must've looked confused because she continued. "This is coca leaf tea. We use it here in many ways as a medicine. It helps visitors acclimate to the high altitude without getting sick. Just relax. I won't be long."

Coca leaf, eh? I thought back to my days as a professional musician. Some of my band mates always had mounds of the addictive white euphoria powder with them. How different it was to sip this mild-tasting infusion instead of snorting the strong powder with a chemical smell. It was hard to believe such distinct forms came from the same plant. These simple green leaves looked so innocent as they floated in my cup of hot water. I knew I had a lot to learn about plant medicine.

The tea seemed to help, but I couldn't shake the fatigue. I had my trip to Machu Picchu scheduled for the next morning, and I wanted to look around Cusco a bit to see the sights first. I planned go out and wander for a short time, and then when the brain fog would set back in, I'd return to my room for more coca tea and a quick nap.

Dying to know what Geraldo had sent me in the email, I looked for an internet place and found one just down the street from my centrally located hotel. I was so excited to find out what he'd sent me that I just couldn't wait to log into my email, and there it was! Was it a photo or sweet message? It was neither. It was simply a short message informing me that he would be accompanying Javier on a five-day lodge retreat somewhere, so was going to be out of communication range for a bit. This made things tricky now. He'd be leaving tomorrow, so I had to decide my plans for the rest of this trip and talk to him before he left. Despite his now lack of romantic overtures, I somehow knew that I had to go back to Iquitos before I returned home.

I found myself in Cusco's main square, another Plaza de Armas, where it looked as if all of the city's travel agents had set up shop around this central space. Most of these businesses offering cheap fares and the usual tours operated out of very small storefronts that had room for two desks and little else. Some were so basic that they seemed like a family had just decided to set up a business in their front room with a phone and a fax; and if they were really fancy, a computer! In order to be able to pass through their doors you usually had to sidestep around the many advertising sandwich boards that blocked the sidewalks.

Despite the near lack of customers, they didn't seem too keen to attend to me. I felt like I was interrupting their favorite television program. With a sigh, a man named Cesar with slicked back hair got up reluctantly from his chair and asked what I was looking for. I explained first that I wanted to go to Puno and visit Lake Titicaca. He handed me a brochure for a hotel in Puno that he assured me was a three star hotel. It looked decent enough so I agreed to go there. I'm sure Cesar got some kind of kickback for directing travelers to this particular establishment.

A first-class bus would take me to this town high in the Andes, stopping at various places of interest. Lunch was included, but I couldn't get too excited about this. Every time I had done one of these bus tours where lunch was included, it turned out to be a low-budget buffet full of bland food that looked more like it had been teleported from almost any cheap restaurant in my own country. You might see a few regional specialties, but the pans with popular dishes were often empty, or the food just didn't look very appealing. I suspected the choice of food was aimed more at keeping the Western tourists happy, being able to recognize so many familiar dishes as they moved around in such a foreign land.

To make things worse, every tour bus in the area seemed to descend on the same places at the same times, including the restaurant. This resulted in chaos as the servers and staff were suddenly overwhelmed with hundreds of hungry tourists all trying to get in the door and find an available table at the same time.

And heaven help you if you weren't a party of four! The frantic servers would split your numbers up and spread you out among the available seats. If you got lucky, you could end up with some great conversations, but more often than not, the other tourists would clam up once they got past "So, where are you from?" as they returned to gaze at their white rice and spaghetti noodles.

To add to the fun, you were given a specific time to meet back at the bus so there was only a limited time to eat. Energy crackled in the room as people shoved their way down the buffet line, cramming their plates full to get a good deal, then stuffing food in their mouths in order to be able to finish it within the allotted fifty minutes. Yes, you could call it lunch, but it wasn't very pleasant.

It seemed to take forever for Cesar to make all my arrangements not only for the Puno visit, but also my tickets back to Iquitos. He would often look up from the ancient landline he was using and tell me the signal was bad or that he was on hold. Sometimes the call disconnected and he'd have to start over again. I was still feeling slightly wacky from the high altitude, so I didn't really mind just watching the traffic pass by the somewhat obscured windows.

Eventually, my full itinerary was completed. The day after tomorrow, I'd be on the luxury bus to Puno, where I'd stay a couple of nights in the recommended hotel, followed by a night on the island of Amantani with an indigenous Aymara family before returning to the city. That sounded easy enough.

Going back to Iquitos, however, would involve an entire day of fragmented travel. Since there was no airport in Puno, I would catch a shuttle to the closest city with an airport, Juliaca, which could take an hour or more. From there I'd catch a flight back to Lima, where I'd board my last flight to Iquitos, finally arriving there after eight o'clock at night.

I decided to call Geraldo before anything else to let him know of my arrival, and then I'd be able to relax and enjoy my sightseeing. Perhaps it was a blessing that he'd be out of range for nearly a week so I wouldn't be distracted by some guy back in a city I'd just left, while I was here in a literally breathtaking part of the world. These were the days before the use of cellphones exploded all over the world, so it was a challenge to make phone calls in some places where the entire protocol was different.

Asking at the hotel's front desk netted me the reply that if I called from the hotel, the charge would be a dollar per minute. When I balked at that, they suggested I buy a phone card for ten nuevo soles, which was roughly about three dollars. Another hotel employee offered to run across the street to the shop for me, so I gratefully accepted.

Feeling victorious after these few successes, I took the card over to a phone but couldn't get it to work. Neither could two other employees. Finally, after about ten or fifteen minutes we figured it out, and I heard Geraldo pick up on the other end. I had just enough time to give him my arrival details and chat for a few minutes before the cheap phone card ran out of credit.

I was up at 4 am the next day in order to catch the 6:15 am train to Aguas Calientes. The four hour ride with a lot of switchbacks was worth the price of the ticket alone. There weren't many people on the train at this hour, so I was able to choose a perfect viewing point. Glued to my window seat, I watched the most stunning landscapes roll into view. As I looked up into the towering mountains, I suddenly felt an immense presence. These peaks were so old that they seemed to hold a lot of wisdom in their being. I wondered if these were the *apus*, the powerful mountain spirits of the Andes.

After disembarking from the train, I had to wait for the local buses that would take me the final distance up to Machu Picchu. I'd bought a guided tour, which took us to the more well-known parts of the site. We did have some time on our own to explore, but it didn't seem like enough. I wanted to find a place to hide and stay within the crumbling walls overnight. I wanted to be able to feel the pure energy of Machu Picchu without having to share it with a hoard of others.

Local boys provided quite a spectacle for us as our bus wound down around the very steep and curvy roads on the return trip. They would suddenly appear at the side of the road, long enough to know we'd seen them and return their friendly waves. As we passed, they suddenly dove out of sight down the nearly perpendicular slope. Several turns later around some impossible scenery, these same boys would suddenly pop up again, laughing and waving as they played their game. I marveled at their endurance in the thin air, although I realized they were well accustomed to it. Although I was no longer disoriented, I couldn't walk too far or fast without having to stop and catch my breath. And these guys were running up and down insane slopes and laughing! I was seriously impressed.

I would have liked to have spent more time in Cusco, but since I already had my return flight to the States paid for, I was up against a time limit. Sure, I could have stayed longer there, but for some reason I knew I had to go back to Iquitos. It's hard to explain the ever-strengthening energetic pull I felt. I had no illusions that Geraldo and I would ride off into the sunset together; all I knew was that I had to return to that jungle town before I flew back home.

The start of the trip to Puno was like something out of an old, black and white TV comedy with everyone running around as if swarms of bees were after them. Cesar from the travel agency showed up at my hotel at eight in the morning. Despite arranging this part of my tour, he didn't seem to know what was going on. He hadn't given me any tickets, and he didn't have them either. When I queried this, he passed it off that yesterday was Sunday, and that the bus company must've moved. Well, that didn't inspire confidence, and I started to wonder if I'd been taken for a ride without yet having put a foot in a vehicle.

Suddenly, Cesar made a mad dash into the street and hailed a cab.

"Oh good," I muttered under my breath. "Finally, I'm on my way."

He loaded my bags into the taxi, closed the door, and signaled for it to leave. He then turned to me and grunted that he had to get the tickets. The car then started to drive off with my bags, so I took off after it, leaving Cesar standing in the middle of the street in astonishment. Running alongside to the right of the taxi, I grabbed the back door handle, flung it open and threw myself on the seat, much to the consternation of the driver. "My bags and I like to travel together," I explained.

I had no sooner managed to be able to sit up and see where we were going, when the back door was suddenly yanked open again and Cesar leapt in. I almost wanted to laugh at the sheer ridiculousness of the whole thing.

While this kind of scenario might set off warning bells for some, I didn't feel there was anything bad enough to set off alarm bells. I have a very good sense of inner vision and was using it now to assess the situation. Deep down, I knew everything was okay even though now I was literally being taken for a ride to some unknown destination.

We continued to drive through the beautiful old city of Cusco until we slowed to a stop in the San Jeronimo District just a few miles outside. Cesar instructed the driver to pull over, then he got out and started unloading my bags.

"You wait here for first-class bus." I looked at him in doubt because this did not look in any way like a bus stop.

"Yes, bus come here. We miss first pickup stop so we get the bus here. You wait." Sure, what else could I do?

Moments later, a large yellow bus bearing a large "first class" sign in the front window came hurtling around the corner. Despite both Cesar and me waving our arms frantically, it didn't seem to be slowing at all. This time it was Cesar's turn to run into the road after a departing vehicle. I watched in amazement as he made an incredible dash to catch up to the bus, all the while waving his arms and shouting. The bus managed to skid to a stop about a half a block away and a man got out. Cesar and the man engaged in an animated exchange as I hoiked my own bags down the street to where they were. I didn't know exactly what was said, although I'm sure it included the fact that there was no ticket issued that could be presented. I was eventually allowed to board, feeling the eyes of all the other passengers on me. Finding a very comfortable, vacant seat, I plopped down and settled in. I was on my way to Puno!

Despite the comical send off from Cusco, the bus journey was wonderful. We stopped at various sites along the way, including the bland buffet with its ubiquitous please-the-tourist food. The only offering that was even remotely local was the coca tea.

Pulling into the Puno bus station, I was relieved to see a formally dressed young man named Nestor waiting for me. He held up a sign that read Señorita Judi. "That's probably me," I thought as I looked around. I still had no paperwork to prove I had paid for the tour or lodging, but this turned out to not be a problem. The connection had been made and I was here. It was a good lesson for me in trusting the process, rather than the details. I'd gotten used to the way the travel agents in my country worked, and they seemed a far cry from the one I'd used in Cusco. Yet the end result was that I did indeed get where I wanted to be, thoroughly enjoying the long ride with its stunning scenery.

Another lesson presented itself softly. *Trust the process. Let go of the details.*

As I'd suspected, the rating for the hotel was based more on wishful thinking than reality. It wasn't bad, but it was more basic than the brochure had led me to believe. Still, it was clean and centrally located.

It was also really cold, so I turned on the room heater. What a difference in climates I was experiencing on this trip!

Although I'd felt I was now fully acclimated to the high altitude, I knew I needed to adjust farther to the higher elevation of nearly another 1,700 ft. from Cusco to Puno. I felt fine, so I decided to find the internet place that the receptionist had told me about.

In keeping with my recent lessons in patience and accepting what I was experiencing at that very moment, checking my email was a non-starter. The computers were so slow as to be virtually unusable. This was another revelation for me. I was used to having pretty fast internet speeds, so it never occurred to me that in more remote places like the jungle or mountain towns that the same service may not be available. It's just one of those things that you don't think about until you experience it.

Deciding to find some dinner, I moseyed down a narrow street with a big question to consider: do I eat the guinea pig, locally known as *cuy,* or not? I'm all for trying local foods and specialties whenever possible, but guinea pigs and I go back a long way. When I was in second grade, my teacher, Mrs. Shuman, had a black and white female guinea pig in the classroom as a mascot for a while. When it came time to find her a permanent home, Mrs. Shuman asked if any of us might like to have her. After begging and pleading with my parents, I became the proud owner of Trixie the guinea pig.

My parents were now obligated to make things equal for my younger sister. She soon came home from the pet store with a brown and white male guinea pig who was promptly named Dixie. Trixie and Dixie went on not only to have ten babies, but they spawned a whole series of adventure stories and mystery books. I created anthropomorphic cartoon characters of the guinea pigs, gave them a family name of Carrosom, and created their home planet of Guiajuania, where they lived lives that bore suspicious similarities to what was either on TV at the time, or what my own human family might be up to. I brought these stories to school, and the teacher would read them to the class. This soon earned me the moniker of the Guinea Pig.

So, could the Guinea Pig actually eat one of her own? That was the question I was now contemplating. My *cuy* conundrum was resolved when a man seated at a nearby table ordered this local dish. Thinking it would be served as either joints or slices, he was rather horrified to be presented with a whole blackened animal, still on the skewer that ran through the length of its body. It was served on a platter and looked like it had been going about its business when it was suddenly hit with a blowtorch and scorched in mid-stride. An immediate fuss erupted from his table, and I turned to see what was going on. The waiter had picked up the offending platter, so I had a good look at the charred *cuy*. Suddenly, I was my eight-year old self, cuddling my little cavies and making cartoons of their imaginary lives on their far-off planet. I just couldn't do it. The Carrosoms had been such a huge part of my childhood; how could I possible eat one of their cousins? I went for the alpaca steak instead. At least I wouldn't have to look into its eyes.

Early the next morning, I set off for my excursion to Lake Titicaca, but not before yet another misunderstanding. Since I would be staying overnight with an Aymara family, I assumed that I would be taking my suitcases with me. I asked Ernesto, the short young man behind the desk if my cases were coming on the boat with me, and each time he responded with a *sí*, and nodded his head. I'd had to check out of my room, so he indicated for me to leave my bags with him. Having already had the experience of having our suitcases travel separately on the Nanay, I thought that someone was going to carry them to the boat for me.

They did not. Despite all the head nodding, I found out later that there was no room for suitcases on the small boats, so they are held in a locked storage room at the hotel. This meant that I was now without my extra layers of warm clothing or any toiletries until I returned the next day. The supply of toilet paper I carried was also locked in a suitcase. In most of the public restrooms I'd been in so far on this trip, there were none of the comforting familiar white rolls that one tends to expect to see in a toilet stall. Carrying one's own, particularly for women, was essential. I sighed. There was that surrender and trust thing again.

As our small boat filled up with European tourists, enterprising local women offered us small bags of coca leaf candies. Since the tea made with these leaves had helped me get used to the elevation quickly, I bought a couple of the bags and tucked them into my purse.

Our first stop was to one of the Uros Islands, which I found fascinating. We were told that these were all manmade using a base of floating loam, which is then layered with reeds. I found walking on this unusual surface to be like walking on a trampoline. Would I bounce off and end up in the cold, grey water? You could even eat the tender, white reed shoots. They made me think of the delicious, sliced hearts of palm called *chonta* that we'd been served in Sacha Wasi and Iquitos.

We were presented with the option of either hanging around on this first island, or for an extra small sum, we could ride in one of the giant reed canoes over to a second island. I decided to go for it. The canoe, called a *totora*, was about twenty or twenty-five feet long, with just enough room for thirteen of us. It looked as if it had started out as one big sheet of the woven reed fabric, then the sides were rolled up to form the canoe shape. There were no seats; the inside was filled with straw. I must admit I was a bit apprehensive when we first started floating away from the shore. How could this thing possibly hold up in the water?

Juan, the boatman, had brought along his eight-year old daughter, Maribel. The little girl had a face that seem to have been pumped up with air, and she was very quiet. As we rowed out into the open lake, Juan told us that she was born with a mandibular disorder. He took advantage of his captive audience to explain that there was no medical help out here, and that correctional surgery was expensive. He was very humble as he said that if anyone felt like helping, he'd be very grateful.

I looked at the little girl, who was the same age that I'd been when I was creating my magical guinea pig stories, and wondered what she had in store for her life. I was touched by the graciousness of the father and daughter, so I was happy to help them. In return, Maribel gave me a colorful, hand-drawn picture with butterflies and plants. She had signed her name in a lower corner like a proper artist. It looked like something another young girl had drawn, many years before, in a land so very far from here.

When Juan pulled back up to the first reed island, I couldn't resist trying out a phrase I remembered from one of my Nancy Drew books. In *The Clue of the Crossword Cipher,* Nancy and her close friends, Bess and George, go to South America and interact with some native Quechua speakers. Searching for clues, she spies an old indigenous man who she feels may have seen something that could help her in her quest. She had been coached in a few basic Quechua phrases, which she now tried out on the old man, provoking quite a shock.

For some reason, the three phrases in that book had remained with me throughout my childhood and buried themselves deep in my consciousness. I'd waited years to be able to casually let a word like *cutimunakicama* roll off my tongue. As a quick aside here, the spelling of this word came from the book, where it was said to generally mean goodbye. Having now studied Quechua myself, I prefer the more common spelling of *kutimunaykikama,* which means more specifically *until you return.* Neither of these was correct to use for thank you, but I didn't know this at the time.

Like the man in the mystery book, Juan looked very surprised to hear this word coming from a White tourist. He made a huge fuss that I spoke Quechua, even though it was only one word and an incorrect one at that. I just smiled and bowed. Nancy Drew would have been proud of me!

The boat ride was a lot longer than I'd expected, but under the grey Andean skies that were reflected in the somber, deep water, I drifted into a dreamy, peaceful state. Since I'd never been given a proper agenda, I wasn't completely sure of what the exact plans were, but it didn't really matter. There I was, drifting along on the highest navigable body of water in the world that had a name I had snickered at as a child.

The next stop was the island of Amantani where I'd be spending the night with a native host family. Representatives from the various families who were accepting guests waited on a small landing just off to the side of the boat dock. I'd been the first one assigned to a host family, and the father, whose name was Facundo, quickly indicated that I was to follow him. Any vestiges of smugness I'd had of acclimation were swiftly crushed as Facundo rapidly took off up a steep cobblestone path, while I gasped and struggled behind. I was now laboring for breath at 13,330 feet above sea level and could barely move. Facundo got quite far ahead of me before he realized I was not right behind him. He came back down to where I was doubled over, and I told him I needed to go a bit slower. He nodded gravely and pointed towards the path that led up to his house, which was mercifully closer than many of the others that my fellow passengers had been assigned to. Not having any pity for the hapless American who was slowly suffocating on his home ground, he turned away from me and zoomed back up the hill, leaving me to make my way up the cobblestones on my own.

I finally made it to the family's small compound, which was a set of mud brick structures arranged around a small courtyard. The entire family was lined up to greet me as I dragged myself into their courtyard. In addition to his wife, Luisa, there was one daughter in her early twenties and another in her forties. The latter also had two children: an eight-year old daughter and a four-year old boy. The four women were dressed in their colorful, traditional garb, which included voluminous wool skirts called *polleras* that were worn with several layers of underskirts. I'd been told back at the hotel that they all spoke Spanish and Aymara, the latter being a language with similar roots to Quechua. I sometimes found it hard to communicate and considered that it had something to do with Spanish being the second language for all of us but spoken with very different accents.

Facundo guided me to a room on the second floor of the living quarters. There were two very lumpy double beds jammed together in the left hand side of the tiny room, which could accommodate companions who were traveling together, so I was delighted to have the entire space to myself. My taciturn host informed me that lunch would be served in a half hour, then he closed the tin door and left me to recover as best I could.

The time zipped by and soon Facundo was rapping smartly on the tin door. He'd brought up a hearty quinoa soup, French fries, sautéed onions and rice. While it was delicious and filling, it was also excessively salty. He told me that all my meals would be served in my room. I thought this was kind of sad because it was such a great opportunity to get to know others from a very different culture. I felt the women were curious about me, a single White woman traveling by herself, and I wanted to talk to them.

I was intrigued by their property and was hoping to be offered a short tour, but they seemed to want me to stay on my floor. The buildings were quite rustic, and there was no electricity or running water. The only outhouse was located a short distance outside of their compound, and I prayed I wouldn't have to get up in the night to use it. There were spider webs in the upper corners of this facility, and their large spinners were still inhabiting them. I also noticed there was no paper of any kind inside. My flashlight and toilet paper were back at the hotel, locked away in my suitcase. Thanks a lot, Ernesto!

Facundo made sure I knew that I must use the outhouse and not relieve myself anywhere else. I agreed but wondered what had happened in the past to make it necessary for this to be made into such a direct instruction.

After I'd finished the salty repast, I thought perhaps it might be a nice gesture to bring my dishes back down to the kitchen instead of expecting the family to wait on me hand and foot. I made my way down the rickety stairs toward an area that looked promising by way of the smoke billowing from the door.

I peeked inside and saw the family all sitting on the floor eating their own meal. There was no light, so the kitchen was somewhat dark and smoky. Scattered straw provided a covering for the dirt floor they were sitting on. On seeing me, they looked quite startled. I held out my dishes and smiled to indicate the reason for my brief intrusion. The younger daughter got up and took the plates and thanked me shyly. Not wishing to disturb them further, I turned around and went back up to my room.

I was fascinated by their kitchen but could understand why they served guests upstairs. While I would not have had any issues with joining them on the floor, other travelers might not have felt the same. I knew I was only here for a brief experience, but I must admit I would've liked to have interacted more with the family. Keeping me closeted away seemed like a lost opportunity to learn about each other's lives.

Back upstairs, I was feeling quite fatigued and would have loved the indulgence of a short nap, but as they say, there's no rest for the wicked or the busy traveler. Facundo told me I'd be taking part in a scheduled hike up to the temple on the nearby peak of Pachatata, and I definitely didn't want to miss that.

The other families who were also hosting dizzy guests led us to a community ball court where we were invited to join in a soccer game against the locals. I thought it was kind of a strange thing to do since we were all gasping for air, and not everyone was able to run around or come anywhere near to keeping up with the inhabitants of this island in the clouds.

The hike up to the sacred site was tough, but the views were stunning--literally breathtaking. I had brought a small quantity of loose tobacco to make offerings with and walked slowly around the ancient temple looking for an appropriate place to honor the ancestors. This was made a bit difficult by the hordes of overeager vendors who dogged me trying to sell their wares. They weren't quite as persistent as the Bora, but they were still difficult to avoid. Every time I would pause at a likely spot, another seller would suddenly appear from around a pile of stones and head straight for me. Sometimes they would ask me what I was doing, so I'd respond by telling them that I was making offering to the spirits of this sacred place. They'd briefly nod as they digested this oddity, then thrust another piece of tourist tat at me.

I did end up making two unique purchases, however. With my suitcase back at the hotel, I had nothing warm enough for the cold night ahead. I was only wearing a T-shirt with a waterproof jacket, and I could feel the cold being pushed through the fibers as the wind picked up. The gods of Pachatata smiled on me, leading me to a vendor who was selling clothing made from native animals such as the llama and the alpaca. I tried on a lovely soft thigh-length jacket made from llama wool. It was vertically striped in cream and black, with occasional maroon-rust colored lines added for contrast. It also had two patch pockets with llamas woven on them. It was cozy and warm, and I felt it would be a neat conversation piece back at home.

The other purchase was purely frivolous. My zodiac sign is Scorpio, so when I found a metal bracelet with a large scorpion on it, I had to have it. Whoever made it had done a good job of cutting the metal pieces to make the character, and I also felt it would attract interesting comments.

All this activity had literally worn me out and I could have easily gone to sleep again when I got back to my room. Facundo announced that there was going to be music and dancing later in full costume, so I was allowed to take a short rest. I was beginning to get suspicious that a lot of the activities for guests who stayed on this island were purposely planned to make us even more breathless than we already were. I wondered if I could decline, but after a dinner of rice and more French fries, both Facundo and Luisa marched into my room to dress me in the traditional clothing of Amantani.

First up was a heavy blue knee-length woolen skirt with a woolen underskirt. The underskirt served as an extra layer of warmth and volume. A three-quarter sleeve, embroidered white shirt was tucked into the skirt, followed by an extremely tight sash belt that was tied around the waist at the back. As Luisa pulled the ties tighter, it felt as if she was trying to cut me in two. I indicated that it was uncomfortable, trying to get her to let the sash out a bit. Telling me that tight was traditional, I saw her smile at her husband and pull the ends even tighter.

A black shawl did double duty as a head covering. Already struggling in the thin air, the extremely tight sash threatened to cut off my circulation at the waist. I was allowed to keep on my thin nylon trousers since I didn't have the stockings they wore to keep their legs warm. Topped off with my hiking boots, I looked ridiculous and could barely move. My hosts seemed to be enjoying themselves far more than I was, taking an almost sadistic pleasure in making me suffer.

But, hey! What's the point of traveling if you can't have adventures and laugh at yourself? Facundo and Luisa escorted me to the community hall, promptly leaving me to join their friends, all of whom were congregated at the snack table, undoubtedly laughing at their own dressed up visitors. All of the female guests were dressed exactly like me, complete with their trousers and shoes or boots. The male guests had it far easier with just a long poncho and a hat.

Not many of the village men showed up, but all of the women did. The hall was jam-packed and there were two bands, one at either end. Facundo made sure I danced and danced and whirled me around like a spinning top. I had to escape outside at intervals to catch my breath and allow my racing heart to slow down. I love to dance, but it was hard to relax with the too-tight belt cutting me in two and a deepening fatigue sucking out any energy I might have stored up. I also felt that the dance was put on solely for us, so it didn't feel completely natural for some reason, kind of like the Bora presentation. Still, I managed to have fun chatting to my lookalike traveling companions and enjoying the music.

Despite the deep exhaustion, I was not able to fall asleep easily. I didn't feel well rested in the morning, suffering from a pounding headache brought on by the thin, very dry air. I knew I was also dehydrated. The lack of toilet paper served to make me afraid to drink too much, which I know was not a smart thing to do.

Breakfast was two flattened white rolls and a delicious pancake. I was given tea made of *muña*, a local herb with a small leaf that tasted subtly like mint. I had seen this plant at Raqchi, an archaeological site that featured Incan ruins during my bus ride to Puno.

After eating, the other visitors and I left the island at 8 am. I couldn't resist practicing my Nancy Drew Quechua again, and this time both Facundo and a woman next to him also responded with *cutimunakicama*. I marveled at the thought of a few very foreign words that had implanted themselves in me as a child could now be used to actually communicate, even if in a somewhat limited manner.

The final stop on our tour was Taquille Island, home of the master weavers. Unfortunately, the heavy rain came in so we had to float around the port for around a half hour before we could land. These mid-lake islands are all extremely steep as if Pachamama herself had violently belched them out long ago. In order to arrive at the main square where the businesses were, there was a forty-five minute climb from the port up a very steep hill. Since this would have been a bit dangerous in the pouring rain, our landing was delayed. A group of Italians had had enough of the primitive conditions and were very vocal in their demands to be taken back to Puno. I must admit this did sound quite attractive, but we'd be there soon enough and I didn't want to miss this last stop on our little mini tour.

Once it stopped raining, we all got out and made our way slowly to the main square. I was surprised to find only two stores open in the plaza. Both offered lovely items that featured the weavers' expertise, but I didn't find anything that I had to have. Since there were no other diversions, I wandered out to a few scenic spots where I could look out into the distance. The views back across the water were gorgeous, and once again the word *breathtaking* entered my mind. A final lunch at a small restaurant was included. Instead of the ubiquitous bland buffet, there was quinoa soup and pejerrey, a local fish, which was very tasty.

We landed back at the Puno dock in the late afternoon, and I returned to my not-exactly-a-three-star hotel. I reclaimed my bags and resolved never to be caught without essentials ever again.

Puno presented me with a few more challenges to aid in this process, although none of them were really that bad. It was just a matter of accepting what was on offer at that moment, and then allowing it to pass. One such trial was the hot water. I really wanted a hot shower before heading downstairs to breakfast and believed this would be possible thanks to the brochure I'd been given by the travel agent back in Cusco. It had very plainly advertised that one of its tourist-friendly features was hot running water, and this was one of the reasons I had selected it. The shower flow started out great, and I soaped up and got under it just in time for the temperature to suddenly drop and turn to a trickle. No amount of twisting the knobs made any difference. It was as if my room had only been allotted about a gallon or so of the precious hot water, and that was it. Oh well, at least I was clean!

As I munched on my simple breakfast of fruit, white bread, and extremely salty cheese, I thought back to something that Harold had said during one of the short meetings at our beach resort. We'd been talking about spiritual awakenings and how these can occur during times of stress, trauma, or even deep suffering. It was the same day that he'd talked about how thoughts and emotions could block communications from the spirit realms.

"You're not going to open up to those special connections while you're safe inside your luxury city dwelling. You can't become a genuine shaman with vision simply by taking a short course where they give you a certificate at the end of it." He'd grunted and added almost in an undertone, "Can you imagine these native shamans proudly displaying certificates of participation or completion? Hell no! They suffered for years in natural surroundings with extreme cold or heat and very little food."

He'd added that being outside in some kind of natural setting somehow facilitated the awakening, as well as periods of quiet introspection. Many cultures and disciplines spoke of such things as vision quests, sit spots, and spending time in nature. I could see a common theme through the different details and words. I'd hoped that the magic of Lake Titicaca would have nudged me a few steps further to this openness, but now I could see that the furious, fast pace of this part of my trip didn't allow time to simply *be*. It was all doing and not much being.

I headed to the reception desk to make arrangements for my transportation to the nearest airport at Juliaca. Ernesto, the eager, young desk clerk, asked me how I was doing.

"Yah, not much hot water for shower. Too bad, huh?"

How the heck had he known about my shower? I didn't even want to know.

I think young Ernie's Spanish was not as good as he pretended it to be, so I had one last misunderstanding with him. Since there was no one else from the hotel heading towards Juliaca, a private taxi would be called for me. The cost was relayed as fifteen soles, somewhere around five dollars, which I thought was very cheap for the roughly twenty-five mile trip by road.

Then, as I was checking out, Ernesto turned on the charm. "You have husband?"

"Not anymore."

"Boyfriend?"

"Not right now."

"Maybe I can be your boyfriend?" he asked hopefully.

I wanted to laugh at this sudden, very absurd proposition.

"Um, gee, thanks, but I'm leaving the area now. Thanks anyway."

When the taxi arrived, I confirmed the cost.

"Fifteen soles?"

The driver looked shocked at first, then gave me a look as if I might be trying to pull one over on him.

"No, *fifty!* Fifty soles to go to Juliaca airport! Is long way to drive."

I sighed for the hundredth time. Okay, *vámonos*. Let's get going.

Back once more at Jorge Chavez Airport in Lima, I discovered I'd somehow lost my debit card. You know that cold panic you feel when you open your wallet and see a space where a card should be? Yeah, that one. I was now short of cash. Thinking furiously back to when I had it last, I recalled using it in an ATM in Cusco. I also realized that in my very muddled mental state I could have very easily left it in the machine. Although I was somewhat alarmed by the missing debit card, I did have a backup credit card with me which I'd used to buy my Puno package, but I hadn't wanted to use it for cash because of the large fees for overseas transactions. In any case, there was nothing I could do about it at this point. I was about to board my flight back to Iquitos, unaware of the life-changing event that was waiting for me in that jungle town.

CHAPTER 7

Shaman's Invitation

As my flight touched down for the last time in the land-locked jungle town of Iquitos, I wondered what would be waiting for me here this time, but I soon found out. Geraldo had hired a motocab to pick me up, sending the driver to wait for me outside of the arrivals door in an area I call the shark tank. I call it that because the moment a traveler passes through those exit doors, a very large group of taxi and motocab drivers pounces and surrounds you, trying to get you into their vehicles. It can be quite intimidating for the uninitiated. The cost for the ride from the airport to the center of Iquitos was only ten soles, but most drivers took advantage of the fact that foreign visitors wouldn't know this in order to charge them a lot more. Having a driver waiting with my name displayed on a sign helped me push past the pesky drivers more easily.

But he was not the only one waiting for me. After all my recent wanderings, I felt like I wanted to come back to a base that had some familiarity, so I booked a room back at the same hotel that I'd stayed in with the retreat group. They told me they would pick me up from the airport since this service was included in the price of the room.

As I stood there looking back and forth between the two drivers, I saw Geraldo making his way towards me, indicating the moto parked nearby. "Come with me! I have a surprise for you!"

The hotel driver understood what was going on and very graciously offered to take my bags to the hotel, so I handed them over and followed my pseudo sweetie over to the moto.

Geraldo presented me with a bouquet of artificial flocked red roses. There was also a cute little stuffed dog with big, soppy eyes. Between its front paws there was a heart with the words *te amo*, I love you, imprinted on the front. Despite the sheer fatigue that was running through me from the long day of travel, I was touched by this romantic gesture.

We arrived back at the hotel just after the courtesy car. I watched the driver unload my bags and take them into the hotel, intending to follow him in. Someone behind me made that kind of throat clearing noise you know is not just for clearing a throat, so I turned around to see what was going on. The motocab driver stood expectantly awaiting his fee, looking back and forth from me to Geraldo.

"Do you have ten soles? You need to pay the driver."

Had I asked Geraldo to pick me up, this would have been fair. He didn't tell me he was going to come to the airport or I would have let him know I had free transport with the hotel. I was very low on cash at this point, and his request popped the romantic bubble I was in. Ten soles is only about three dollars, but until I could sort out my cash flow situation, I needed to be careful about every expenditure. I explained to him about my situation and that I didn't have it just then. Did I detect a brief look of annoyance crossing his face?

He paid the driver very reluctantly and followed me inside. I went up to my room and dumped out my suitcase hoping to find the misplaced debit card but had no luck. While I was putting the items back in, Geraldo's phone rang. He told me that before meeting me at the airport, he'd been out with some friends celebrating one's birthday, but he'd disappeared suddenly to come meet me. They were now calling to find out what had happened to him.

"Let's go meet up with my friends! I told them all about you!"

Seriously? No sweet reunion *a deux*? I was totally exhausted and would have preferred a quiet night in with my jungle honey, but once again decided to participate in what the universe was presenting to me. Taking a quick hot shower, I changed into the same outfit I'd worn only recently on our fateful first night together. This consisted of a flowered tank top, the black miniskirt, and some low heels I'd also bought for that night. It wasn't particularly sexy or clingy in this sweltering town where you could feel the sexual tension always hanging in the air. Most of the local girls were wearing far less than I was.

Geraldo looked me up and down and shook his head. "You put on more clothes. I don't want my friends to be interested in you."

No one besides my mother had ever told me what I could or could not wear, and normally I wouldn't let anyone else tell me what to do. This was a novelty to me, so I wanted to go through with it to see what it felt like, how it played out. I must admit I was also a bit flattered!

We met up with his three friends at a local bar, then moved on to a club because the guys were hoping to score some action. Some of them, like Geraldo, spoke English with varying degrees of proficiency, so we went back and forth in that strange mixture of two languages that often happens when speakers of different mother tongues converse together.

One of them told me that he thought American girls were really pretty, but very stuck up. He pointed his nose in the air, and the rest of them imitated him for emphasis. I could only imagine this had to do with their pickup attempts: whistling and snapping their fingers at my countrywomen passing by, while saying something along the lines of, "Hello, baby! You want to drink beer with me?" Not the most effective ways to meet a girl!

Geraldo pulled a bottle out of his backpack. I smothered a smirk as it turned out to be an Amazonian ginger aphrodisiac potion, which was now being added to the communal sangria we were drinking. The guys obviously had a lot of confidence in their pulling chances with the *chicas*. My pseudo partner knew of my money issues but still applied some pressure for me to contribute twenty soles out of the fifty I'd told him I had left. I felt it was fair to contribute something but given that he'd told me what to wear I would have liked to have been taken care of for a few hours. I guess he had other ways of taking care of me, which he'd save for when we retired for the night. That is, when I could get him to turn off the TV.

Since I'd come back to be with Geraldo, he'd used my place as a base for as much as possible even though he retained another room elsewhere. I watched him use my room phone to make all his phone calls so he could save money on his own mobile bills. He didn't even ask, and it's likely the cost of the calls on my room far exceeded his. It didn't matter because I was paying for it all. I recalled Edwin's comment about what Harold had told him, and now I could see what he meant. I wasn't surprised or really disappointed because I had signed onto this supposed relationship for the feel of it. I'll do things like this as long as they are not dangerous or harmful to anyone, including me, and they always turn out to be valuable learning experiences.

Geraldo must've figured he'd milk the situation as much as possible, so he tended to hang around more than I would have liked. Not long ago I was so enamored that I couldn't wait to get back to him, but now I started feeling like I wanted some alone time. What's that saying about how it's a woman's prerogative to change her mind?

The next morning, we wandered over to Ari's Burger for breakfast. There was just something about Ari's that made me feel at home. It could be noisy and chaotic, but I still have a great fondness for the place to this day.

He wanted to go back to his place to change and pick up a few things, so I slipped into the internet place next door to the hotel. I checked on my bank account and card status and was relieved to see there'd been no activity. Phew! I sent my sister a long email to explain what happened and asked her to contact my bank for me. That done, I was able to relax a bit.

I returned to my hotel room and got a surprise when I unlocked the door: Geraldo was waiting for me inside. How had he gotten in without a key? The room was in my name and I had the only key.

"They know I'm with you, so when you didn't answer the door, I got them to let me in."

There was something mildly creepy about this. While I didn't feel that Geraldo might be dangerous, this was a kind of boundary invasion. I hadn't left any valuables in the room anyway, and probably needn't have worried. The most important thing to him was neither me nor anything in my bags: it was the television in my hotel room. I noticed how the energy between us had changed from when I was here previously. Then, he had seemed more caring and solicitous and hadn't asked for anything, but now it felt like I was being taken for granted. I was fascinated with the process and to see how it would continue to unfurl.

I needed to sort out my return ticket to Lima, so he directed me to a little travel agency on Prospero. They said they'd be able to accept my credit card, and the charge went through successfully. Very few of the businesses in Iquitos accepted credit cards because of the fees involved. And in some cases, the charge would not go through even if they did accept that method of payment. The internet connections in some parts of the country were not very good, and without that there could be no credit card approval. It was always best to have some cash on hand.

It had started to rain so we went back to the hotel for a bit. He had the TV remote in his hand before I could even close the door. I could feel the resentment building, but I bided my time.

A little while later, we went down to the bar, where he suddenly got very serious. I had a feeling that buying my departure tickets would cause some kind of response, and I was right. He wanted to have a talk about us, and how he was afraid that I'd forget him once I got home. He'd told me this had happened with another girl he'd met here years ago. I had my own thoughts as to why that had happened, but I kept them to myself.

After a delicious lunch at his friend's *cevicheria*, we returned back to the room for a siesta. Geraldo made an immediate dive for the TV remote and turned the unit on. I tried to engage him in conversation, but he was quickly wrapped up in some stupid game show and would grunt responses without even turning his head. Yes, I should have made a scene right then and there, but we don't always do what we should, do we? I changed into my bathing suit to cool off in the hotel's pool and stomped out of the room.

Game show or girlfriend? Geraldo was smart enough to realize I wasn't happy, so he bolted out after me, demanding to know what was up. I told him that being trapped in a room with a constantly blaring TV was one of my worst nightmares. I was trying to find a balance between indulging him a little, but also spending these last few days together.

"I'm picking up all the bills, but the moment we get back here you dive for the TV and it's like I'm not even here."

He thought he'd placate me with a bit of bungle in the jungle. Funny how so many couples follow a fight with a cuddle.

The next time his phone rang it turned out to be his younger sister. She wanted to see him to discuss a family matter. Without asking me, he invited her to the hotel, where the two of them decided to arrange a *parrillada* at their mother's house. These barbecues were quite common around Iquitos, and they were a way for their hosts to make a little money by turning their home and yard into a restaurant for as long as the food lasted. The biggest investment for the host to make up front was for a large number of chickens. The grilled meat was always accompanied by various side dishes, such as the huge piles of French fries that seemed to be very popular here. Tables were set up in the yard and people could come by for a meal or take their food away. Of course, these plans necessitated the use of my room phone to make all the arrangements. Two more days; I can wait.

Geraldo started going on about how hungry he was, so I suggested we go downstairs and eat in the hotel's very decent restaurant. He complained about this, saying he was used to eating more casually in the Belen market stalls. I had no objection to this, but I was trying to preserve what cash I had, so I explained that by eating here I was able to put everything on my tab and then pay one bill with my credit card. As he continued to grumble a bit, I thought of the old saying about not biting the hand that feeds you. Or how about not looking a gift horse in the mouth? I hoped his sister would take off so I didn't have to feed the two of them, and fortunately she did.

Finally, in the late afternoon he said he wanted to do some errands. He gave me the impression that he'd be back soon, but in fact he didn't turn up again for another five hours. He told me his boss had called him into the office for some translation work. I asked where this office was and he evaded my question. He said he was tired, but then he suddenly jumped up, saying he had to run around the corner to talk to his sister.

After he left, I went into a weird sort of trance state where I saw this simplified version of reality, something that had presented itself to me during the earlier part of my trip with the group. I also was able to look remotely at a few people I knew, seeing the energetic blockages that caused their respective physical challenges. While this took me by surprise, it also felt very natural and comfortable.

When he finally returned, I was already in bed, indicating there'd be no TV. Just shut and go to sleep!

My relationship with Geraldo continued to weaken, at least from my point of view. His initial pretense of caring about me had all but vanished. I only had two more days left until my final flight home, and despite the desire to throw him into the nearby Itaya River, something told me to just go along for the ride.

Yes, sometimes we do things that initially seem like they aren't going to benefit us at first sight, and it's only later that we are able to step back and see the big picture; how the universe put things in motion and set off a domino chain of events that we could not have ever imagined. I somehow knew my relationship with him was not the main event: it was only a side trip. In fewer than twenty-four hours I was going to see why I'd gotten involved with Geraldo.

The next morning, we had breakfast at Ari's again. I just loved their sugary guarana-based drinks, particularly the *Infiel*, and I found them to be a great way to get the day's juices flowing instead of coffee. And they definitely tasted a lot better than the instant coffee that seemed to be on offer everywhere.

As we were finishing up, my strange companion suddenly announced that he wanted to go visit Javier. I was keen to join him and see Javier again. Jav was a very likable character, seeming to always be jolly--almost childlike—and I'll admit I was curious to see how he lived away from tourist retreats. We flagged down a passing moto, which of course I paid for in addition to breakfast.

The young shaman seemed genuinely surprised to see me, saying that he usually had visions of visitors and patients, but that somehow I'd eluded this process. Of course, he wanted to know how I came to be with his associate and occasional student, so Geraldo and I gave some kind of simple explanation about being together. Jav was thrilled, apparently since it seemed that Geraldo had not had good luck with women and had been wanting a partner. I bit my tongue.

My moochy partner asked for several soles to buy a large cola to share, a common practice. Sure, why not? I'm just made of centavos and soles! I knew that in addition to his own expenses, Geraldo, being the only son, was also helping his mother financially, as well as several of his sisters, none of whom had any kind of employment. I'd also found out that he had a daughter who lived with her mother in another city. This ex-partner and he were not on good terms, but he also had to send money for the girl's upbringing.

The visit with Javier and his wife, Julieta, went on into the early evening. Geraldo's reason for being there had something to do with having Jav prepare him some kind of medicinal potion, so I chatted with the members of the household while the two men had their consultation.

I had the feeling that Javier was peering into me, seeing something that lay far below the surface. He began bringing up shamanic topics, and I listened with rapt attention. He recalled our conversation in Sacha Wasi about my wanting to be a healer, so he started asking more specific questions about this. I told him that I was considering coming back during the summer when Harold and Patrick would be running another retreat. I felt that I had not honored the tradition and practices as much as I should have due to my sheer ignorance, and I wanted to start over. This sparked off a very animated discussion.

He peered at me again. "You have a very strong spirit. I am looking for an apprentice. How about instead of going to another lodge retreat, you come back and live in the jungle with me while I teach you this path?"

I had to shake my head to clear what I thought was another misunderstanding. Did he just say what I thought he had? Was he really offering to teach me the path of the Peruvian Amazonian jungle shaman? Me? A klutzy White mosquito magnet?

Yes. Me. When I asked him why he would want someone like me as his student, he told me that it was because of what I had *not* said, as much as what I had. "You told me how much you wanted to be able to heal others, not that you wanted to be a shaman. There's a big difference there."

He explained further that while he had received requests from foreigners, mainly young men, to be trained, they were almost always in the form of an ego-based statement of wanting to be a shaman, a person with all the power and admiration.

"They think it's all about sitting behind an altar, serving ayahuasca, and singing some songs, but they can't see what is really going on because their focus is in the wrong place. They are looking out when instead they should be looking inside." He tapped his chest.

Aside from the few ceremonies I'd taken part in, I also didn't know what was involved. I was totally naïve, which was probably a good thing because I had no idea of what I was getting myself into. At that point, it just seemed kind of cool. I pictured myself as Carlos Castaneda meeting up with don Juan Matus.

We spent hours talking about fine points of the training, some of which I just couldn't imagine. He picked up a blue plastic container, the kind we'd used as chamber pots in the camp and brought it over to me. Inside was a very large rock submerged in water.

"This is an *encanto*, a magical healing stone that is passed down through the lineage; one shaman to another."

The large grey rock was unremarkable in appearance, yet it seemed to exude a tangible energy. I liked it, and for some strange reason, I felt that it liked me too.

Javier decided I needed a *limpia*, a cleaning of my energy field. He handed me seven black stones and instructed me to hold them while I sent all my negative energy into them. As I was doing this, he prepared a bed of leaves on small side table, telling me to lay the stones on the leaves as I finished with them. I was then instructed to choose one leaf and use it like a bar of soap, washing my hands with it. This was then thrown over my left shoulder with my left hand.

Next, he handed me a white stone, which I passed over my face as I visualized good things. He enlisted my *enamorado*, Geraldo, to use another stone on my back. Several other practices were done, then Jav handed me the magical ancestor stone and gave me instruction on how to use it next. I aimed all my intent and focus at the *encanto*, recalling my days as a magician. When I passed it back to Javier, he made a fuss about what he felt was an incredible amount of energy that I had put into it. Again, he remarked on my strength, and I felt grateful at last to be seen.

The talk turned to what form the apprenticeship would take. I had no job or obligations back in Southern California, so was open to however this played out. He kept returning to how thrilled he was that I and Geraldo had hooked up. I talked a bit about the huge age difference, something that is not as common in my country.

"In the jungle, we don't look at things like that. When I was thirteen I was in love with a woman who was thirty years older than I was, and both sets of relatives gave us their blessings."

Wow. Thirteen? That woman would have been arrested for rape and child abuse in my country!

I started to feel like they were keen for me to seal the deal with Geraldo. He had talked about our tying the knot after only our first night together, which I though was utterly ridiculous. I was beginning to feel a sort of pressure to marry him and it was putting me off. I didn't know what their practices were like here, but in my country we generally don't get married after spending only one night together!

Julieta made us all a nice lunch of rice and *tortuga*, a local tortoise, something I normally wouldn't have chosen to eat. But if I was going to return to live in the jungle, I might have to eat other things that I wouldn't normally put in my mouth. In the quiet corners of my mind I heard Harold again, talking about people who wanted to be shamans in the comfort of their own surroundings. I ate the *tortuga*.

The hours passed quickly in the convivial company, and in the evening, I was whisked away with Javier and Geraldo to a local street party. It was a raucous affair with a lot of beer. Everyone was up dancing to the very loud *cumbia* music. I was the only non-local there, but any self-consciousness quickly disappeared. Beer after beer appeared and I was yanked up to dance in the steamy evening heat. Two women seemed to take particular delight in teaching me how to dance Latin style, and I won an enthusiastic round of applause for my ability to lower myself to the dirt floor and get back up again.

It'd been hours since the lunch at Javier's house, and the heat and loud music were starting to make me wish for a little peace and solitude. I used my apparently strong spirit to continue to just be, marveling at what was taking place. Javier continued to profess being utterly thrilled at having me as his student, something I was still trying to wrap my head around. He also kept expressing how happy he was that his friend had found such a great partner. How did I feel about this?

Despite my now well-inebriated state, I told him the truth. I explained that in my country, a commitment like marriage usually happens after a longer period of time, especially in order to be lasting. I told my new teacher that for me, we simply had not spent enough time in each other's company in order for me to be able to commit to something serious like marriage. He understood this and suggested that we should just live together instead. Yeah, and yours truly would be paying all the bills while he ran around doing this and that.

For a short while I pictured what was being presented to me. I could move down here and enter into an entirely different life. On one hand, I'd be training in the ancient traditions of Javier's lineage. On the other, I'd be Geraldo's wife. *¡Otra cerveza, por favor!* Gimme another beer, quick!

The party wound down and Javier told us there was another one we could move on to. Geraldo asked how I was feeling, telling me it would only cost me about sixty soles, roughly another twenty dollars, meaning I'd be the one financing the entire rest of the night for the three of us. Twenty dollars in my culture is not a lot, but here it could buy a lot more. I was vacillating between resentment at being expected to pay for everything, yet also feeling I didn't want to be the one who just took things from them. I knew this was an important turning point in my life and I wanted to celebrate this sudden turn of events, but my head was pounding and it felt like the right time to head back to the hotel.

So, I told him I could do with a bit of quiet. He said he wanted to go back to his room to shower and change, then he'd return to the hotel, and we could get something to eat in the restaurant. I wondered about the fact that I had a really nice bathroom with hot running water that he could use, and I couldn't imagine the one at his boarding house would be the same. Ah well, not important. It's really what we are used to, isn't it?

We agreed that I'd head back to my hotel, and he'd join me when he was ready. As the motocab pulled up, I stepped into the back seat. Geraldo leaned in and instead of a nice, romantic kiss, he asked me for ten soles instead.

"What for?"

"To pay my driver and get something to eat."

"Um, didn't you just suggest we'd eat together back at the hotel?"

Something shifted inside me, and I looked at him like he was from another planet. Despite all the beers, his intuition was sharp enough to see that he'd be wise to back off. He told me to go on and he'd see me later. I fumed, thinking we'd have to have a little chat. I'd spoken to him of having limited funds, yet he continued to treat me as if I were a cash machine. He never asked if it was okay or if I minded at all.

I then recalled something that had happened the day before. I needed to buy more bottled water so we went into a small shop. As I was starting to pay, he casually added a few things to the items I had selected for myself. He didn't even ask me if it was okay. He just snuck them behind mine and then sneakily pushed them forward so as to make it look like everything was on my tab. The cashier saw this and looked at me.

"Are these all together?"

I turned around to look at Geraldo, who gave me a fake smile.

"Yeah. I'll take care of it." I probably rolled my eyes.

I was glad to get back to my hotel room alone and take stock of everything that had happened to me earlier in the day. After a cool shower helped to settle my swimming head, I sat down to make some notes. Writing helps me think. Seeing things on paper can sometimes be like psychotherapy for me. I realized that if I made the decision to move in with him, married or not, I'd not only be supporting him, but very likely his mother and his sisters and his daughter, and paying for absolutely everything without getting much in return. I could feel the truth resonate in my body and it was a real passion killer.

I let my mind wander back to those difficult times when I lived with Liam in London as my marriage was dying. Like Geraldo, he was a very interesting man who didn't work enough to support himself. Part of my intention when I had moved in with him was to help take off some of the pressure, to keep the wolf from the door, in the hopes that this would then allow him to get his life in order. But what happened instead was that once I was holding down the fort, he stopped trying to get more work for himself. It was the opposite of what I had intended and was a driving force in my decision to leave. While I knew I was drawn to interesting men, I vowed that I would never do this ever again. I had recognized the same kind of energetics around my relationship with Geraldo and remembered my promise to myself.

Even in these few short days I saw behaviors that I found unacceptable, like the way he'd vanish for hours and then be evasive when I asked him what he'd been up to. I didn't expect him to push the pause button on his life just because I was there, but communication is very important to me. Long lasting relationships tend to be that way because those involved really speak to each other. Shoot, why not just tell me the truth?

I also watched as several of the conversations I'd had with Javier during the day resurfaced. One of the important aspects of the apprenticeship, he told me, was intelligence. Did I consider myself to be intelligent? I felt a bit funny saying I did because it felt like bragging. I felt the actual answer wasn't so important as that I believed it. Over the years, through all I've experienced, I've found that self-belief is a huge component of successful magical work, if not *the* most important.

Javier also firmly believed that my background as a professional musician was going to help me in learning the icaros, those wonderful sacred songs that drove the ayahuasca ceremonies. There was one song he'd sung in Sacha Wasi that had bored itself into my brain, so I sang it back to him.

No me dejes, no me dejes, Madre mía Naturaleza…"

His eyes had opened wide in surprise at how much of this had remained with me. I told him it was as if the icaro had chosen me, and that I felt it wanted me to learn it for some reason. It was like when that dear soul, Jim, years before back in Liam's magic class, had said that one word: *ayahuasca*, and it had bored into my being like a super worm. I'd felt my whole body recoil as if I'd been hit with some kind of energetic spear, only to be told to just store it for later, when it would all make sense. That was now six years ago, but suddenly seemed like it had only the day before.

We'd gotten into a discussion about how the shaman enters into a marriage with Mother Earth, and he asked me how I felt about that. I told him about that fateful ceremony back at the lodge where I'd seen Mother Earth, and how at that point I knew I was just fine. He nodded in understanding and told me this had been a sign for me. A good sign. In fact, a *really* good sign. He said he was also going to attend the *parrillada* at Geraldo's mother's house the next day, so we could continue our conversation then.

By the time Geraldo finally returned, I was already asleep. He banged on my door several times, forcing me to get out of bed to let him in. I was not happy! Sure enough, he'd made sure he'd gotten himself dinner, while I had not. He didn't even think to either call me to see if the restaurant had closed and if I might like a little something. Grrr. Just shut up and stay on your side of the bed!

It did occur to me to not allow him to come in, but this was the penultimate night of a long, amazing trip, so I decided to let everything play out. Before I fell asleep, I said a silent prayer of thanks for how everything had worked out. Spirit had waited until almost my last full day to make the connection with Javier. I briefly wondered what might have been had Geraldo not suddenly decided to go see his shaman friend, or if I had not gone with him. But there was no use in giving energy to that past. What was important was only what *did* happen.

The next day started with the same routine of him going back to his room, although this time he didn't mention taking a shower and changing his clothes. He swore he'd be back for 11:00 o'clock, but by noon he there was no sign of him, so I went next door to send my final emails. He suddenly appeared next to the computer I was using and said he'd been looking for me in the hotel. I told him I'd gotten tired of waiting and was going to finish what I was doing, so he decided to check his email too.

"Can I have one sol for the internet?" I rolled my eyes.

The detective in me was curious about what he wanted to look at for such a brief time. It wasn't email. It was porn. So, here's this guy who's been given a ticket through heaven's gate, and what does he do? Call up cheap, soft porn.

"Can I have the key to the room? I want to go up and take a shower."

Oh, really? After all this time you suddenly want to use my shower? I asked inside my own head.

I gave him the key but came up very soon afterwards myself. Did I hear the shower running? No, of course I didn't. The television was on and blaring once again.

Another strange thing about him was that his phone rang frequently, and when he looked at the screen I had the feeling that he knew the caller, yet every time he'd say he didn't know who it was. My guess was that it was the mother of his child calling to try to get more money out of him, or perhaps it was some dodgy associate. Why all the deception?

Anyway, we were about to head to the *parrillada* at his mother's house, and knowing there'd be costs for transport, I let him know that all I had left for the rest of the day was twenty soles. Despite saying this, once again I had to cough up for the cost of the ride. I'd fudged about the actual amount of cash I had left to make sure I had enough to get me back to Lima and onto the final flight. I was annoyed because while Geraldo was now always asking me for money, even when I didn't give him any he still managed to eat or take a moto or whatever. I know he didn't have a lot, but it seemed that he was definitely keeping his own for himself rather than sharing expenses with me.

The barbecue was fun despite all this nonsense. I volunteered to help man the grills because this is something that I love doing. As neighbors stopped by, they seemed to be taken aback to see a strange White woman cooking their lunches, but it was a great way to meet the locals. I also got to meet his sisters, some of whom started calling me *cuñada*, sister-in-law. They explained to me how the *parrillada* worked. His mother was charging eight soles for a plate of food, which included a generous portion of chicken and some sides. Drinks were also available for a price: a large beer cost three soles. We had a plate of food and one beer each.

The beer custom here had really confused me at first. I was used to the practice of each person buying a drink for themselves or someone else, but they alone would drink it. Here, a beer was bought and shared among several people by passing one single glass around. When it was your turn, the bottle and the glass would come to you; you'd fill the glass, drink it down, shake it out and pass both along to the next person. Once I got used to this I could see its value in that a quick bottle turnover would allow for a colder beer going around.

Since I was no longer enamored of my *enamorado*, I really wanted to knock back one of the large beers on my own. But no sooner had I poured myself a glass than someone would appear next to me, looking expectantly at the bottle and glass, then at me. I think I got one whole glass out of those two bottles!

Javier and Julieta also showed up, so I had someone to talk to since Geraldo kept disappearing. After one such absence which I queried, he said he'd gone out to get cigarettes. Funny, I'd not seen him smoke even once during the entire time I'd been with him. If this had been Southern California I'd've suspected him of doing drug deals.

In my late teens and early twenties I'd gone out with a couple of guys who worked in this arena. While it initially seemed exciting to hang around in such a clandestine atmosphere, the novelty quickly wore off, and I decided that I would not date any more drug dealers. We could never make any plans because they'd always be broken by some deal that had to go down. People would come and go, or my partner would come and go, and I just got fed up with it. Whatever Geraldo was doing may not have been drugs, but it was just as irritating.

The final straw came when it was time for us to go. Walking over to me, he asked if I'd paid for our food and drinks. It seemed odd to me that his mother was charging her own son for his lunch. Was it because I was there? I reminded him of what I'd told him earlier: that I only had twenty soles left and asked if he could make up the small difference. He gave me a funny look and then explained to his sisters that I didn't have enough cash on me, so I'd have to go change more money to take care of the bill. I took that to be a no.

I paid for the moto back to the hotel and discovered that he'd made other plans for the day that did not include me. This time, he said he was going to go see his soccer team play. Apparently, he was a member of the team but hadn't played any games since he did the Sacha Wasi trip with our group. He told me that he wanted to go talk to his coach because he was afraid of being dropped. I wondered how he could be a part of an ongoing team sport when he made his main living as a jungle guide, meaning he'd frequently be away for days, if not weeks. I didn't bother to ask him about this.

I spent the time tidying up and relaxing a bit, just happy to have the room to myself without a TV blaring in the background. Geraldo made a sudden appearance just before 7 o'clock, then dashed off again to take a shower and change his clothes. For all the showers and clothing changes he supposedly made, my young jungle lover must have been the cleanest man in Iquitos!

Remembering how late he'd returned the previous night; I wasn't going to wait up for him. I was very tired at the end of this transformational journey, and I hadn't slept well the night before, so I wanted to get a good night's sleep. I took an antihistamine to knock me out and fell into the deepest sleep ever.

Sometime later, I was awakened by an insistent banging on the door. I was tempted to let Geraldo stay out in the hall this time, but he was making so much noise that I worried he'd was disrupting other guests.

"Why you not answer? I call you three times!"

I found this quite astonishing as the phone was right next to my bed. If he really had called, I can't believe I didn't hear it. I told him I was in the middle of a good sleep and promptly went back to bed and zonked out.

I woke up about 5 am and saw him still in his T-shirt, lying on top of the sheets. He told me that I'd totally wrapped myself up in all the bedclothes like a mummy, so he was cold. I'd never done that before, but I understood the subtle message my subconscious was telling me.

Sometime later, at a more reasonable hour, he told me he didn't feel well. He had alluded to some kind of kidney problems, and this is why he'd wanted to see Javier. He felt he'd had a fever in the night and needed to get more medicine from Javier. I gave him some Tylenol and let him go back to sleep, this time under the covers.

I'd been thinking that even though this was my last day, I might try to go into a bank and see if they'd allow me to get some cash off my credit card even though I didn't have the PIN. Since we were going back over to Javier's, where I knew we'd both be presented with something, I wanted to make sure I had enough money for a proper energy exchange.

In my years of travels and workings with shamanic healing I have frequently come across the notion that someone who has the healer's gift shouldn't charge money for their treatments, ceremonies, or medicines. The Divine is said to be giving them these magical healing gifts, so how can you monetize something like that? I believe this was likely to be more of the case in the years before cash became king when people traded and bartered with goods.

I know there are still places in the world where the village healer lives in abject poverty along with his or her constituents, so they will accept non-monetary goods for providing services. While there is no one size fits all answer, my experience is that modern day indigenous shamans prefer to receive cash. They have to feed their families, buy clothing and other items, so they need money just as we Westerners do. For this reason, I wanted to be able to give Javier money for all the time he'd spent with me.

Once Geraldo was up and about we made our way back to Jav's. He and the shaman chatted for a while, then a two and a half liter bottle of some herbal infusion was brought out. Javier had Geraldo drink a cup, and judging by the latter's facial expressions it must have tasted awful. I felt a brief pity for my soon-to-be-ex jungle lover because apparently this was only the first of such eight bottles that he'd need to consume for his kidney issues.

His phone rang as he was sitting quietly after taking his medicine. This time it was one of his sisters informing him that their mother's electricity had gone off again. Although he hadn't been very forthcoming about his family situation, from the parts I could piece together it seemed that he was the sole provider for not only his daughter, but also his mother and seven sisters, hence my strong objection to getting seriously involved with him. He did tell me that he'd paid to have electricity installed in his mother's house because there hadn't been any there until he did this. I had a strong feeling that many of the calls he'd received when he was with me may have been from someone wanting something from him, either cash, help or some item. Every now and then he would grumble about the laziness in his family and how no one even tried to earn any money. Perhaps that's why at times he acted like it was a wrong number and he didn't bother to answer.

I knew my jungle boy had a good heart despite the now constant requests for cash. I had learned something else from him that really touched my heart. One night after leaving a restaurant with a bag of leftovers, two young boys ran up to him. I didn't catch what they were saying but he handed the bag over to them. As they ran off I asked him what had just happened.

"Here in Iquitos, there are a lot of street kids with ignorant mothers and deadbeat fathers. The only way they can eat is to beg for leftovers."

I digested this for a moment while he continued. "Most of the restaurants here put your leftovers in white bags, so the children know what they are. So many people, particularly tourists, order too much food and then they can't finish it for whatever reason. Instead of throwing it out, we suggest they give it to the kids so they can get something to eat."

I thought of my own country, with its overflowing food offerings from coast to coast. Every street was lined with the same chain restaurants, and in addition to grocery stores, food could even be bought in such places as hardware and auto parts stores. I made the decision that from that moment on, whenever I was in Iquitos, I would order a little more than I knew I could eat. I would then ask the server to wrap up the leftovers for the kids, and I have continued to do this through the years. When I walk out with my white plastic bag, I hold it prominently and sort of swing it in front of me, and usually within a minute someone comes up to ask for it. It's a small gesture, but one I feel I can easily do.

Javier had made up a small amulet for me to use whenever I needed a boost of positive energy. He told me it was to remain out of sight in order that it not pick up any negativity that might be floating around in the atmosphere. It was a small bundle tied up in a square of cloth, very similar in appearance to the prayer ties I had made at the various sweat lodges I had participated in. I was curious as to what was inside the little bundle, but Javier just gave me one of his face-splitting grins and told me never to open it.

He also brought out his *encanto* again, still in its container of water. Only now, the water was not clear; it was cloudy, perhaps even a little dirty. Jav told us this was the way it cleaned itself after having been used the previous day. The water was to be thrown out into the street or wherever it couldn't contaminate anything else. He told me that when I return to begin my apprenticeship with him, he would give an *encanto* of my own from his uncle's lineage.

Unlike his protégé, Javier never asked me for a thing. I told him I wanted to give him something in exchange for not only what he'd taught me so far, but also for Geraldo's medicines. What did he need for the house? What was needed to make his family's life a little easier? He consulted with Julieta and the answer came swiftly and firmly: a flush toilet!

While we in the more developed countries take our flushing toilets for granted, they do not exist everywhere else in the world. So far, in the more rustic areas of my trip I'd seen a base toilet unit—usually with no seat—and a large cistern of water standing next to it. Since there was no flushing mechanism, you'd have to dip a bucket into the cistern and chuck it into the bowl in order to vacate the contents. Jav and Juli had two young boys and were caring for her mother who had dementia, so a flush toilet would make their life a lot easier. I enquired as to the cost and found it well within my budget. I think Julieta was a lot more thrilled than her husband was!

I would have liked to have stayed and visited for much longer, but I had to get back and pack up my room, so we bid our farewells to Javier and Julieta. Javier and I had exchanged contact information and would be staying in touch until I could return to start my new life.

Once back in the room, Geraldo asked if he could watch TV while I packed. I agreed, knowing he would soon lose this facility, but instead he started looking through a book I'd brought with me, a collection of stories written by the Argentinian author, Julio Cortázar. Next, he picked up my book of cryptograms and put it over his heart as he stretched out on the bed and closed his eyes. I had the strong feeling he didn't want to watch me pack.

I had so many emotions running through me as I neatly folded the clothing that had kept me cool in the jungle and toasty warm in the mountains. The plant spirit medicine retreat had become something way more than it had started out to be. My mind flew back in time to that cold night in London when I'd first heard the word *ayahuasca*, and something unseen had embedded itself in my heart. Then, a few years later when I knew I was going to meet the plant spirits myself, I trusted my inner vision again and look what had happened!

From the wreck of an unrequited life as a rock star, I was going to be a jungle shaman's apprentice. Me! A jungle shaman's apprentice!

But what did that really mean? I realized that once again, I'd dived into the unknown. Without Geraldo, this might never have come about. The almighty Creator had put him in my path so that this connection could be made. Instead of feeling sad at leaving my new friends behind when I returned home, I felt I now carried the seed of the new life that was to come.

CHAPTER 8

A Mighty Fine Tent in the Meadow

My first trip to the Peruvian Amazon was now behind me. Javier and I had agreed that I'd return sometime in the summer, and that we'd stay in touch until then. Geraldo had accompanied me to the airport, where we both pretended that our parting was truly a great tragedy. But deep down, I believe neither he nor I really felt a thing. We agreed to email each other, but I knew this too would fade over time just as we had. When there is no heartfelt sentiment, there can be no close relationship. I wished him prosperity and passed through the departure gates.

As spring approached Southern California, I found myself spending more time working outside in the yard. I now felt a stronger connection with the plants I was tending, and they seemed to help me stay connected to the jungle. As I pruned and weeded, I considered that we humans can be such funny creatures. We have our families and friends, homes, work, and daily routines, some of which never change from year to year. We may briefly alter the energetics of our day-to-day lives, perhaps with a nice vacation, spiritual retreat, or self-improvement workshop, and then we come home expecting to see that everything else has changed along with us. When we finally realize this hasn't happened it can be like having a bucket of cold water thrown on us.

My own realization was more like being subjected to a constant dripping water torture. After spending more than a month in a world so different from my own and having experienced such profound changes in myself, it was hard to adjust to being back home. But what exactly were those changes? How had I shifted? If pressed to answer, I would say that I was now able to see the incredible inner strength that had been hiding for much of my life. I'd also started to realize that it was okay to consider letting my life's dream of musical stardom take its final bow. I had never before thought of giving up that intense desire because there was never anything else to take its place until now.

For a brief time, I'd felt like Cinderella: one night I was flying with my prince in a magical coach, and then I woke up in my single bed back in my parents' house. I was in a strange place between various people trying to get me to do something constructive with my life and my secretly knowing that I'd be sleeping with the snakes and the sloths in only six more months. For this reason, I was reluctant to get involved in any other long term commitments like a job.

I believe that many people who have lived away from the family home as an independent adult can have a hard time moving back in with their parents, and it works both ways, of course. We follow our own rhythms and do what we truly believe is the right thing, but sometimes it all goes horribly wrong. Partners leave, jobs end; any matter of serious events can cause one to lose their sure footing in this world. I was very grateful to have had the safety net to catch me when my life in London spewed me out so rudely, but after nearly twenty years of making music and globe-trotting, I had come back to the same issues I'd left all those years ago. I was now in my forties, yet it seemed as if nothing had changed.

A good lot of my perceived problem had to do with feeling I couldn't be open with my parents about who I was and how I experienced the world. I wish I could have really explained to them about my shamanic worldview and practices, but they were from a very practical generation that only trusted what they could experience through their five senses. They believed in a man who walked on water and could change water into wine, but not in ancient practices that could heal someone without doctors in white coats and high tech medical facilities. Every time I tried to introduce even a small snippet of my world I would get shut down and ridiculed, so I stopped trying after a while. I didn't know at the time that hiding who I was in order to keep peace in the house was a major hindrance to my spiritual development.

So, while I struggled to adjust to the energies of my new life within the cradle of my old one, I continued to keep in touch with Geraldo and Javier by email. They were my lifelines to the magical month I'd spent during my first trip to South America. They were my secrets. When my mom would continually ask me when I was going to get a job or start shrieking at me for something petty, I would hide upstairs and write to these two jungle men who'd made my life so exciting. How could I explain them? Or even more, how could I explain that they were a part of my life and I'd be going back to see them in the very near future? I wanted to be able to share my stories and experiences openly with my parents but I couldn't.

Geraldo told me that he'd been diagnosed with malaria and spent some time in hospital. The area he had been in during the five days we were apart had been heavy with mosquitos, and it was hard to avoid being bitten, even for a native. He asked me for money for these expenses and I thought about the Iquitos Money Extraction Method number one: going on at length about serious medical issues that could be healed if only this or that treatment could be bought.

I had seen him start to exhibit some of malaria's symptoms in our last few days together such as the headaches and various pains, so there may have been some truth to what I was reading. I wanted to help him, but I was also leery of opening the floodgates.

I told him to give me a list of what he needed and how much it would cost so I could assess whether I wanted to send him anything. In the end, I did end up wiring him a little more than fifty dollars, which would have gone a long way in Iquitos. I also put it to him that this was not going to be a regular thing. I still had so many questions about his mysterious life, and until I was able to get a clear picture of this man, I was not going to get any more involved.

One thing I did know for certain was that I had to improve my spoken Spanish before I went back. My ability to converse and understand was decent, but I knew that during that first foray to South America I'd also had the advantage of being around others like Geraldo who spoke some English at times. While I agree that total immersion is the best way to learn another language quickly, it can also be quite tiring until you reach a certain level of proficiency. I knew that when I went back I would be living with people who didn't speak a word of my mother tongue, so I had to improve my ability to speak theirs. The search for a tutor was on!

While I have always been open to signs and phenomena from what we might consider to be parallel dimensions, these things seemed to ramp up in the coming months as Javier and I stayed in contact. One night after going to bed, I turned out the light and was in that relaxed phase before sleep. All of a sudden, I felt something leap from the floor and land heavily on me, sinking sharp claws through the layers of bedclothes. I knew there was nothing physical in the room with me, so I snapped on the light quickly to see what had jumped on me. *There was nothing there!* Did I imagine it? No, I was still awake enough where I couldn't confuse it with a dream. But what was it? To me it felt like a very large cat, especially because of the claws. I didn't feel that it was trying to attack me, but it was more like when a domestic kitty leaps on you as you're snoozing, only a lot heavier.

I sent Jav a note about this and asked for his thoughts.

"Always remember, Judita, that anything can happen in our world. Do you recall the floral bath I gave you back in Sacha Wasi?"

I paused reading his message as I allowed my mind to flow back to the first of the lovely plant baths we'd had. Javier had given me the power of the *yana puma*, the black jaguar, during that bath, and I had felt it coming in through the scented water. Had this spirit animal been the one to leap on me in the night? Yes, I believe it had been. Cool!

"This puma wants to escape the negative energy that is in your house. It is telling you that you must do something about it. It is a sign, bringing this important thing to your attention."

As time went on, I could sense my teacher's presence ever stronger around me. The feeling wasn't as strong as it had been that night I could have sworn he was rattling over me in person in Sacha Wasi, but I felt he was with me, nonetheless. He'd picked up on the negative energy in the house and told me I needed to do something about it because it was in my way.

The feeling of being trapped was soon to be relieved with a trip up north to California redwood country. For several years, I had volunteered at a nearby nature reserve in Southern California doing park patrol, and while traversing this wonderful park I became interested in animal tracking. After one grueling hike, my patrol partner, Dan, asked me if I knew about Tom Brown Jr., the tracker. I shook my head.

"Well, you must check him out. Read his book, *The Tracker*."

For me, *The Tracker* was a true gift from Spirit. It satisfied my sense of adventure and mystery. Following my usual pattern, I promptly ordered more of Tom's books and knew I had to experience his classes in the flesh. My luck continued on finding out he was going to be at a camp up in Northern California. I jumped in and registered for three classes in a row, each one being a week long. Tom had spent his youth growing up under the tutelage of an Apache medicine man, so he offered courses in the many aspects of what he himself had experienced. I felt that the opportunity to learn about wilderness survival and the structure of reality went along quite nicely with my upcoming apprenticeship with a jungle shaman.

While I waited for the first week in Tom's camp to arrive, I continued to live an uncomfortable existence at home. I'd had this utterly mind-blowing adventure in Peru, yet I'd returned to cloister myself in my room with the three cats that I'd brought with me when my marriage to an Englishman had ended. It was just safer than sticking my head out and constantly being attacked for one thing or another. I felt that my regular communication with Geraldo and Javier was my only salvation.

Yet despite my feeling that they were my saving grace, I was becoming increasingly annoyed with Geraldo even though I knew we weren't going to ride off into the sunset together. I felt that when he read my emails, he would only skim to the parts he was interested in and ignore the rest. I would ask him questions that went unanswered, and this didn't sit well with me. His increasing requests for money also did not sit well with me. There was this thing and that one, and if he only had a certain amount of money everything would be just fine. I wanted to help him, but I also didn't want to be seen as nothing more than a human ATM.

And unfortunately for him, I had already experienced this kind of one-sided relationship with Liam back in London. Looking back now, I can see how the wonderful universe gave me that experience so as to not be taken in by anyone else. As I've said, I knew full well what I was signing up for when I went after my jungle boy.

There is a lot to be said about personal experience versus hearsay, or something that is read in a book. I find that when I actually experience something firsthand and can feel the energetics in my body, it helps me to deal with other situations that may come along later. So, although the details of my liaison with Geraldo were vastly different than what I had with Liam, the underlying energetics were quite similar.

I had allowed myself to get involved with Geraldo because he was from a different culture; a culture that I subconsciously knew I would be spending a lot of time with in the coming years. Thanks to comments I'd heard either directly from our retreat leaders or from others in the group, I knew this kind of trickery was common here, so I wanted to train myself to recognize the kinds of deceptions I didn't experience in my home country.

I wish I could have made him understand that if he were able to be a genuine friend instead of just throwing out hollow words, his life could be vastly different. Sometimes, when Spirit gives us a nudge, we may not understand the details of those instructions at the time, but if we have faith in our inner vision we will surely see the genius of the master plan somewhere down the line.

On one hand I had him professing his undying love for me, but could I send some money for his daughter's school supplies? On the other hand, I had my new teacher introducing me to the world I was about to share with him. In between those two, I had the horribly depressing day to day mundane tasks of living in what I dubbed White Bread Wonderland. It was just weird.

The beginning of the end with Geraldo came when he asked me to send him some American sneakers. During some of our time hanging around Iquitos he had mentioned that he needed some new shoes. I was happy to purchase him a new pair of perfectly good sneakers from the Belen market for a good price, but he didn't want those because they were Peruvian; they weren't something his friends would envy. He would drag me into the stores selling well-known American brands for three figures and point to the ones he wanted. This alone told me that it wasn't just a new pair of sneakers he wanted; he wanted a status symbol he could impress his friends with. When I pointed out that he could get perfectly good shoes in the market, he would get petulant, and this had then caused me to stop offering the gift. *A caballo regalado, no se le miran los dientes.* Don't look a gift horse in the mouth!

He had also repeatedly asked me for a T-shirt from my city, so when I asked him for a safe address where I could send this to, suddenly he decided this wasn't good enough because he still wanted those damned sneakers. Knowing I was treading on shaky ground, I told him that I felt like I was being considered as his personal shopping service. He'd never answered any of my simple questions about how his life was going, yet his requests were becoming more and more materialistic. Never mind the cost of branded sport shoes; the shipping costs would also be exorbitant. He'd send me these ridiculous emails about how he loved me and what he was going to do to me, then he'd ask me to send him things. I allowed myself to feel all the energetics of these stupid exchanges, recording them for some nebulous future.

He responded with a message that I had to read several times to make sure I was really seeing those words on my screen. I went cold.

"Yes, my baby, my friends told me to get everything I could from you."

His admission surprised me in that while I really wasn't a gullible fool, I still couldn't believe he could be so blatant. What did he hope to gain by this? He then went on to confess that he was also communicating regularly with Joan, she of the magic potions that were supposed to bewitch her reluctant husband. I could only imagine he'd been sending her messages similar to those he'd sent me. They were not about building good relationships; they were only about things. While I had gone into the liaison with open eyes, I had also hoped that we might have developed a real friendship. We both had a lot to offer the other way beyond just stuff.

I decided to make one last reply, saying things to this effect. While good relationships should swing back and forth, there was nothing in this for me anymore. I realized his emails had simply become an unrealistic fairy tale escape for me. He didn't love me—heck—he didn't even care about me at all. Harold and Edwin had been right, and I was grateful to have been able to get their messages early on. As I pressed the send button and turned away from the screen, I felt a little deflated.

"Cheer up, little one. Sometimes people come into your life only for a short time to teach you lessons. You learned a lot from him, didn't you?" The voice of the Divine was speaking to me gently.

"Yes, I did. We had a good time, and it was through him that I made the connection to Javier. But why did it have to be this way? Why could we have not been genuine friends?"

There was no answer.

After a long but scenic drive, I finally arrived in the camp up north near Santa Cruz. I had signed up for three consecutive weeks, each one with a different theme. I had to do the Standard class first, which taught basic skills that would be used throughout ensuing classes. This class was made up from several areas that a student might choose to focus on such as tracking skills, wilderness survival, spiritual practices and more. My next two, Philosophy 1 and Healing, were more specialized and aimed at developing the important inner vision gifts that we are all born with. I particularly wanted to work with Tom in order to be able to pick up some useful skills that I might need when I eventually went to live in the jungle with Javier.

I'd brought a lot of equipment with me, not knowing exactly what I might need. I had been camping before, but this was a bit different. I'd borrowed a family-sized tent, which I thought would give me a little space for the duration. It was an inexpensive tent with a postage stamp-sized rain fly that was obviously meant to be used in sunny climates. I was still in California, so I'd be just fine, wouldn't I? As I looked around the meadow at the other tents, I saw smaller, sturdier structures. No one else had hauled in the load of stuff that I had. Still, I'd found a nice spot near some trees so I decided to push my feelings of being a klutz aside for now.

There were a lot more people registered for the first week than I had expected, well over one hundred. This first week was required of every student regardless of which area of specialization one wanted to eventually pursue. It was for building a common language and skill base, and after the welcome introduction the first lecture dealt with the subject of knives. I think the only thing I'd ever used a knife for was to cut food, so I was looking forward to learning how to use the nice blade I'd purchased to actually make something useful.

Not long afterwards, it started to rain and continued to do so throughout the night. Without a full-sized rain fly, the water seeped into my cheap tent, soaking everything inside that I had so meticulously laid out. A strong wind had also picked up, so the falling drops not only came in from the top, but also through the side seams. My sleeping bag and pad hadn't escaped these leaks, and I huddled inside trying to stay warm.

Fortunately, I'd paid meticulous attention to the list of things to bring, one of which included a rainproof tarp. Since I hadn't ever needed a tarp before and therefore wasn't exactly sure how I'd use it, I'd bought one that was ten feet long by ten feet wide. Okay, so I'm not great at estimating sizes.

Feeling confident in the early morning light, I ripped open the plastic packaging and pulled out my shiny new silver tarp. It was only as I laid it on the ground and unfolded it that I realized exactly how large a ten by ten foot tarp was. It was not a job for one person, but as usual, I was on my own so was I determined to get my poor sad tent covered up from the elements before breakfast.

The material was heavy and unwieldy, and with only one set of hands I wasn't able to get it stretched out properly over the tent. Since I had found a cozy little nook instead of setting up on open, level ground, there were also trees and bushes in the way. The tarp had been folded up into a small package, and it sure seemed like it did not want to be disturbed from its rest inside the plastic shrink-wrapped packaging. When I finally decided I was finished, my living quarters looked like a cross between a giant canned ham and some kind of mutant spaceship. You couldn't help but notice the massive silver blob shining forth in a corner of the meadow. Maybe I should have chosen a more hidden spot, huh? I was sure everyone in the camp would be snickering at my ridiculous campsite.

To add insult to injury, I quickly felt as if I was way out of my element. There were guys who showed up in full camouflage gear despite this first week being mostly lecture and short exercises. When we did work with our knives, they were able to quickly carve out whatever was being asked for with great proficiency, while I grappled with grip and blade angle. We were supposed to be making bow drills, which are useful tools for creating sparks with friction to light a fire when one didn't have a lighter or matches. I'd never even heard of a bow drill, much less have to carve my own!

"It's time to lose some wood!"

I looked up to see one of the camp's young male helpers staring down at me with a slight curl in his upper lip.

"I've never done this before. I'm just learning how to use a knife!" I protested.

He looked at me like I was an idiot who should never have registered for this camp in the first place. "Well, see if you can move a little faster then! You've got to get your bow drill made!"

I wasn't off to a very good start!

My first week in this basic skills camp really took me way outside of my comfort zone. I'm not overly fond of crowds because if I'm not attentive I tend to pick up a lot of energies that are floating around. It's as if there are multiple radios blaring at the same time but all tuned to different stations. I also felt there wasn't enough time for me to get the hang of these very basic skills. I'd start something with good intentions to be patient with myself while I learned unfamiliar new skills but then I'd end up miserably hacking away as I watched all these beautifully finished products forming around me. It was quite intimidating, so eventually I just gave up. Whenever there was an exercise that I knew I needed more time to work with, I would just go for a walk. Were I to ever find myself stranded alone in the wild, I'd certainly be in trouble. Hey there, big hungry bear! Over here!

I think part of what was affecting me was just the sheer number of people in the space. There were lines for the shower, lines for the bathroom, and lines for each meal. I felt like I needed a little breathing space away from all the activity, so one evening during a break I decided to walk quietly down the dark road that led into the camp.

Allowing my eyes to adjust to the darkness, I thought I saw movement on the slope to my right. Peering into the shadows, I watched as a tall figure silently made its way down the hill. Really? I can't even sneak away on my own into the darkness without someone else invading my space at the same time? What were the odds of this? Feeling really annoyed, I pressed myself into the shadows and watched as the figure swung itself up into the branches of a tree. I knew that there were apprentices who practiced their scout skills like this, and I wondered if he'd even seen me, but I didn't think he had. I thought it was kind of funny that I'd seen him sneaking around, while I felt pretty sure he hadn't seen me because he hadn't made any evasive maneuvers. With a deep sigh I returned back to the main lodge to continue the evening's work.

Despite my own little niggles with the crowd and the manual skills, I found the introduction to the spiritual work utterly riveting. This was usually taught in small groups or with a partner. For example, we might go out into the woods for a sensing presence exercise to see if we could feel our partner sneak up on us, and if so, how close could the other person get before we felt them, and what kind of energy did they exude? I just loved this stuff and was very good at it.

In the deepest reaches of my vivid imagination, I was already a master scout with the most advanced survival tactics, yet I knew the reality was quite the opposite. While I could acknowledge that the techniques being presented were truly valuable ones to know, I'd come for the spiritual component of the teachings. I could not wait for the following week, which would be all spiritual work, and I didn't have to feel like a klutz for carving a piece of wood to form my bow drill too slowly.

One of the things that Tom told us seemed almost like a personal message for me. It had to do with coming out of the closet in order to be able to let your light shine and be of service to others and the earth. I thought of how I was keeping myself in this safe closet at home so I could avoid what I perceived to be inevitable criticism and negativity. Perhaps it was my own mind that was creating many of these scenarios!

During the next two weeks we dove into magical worlds, following lectures with practical exercises which allowed us to experience short forays into other dimensions. Tom was a master of the flourish and the dramatic, suddenly appearing through a door as we all waited in anticipation. Whenever he would speak, I would be so entranced that I would sit on the edge of my chair and hold my breath lest I miss even one word. I could have sat there for years listening to him and his teachings, and when he'd come to the end of a lecture—or even worse, the night—I would yell "No! No! Don't go!" silently in my own mind. The sheer energies of the subjects forced me to remain in my seat until I could gather up enough willpower to walk back to my mighty fine tent in the meadow, still covered with the unruly silver tarp. I was no longer an out of place klutz; I was in the groove at last!

¿Qué? What? I stared across at my new Spanish tutor, Claudia, in confusion as I struggled to find the words to respond. During those final days in Iquitos after accepting Javier's apprenticeship invitation, I felt I needed to sharpen up my language skills before returning to the jungle in the summer. So, once I got home I'd looked around for a native Spanish speaker with whom I could practice. I found that I was not as fluent as I thought I was, and I was really concerned about being able to communicate well.

As agreed, she and I would not work with formal lessons, but rather discuss subjects as they arose in an attempt to mimic what I would experience with my teacher and any others I'd be with. I was fine when I had time to think and mentally translate, but I had to increase my speed of comprehension and response. I had no idea of what kind of situations I'd find myself in and I didn't want to miss any of the magic. As with the basic camp skills, I felt squirmy and a little inadequate.

As I drove home my mind floated back to my first semester in college. I'd been a slacker student in high school, taking things like jewelry design and personal development to fill my electives instead of meatier subjects like languages. Yet as I was choosing my college courses, I found myself signing up for Spanish I. "This is absurd! Why am I registering for Spanish?" I asked myself.

"Someday you will know the answer to this. Just take this step and do the best you can." Ah, that inner voice again. It had obviously been with me longer than I'd thought.

I ended up earning top marks in that class, so continued to refine my Spanish, both in the States and in London, but not really knowing why. Now I had my answer. How could that teenager have possibly known that she would end up in a South American jungle communicating with people from an entirely different culture? The physical being could not have known, but her higher guidance certainly did! As when I went to London on that one-way ticket many years before, the magnitude of the situation didn't really seem to occur to me. Somehow I just made it work.

As I counted down the days and gathered the equipment for my big adventure, I continued to face opposition from some of those closest to me. It was almost as if they could feel the change in me, and that change made them uncomfortable.

I've seen this a lot in the work I've done through the years as a shamanic practitioner. One member of a partnership or family wants to make what they believe to be positive changes in their lives, but as they alter their energies those effects ripple out to those around them. This is where the backlash can occur. Loved ones will perceive these energetic changes as threats even though they don't see anything concrete, and they then attempt to return the situation back to where they felt comfortable. The usual methods for doing this involve criticism and undermining the person who is working on themself but can even take on stronger forms such as making ultimatums.

When one friend accused me of using travel to avoid getting a job, I explained to her that I was doing this training for some future work, even though I didn't know in what form this might take.

"My excursions are not diversions!" I replied with some heat at yet another attempt to keep me in White Bread Wonderland. I couldn't seem to make anyone understand that I was following my heart. Just because my heart had a different plan for my life besides slowly dying of boredom in an overcrowded, materialistic city it didn't mean it was wrong. It was just different.

From the day I'd arrived back from the devastating end of my life in England, I'd taken on an increasing amount of household and support work as the years went by. I cooked dinners, cleaned the kitchen up afterwards, kept the yard in good shape, did all the grocery shopping, and accompanied my elderly parents to their various appointments. I was happy to contribute and give back while I was finding my life's direction, but I knew one day this would all come to an end and I had to find something for myself.

I've had some of my greatest downloads and inspirations while standing at kitchen sinks. One day, while rinsing some dishes, I thought of Geraldo and Javier yet again and then heard my inner voice speak to me.

"Don't look outside yourself or to another person for happiness. Completion comes from within. That is where you will find the truth."

I finished wiping the pan and put it down, thanking my inner guidance for that golden nugget. I vowed to take this advice onboard from that moment onward.

PART THREE

Río Momon

CHAPTER 9

The City of Eternal Noise

The day I finally boarded the plane for my return to the magical country of Peru, Mother Nature reminded me of her immense power. It was August of 2005, and Hurricane Katrina had forced a slight change of flight plans, but we arrived in Lima just a little later than originally scheduled. Somehow, the idea of a powerful wind to blow away my old life at the beginning of a new phase seemed very fitting.

Since my internal flight to Iquitos the next day was in the afternoon, I'd booked a hotel room in Miraflores for the night. Based on my previous experience, I knew not to expect much for the included breakfast, although this time I was able to negotiate the *concentrado* routine like an expert.

There was a television in the dining room, and it was playing music videos from Mexico. I was glued to the screen in case any of my then current *rock en español* obsession, Maná, came on. The sweet waiter looked relieved that I spoke Spanish, and seemed concerned that I was dining alone. He mistook my interest in the television and asked me if I'd prefer watching the American news channel, CNN, instead.

"No, thank you. I am now in Peru, so I prefer your local programming."

He bowed graciously, saying that most American tourists want to watch CNN while they eat. I smiled into my coffee and thought to myself that I was certainly not a typical American tourist.

After finishing my white roll and motor oil disguised as coffee, I wandered around Miraflores looking for a good bookshop. I'd been getting some of those invisible pokes that I now recognized as spirit input, telling me I should learn some Quechua. I'd looked for anything related to learning the language of the Incas in my own country but was unable to find anything in Southern California apart from tourist guides. I figured I'd start with a good dictionary and thought I'd be able to find one in Lima. Luck was with me, and I found a large bookshop on Avenida José Larco, located on the ground floor of a two story mall. After some discussion with the helpful salesperson about what I was looking for, I walked out with a rather large, heavy dictionary. I was so excited for my find that it didn't occur to me that I'd now have to carry this heavy tome through the jungles with me for the next several months.

The idea that I could easily pick up the main local indigenous language was not borne out in my trying to master a few phrases. I find native languages to be in a very different format from the more formalized Western ones I was used to studying. So why *Runasimi*, this language of the Incas?

As I'd mentioned before, I'd heard some icaros with Quechua lyrics during the few ayahuasca ceremonies I'd participated in on my last trip. Since I was now going to be training in a tradition that included this language, I thought it might be a good idea to learn the meanings of some of the more frequently repeated words. For me, it's very important to understand what I am singing and not to just parrot what I've heard.

Javier was waiting for me outside the arrivals hall in Iquitos, but he wasn't alone. He'd brought along the young man who'd I'd met very briefly when he and Julieta had arrived at Geraldo's mother's home for the *parrillada*. Olaff was Julieta's nephew, and his family owned a motocab, so that day he'd been conscripted to take them to the gathering and then for today's airport run. A tall and slender young man with dark eyes and a serious expression, Olaff was only twenty-three and studying for his first degree in Amazonian biology at a local university.

They strapped my bags onto the back of the motocab, and Olaff zoomed off with Javier and his trusty student in the cab behind him. I was looking forward to relaxing and visiting peacefully after six long months of fantasizing and wishing for this day, but it wasn't to be.

The noise of Iquitos is not confined solely to its central area. It reaches out away from the Plaza de Armas and oozes down the back streets into the residential areas, where it is furthered along by the presence of thousands of radios and televisions all turned up to maximum volume.

Javier's house was part of a row of cinder block structures with shared walls that framed both sides of a very uneven dirt street. I briefly compared them to the terraced houses I'd seen in England, but that was as far as any similarity could go. There were no ceilings, and the shared corrugated metal roof, made with panels called *caluminas*, was set up high to allow air to circulate through the rooms.

Unfortunately, this kind of arrangement also allowed noise to circulate just as easily. As soon as a household would wake up in the morning, someone would turn on a radio or TV, or both or all of them, and crank up the volumes. The sound would rise up to the metal roof, bounce off and reverberate into the next house, where it would then mix with that property's own electrical noisemakers. I was glad we wouldn't be spending a lot of time here because I was sure the cacophony would drive me insane.

Javier had promised me a surprise in one of the last emails, and I knew I wouldn't be able to get any hints out of him so I didn't try to fish for details. The surprise turned out to be a party to celebrate the combination of his mother-in-law's birthday and my arrival. It was also a chance to christen the little house he'd made for me. Since they didn't have any festive ribbon, Jav and his family had totally wrapped up the front of the house with toilet paper in their attempts to make it look special. Yes, it certainly did look special!

Although it was a simple structure, I was impressed. It had a concrete front patio that was about the size of the house itself with a sloping ramp leading up to the door. It had been built into the rear right hand corner of their property, so the fences served as my back and right side walls. The front and left side walls were covered with cheap curtains printed with sweet little cartoon animals that wouldn't have been out of place in a child's nursery.

The roof featured the usual woven irapay panels, and simple wiring brought in a single, dangling, overhead light bulb that served as the only lighting in the hut. I was also taken aback to see a small television set because this seemed to be totally out of place. Jav mistook my look of surprise at seeing the old apparatus to be one of delight. I didn't have the heart to tell him that I would probably never turn it on. A double bed with a straw mattress and a small set of shelves completed the furnishings.

After taking a quick bucket shower to rinse off the sweat from my journey, my new teacher sidled up to me and looked like he wanted to discuss something of great importance.

"Can we go to the store to buy a case of beer for the party?"

Upon finding that the price for twelve large bottles was less than twenty-five dollars, I agreed. It was a momentous occasion after all. With Olaff once again at the helm of the moto, the three of us headed to a nearby beer store. These stores were nothing like our well-stocked liquor marts back home. They were literally just corner spaces on some side street, stacked high with crates containing only one or two types of bottled beer. But like in the States, you pay a deposit on the bottles, which you would get back when you returned them.

Despite the large gathering, it actually took quite a while to go through the first lot of cerveza. I'd mentioned before how one bottle at a time was opened and shared via a single glass that was passed around. Somehow, this worked even in a large crowd and served to make the supply last longer. Once all the bottles had been emptied, I was pulled aside again and told we now needed another round to toast my new *casita*, my little house. Why not? It somehow seemed right to begin our journey with a good send off.

I'd also brought along some CDs of some of my favorite *rock en español* bands. I made a deal with Javier: I'll buy the second case of beer if we could play just a few of these songs, because I really wanted to hear them blasted out here in these jungle town backstreets. Suddenly, the music that I had samba-danced to in my room back home after several tequila shots came alive in the Iquitos night. Many of the young men mimed air guitars and I joined in with complicated, imaginary solos. The older folks watched in amusement and tolerated the noise for a short while, then the CDs were replaced with the local *cumbia*, and everyone danced for hours.

Despite the fatigue from two days of travel with very little to consume except a lot of alcohol, I was asked to make a speech. I silently thanked my current tutor and the voluminous quantities of beer for giving me the confidence to pull off a comprehensible speech, then thanked everyone present for the party honoring Julieta's mother. *¡Salud!* Cheers!

Pulling me outside to sit in the motocab to be away from the center of the noise, Javier was in full flow. He was quite drunk but still in that deliriously happy phase where he just wanted to talk a lot. He began describing the exact process that his Jivaro friends had used in the past for making shrunken heads. I shook my fogged head in a feeble attempt to clear it, thinking that I was surely misunderstanding what was coming at me so enthusiastically. I mean, where else can you go for a few beers and get a first-hand description of how to make a shrunken head? I was fascinated and wished I had my little recorder handy, but it was still tucked away in my pack.

Next, I was regaled with how to make *masato*, the famed yucca beer. I told him I really wanted to try it, and he said we'd be able to make some at our first training station with the Jivaro.

I must admit I was somewhat taken aback to see Javier in such a state, thinking that if he was a shaman then he must certainly be an enlightened being who eschewed alcohol and wild parties. But the fact is that jungle shamans and other healers are just like the rest of us. They work very hard in conditions that most of us would not tolerate, so when they have an opportunity to forget about the weight of the poverty they live in even for just a few hours, they can be big party monsters just like the rest of us.

The fiesta went on into the wee hours, and I finally decided it was time to try out the new bed. All the dancing and tasty Peruvian beer had energized me, but eventually the two days of travel and the heat finally convinced me to call it a night. As I stretched out and sighed, I realized that I could hardly hear all the racket from the front of the house and the street. This surprised me because even being in the kitchen at the back of the house one could hear everything that reverberated through the building. But my *casita* wasn't part of the block long building which shared the metal roof. I said a silent prayer of thanks and fell asleep, only to be awakened a few hours later by that scourge of country life: a group of roosters who seemed to be competing with each other for the title of the loudest bird in Iquitos.

Through my sleepy haze I sensed that someone was moving around stealthily in my little house. I remained motionless, carefully cracking open an eye to see if I could recognize the intruder. There was no one in my line of sight, but the noises continued, forcing me to raise my upper body a bit so I could get a better look. A startled clucking ensued, and I saw three chickens wandering around in their quest for breakfast.

"Well, hello there! I can't say I've awakened to this kind of greeting before."

The three birds cocked their heads at me and flapped their wings in alarm. I kept still so as to not scare them, and they eventually waddled away down the ramp to the yard. I love chickens. There's just something funny about these sweet creatures; and when they run, rolling their bodies from side to side, I just crack up laughing.

Easing myself off the straw-filled bed, I thought about a nice hot cup of coffee as I crossed the yard towards the back door of the house. I pictured an inexpensive coffee machine in the kitchen with the fragrant black brew dripping into a glass decanter. Dare I hope?

"Buenos días, Judita. ¿Cómo amaneciste?" Here was Jav, asking how I'd slept.

Pretty darned well, for my first time on a straw bed. So, what were the chances of some caffeine? The look on his face told me everything. I might as well have asked if they had a private plane. We both went into the small kitchen and he inquired of Julieta about my request. She rummaged through their cupboards and pulled out a single envelope of instant coffee. It looked like it had been tucked away in there for years.

"No one drinks coffee here. It's too hot. We drink sodas or juices. You can buy what you like at the market later today."

Sure, but what do I do right now? We boiled up a small amount of water, and Julieta handed me a cracked cup. I tore open the packet and dumped in the miniscule amount of fine brown powder and poured the water into the cup. Stirring, I hoped it would at least be drinkable. It was not. Despite being desperate for that sweet morning buzz, I couldn't get past a few sips. It really was that bad. I decided right then that I would adopt the ways of those I was with rather than trying to hold onto my usual desires. If they didn't drink coffee, then neither would I.

Breakfast was a simple meal of fruit and leftover rice. As we ate, Javier outlined his plan for our training over the coming months. "We will work in three different places in order to give you a chance to see and experience more things. In between, we will return here."

I felt my heart sink a little at hearing this as I had thought we were going to go out and spend the entire few months away from the city. It was so noisy here! Jav explained that we would need to return to replenish our supplies, which was something I hadn't thought of. He gave me one of his brightest smiles as he continued. "I can go out into the jungle for three months without coming back, but you cannot."

I protested mildly even though I didn't really know what it was like to be out in the wild jungle for months, surviving on one's own skills. I thought back to my first Tracker camp and how I'd failed miserably to even make a simple bow drill. I'd felt a knot in my stomach as I recalled seeing everyone around me making sparks and creating small fires, while I'd been unable to even carve the wood well enough to make something useful. I had to admit he was probably right.

I felt another question bubbling up and hesitated to ask it because it seemed kind of stupid. "Why do you even have to go out into the jungle anyway if you can see patients here?"

He considered this for a moment as he swallowed a piece of juicy papaya. "To rest and restore. After I see sick people for weeks or months, I have to get away to clean my energy, so I go out into nature. This is something you will understand with time. It's very important. If you don't clear your energy you will also get sick and not be able to work."

I nodded even though I realized I didn't quite understand this completely because I hadn't experienced it myself yet. I hadn't healed any sick people, so I didn't know how that would affect my body. Yet deep down, I felt that click, and I somehow knew without a doubt that he was right.

One of my first tasks as a jungle shaman's apprentice was to make a pot of ayahuasca, the famed master plant teacher medicine. Normally, we'd cut the vines ourselves, but to save time, Javier had done this himself before my arrival. Later on, I would have the chance to do this under his guidance. That part of the process is probably the most physical of all. You have to hike into the jungle with machetes and cut down the amount of vines you need. The vine depends on other tall plants such as trees for its support, so sometimes one has to climb up to where the vine is in order to harvest it. Depending on the amount needed and how much is available, this can be an all day job.

Javier told me that there are very definite steps to follow when brewing this sacred medicine in the traditional ways. Cooking it over a wood fire is one of these steps, so we'd bought enough for the task after we'd finished picking up other necessities such as a new machete for me in the Belen market. Following my teacher as he wound very quickly through the alleys and crowds of this covered facility, I mused at how much had changed in my perception since the previous trip when I'd visited this labyrinthine market for the first time. Then, our small group had banded closely together to protect ourselves from the many purported dangers we'd been told about. I'd felt like a target, being an obviously foreign tourist who didn't know the score. Now laughing at my baseless fear, I slid past the locals as if I were one of them. For the next few months, I *would* be one of them!

My teacher also warned me that the brewing process was an all day job--sometimes two—so I needed to get everything prepared and ready to go for an early morning start the next day. This meant cutting the sections of the vine so they would fit in the large pot. This was also a labor intensive job. Laying an old sheet on the ground to catch all the pieces, we brought out the vines that Javier had previously collected and set them to one side. He handed me a triangular shaped log and a heavy mallet, although I wouldn't need these until tomorrow when I would pound open the cut sections of the vines.

Next came that ubiquitous piece of jungle equipment, the machete. Available in a range of sizes, these long blades are used frequently to clear paths through dense greenery and maintain gardens where food is grown. They can also act as a defensive weapon when one suddenly encounters a poisonous snake or other aggressive animal.

I must admit I rather enjoyed whacking the vines to pot size with the machete after Jav demonstrated the technique with a few vines. Casting my thoughts back to my failed attempts at wood carving in the California camp, I felt more proficient with this big blade than the much nicer, smaller knife I'd struggled with. Once the pieces were all cut, we wrapped them back up for the rest of the day. Javier then showed me how to use the mallet and log to split the cut pieces of vine open.

"You don't want to crush them, Judita, you just want to open them up to expose the inner fibers to the water. Ya?"

I nodded my understanding as he continued.

"You must get up at dawn tomorrow morning to finish preparing them by splitting them open before cooking. That way, they'll be fresher when we add them to the water."

Having instructed me on these preliminary steps, Jav stood up and walked back into the house. Looking around to make sure that I was alone in the yard, I picked up my new machete again. It was a simple, inexpensive blade, but something happened when I grasped its orange plastic handle. Suddenly, I was a super hero with magic powers. I was sure that if I held the machete up and pointed it at the sky, lightning bolts would shoot out from the tip and reach beyond the clouds. My mind flew back to the Arthurian legends that had led me to England. For a brief instant, I and the Once and Future King were superimposed upon one another, raising our powerful blades to the heavens. I could hear the thunder and feel the lightning bolts crackling overhead. From that moment on, I was Machete Woman, jungle master and accomplished *curandera!* Now I just had to live up to my ridiculous imagination.

In between errands and getting to know the extended family more, I received a great gift: my very own *encanto*. I recalled the large stone that had been introduced to me when Geraldo and I had visited Javier on that fateful day, when the latter had asked me to be his student. That stone already had its own caretaker, so this new one was to be mine.

In this tradition, an *encanto* is a large stone that presents itself to a shaman and is used for healing purposes. What makes this remarkable is that in many areas of the Amazon jungle, it can be difficult to find rocks of any size. It's not something you notice until you decide to look for a few stones but can't find any. So, to have a large, hand-sized stone suddenly appear in one's path is taken as a sign that it is an *encanto* that wants to work with you.

Javier told me that these magical tools originate deep within the earth and slowly make their way to the surface. When a shaman seeks an *encanto*, it will somehow appear in his path, frequently in water like a small stream. The stone he presented to me had come from his uncle. It was sitting in a few inches of water in a plastic bucket with a handle.

"The *encantos* should always be kept in water. They need the water," Javier told me solemnly.

I fished the heavy grey stone out and examined it closely. It exuded a sweet energy, and as I continued to gaze at it I could see a face emerge. It looked like a kindly old grandfather, and I felt that it was happy that I was going to be its caretaker now.

"You will carry this stone in its bucket all through your apprenticeship," he told me. I nodded, feeling very humbled and honored.

The next morning, I arose early and spread out the blanket once again. I sat on a low stool behind the log and began to work with the vine pieces I'd cut the previous day. Javier had left everything I'd need on my porch, including the very large heavy cooking pot called an *olla*. Holding one end of the vine to keep it steady as I placed it on the edge of the log, I would hit the plant with the mallet until it flattened somewhat, opening up to expose its fibers. The prepared sections would then be layered carefully in the *olla*.

Each shaman has his or her own recipe and method for brewing their ayahuasca. For my initial batch, Jav had told me to layer these *lianas* in the pot and then cover them with water up to the point he indicated. I then had to fetch buckets of water from the primitive bathroom and at first, this concerned me. Coming from a more developed city where the tap water contains such chemicals as chlorine and fluoride, I'd assumed that all domestic water supplies were the same. On expressing my doubts about making a sacred medicine with such liquid, Javier looked at me as if I were a child that needed to learn an important lesson.

"No, Judita, our water here comes from the river. There is nothing in it as you say."

As I poured the river water into the giant pot, I began to feel the magnitude of how much I had to learn. Not only to learn, but also to adapt. My supposedly civilized, Western train of thought had led me to question making a medicine from unsanitized river water. Yet it had been done this way for centuries, hadn't it? And surely the long boiling process would kill off any germs that might be present, wouldn't it? I sucked air through my teeth and bent to my task, not wanting to be one of those oversensitive types who insist on wiping everything down with antibacterial wipes before making any kind of physical contact. I was in a jungle town, after all. A jungle that was full of germs and microbes and other larger things that probably wanted to eat me. I was going to be just fine.

"Trust the process. Get out of your head. The world of the shaman is not built on logic," my wise inner guidance piped in.

Yeah, I know. I know.

The ayahuasca cooking process is an exercise in mindfulness. Because of the size of the pot and the slight dampness of the wood we'd bought, it took three hours just to bring the contents to a boil. At that point, we added the companion *chacruna* leaves and a few other ingredients that were part of Javier's own recipe. This was also when we started using the *soplas* to enhance the brew. The Spanish verb *soplar* means to blow, and the breath is an important element of almost any magical process.

"We must attend the pot for the entire cooking time," said Jav as he gave me a piercing gaze. "Don't leave it unattended for a moment, because if that happens, the evil spirits can sneak in and ruin everything. They can cause horrible visions."

And just how do we keep away these vision spoilers? With tobacco, of course! Jav had already informed me that I absolutely had to form a relationship with Grandfather Tobacco if I wanted to be a successful healer in his lineage. This was something else I had some difficulty with at first. Being from the United States, never mind the trendy West Coast, tobacco was practically considered to be something as vile as anthrax. To be anywhere in the vicinity of a lit commercial cigarette was said to be as bad for the health as inhaling mustard gas. How on earth was I going to be able to completely shift my outlook one hundred and eighty degrees?

The tobacco plant is considered to be very sacred among many indigenous peoples of the Americas and beyond. While there are many variations in its ceremonial and healing usage, it may be used as a vehicle to carry prayers, clear out negative energies or gain wisdom. Only the pure leaf is used without any processing or additives, and there is always some intent for its use; it is not smoked gratuitously. Used respectfully in this manner, it doesn't become habit forming.

Making our pass through the market the day before, we'd stopped at the tables where the tobacco vendors offered their wares. We'd picked up a large supply of the pre-rolled cigarettes called *mapachos*. I was told that this was also the general name for the local tobacco.

During our stay in Sacha Wasi, the two shamans had brewed a pot of ayahuasca on site and encouraged all of us to help in the process of keeping it safe. They'd demonstrated the technique of taking the smoke into the mouth and mixing it with prayers, then bending over the pot while forcefully exhaling.

"The good spirits love tobacco, but the bad spirits don't like tobacco at all. You want to keep them away by blowing the *mapacho* smoke all around and into the brew."

I nodded as he continued. "Do you remember how I walked around the room during the ceremonies and blew tobacco smoke all over? I was keeping away the evil spirits so they wouldn't make you all have ugly visions."

"Okay, Javier, I understand. But what are these bad spirits and where do they come from?" I asked.

"You will learn more about these as we go. For now, I will tell you that they may be sent by a *brujo*, and they get into any space that isn't well protected. They cause a lot of trouble!" His eyes widened and he flung his arms out dramatically to the sides. Lighting the first cigarette, he continued. "We must give three strong *soplas* into the pot every thirty minutes. I'll start; you watch me. Ya?"

And so went the long day. In between keeping the bad spirits away from my first pot of medicine with the *mapachos,* I had to keep the fire going by fanning it with the pot lid. Javier would occasionally come by to inspect the progress and give a grunt of approval before wandering back into the house. Eventually, he deemed the cooking process to be complete and we filtered the jungle tea into clean two-liter plastic soda bottles.

My young teacher then instructed me to take a bath with the filtered solids the next morning at dawn. This simply involved putting the leftover plant material into a large basin filled with water, and completely bathing the body from head to toe with the infused liquid. The thought behind this is to clear one's entire being. Drinking a plant medicine works from the inside out, while bathing in it provides even more healing and protection by strengthening the body's energy fields. Nothing of this sacred medicine was to be wasted!

All this time I had been wondering if anyone else would be going with us when we left the city to go into the jungle for our first training location. Did Javier have any other students? Who would help us carry all of our supplies? While traditionally the student and the teacher would go together up until the day when the pupil went alone, I had the feeling that at least one extra pair of hands would be helpful for the long excursions, especially since I didn't have any jungle survival skills yet and could potentially be a liability. I knew Javier worked a lot with Geraldo, but since he hadn't mentioned my moochy ex at all, this added a bit to the suspense.

"Olaff will be our cook and helper!" Javier drew himself up proudly in response to my query the next day. My teacher rattled off many of his nephew's accomplishments, particularly in the jungle camping and survival arts. The jungle biology he was studying at the local university meant that he not only knew which bird or plant I would inevitably ask about, but its scientific name. I knew part of my training would involve plant identification walks and making up medicines from certain plants. In addition to the local names, I also was hoping to get their proper Latin names if I could.

Having just met Olaff, I didn't know about these abilities, but I trusted Javier. I also liked Olaff. He had a sweet, sincere air about him and I felt that he was a good man. He had a young wife and a new baby, so with his full time university studies and side gigs to bring in money, I was impressed with his work ethic. He had a chance to prove himself later that day when a fierce windstorm suddenly sprang up. The strong current raced through the cute animal print curtains that served as my walls and doors and started knocking leaves and fibers off parts of the structure. Before I could even ask for assistance, Olaff was on it. He had everything under control while I just stood back and watched what he was doing. Just in case. You never know.

Our handyman joined us on another foray into the Belen market to pick up more food and supplies. No matter how many times I went to that city-size market, or will go through it, there will always be something new and fascinating to catch my eye. There were scores of creatures that I'd never seen before—alive and not—and I had to stop and gape at each one: unfamiliar-looking fish and small mammals and reptiles. For me, a traditional apprenticeship is not just about learning the ceremonies or healing work: it was also about the history and the culture where the tradition developed. I wanted to know everything about this world I was entering—its legends, myths, food, languages, view of the world and much more! This is what brings the magic to life.

"We must bring *víveres* to the Jivaro," Javier informed me as we zig-zagged through the crowded lanes.

I had not heard this word before and asked for clarification.

"Food and supplies. The people of the jungle are poor. The Jivaro are helping your training by allowing us to share their space so we must bring them gifts." He looked at me very intensely and added, "You should never go visit the native people empty-handed."

I was beginning to realize that whenever my teacher gave me that intense look, he was making an important point that I needed to remember and take on board. Nodding my understanding, I asked Jav to suggest what might be useful.

"There is no electricity or refrigeration so we will bring things that can be stored like rice and beans and sugar."

Sugar? Jav nodded vigorously and that Cheshire cat smile spread across his face. "And you must buy bags of *caramelos* for the children." I had a feeling the children would not be the only ones dipping into the candy bag!

Although I was sure Javier knew what we'd need, my orderly Western brain demanded that we have a brief chat about what we had to have, at least on a basic level. I considered that there were unlikely to be many shops in the middle of the forest, so what did we absolutely have to have with us until we returned to the city to restock?

Part of this was just logical. I didn't grow up in the jungle, and while I describe my overall style as sleeping-bag chic, there are a few crucial items that I felt I'd need in order to survive such as toilet paper. I'm a woman without the bacterial resistance a local might grow up with, so I am not going to use some random leaves or other biological material in certain parts of my anatomy.

Another part was economical. I had a finite amount of money with which to finance this expedition, so I was hoping to avoid surprises as much as possible. Although it was early days, I was already seeing the pattern of requests for some very important item that was needed *right now*, even though I had asked what all was needed prior to that and had been assured that that was it. ¨*Sí, Judita. ¡Es todo!*¨ That's it! That's all we need! Yeah! How many times would I hear that?

I believe there was yet another reason. I am guilty of having one of those brains that wants to know as many details as possible, and then it likes to construct its own version of reality based on those external factors. "Okay. I got this. This thing is like that thing I did before, so this new thing will be like that." This is quite detrimental for a student of any magical path. When you create a scene based on what you think it should be like, you are then blocking out what is really flowing in the universe. In this case, we miss out on a reality that is far more stunning than anything we could have ever imagined.

On returning to the house with all of our supplies, we added them to the growing pile in the front room. I picked up my machete from where it was resting against a large pack of toilet paper and looked at it thoughtfully. I'd been told that if you're going to go out into the jungle, you have to wear knee-high rubber boots and carry the long blade to not only clear the path in front of you but also to protect yourself from any aggressive snakes that might strike out as you walked by. I patted the new boots that I'd bought and felt a sense of satisfaction. Machete Woman was now ready for whatever was in her path.

Javier came in and told me that I needed to make up some *camalonga* with ingredients I'd just purchased. We had used this *preparado* before the ayahuasca ceremonies at Sacha Wasi as a protective psychic shield around the body. While I had been uncertain as to why Javier had prescribed this jungle potion for me during one of our consultations in Sacha Wasi, I now understood. Someone who steps off the physical world needs to be spiritually strong and very well protected from the unseen entities that might not have our best wishes in mind. *Camalonga*, with its large proportion of onions and garlic, in addition to camphor and other ingredients, packs a powerful punch that's strong enough to keep an entire legion of evil spirits, zombies and vampires far, far away!

Later that night, we held our first healing ceremony for local people. The little hut I slept in was now going to become an examination room. One of the original traditional uses for ayahuasca was that of a diagnostic tool. Only the shaman and any apprentices would drink the medicine, unlike current practices where every participant drinks for one reason or another. Javier and I would each drink a small quantity of my newly made brew, then we'd sit and wait for the spirit of Madre Ayahuasca to let herself be known. This can be through feeling a shift in consciousness, seeing bright geometrical shapes, feeling nauseous, or any combination of these.

My young teacher's patient was suffering from diabetes, but Javier had purposely not told me about this beforehand. The woman had brought along her daughter for support, and there were two other men that Javier knew who had also come along for healing. The diabetic patient laid on my bed, and the others took chairs around the room. I was assigned to the very low, uncomfortable stool I'd used earlier in the day, which was placed next to Jav.

While a true person of power does not need any special clothing or tools, any of these can serve to connect with the patient's subconscious that something out of the ordinary is happening. I'd come of age in an era where rock stars did not look like your average Joe or Jane off the street. They dressed in glitter and satin. For the audience, it was a sign that you were in the presence of the gods. For the performers, changing into stage clothing was a signal to the subconscious that it was show time. So whether it was for a ceremony in a small jungle *maloca* or a huge stadium on another continent, changing your outfit changed the energy, and everyone present was aware of this.

But on this night, although Javier had donned his cushma, I was dressed in my regular clothes. Earlier in the day, one of our errands had been to a fabric shop where I'd chosen the material for my own ceremonial cushma. While Jav favored flowered prints because they represented nature, I went with starlight and a pattern of light points against a dark sky background. We'd taken the material and thread to a local seamstress who promised that the garment would be ready before we left Iquitos.

The hardest thing for me was sitting on that very low hard stool for hours. When I would occasionally shift, I would get a stern look from my teacher, which I clearly understood to mean that I must sit absolutely still, but I just could not. There was so much energy running through me that I had to stand up once in a while to help it move through me. Occasionally, he would rattle over me briefly which helped to calm my agitation.

As the medicine spirit made her presence known, I could see a cloud of what looked like red smoke spread out above the patient's body. It reminded me of the human circulatory system that I'd studied in an anatomy class a few years earlier. As I watched Javier shake his leaf rattle *shacapa* over her I saw more red smoke start to come off the woman. Other images followed: a jaguar and a very large snake which superimposed itself over my body. Even though I had only taken a modest amount of medicine, I was astonished to see myself as an almost room-sized anaconda. It briefly reminded me of the trance posture that had allowed me to shape shift into a large angry bear all those years ago in North Wales.

The two men, whose issues were more emotional than physical, received energetic cleansings to remove the negativity that Javier saw in their energy fields. When I had looked over at them from time to time, all I could really see were what looked to be nebulous shadows. As my teacher worked on them, passing his leaf rattle around their bodies as he sung healing icaros, it looked like the shadows quivered and then faded.

When the ceremony concluded after about two hours, he counseled those present before they made their way out into the humid Iquitos night. Once they had gone, he turned to me and instructed me to sit cross legged on my bed, whereupon he proceeded to press down on both of my shoulders. He told me that we had begun to work with my very first spirit, *Sachamama*, the Earth Mother, who in their lore is a giant anaconda. My mouth dropped open and I told him what I'd seen. Javier gave me one of his face-splitting, ear to ear grins and nodded.

"You have been brought here because this is your work. You have been here before. Not everyone can do this work because it takes a lot of strength. You have the grounding of the *Sachamama*. You will go on to be a very powerful *curandera*."

I felt a brief sense of awe at the great responsibility that this would entail, but I was not allowed to revel in my awesomeness for long.

"You must sit very still throughout the entirety of our work so that we present a united front. This is how you harness the power, not by frittering it away with physical movement. It is a way to master the physical. *¿Me entiendes?*"

Yes, I do understand you.

We then went on to have the *brujo* versus the *curandero* talk. I knew that one of the things a teacher looked at before accepting an apprentice was their intent. The master would confer with his own spirit crew about the potential student. These guides would tell him about his pupil's character. A true seer can tell you things about yourself that no one else knows, and it can be very squirmy. There are no secrets because in this work there are no places for them to hide.

I want to explain briefly about the two opposing forces that hold court in the magical jungle traditions. Like everywhere else in the world, the Peruvian Amazon has its own version of good versus evil. The *curanderos* are those who have mastered their self-discipline through the challenging years of apprenticeship. They work for good causes such as healing and prosperity, and many claim to follow a Christian religion, although they do this in their own ways.

Mastering one's self-discipline through such ascetic practices as abstinence from all forms of sex, including even thinking about it, can be extremely difficult, but it is crucial for those who wish to manipulate energy in a good way as a shaman, healer, or magician.

Energy itself is a neutral force, but it can be manipulated according to the intent one puts into it. If someone leading a magical ceremony has not mastered his or her self-discipline, there is a chance that their own nonsense will arise during the work and be spewed out into the room, adversely affecting the innocent participants.

On the other side of the coin is the *brujo*. While this word doesn't always have negative connotations in the general sense of being a practitioner of some form of magic, in the Peruvian Amazon it refers to someone who was unable to master themselves through the strict observances required of an apprentice, so they tend to operate in the dirtier areas of the magical realms. They have enough knowledge of energy manipulation to make them dangerous, but they don't have the self-discipline to stop themselves from using the forces for harmful purposes.

Thus, we have the jungle version of good versus evil, with the *brujos* casting nasty spells and the *curanderos* working to counter them. I'd learned about these otherworldly battles during my time studying magic in London, but I was now entering a world where it all seemed more real.

Early the next morning, we were ready to move on to the first part of my training out in the wilderness. We were going to be staying with some indigenous Jivaro people in their camp on the Momon River. They were close friends of Javier's, and he'd managed to talk them into providing a space for his new foreign apprentice to start her jungle training.

We arrived at the port of Bellavista late the following morning after picking up some last minute supplies from the market. We'd had to make two trips to the port because we couldn't fit the three of us and all of our supplies in the small motocab. Olaff conscripted his friend, Carlos, to do the driving, so the two of them loaded up as much as they could fit in and took off. Once unloaded at the dock, Olaff stayed with the pile and Carlos returned for Javier, me, and the rest of our equipment.

Our next task was to search for a boat and driver that would take us up Rio Momon to our destination. A long, woven palm leaf covered motorboat called the *Rey de los Reyes*, King of Kings, caught Javier's trained eyes. This particularly craft was called a *pecamari*. It, and its even more compact relation, the *peque peque*, get their names from the sound that the small motor makes as it chugs through the water. The motor itself reminded me of those hand-held blenders that you can insert into a glass or pitcher to make your morning smoothie. It has a very long shaft attached to the small rudder and rotating blades, which allows the whole thing to be lifted out of the water when necessary to avoid obstructions and thus avoid costly damage.

Its owner was lazing on the cushioned seats smoking a cigarette, while his teenaged son coiled a length of rope. The boatman shifted his gaze from Javier to Olaff, then to me, and finally to the huge pile of equipment and supplies, an obvious question in his eyes. His curiosity finally got the better of him, and sizing up Jav as the leader, asked him what we were up to. What was this White woman doing with two locals and all this stuff? My overactive imagination created a feeling that he thought my two jungle brothers might be kidnapping me and were planning on keeping me hidden away in some leafy labyrinth while they made their ransom demands.

"She's my apprentice. We're taking her to the Jivaro camp to begin her training as a shaman," Javier explained.

Once more, the boatman looked me up and down. I nodded and smiled, indicating that I was indeed in on this caper and all was well. Somehow, the idea that I was being spirited away for nefarious reasons struck me as kind of funny. I had wanted so badly to be here that I might have been the one doing the kidnapping!

A price for carriage was agreed on and the equipment was carefully stowed aboard. As we climbed in and sat down, I turned to look one last time at the bustling port as we left Bellavista. I didn't want to fall into my usual pattern of imagining what I thought might be lying ahead, but I somehow knew that I would be a different person when I returned to this port. I felt no fear or apprehension, only a sense of anticipation. As our little craft navigated the shallow river, I realized that what I did feel was that I belonged here. I was home.

CHAPTER 10

Hanging with the Headshrinkers

As we chugged up the river towards the Jivaro settlement, I wondered if my soon-to-be hosts still practiced head shrinking. I'd understood from Javier that they mainly did this with vanquished enemies, but what if they wanted to add my head to their collection? I was afraid to ask my teacher about this possibility because he was such a joker that I doubted I'd get a straight answer out of him. I could even picture his response: eyes wide and arms flung out to the sides for dramatic effect.

"You must be very careful not to make them mad, Judita. They would probably want to add your beautiful blond head to their collection!" He'd then make a sweeping motion with the side of his hand across the front of his neck.

My musing was broken by my stomach letting out an audible growl, reminding me that I hadn't eaten yet. When I'd asked about breakfast before leaving the house, Javier told me we could pick up food for the journey at the *puerto*. In addition to boat rental, the Bellavista port area was full of stalls selling all kinds of local dishes. Each stall had small tables and benches for those who chose to sit and eat there, but most dishes were also available to go. And there was no better food to take with us than the classic jungle dweller's portable snack, the *juane*.

In the Peruvian Amazon jungle, *juanes* are eaten with gusto each year on June 24th, the Feast of St. John the Baptist. Local lore says the shape of the packet of food resembles poor St. John's head after it'd been detached by the order of King Herod of Galilee. Despite the somewhat grisly comparison, the contents of the *juane* are such tasty ingredients as spiced rice, a small amount of meat, and a hard-boiled egg. This mixture is then wrapped up in the long green *bijao* leaves, which come from the macaw flower plant, then the whole thing is boiled or steamed for about an hour and a half. To eat it, all one has to do is to carefully open the packet and fish out the ingredients with a plastic fork if you have one; fingers if you don't.

Doing my best to make sure the rice and other ingredients packed into the *bijao* leaves ended up in my mouth instead of all over the vinyl seat, I allowed myself to settle into a pleasant reverie. I was really enjoying the much slower-paced river travel in comparison to the frantic racing through the noisy city streets in Iquitos. It was quite soothing to watch the interminably long shorelines slide by, with occasional riverbank villages coming into view, as the breezes broke up the intense jungle heat and humidity. It was fun to see the other watercraft slipping by us. Some of these crafts were truly amazing to look at, ranging from tiny one man canoes to huge *lanchas* that were reminiscent of the old riverboats from the past. In between those two extremes, there were some very strange looking vessels that looked like floating forests or even little villages. These precious waterways were the super highways of the jungle where just about anything could be transported.

In this region, the locals will tell you that they really only have two seasons—the rainy season and the dry season, although sometimes it can be difficult to tell them apart. While the exact months for each can vary depending on who you talk to, the rainy season generally begins around the end of November and lasts through to around the end of April; then the dry season kicks in through the remaining months. So, this being the beginning of September meant that we were currently in the dry season.

As we puttered along, Olaff told me that we had to watch out for any *palos* that might be ahead of us. *Palos* are the dead trees and floating logs that have fallen into the waterways, making navigation tricky, particularly in a fast moving current.

The water level of the river is also very important. Apparently, this had been an exceptionally dry season, with the river reaching a low that had not been seen for many years. Several times, the boatman's young son had to jump off the front of the boat and push us off a sandbar. I'd never had to consider things like this before when boating on lakes or the ocean, so I was learning about these important jungle practices as we went along.

Secretly, I was glad that it was so dry. Once we got off the boat we had a long hike through the jungle to get to our encampment, and we were packing a lot of gear. At least we'd arrive at the camp nice and dry.

A few clouds had meandered overhead as we putted through the shallow water. I was so engaged with my companions and observing the passing landscapes on either side of the river that I didn't notice the cloud cover thickening above us. As our boat angled in towards the bank, the sky darkened and it began to rain. Of course, it did: this was the tropics! I covered my heavy pack with plastic and helped to unload the equipment. We pulled on our rubber boots, which along with a machete and a mosquito bed net are essential jungle gear as Javier had told me several times already. From the landing, the three of us had to haul our belongings up a steep hill, which by now had now turned to soft mud.

"Oh well, at least it's not cold," I muttered to myself.

We continued on until we came to a small, deserted village. This might happen when their dwellers decide to move on to a new place that has more resources, or if they simply want to get a fresh start somewhere else. Javier instructed us to store everything inside an empty hut while he went to let his friends know we had arrived. A series of vocalizations followed, and they sounded like an odd echo.

"Hooooo!"

"Hoo!"

"Hooooo!"

"Hoo!"

A wizened old man in his seventies with intense eyes appeared and was introduced as Augustin. Augustin and Javier greeted each other enthusiastically, and then Olaff and I were introduced. I was last, and he seemed to suddenly lose his enthusiasm for animated greetings. He half nodded his head, grunted, and turned away. From that moment on, Augustin would never look me in the eye. I never found out for sure why, but I believe some indigenous people avoid eye contact with those they deem unsafe or who might taint the pure tribal energy they live with.

The old Jivaro loaded himself up with more equipment than any of the rest of us carried, then bolted forward to be lost between the trees. Javier took off behind him, and soon the two of them were out of sight. Olaff and I grabbed our share of the supplies and hurried after them. On my back, I was wearing my fifty pound pack filled with all the jungle necessities I thought I'd need for the weeks ahead. My left hand was wrapped around the thin wire handle of the white plastic bucket of water containing my precious *encanto*. Under my right arm was tucked a multipack of toilet paper, which was something I had insisted on. The thought of using dirty leaves in the delicate parts of my anatomy didn't seem like a great idea, particularly being so far away from a pharmacy. To finish off, I carried a black plastic bag in my right hand, this one containing rice, sugar and a few other food stuffs. All of this ensured that my body was somewhat off balance.

The jungle around us was very humid, and I was beginning to be grateful for the rain. I had considered myself to be a strong hiker, but I was struggling to keep up with the two men in front of me. Eventually, the distance closed somewhat as the path became narrower and more filled with obstacles like low hanging vines and fallen trees.

I found it to be somewhat of a challenge traversing the jungle paths. In addition to the heavy rain, the humidity, and being loaded down with equipment, there were more *palos* to deal with. Sometimes two or three of these thin logs were laid lengthwise through a patch of mud; sometimes there was only one to navigate. I was having a hard time trying to keep my balance on these makeshift bridges because the rain was running into my eyes and my hands were full, so I couldn't throw them out sideways to aid my balance. The clunky rubber boots I wore also did nothing to help. How I wished for a lightweight pair of running shoes! I decided it had to be a lot easier just to step off to the side briefly rather than risk rolling off the precarious wobbling logs that became more frequent as we moved deeper into the jungle. After all, this is why we wore knee-high rubber boots, wasn't it?

As we walked along swiftly, one behind the other, I saw another one of these cut tree trunks laid out just ahead, with a small area of mud just off to the right side. It looked safe enough, so I stepped off the log and confidently put my right foot down on the ground. Instantly sinking in up to my knee, I flailed wildly in an attempt to regain my balance. Without thinking, I now put my left leg on the ground where it too disappeared into the deceptively deep mud pit. I fell forward onto my hands, totally immobilized like a roach in a glue trap. For some reason this struck me as hilariously funny, so I started laughing and soon my jungle friends joined in. They pulled me out of the mud pit with some difficulty. The combined weight of me and my load against the deep mud and gravity required someone on either side of me to pull up and out, all the while balanced on that damned *palo*. I had wanted so much to show these native guys that even a White chick from California could be tough. So now, in addition to being totally soaked from the rain, I was covered with mud and filthy. And not only that, but I was also about to be presented to Oscar, the local Jivaro chief. I had heard for many years from different sources that the deeper one dives into the world of Spirit, the greater the sense of humor one must have. What else could I do except laugh?

Shortly afterwards, we entered a clearing and saw Oscar's *albergue*. This large open structure was basically a platform raised about six feet off the ground and covered with thatched irapay palm leaves. Although Oscar and his family lived in a small village deeper into the jungle, he preferred to spend his days in this separate location because it was quiet, and anyone coming along from the river paths would have to pass by his shelter and stop for a visit. This was one way important news travelled through the jungle.

Oscar was a lean man in his late fifties with kind twinkling eyes and he immediately invited us to get out of the rain. Our own private shelter was nearby, but we could rest there and wait until the rain stopped before transferring our equipment. I saw him look in question to Javier for an explanation of my extremely disheveled appearance, so the amusing tale of my immersion into the mud pit was told with great relish. I could sense his initial concern for my wellbeing, while at the same time trying to hide a faint smile. Oscar presented his partner, Luzmilla, a sweet, graceful woman about fifteen years his senior. Large age differences between couples are simply not an issue in the jungle. They have a very different way of pairing up than those of us from the more northern countries, and I'll get back to this in a bit.

Javier jabbed me in the ribs and nodded towards his friends. I was still trying to catch my breath, so I wasn't paying full attention to what he was saying.

"The *víveres*! Give them the *víveres*!" he forcefully instructed under his breath. So much for the idea coming from me.

I found the bags containing the food supplies we'd brought along as gifts and ruefully noticed that they now sported a thin coating of mud in some places. Hoping no one else would notice, I ceremoniously presented them to Oscar and Luzmilla, who accepted everything with their own huge smiles. If they had seen the mud patches, they graciously gave no sign of this. Although I'd had to be prompted, I could see that this gesture went a long way to establishing a good relationship with these lovely jungle people. I knew it was a lesson that I would never forget.

As we settled down on the hard wooden floor of the shelter, I began to see movement through the dense foliage surrounding us. These Jivaro were very sociable, so when word of visitors--particularly a klutzy *gringa* covered in mud who was traveling with two local men, rippled through the village, a steady stream of extended family members passed through the rustling green gateways and climbed up the ladder to join us. Among them were Abusha, a hunter, and Juanito, Oscar's five-year old grandson. Juanito was a wiry child with a head of unruly, chestnut colored hair above an attractive face that always seemed to be smiling in great joy. No advanced yoga master sitting in bliss could have outshone little Juanito!

Introductions were made all around, and most of the people had trouble with my name. I'd encountered this before in my travels around Latin America, and allowed people to call me Julia if they find it easier. I mentioned this to the group and Oscar looked thoughtful. He leaned over to his wife and I saw them discussing something briefly.

"We have decided to give you a Jivaro name!" he said proudly. "We will call you Juyushi. And of course, Javier is always Javicito to us."

I liked my name, but thought it was more complicated than my real name. Still, here we were at the start of a new adventure, so it seemed appropriate to have a different jungle name. I thanked the Jivaro chief and said I was honored.

As we all sat sharing the latest news, I noticed little Juanito to my right, and he was playing with what looked to be a large white caterpillar. Earlier, as we were traversing the final leg of the path here to the *albergue*, we had seen him and another boy collecting these from a fallen tree stump. Olaff had called my attention to them and asked me if I was hungry.

"*¿Tienes ganas de comer suri?*"

I looked at him and made a face, and he laughed in agreement. No, I do not feel like eating *suri!* I recalled that Javier had shown me these things in the market recently as we were kitting up for our expedition. There had been piles of the fat three-inch long squirming grubs, all wriggling together as if they were a mutated horror out of a science fiction B-movie.

But you weren't just limited to squishy, raw *suri* shooters who, if not taken home for dinner in one of those ubiquitous black plastic bags you see all over Iquitos, might grow up to be adult palm weevils that bored holes in the local aguaje palm trees, the latter of which are prized for their "cheddar cheese" fruits. The adults drill their way in to lay their eggs, and their grubby offspring munch their way out. In many of the same stalls, the palm grubs could also be found in deep cooking pots, floating in some kind of mysterious liquid, which was sold as soup.

So! Raw or cooked, your choice. I was told that *suri*, whose proper name is Rhynchophorus palmarum, reduces fat in the blood as well as providing a protein source for the jungle people. I've eaten oysters and I like sushi, but I just couldn't quite get past the idea of popping one of those things in my mouth. It was just too big and just too ugly!

The jungle Indians have a great sense of humor and it wasn't long before they were testing me to see what I was made of. Javier stood up and declared that I should be allowed to hold Juanito's little buddy so that I could begin my lessons in jungle culture. I'm not too squeamish about holding bugs or worms but I had to steel myself up to receive the wiggling grub. I held it between my thumb and forefinger and was amazed at its strength. I could've sworn I felt muscles rippling underneath its wrinkled skin. Perhaps it sensed that it was being held in some clumsy foreigner's fingers where it was in danger of being squished to death. The *suri* opened its mouth widely, and I'm sure if it had had vocal cords I would have heard it roaring at me to put it down. Olaff had also told me that they have quite a bite, and I was not about to let that repulsive, oversized maggot sink its teeth into me. Everyone on the platform watched me as I inspected the grub and tried to keep it from escaping my tentative grip.

"Please don't make me eat it. Not yet. Not just yet." I prayed silently, trying to look cool.

"*Muy bonito. Gracias, Juanito.*"

I handed the ugly thing back to the jungle boy, wondering if I was off the hook. Juanito flashed me a broad smile and accepted the grub. We all resumed our conversation and I relaxed. But moments later, I looked over at Juanito and saw the grub hanging out of his mouth. I was fascinated and horrified at the same time and wanted to watch, but I had to act as if I saw this kind of thing every day. He bit the head off the *suri* and then sucked out the contents of its body as if it were a drinking straw. I managed not to react, but when he then slipped the empty skin over his little finger and began licking it like the most delicious ice cream cone, I had to get up and look for something in my bag.

I'd noticed that Oscar's structure had the foliage cut away for several yards around its base, so it looked like a small island floating in a leafy green sea. On questioning this, I was told that's common to clear the land around houses and structures for safety reasons. This not only helps cut down on concentrations of smaller pests like insects, but it also removes hiding places for larger space invaders like poisonous snakes.

Suddenly, Abusha was alert and he stood up quickly. There was a quick consultation with several of the others, and I saw Javier listening in. My Spanish was good enough to allow me to travel into areas where no English is spoken, but I still had trouble comprehending some regional accents. The Jivaro have their own language, and like me, Spanish is their second language. Their spoken Spanish reflected an accent that I had a hard time understanding at the beginning of my stay with them, so I couldn't tell what was going on.

They had somehow sensed that there was an *afaninga*—a deadly viper–somewhere out there in the grass. I'd had some basic experience with animal tracking, but now I was seeing it in its purest form. Not only had Abusha been able to hear a snake on the ground some thirty or forty feet away, but he was also able to identify the type of snake it was! A mad hunt for the viper ensued, and I just had to get in on it too, even though I didn't have a clue what an *afaninga* looked like.

Abusha was able to pinpoint the greyish-brown snake's location under a bush, and after a quick whap on the head to stun it with the top edge of his machete blade, he grabbed a long stick flipped it up into the air. The spectacle was not unlike that of a pizza chef flinging and spinning the base of dough high in the air. As soon as the poor snake landed, he was sent up again and again. That *afaninga* was not happy!

When I asked why they were even bothering with the four-foot long serpent, one of the men declared that they had to move it out of from the shelter area to keep it away from the children. While this was surely a sensible thing to do, I thought their method seemed to be a bit over the top. I was a little suspicious that perhaps that they were putting on a show for me, something that Javier later confirmed.

After about fifteen minutes of this, the *afaninga* had only been moved about twenty feet from the bush. He was now even closer to the shelter, hence my thoughts that this display might have been to show off a little. I certainly was impressed! The children thought the snake flipping game had been hilariously funny, and they would get a lot closer to it than I would have. While I was fascinated, I thought that standing within striking distance of a mad viper didn't seem like a good idea. The unfortunate serpent finally decided it had had enough and quickly slithered off into the greenery before it could be given another flying lesson.

We all climbed back up onto the platform and continued to enjoy our visit. I relaxed against my pack, feeling safe for the moment from silently screaming grubs and flying vipers. Freshly picked papayas were sliced open and passed around. There were several papaya trees in the immediate area, and in the days that followed I would see Juanito and another boy climbing up the trunks to harvest the fruit. They would reach up and place their hands around the tree with a firm grip, then climb by angling the outer edges of their bare feet against the tree to prevent them from slipping. As someone who was never able to climb ropes or do pull-ups in gym class, I knew this required an upper body and arm strength I certainly didn't have. At other times, I would see very young boys carrying machetes as they followed after the older men who would teach them the skills they needed to survive in the harsh environment. I tried to imagine a six year old being allowed to run barefoot on a dirt path with a long sharp blade in Southern California while his parents looked on proudly, shouting words of encouragement, but I could not.

All at once, something dropped right down onto my head from the overhead beams that supported the woven leaf roof. After the recent experience with the *afaninga*, I thought it might be another snake. I jumped up off the hard wood floor, shouting in alarm. Amid everyone's delighted laughter, I discovered that my attacker was not a deadly serpent intent on squeezing the life out of me, but a small white-faced monkey. I soon realized that the little capuchin was really more interested in my food than in me. He scrambled from shoulder to shoulder while trying to reach over and grab my snack as I shifted it from one hand to the other. Everyone was in an uproar, and I was told that the pesky little chap was Oscar's pet. He did not have a name, so I promptly dubbed him Mr. Pickle. During our stay here with the Jivaro, I became quite attached to Mr. Pickle, but at mealtimes I always had to be on the lookout for him. His signature technique was to drop and grab, and he could be very fast.

When the rain finally stopped, I was told to follow Javier, Augustin, and Oscar to the separate shelter that would serve as our base camp. It was located only about a ten minute walk away from this more public gathering area. Javier told me that the two Jivaro men were also shamans, and that we had to engage in an old initiation ritual. Our own *albergue,* or shelter, turned out to be nicknamed *La Casa del Shaman* because this little house was where their own people did their spiritual training. I felt honored to be there following in their tradition. The *casa* was fairly small and built in the typical local jungle style. The floor was made of planks of the very hard wood *tahuari* tree, set on vertical supports about three feet off the ground. It was open on all sides and covered with the ubiquitous intricately woven irapay palm leaf roof that slanted down at a sharp angle to help deflect the rain.

The initiation consisted of them asking me questions to which there were formal answers. Augustin, being the oldest, was the one who would ask the questions. Unfortunately, he was also the one I had the most trouble understanding. It was almost as if he was speaking in his own dialect. He would ask me a question, looking at me with that piercing intensity in his eyes, yet at the same time avoiding eye contact as he waited for my reply. I would look over at Javier for help. He would tell me the correct answer that was expected and I would repeat it to the two Jivaro men. Javier also had to explain to them that my Spanish wasn't very good right now and I needed a little help from time to time. They nodded, and I was told I had to work very hard so I wouldn't have so much trouble understanding what was going on. I stood there suddenly feeling very inadequate and out of my depth. I felt like an idiot for having thought earlier that I would certainly impress them with my excellent physical condition and Southern California camping skills, yet the jungle had humbled me shortly after we'd left the boat. I suddenly felt very unworthy.

Once this ritual had been completed, we had to move all our equipment to the *Casa del Shaman*. I was glad to be doing something that I couldn't mess up and further prove to my companions that I was a typical, inept city person. Once everything was neatly stowed away, I decided to dig a hole for a latrine behind some nearby bushes but realized that we'd forgotten to include a shovel in our supply list. In the middle of thinking I might create one with a long branch and my machete, I spotted a length of wood that looked like a ready-made handle. Someone had built a very basic set of shelves for those occupying the training tambo. The stick I wanted was standing upright underneath the right front corner. I tugged on it, expecting it to move easily, but when it resisted, I pulled harder. To my surprise, the reason for its reluctance to shift turned out to be that it was a flat-blade shovel that had been jammed into the dirt. It looked like it had been there for a long time, and I figured all the mud had glued the blade in firmly as it dried.

Thrilled with my discovery, I moved into the small clearing where I'd planned to build my pit and began digging. Suddenly, I heard some loud cracking followed by a big crash somewhere behind me. Returning to the tambo area I saw that all of the shelves had collapsed. I then understood that the shovel hadn't just been stored there for use: it had been used to prop up a weak support area of the shelf unit. Attracted by the noise, Jav, Olaff, Oscar and Luzmilla came running over, certain that I had already managed to mortally wound myself by getting crushed beneath the heavy weight of the shelves and their contents. Seeing me standing safely nearby, I thought I'd better 'fess up and reveal that the shelves had not in fact fallen on their own as they'd initially thought.

Jav tried to look stern but he couldn't stop laughing. "You will rebuild the shelves and put them back the way they were." Then, realizing that putting this project in the hands of his klutzy apprentice might bring about the demise of the entire jungle, he added, "Olaff will help you."

Looking a bit sheepish, I told Javier that this was his chance to escape now and run for his life before I could wreak any more havoc. Somehow, this made him laugh even harder, and soon all of us were sharing the joke.

We were due to have our first short ceremony later that night. Its purpose was to introduce me to the jungle spirits and start to become familiar with the various phases of the work. I was exhausted and had fallen dead asleep, hoping that my teacher might either take pity on me and let me sleep or simply forget about it. I should have known better. I didn't come all this way to snooze, did I?

Feeling a rude jab in the ribs, I was told to get up and put on my cushma because it was time to begin. I paired the beautiful night-sky printed garment with my clumsy rubber boots. Javier told me that I would not be given everything at once because I wouldn't be able to take it all in. It was important to take time with each step so as to really understand what was happening and why it was done. This sounded good to me!

While the rituals vary from shaman to shaman according to their different traditions, there are certain items that are an important part of the work. The ayahuasca brew is of course the centerpiece, along with a small cup for serving the medicine.

Next on the list is tobacco. Some shamans use only the prerolled mapachos, while others like to add loose tobacco and an intricately carved pipe.

You also likely find a bottle of *agua florida* on the altar. As I mentioned before during the ceremonies with San Pedro, this commercial cologne is used for purification and cleansing. While to me this product bears no resemblance to anything with flowers in it, there is something about the smell that transports me across time and space. It's very alcohol-forward, and when inhaled deeply after rubbing a quantity of it vigorously between the palms, it can really open up the energy channels in the body and clear them out quickly.

Another important item is a rattle of some kind. The shacapa, which I introduced in a previous chapter, is a bundle of leaves tied at the base of their stems to form a rattle. They are shaken to give rhythm to the songs, as well as to beat away any negative influences from around the body's energy fields. Some shamans prefer to use rattles made from small local gourds, while still others use no instruments at all.

While I was certainly no authority on these long-practiced jungle ceremonies, I had tended to think that they were all in a format similar to what I had experienced back in Sacha Wasi, being somewhere around the four hour mark. Not so! The length is determined by the purpose of the ceremony. Those used for training and patient healing are usually much shorter, even as brief as one hour. As with everything magical, it is the practitioner's culture, training and intent that sets the format.

This first ceremony lasted a little over an hour and was celebrated with a small quantity of my self-made brew, perhaps only about one or two ounces. The idea was to make the connection to the spirits without being so affected that I was unable to retain anything that was being taught to me. I learned how to put prayers and intentions into the tobacco and then blow the smoke over myself and my ceremony tools for blessings. The precious icaros would come later.

After we finished sometime after midnight, I was tired and longing to stretch out on my self-inflating mat under the mosquito net, but I took some time to look around at where I was. Despite the late hour, it was still humid, with the damp air starting to draw in a little bit of a chill. Shadows of the leaves and trees rose all around to enclose us in our own little corner of the jungle. Thousands of crickets and frogs and whatever else joined in the most amazing chorus I've ever heard! What happiness! When I finally could not keep my eyes open any longer, I crawled under the net and laid down, tucking the lower edges of the net underneath the mat. As in Sacha Wasi, I once again fell asleep listening to this enchanting jungle choir.

I awakened early the next morning in the *selva,* my first time doing so outside of a retreat center. Olaff and Javier were already up and organizing things around the tambo. On seeing that I was awake, Javier shook my mosquito net and said,

"In the jungle we always get up early, Judita. You will have to adopt our habits if you want to be a real jungle woman."

I threw a towel at him in response and we all laughed.

Today, it was time to begin my *dieta* in earnest. I was told that when available, my meals would be a small, local fish called a *bocachica,* and a few pieces of boiled yucca or small mound of rice. For those times when I felt I was dying of starvation, I could also have some farina, which had already been prepared by someone else. Soaked in water, this was the perfect *dieta* food because it would swell up like a sponge and help fill the hole in the hungry student's midsection.

Jungle farina is quite different from the refined wheat product that can be found in our favorite grocery stores in the United States. This local cereal is made from the yucca root, a very versatile plant part. It has to be peeled and cut up, boiled until soft, then drained and mashed. These would also be the first steps in making *masato,* the highly prized yucca beer.

The mash is spread on a flat metal pan like a badly made pizza dough, then set to dry in the hot jungle sun for hours. If there is no sun or time is short, it can be dried over a cooking fire, but it would then need to be attended to keep the cereal from getting burned. The resulting hardened pieces are then smashed up with a mallet to achieve the final granola-like grains. For a bland, one-ingredient food product, it was amazingly labor intensive.

Jav, Olaff, and I preferred to join Oscar and his group for meals rather than eat separately in our own area. It was a chance to share a unique togetherness and pass on the gossip. For being such an obvious outsider, these lovely people accepted me right into their lives. They included me in conversations and activities, and I felt their genuine concern that I have a good experience during this special time in their camp.

Since we were a good distance away from the river, Olaff hadn't gone out to fish yet. Todays' breakfast was dried fish, yucca, and farina. I knew things like dried fish and cured meats were wilderness essentials, so I tried to be grateful that there was at least some kind of protein, but that danged stuff was grey and chewy and didn't bear any resemblance to fish in my opinion. It was also very salty, something I'd been told was a no no for dietas, but I was not about to question this so soon. If that was the only thing available to eat, and my teacher said it was okay, then I'll eat it now and question it later.

After finishing my modest meal, I wanted to make some journal entries in the voluminous notebooks that I'd brought along for the purposes of documenting my journey. I told Javier that I was going back to our tambo and asked if he needed me to bring anything back for him. He shook his head.

I ambled along the overgrown path, lost in my thoughts and twirling my machete like a baton. I was definitively not practicing keen outdoor awareness, so I didn't notice the subtle movement in the greenery in front of me. All of a sudden, three male commandos rose up from the grass only a few yards in front of me. I don't know who was more shocked--me or them!

All three were younger than I was and had those handsome good looks that I see on many jungle men. They were dressed in full camouflage with black rubber boots that were definitely more stylish than my own. They looked at me brandishing my mighty machete and hands dropped slowly to weapons, not sure of my intent. All I could think of in that moment was that they were members of the dangerous Shining Path group that I'd heard about in the news years before. Was I about to be kidnapped? When you're confronted with a potentially dangerous situation, you don't always think clearly.

While they didn't seem to be aggressive, I thought I'd better err on the side of caution. Very slowly, I bent down and laid my weapon at my feet and then rose up, showing them my empty hands. Suddenly, there was no fear, and I think the Spanish for "Hey, dudes! What's happening?" rolled off my tongue without thinking. This then made me smile, which is exactly what was needed. I could see three sets of shoulders drop in relief, and we all approached each other with smiles and greetings.

"Who are you? What are you doing here?"

"And who are *you*? What are *you* doing here?"

Hah hah hah. Phew!

The men turned out to be military patrollers who move around through all sorts of areas in order to prevent or combat any possible guerilla action that might be gathering steam. They were also on the lookout for drug or weapon runners who might be taking a detour through the wilderness in hopes of avoiding detection. These guardians of the peace had been working their way down from the Colombian border through the jungle. The men explained that it was a very stressful life, so they sought shelter in the indigenous chiefs' shelters where they were able to relax and pick up on local happenings from the very ears of the forest itself. No wonder my subconscious had picked up on the energy of the *Sendero Luminoso*, a terrorist group formed in the late 1960s in Peru that espoused Maoist principles and violence. I didn't know a lot about this movement but had only read briefly about it in the past. The captain of the men asked me where the chief's *albergue* was, so I pointed in the direction behind me to my right.

Back at our small shelter, I briefly caught up on my notes and then returned to Oscar's lodge. The three young patrollers were sitting at the rear, chatting animatedly with the Jivaro chief. Although I understood they were discussing the security of this precious area, I could also hear a lot of guffawing and hooting. To me, they seemed like old friends who'd run into each other after a long absence.

All talk ceased as I climbed the short ladder to the deck, and I could feel their eyes on me. "Please don't trip. Please don't fall off the platform," I silently wished to myself. Sucking in my breath, I summoned my confidence and turned around to wave at everyone. My dignity was soon to be doomed once again.

"Judita!" It was Javier. He was carrying a large stone that was somewhat curved inwards on the top. He set the heavy object down near the front railing and summoned me over. "Time to learn how to sharpen your machete!"

"Okay, piece of cake. This should be easy," I thought as I sat down on the hard *tahuari* wood deck.

Javier reached his hand out to indicate he wanted my machete, so I handed it over. He sat down easily and indicated the bowl of water near the sharpening stone. "Watch me." He showed me how to drip a little water on the edge of the blade as he moved it in small circular motions at an angle to the stone. I watched intently, feeling as confident as I had been before the bow drill carving assignment.

Setting to my task under Javier's critical eye, I noticed the three patrollers watching me in undisguised amusement. One of them leaned over to Oscar and whispered something in his left ear, making him smile. Was it about me? Surely not!

Javier indicated that I was to continue with the task as he walked back to rejoin Oscar and the patrollers. As I slowly swirled the edge of the blade I couldn't shake the feeling that I was being watched. I realized I was not a common site in this area at his time, especially being a single woman. Okay, I was a single, White woman in a Jivaro camp learning to sharpen a machete in the traditional way with water and a stone.

It wasn't until later that the joker who was my teacher told me what they'd been talking about. He'd noticed their undisguised interest in me so he decided to have a little fun with them. He'd informed them that because we were a team, the three of us slept and bathed together, embellishing the tale with great detail to pull them in as far as he could. No wonder I'd felt so many pairs of eyes on me! I thanked the stars for my sense of humor. It allowed me to laugh along with anyone else who was laughing at me!

The ability to laugh at yourself is one of the most important skills in any magician's training. I firmly believe that the universe has a great sense of humor and is constantly inviting us to join in sharing a few laughs. True spiritual training is not about waving a sage wand and flitting about in floaty garments like a fairy. When you go in deep, you're absolutely going to be facing your own inner demons or mud pits. Without that sense of humor, the challenges might be far more explosive than they need to be.

"Judita! Come and see this! I think you'll be interested in this." Jav interrupted my task.

"This" turned out to be Augustin's private masato stock. He had several containers of the yucca beverage in various stages of the fermentation process. I'd done some reading about how this mildly alcoholic drink was made, and the part where the women would chew mouthfuls of the cooked root and then put it back into the pot fascinated me. As I told them what I'd read about, Javier and the grim-faced Augustin exchanged what looked like approving glances.

"I love anything to do with food and its preparation," I explained. Not to miss an opportunity, I added, "and I'd really like to learn from you how you make your masato while I'm here."

Augustin grunted with what I took as some sort of agreement. He poured a large bowl of masato for himself and drank it down quickly. I was hoping for a taste of the thick drink too, but the bowl was not offered to me this time.

Next up on the day's agenda was a plant walk. Jav and I were joined by the now masato-sated old shaman and his sweet grandson, Juanito. I made sure every inch of my skin was covered with a long-sleeved T-shirt and long pants, the usual knee-high rubber boots, and a hat. Things do fall from the trees, you know.

In contrast, little Juanito wore shorts and a T-shirt, and nothing on his feet. I thought that it must be wonderful to have that immunity, but I wasn't about to take any chances. Despite keeping myself fairly covered up, bug bites were starting to appear even in places where my skin had certainly not been exposed.

As we walked, Jav and Augustin pointed out some medicinal plants and their uses, and I duly made notes in the fat notebook book I'd brought along. Standing in front of a coca bush, I recalled a walk I'd done through a spice and herb garden in Sri Lanka some years before. I'm an avid chef with a well-stocked cupboard full of yummy ingredients to add into my culinary creations, so to see how they grew — what they looked like in their own environment--gave me a thrill. There had been a coca bush in that garden too. I smiled as I recalled sneaking away from the guide to surreptitiously pick a few of the leaves.

"You can take some of the leaves if you want," Javier let me know. "It will give you strength for the jungle walk."

I decided to pick a handful of the leaves and chew on them. As we walked deeper into the walls of greenery, I could feel the coca giving me a subtle sense of renewal. I love to walk and can keep going for hours, but I do struggle on long jungle treks. Part of this is due to the heat, the high humidity, and the bugs. The ground is also very uneven, and it can be surprisingly steep in places. It's also not uncommon to encounter a path blocked by a fallen trees that must be clambered over. A trek through the dense forest is a real workout, and the term *jungle gym* takes on a whole different meaning out here. I silently thanked the coca spirit, feeling a little sad at how our supposedly more sophisticated society has abused these precious plants.

As we collected some plants and barks so I could make up a batch of medicines, Jav told me, "It's important for you to not only learn how to make them, but to also try them yourself. How do they feel in your body? What are their effects? Only then can you know how to use them with others. Do you understand this?"

I nodded as I took in this teaching.

Coming upon an old, dilapidated tambo, we paused briefly. Augustin said something to Javier which I didn't catch, and the latter turned to me.

"He says that when you come back here one day, this can be your house. They can fix it up and you can live here with them and learn their ways."

I turned to look at the inscrutable, old Jivaro. He had already turned away so as not to face me, but I sensed a sort of softening in him.

"Wow. That is a really amazing thing to know. Thank you."

I looked at the structure that really did need to be rebuilt, and pictured living there with these lovely people. Once again, I was touched.

CHAPTER 11

Swinging Like Tarzan

"Wake up, Judita! You have to come to the *albergue* right now!"

I shook my head to clear it and looked at my watch, dismayed to see it was now late in the afternoon. After we'd returned back to the camp from our hike in the late morning, I'd gone down to the bathing stream to rinse off and then planned to enjoy a short siesta to recharge my batteries. Instead, I'd fallen dead asleep, only to be awakened well past lunch time by my teacher insistently tugging on my foot. I'd not only missed lunch, but now would not get anything until the following morning. Why didn't anyone come get me? We were planning to get started with the ceremonial training later tonight, and with no dinner allowed it was all the more important not to miss lunch.

Wondering what the urgency was, Jav explained that I need to work on my ceremonial regalia. He explained that Luzmilla had various items I could choose from—*collares* and *pulseras*—the necklaces and bracelets that were worn along with the cushma. These typically include the attractive red and black huayuro seeds, cream or light blue prayer bush seeds and small anaconda bones. I was told that in addition to providing protection to the wearer, the sounds they would make as the body moved would add additional juice to the leaf rattle.

We headed back to the central structure and I bought several necklaces and bracelets, as well as a small bag made out of various seeds strung through like beads. I really resonated with this sweet, older jungle woman. She seemed so solicitous of my well-being. "You did not want to eat the mid-day meal?"

I sheepishly replied that I'd fallen asleep. I explained that I wasn't used to the heavy, wet heat so I had to take little breaks here and there. I admitted that I was hungry. Javier laughed at me for being too sleepy to eat, and asked if I wanted something. I questioned this, and he told me it was okay to have something light.

A plate of rice, fried yucca strips and the rubbery, dried fish appeared. Fried yucca chips? Oh boy! Are those acceptable for the *dieta*? Nodding, Jav said a little vegetable oil was fine. All right! What a feast! I think I'm going to live after all!

As I savored my snack, Oscar shared with me about their ways. "In the past, the men had more than one wife or partner. Each wife would have her own chores, as well as her own allotted animals and even land." He looked lovingly at Luzmilla. "Now, we usually only have one."

He went on to say that in their culture they considered it very important to be paired up, that no adult should be alone. As soon as someone would come of age, somewhere between sixteen and eighteen in their tribe, they would be paired up with a mate. They were free to find one for themselves, of course, but if they needed help they could always ask their elders.

"And what about you? Do you have a husband?" Suddenly, everyone was peering at me, waiting for my response.

"No, I'm not married anymore," I replied as I munched my delicious yucca chips.

"What about boyfriend?"

I shook my head, feeling a bit like a total loser for some reason.

Oscar sat back looking pleased with himself as if he had just come to a decision. "We have a mate for you! You do not have to be alone anymore!"

Someone pointed to a very cute and very young teenaged boy and motioned for him to come forward. "This is Miguel, one of my nephews. He is seeking a wife. You can be his wife!"

Trying not to choke on this latest surprise, I looked at the young man who smiled shyly at me. I had read about how in some cultures, young women are given to esteemed male visitors, but I had not read about the reverse case. Yet here it was: a sixteen year old boy was being offered as a mate for a woman who was old enough to be his mother. Like I said, age is pretty irrelevant in the jungle.

The shock of what was happening really threw me off. Because of the *dieta*, I was supposedly not even allowed to think about sex, and my hosts were trying to get me to teach young Miguel the ways of the world. It was really awkward with everyone looking at me expectantly, waiting for my answer. I looked at Javier for a clue, but he just gave me one of his face-splitting grins. Was this one of those tests I thought he might pull on me?

"Oscar, I thank you very much, but I don't think I'm allowed to do this during my training. You know, the *dieta*?"

He smiled and looked at Javier. Something very subtle passed between them.

"Are you sure?"

"Yes. It really is very generous of you to not want either of us to be alone," I indicated Miguel who was looking at me with big, adoring puppy eyes. "But I've come a long way to do this work and I need to do what is right, what supports it for now. I think it's actually better for me if I am alone right now." I smiled back at young Miguel. I didn't want him to feel rejected.

Oscar continued to smile as he nodded in understanding. He said a few words to Luzmilla and another woman who I thought was Miguel's mother. They spoke to the attractive boy and the three of them melted softly back behind the rest of the gathered group. I hoped that I hadn't committed some grave offense by refusing to marry the chief's young nephew.

I was dying to change the subject and ask if they had any shrunken heads I could look at but had the strong feeling not to do this. I felt it would be better to ask Jav about it away from the group. When unsure of local protocol, best to err on the side of caution. I was presented with a perfect opportunity later on when Jav and I were on our own for a brief period.

"Javier, do you remember that you told me how the Jivaro made those shrunken heads?"

"Ya, Judita."

"Well, am I going to get to see any while I'm here? I think that'd be really cool. I didn't notice any around the *albergue*."

Jav shook his head vigorously from side to side. "No. Those old things are kept where the people actually live, deeper in the jungle. They keep them out of sight now. Since they don't do this anymore, it wouldn't look good to have something like that dangling in a common area where they welcome visitors."

Yeah, probably not. I allowed myself a quick moment to imagine how I'd feel being welcomed into a camp that had a bunch of shrunken heads hanging around or impaled on posts. They wouldn't exactly be a great advertisement for good guest relations, would they?

The area around our little house served as our ceremonial space. There were no chairs or amenities such as those we'd had at the retreat center, so we worked out in the open. Large logs had been placed in a small circle for seating and the earth served as our altar.

I got myself ready for the night's work, pulling on my cushma over a long-sleeved T-shirt and long pants. I thought this looked a bit silly, but I needed protection from the mosquitos. I then added the seed jewelry I'd bought earlier and practiced making a few movements to allow them to rattle audibly.

I'd been able to have the late snack because tonight's medicine wasn't ayahuasca: it was camalonga. I've already described this potent *preparado* as a sort of liquid psychic shield. My teacher had chosen this medicine to begin with, telling me that the purpose of tonight's work was to bestow protection against *brujos*, as well as the negative energy that may come from working with patients. Sometimes, no matter how well you clear the energetic fields and the people, some toxic psychic dust can still cling to you. You definitely don't want this stuff hanging around so a little help from some jungle spirit Teflon can come in handy.

While I'd previously mentioned camalonga's potent smell and external use, I hadn't had the opportunity to try drinking it yet. Javier had told me that throughout my training we'd be working with other medicines that I had to drink besides ayahuasca such as tobacco, agua florida, and tonight's camalonga. Each one had its own purpose and protocol. I thought to myself that jungle shamans sure had to consume some strange things!

Javier poured a small amount into the little gourd cup and blew smoke into it before handing it to me. He warned me to just take a small sip to start. I probably took in no more than a teaspoon, but it had the effect of a quickly knocked back shot that hits you with a *wham* and then lights up your entire insides. I was sure that no evil spirit would be able to withstand getting anywhere near this stuff.

After drinking, Jav indicated that I was to rattle along with him. During our plant walk we had picked the special leaves that are used for the rattle, and I was shown how to make a nice bundle and secure it with red ribbon. I now had my first, very own shacapa. Like my stone *encanto*, this felt very precious to me. He came around me singing an icaro, and using his shacapa, finally blowing into the top of my head.

"Now you sing!" he commanded.

I froze. I didn't really know any of the sacred songs aside from some phrases that had really stayed with me from Sacha Wasi. I think my teacher sensed my question so he added,

"Canta sin letras." Sing without words. Just let a tune come through. He started off with a simple melody and suddenly something popped into my head. Hesitant at first, I allowed the celestial singer to come through and a part of me listened in astonishment as an entire melody sang itself.

After singing this several times I was instructed to do the *sopla*, the somewhat forceful, but controlled exhale that many shamans do at the end of a song. I had to practice this for a while until Javier was satisfied with my form. He told me that it's not about making the loudest, strongest hurricane force possible.

"You're not trying to blow down a wall with the *sopla*. Real power is subtle, Judita. Always remember that."

I nodded solemnly, silently acknowledging once again how much I had to learn.

We did some work with the leaf rattle, using it not only to accompany the songs, but also to beat gently on the crown of the head and down the body to help cleanse the energy field. This short work only lasted about an hour, then we crawled under our respective mosquito nets and quickly fell asleep.

Another part of the shaman's dieta is daily bathing. There are many streams running through the jungle that the locals call *quebradas*. Some had formed pools large enough to wade in to waist level, while others were only a few inches deep. I noticed that my two male companions, as well as the locals, were all meticulous about bathing and keeping clean. I, however, was not. My sleeping-bag chic habits served me well here: no makeup, no shaving, no toiletries; just all natural. *¡Todo natural!* I'm not quite this raw at home, but let's be honest: I was a little leery of stripping off without knowing what might be lurking around in the bushes and perhaps more importantly who might be around.

The bathing spot I was using was quite shallow. Since there hadn't been a lot of rain and the river was very low, this also had affected the jungle *quebradas*. I'd have to sit in only few inches of water, well aware that I was a glowing white beacon to every biting jungle bug in the vicinity. The mosquitos weren't really the biggest problem: it was a tiny fly the locals called *manta blancas*. They were fast enough that I couldn't slap them when they landed on me, and they'd crawl up under my sleeves and even under my watch. Let's just say the stream baths were not leisurely affairs. Strip off, rinse off, and get dressed again very quickly.

However, being an apprentice, I had a specific requirement to bathe at dawn. And not only that, but I also had to bathe with the water in my *encanto* bucket. Jav had instructed me to not only keep the *encanto* submerged with river water, but to also add tobacco, agua florida and camalonga. This fragrant mix would steep all day and through the night, then I would carry the bucket down to the stream on rising and bathe with it. At the end of the bath, I would refill the bucket with the stream water, then carry it back and add in the other things.

It wasn't that I didn't like the stream water either. It was just that it was cold at such an early hour. The jungle, being quite humid and damp, can get chillier at night than many people realize. It's fine later in the day when the temperature rises, but for a cold water wimp who was raised on long hot showers this required quite an adjustment.

"You better get used to it and toughen up, Lemon," I'd say to myself. "I have a feeling we're in this for the long haul. There's going to be a lot of cold water in your future!"

Masato making lesson part one commenced casually after breakfast. I had been thrilled to be presented with a very large bowl of the yucca brew for the morning meal. After carefully watching Augustin's bowl-tipping technique the day before, I now tried to imitate him. I managed to successfully get all of the thin oatmeal-like consistency into my mouth instead of all over my face. As I drank, the family watched anxiously for my reaction. I genuinely liked the masato and promptly gave it a thumbs up. Big smiles broke out and I saw Oscar say something to Augustin. They quickly relayed the message to Javier.

"They said you are now one of them—a real jungle woman! Ha ha ha!"

I think I did something geeky like flexing my biceps, which caused more guffaws. I felt a very mild buzz somewhat like a light beer from the large bowl,.

Thus fortified, I sat on the hard wood floor of the *albergue* with the women and began the laborious task of cleaning and peeling the large tubers. Watching them deftly slicing off the thick brown skin and cutting the now bare cream-colored roots into chunks, I felt a bit like I had back in the Tracker camp. I wasn't used to using such a large blade to perform what I thought of as a fine action, but after a few tips on how to hold both the machete and the roots and watching the others, I slowly started to get the hang of the preparation.

Once all of the yucca pieces had been cut to the required size, they were put into a very large pot, another *olla* like the one we had cooked my ayahuasca in and covered with water.

"It will be a long time cooking," Jav told me. "Many hours. Today is Sunday, a rest day so we're not going to do any training. Would you like to walk into the pueblo and see it? Olaff wants to pick up a few things."

I responded eagerly and told him I wanted to grab a few things to bring with me. While they may have joked about my being one of them, I knew I would need such important things as a bottle of water and toilet paper, so I stuffed these items along with my camera into my small daypack.

I had never been backpacking before, so this was the first trip where I was using one. During our interim communications when Jav had loosely described to me about walking through the forest to get to the training areas, I thought a large wearable pack would be far more sensible than the suitcases with wheels I normally carry. Like so many other things for this adventure, there was a steep learning curve regarding how to wear it properly balanced and secured. The sales assistant that had helped me select the pack advised me to load it up long before I got on the plane and practice being able to put it on and take it off, as well as walking around with it fully loaded.

With a month or two to go, I'd decided this was good advice, so did I trial runs with everything I thought I'd be carrying. In one attempt to remove it, I fell backwards onto my bed and got stuck like an upside-down bug. I was half on, half off the bed with my lower body still braced against the floor and the bed, but my top half with the heavy pack lying crosswise on the mattress. I'd found it difficult to push my upper body up high enough to get my arms out, so ended up sliding to a heap on the floor in a tangled mess.

My mom had heard the commotion down the hall and now stood in the doorway. "Oh gawd, Judy," she started with one of her favorite expressions. "Are you alright? What are you doing?"

"Yes, I think so. I'm learning how to use my new backpack," my muffled voice answered as I tried to extract my arms from the loops.

"Oh gawd. Why can't you just travel like normal people and go to Europe with a regular suitcase?"

For just a moment, that did seem attractive, but I knew I had to master this crucial piece of equipment before even stepping out of the house. I'd chosen this particular pack because there was a top section that could be removed to allow use as a separate, smaller daypack. This is what I was now loading up for our hike.

With the yucca beer left to simmer for several hours, I strapped the small bag around my waist, closing the fastener with a satisfying click. The pueblo, a very small town, was about a half-hour's hike away from our site on narrow, cleared trails. On arrival, I was surprised to see satellite dishes pointed towards the sky.

"Those are for the televisions and the phones. Look! There's even a restaurant!" Jav showed me proudly.

The three of us entered a bodega at 9:30 am and found all of the young men inside already three sheets to the wind. They were having such a hilariously fun time that I wanted to know what they were drinking, so I asked one of the men.

"*Aguardiente* infused with *chiricsanango*! Wanna try it?"

Of course I did! I looked to my teacher. "One sip to try it. No more!" he admonished sharply.

The clear, fermented, then distilled sugar cane liquor was a taste I was still getting used to. Its strength can vary greatly depending on where and how it's made. While it does have a particular signature taste, it can also be infused with herbs, spices, and other ingredients to make a unique tipple. *Chiricsanango* is a green leafy plant also known as Fever Tree. It has several uses, one being as its namesake, to treat fevers. *El Chiric*, a Quechua word meaning cold, as some locals call it, has some strange physical effects such as first numbing of the face and body, then making the imbiber feel extraordinarily cold, even in the middle of the jungle heat. One sip of the potent potion was enough for me. I'd already had my lovely bowl of *masato* and I wasn't supposed to be getting drunk even though this was a day off.

One of the items that Olaff purchased was a small quantity of white bread rolls. The plastic-wrapped package looked as if it had been sitting on the shelf for a few days, and a hasty consultation with his uncle was needed to see if they were fit for us to eat. No matter how small the pueblo shop, wherever we went in our travels there always seemed to be those horribly bland bread things lurking on a shelf, waiting to entice the desperately hungry customer. While I generally prefer whole grain breads, there are some white breads that are very tasty, especially when slathered with good butter. These were nowhere near that category. I don't know how they were made to be so completely tasteless, and even with my prodigious appetite I found it difficult to finish one because it was so awful. But in the jungle, without refrigeration or an abundance of food stores, you can't be too fussy.

As we walked back through a clearing, a small boy sidled along with us. He looked smaller than Juanito, and definitely thinner. With a mop of hair like many of his young peers, he almost looked like a character out of a Disney movie. I found myself falling in love with the jungle children because they seemed so sweet and pure. He looked at Javier, then at me, as if waiting for permission to speak. Javier, obviously knowing him or what he was going to ask me, nodded to him. Encouraged, he tugged on my hand and looked up with big, soulful eyes. "Miss? You want have the jungle experience? Swing on vine like Tarzan?"

Wait, was I hearing this correctly? This boy was asking me if I wanted to follow in the footsteps (or vine swings!) of that well-known jungle hunk, Tarzan? Where had he heard of this fictional jungle character? Of course, I was going to go for it! I was safe with Jav and Olaff by my side.

"What's your name?" I asked him.

"Stefano. Please, Miss. You will like it. I show you. Watch!"

It obviously hadn't occurred to him that I was not a slim young denizen of the jungle and had very likely never swung from a vine before. The three of us halted as we watched little Stefano quickly climb up a large tree from which a long, sturdy-looking vine had been draped over a branch. It hung freely in the space below it with enough room to swing widely and not hit anything.

When Stefano was level with the top of the rope he reached up and grabbed the branch it hung over, scooting over to it by sliding his hands sideways. It was the same technique that children all over the world use when moving along on the metal bars of a play structure in a park or schoolyard.

"Look, Miss! Very easy. You watch!" He now reached over and grabbed the top of the vine, first with one hand, then the other. He held on tightly as he managed to create enough motion to approach the trunk, where he then kicked backwards and started a good swinging motion. I was sure he was making it look a lot easier than it would be for me; after all, he'd probably been doing this for years and he was a lot lighter than I was.

He allowed the vine to slow and climbed down slowly, hand over hand. With Olaff and Javier cheering me on, I approached the tree and attempted to climb it as expertly as Stefano had. My tree climbing skills were a little rusty, but at last I made it to the branch. Feeling foolishly confident, I copied the boy's technique of first hanging from the branch and then moving my hands sideways. It was about at this point that I remembered that I had no upper body strength. Although I had been bodybuilding for years, I just was not able to get the hang (pun intended) of things like chin ups and pull ups, never mind climbing up and down ropes.

I grabbed onto the vine and managed to hang on for a few seconds. Stefano held the bottom of the vine and pulled it back and forth to give me momentum, and for a few brief moments I was really swinging on a jungle vine! Wheeeee!

Then, thud! I was lying on my back on the ground far below with the wind knocked out of me. Stefano sauntered over and look down at me with an expression of hope on his face. "You try again?"

Olaff extended his hand and helped me sit up. *"¿Estás bien?"*

I assured him that I was fine.

"Ha ha ha, Judy! You looked so funny! Ha ha!" my teacher was bent over, grabbing his sides with undisguised glee. So much for sympathy!

Thinking I was lucky not to have broken anything, I thought I'd give it another go, weak upper body or not. After all, I may not ever get another occasion to swing on a jungle vine again, so I didn't want to pass up this great opportunity. I lasted even less on this round than on the previous attempt. With my underused hanging muscles already fatigued, there was just nothing left to keep me clinging to the thick vine. No sooner had I grabbed the top of the rope when my hand strength gave out and I fell vertically along the rope's path. I landed on my feet and instantly rolled to break the fall.

Javier was still laughing heartily, and Olaff was trying to look concerned, but I could see that he, too, was fighting a smile. Stefano came running over and stood in front of me expectantly.

"One sol!" He demanded as he stretched his hand out expectantly. Apparently this hadn't been a free ride. I was expected to pay for my fun new jungle adventure. Javier indicated that I was to give Stefano a coin to pay for my experience. Fortunately, I had brought along some change and small bills, not knowing what to expect in the pueblo. I handed over the coin and Stefano examined it carefully, turning it over to make sure it wasn't counterfeit. Satisfied, he suddenly took off and ran back up the path we'd come from.

We made our way slowly back to camp and stopped at Oscar's headquarters. The tale of my failed attempts at a classic jungle skill was recounted with great embellishment and a lot of hooting. Although Jav was laughing, Oscar and his relatives looked at me with that concern I'd noticed before, not sure whether to join in laughing at me or not.

"It's okay! I had fun trying. I guess I just need more practice," I told them. Then a thought crossed my mind. "I'm sure I'll feel a lot better after some masato."

Oscar gave Javier a hearty slap and ordered one of the women to get me a bowl. Like the first, I downed it slowly, relishing the taste and the experience. While it didn't pack the punch of an *aguardiente*, the slight buzz did help take my mind off the soreness in my back.

I went back to the *Casa del Shaman* and decided to take a little break after the morning's silly adventures. It didn't last long. Less than an hour later, I was once again summoned from a nice siesta under the *mosquitero*.

"Come, Judita! We have another jungle skills lesson for you!"

It was my teacher and judging by his energy and movements I suspected he'd been into a few bowls of the masato.

Now, I'm all for learning new skills but I felt I really needed to stretch out my back a bit more. I could feel more soreness and pain coming in. Groaning like an old lady, I rolled sideways to sit up and emerged from my little shelter.

"So, what fine task have you got for me this time?" I asked.

"You'll see!"

We walked to a short path leading to a small clearing not far behind Oscar's shelter accompanied by a girl of about eleven and her younger brother. There was a small structure that looked like the jungle version of a bus stop: a bench covered by a small palm leaf roof. On the bench was an interesting cap with long, colorful feathers sticking upwards from the band. There was also a long pole that turned out to be hollow like a giant straw.

"This is the long-distance blow pipe for use with *pucunas*. Want to see how far you can blow a poison dart?"

"Sure! But only if I can wear that amazing hat!" I indicated the feathered band.

"That is a chief's headdress." Jav inspected it carefully. "I think it is an old one that he doesn't use anymore so it would be okay for you to try it on."

Donning the cap, much to the delight of the two children, I picked up the long, hollow shaft. Jav handed me a dart, trying to look solemn.

"Be very careful, Judita. Tip is very poisonous! One stick and … "

He made a dramatic motion of putting his hands around his neck, making horrible gurgling sounds, and finally falling to the ground.

Yeah, I'd read all about curare and some of the other poisons that were used to coat the tips of hunting darts like this. They're not something you really want to mess around with if you don't know what you're doing. Deciding to ask for a demonstration first since I can't say I'd ever fired off a poison dart before, I gingerly handed the venomous *pucuna* back to my teacher. He loaded it into the shaft and aimed at a nearby tree trunk. A quick, forceful blow sent the deadly thing straight forward to stick into the tree.

"Ya, Judita?" I nodded.

I actually had better luck firing the poison darts than I'd had swinging from the vine. Feeling somewhat proud of at last being able to do something without landing on the ground in pain or in a mud pit, I did a little circular dance, at which the kids laughed in amusement.

We all trooped back to Oscar's shelter where Javier reported on my ability to kill trees with one ferocious blow to the pipe. Oscar leaned over and I heard him ask Javier something, after which the two of them started chuckling. I looked at them with a question on my face.

"Ha ha ha, Judita! The darts were not poisonous after all!"

I wish I could have seen the expression on my face as I realized I'd been tricked yet again. What else could I do but laugh at myself along with them once again?

After this latest caper, I decided to make good use of the break to wash some clothes. I was hanging up the freshly stream-washed laundry when Jav suddenly appeared once again through the greenery.

"Do you have any medicines with you? Luzmilla has diarrhea and is sick."

Although I'd been told not to use anything that wasn't natural during the *dieta* periods, I did bring my medicines along with me because you just never know, do you? I nodded and dug around in my pack for the bag containing the commercial remedies.

When we got to the large shelter, Oscar approached us with a deep look of concern and hope on his face. I held up my bag and assured him that I did have medicines, but I needed to talk to his wife first to see which one would be best to offer her.

Luzmilla was lying quietly at the far end of the communal area, looking a bit pale. My heart went out to see her suffering after she'd been so solicitous of me. After asking a few questions, I decided to start out by having her try some Pepto Bismol tablets. I always travel with these and other medications, and more often than not I end up handing them out to others in need rather than having to take them myself. She took two of the chewable pink tablets right then, and I gave her two more to take later if she needed them.

Giving her instructions to remain quiet to let the medicine work to settle her system, Jav and I made our way back to our little settlement.

"Okay, Javito, now I have a big question. If I am here with all these master shamans who live in nature's pharmacy, why didn't someone whip up some kind of infusion or decoction? Surely this must happen from time to time, and there must be plants that would sort this out."

"Ya, Judita, there are. But sometimes it is better to take commercial medicines if they're available because it's faster than having to prepare something from scratch. It takes time to go out and look for the right plants and then make up the medicines. We would normally infuse the plants in a tea and in this form it will only last a day or two, so we can't keep them on hand like in a pharmacy. Sure, we can keep making up fresh batches, but we just thought it would be easier and quicker to give her something that you already have. If you weren't here, yes, we would have gone out to gather plants for her."

"Okay. That makes sense. It just seems kind of ironic that I'm here learning about plant medicines and there are all these plant experts in one place, yet I've just handed over some store bought medicine that I brought from the States."

He nodded and walked away, leaving me to continue with my domestic tasks. Once these were all completed, I wandered over to the house to see how Luzmilla was doing. Seeing me approach, Oscar walked quickly towards me, beaming happily.

"She is much better, thanks to you! She does not feel so sick anymore!"

"Oh, that's great! I'm so relieved!"

We climbed back up the short ladder together and I found his partner sitting up and smiling. The color had already returned to her face and I could tell that she was on the mend.

"The diarrhea has slowed so I took the other two tablets," she told me.

"Good. They will help. Do let me know if you need more but let those do their thing and we'll see how you feel."

I felt happy at being able to help in this small way. After all the bumbling and failures, it was nice to succeed at something for a change!

CHAPTER 12

Sex and Bugs and Icaros

Another week had passed in the Jivaro camp. Javier had told me that Sundays were supposedly a day of rest, but sometimes I thought he just wanted to take a break from working with me, because in the jungle there is always work to do.

We were called to join in a very labor intensive work called a *minga*. This Quechua word refers to a shared work originating from someone who needs help with a particularly large task. For instance, were I to return and take residence in that run down *casita*, I might call a *minga* to get help in rebuilding it since it's something I can't do myself. The community would turn out to help, lending whatever skills they have in the knowledge that I would provide food and drink and a big celebration once the work was completed. While it was not a requirement to help, most of the villagers would join in some way and contribute whatever help they could. This was partly because of the social aspect, but it also allowed them to call their own *minga* should the need arise.

Today's task was to collect huge bags of charcoal from someone's *chacra*, or private garden, and transport them down to the river, where they would be stacked up to await transport to Iquitos by boat. From there, they would be taken to the market where they would be sold. I recalled the long hike we'd had to get from the river to our camp, and realized we were now even farther away from the water. How were the heavy, body-sized bags weighing around eighty pounds apiece going to be transported all the way to the river? I was soon to find out.

Sometimes, as you journey along the jungle rivers you will see smoke rising from pyramid-shaped pyres dotted not too far from the shores. In these, the locals are making a form of activated charcoal from wood, some from fallen trees as long as the wood is of suitable quality, while others are cut to order. Being intrigued with this unfamiliar operation, I had a lot of questions. Javier and Olaff explained how to make the charcoal that was derived from local trees and provided the jungle residents with a source of income.

"Ideally, you start with good wood. A dense wood like *tahuari* is the best because it yields more *carbón*. You have to cut it into pieces that are all about the same size, just like you did with the ayahuasca vines, so they will all cook at the same rate," Jav explained.

Olaff nodded in agreement. "The other important thing is that the wood has to be heated without oxygen or it will burn up just like in a camp fire."

Since I had shown a lot of interest in the procedure, they decided we needed to hike around to find one of these pyres so I could understand how the process worked. I strapped on my small waist pack, making sure I had my camera and other essentials.

It didn't take long to find one of the tipi-shaped pyres. As we paused next to the vegetation-covered structure, the inhabitants of a nearby hut strolled over to see why we were so interested in their project. Javier took over and greeted them in the local fashion, answering their questions about who we were and who I was, and why we were so interested in their source of income. Once they realized that we were not there to steal their charcoal, they were happy to answer my questions about the process.

"After you cut the wood into same-sized pieces, you have to cover the fire with plants that don't burn. Inside the structure, the lack of flames is what makes *carbón. Mucho tiempo.*"

So, in order to make charcoal from wood, many hours were required. Olaff indicated the small hole in the top of the "tipi" where the smoke was emerging lazily towards the sky.

"You want to get rid of the moisture in the wood pieces. Everything that is not needed will burn off and come out through that hole," he explained. "You wait for no more smoke, then you check the progress. Once things settle down you can leave it all to cool overnight, or longer if there's a lot of *carbón*. The finished pieces are all black and much lighter in weight than the original wood was."

I was fascinated. Picturing the many family barbecues where my dad had dumped bags of easily purchased charcoal briquettes onto the grill, I remembered picking up the very lightweight pieces and using them to draw childish pictures on the cement floor of our patio. How on earth could they have figured out how to create this method of making what we can easily buy in bags at our local stores? I was beginning to be very impressed with the skills and talents of these supposedly less-civilized people. If there were ever some catastrophic event that threatened the structure of human civilization, I knew who would be able to live off the grid and survive. It wouldn't be someone like me.

So, was I up for it? There was no pressure for me to participate in the *minga*, but Javier suggested it might be a nice gesture. Before giving my answer, I asked to understand what was going on. I was shown the bags, made of a strong, plasticized paper, and when filled were somewhat taller than my backpack. Each bag weighed at least thirty-five kilos or just under eighty pounds, which was more than my full backpack weighed. A long strip of cloth was tied around the bag and then looped across the forehead once the load was placed on one's back. Each person would take one or even two of these bags, meaning they could be carrying a load of up to one hundred and sixty pounds. Considering that these slim people weighed a lot less than this, I was having trouble believing that they could haul even one of the full, body-sized bags all the way to the river port.

I stood aside and watched as a steady stream of both men and women walked quickly by, the huge bags filled with blackened wood pieces strapped to their foreheads and tied to their bodies. Heck, I lifted weights. I'm strong! No problem! I'll be glad to help out. Sure!

Not even trying to stifle a grin, one of the villagers brought over a smaller bag, and it was positioned on my back with the carrying strap placed across my forehead. It was a lot heavier than I thought it might be, but I was determined to carry at least one bag to the river to show my solidarity with these good people. Javier pointed to the trail and I took a few steps. I knew I'd been given a lighter load than the natives were carrying, much less only one bag to their two, but I could already feel it pulling me down. There was a tremendous force in my neck and I was a bit worried about this. My hips and knees started to protest at the unaccustomed load but I kept going, getting slower and slower. My heart rate soared dangerously and I started to be concerned. I paused, doubled over, gasping for breath.

"Ya, Judita?" It was Jav at my side.

"I'm fine!" I lied through gritted teeth.

I managed to stagger a few more steps, then I heard the voice of my inner wisdom. "Know your limits. Giving in to your ego will kill you. You have nothing to prove here."

I stopped and told Javier that I wasn't going to be able to carry the bag after all. Feeling defeated and deflated, I asked if he could carry it for me. In place of answering, he told me to bend over slightly while he released the knots that held the bag along my back. One of the men came rushing over and grabbed the bag, hoisting onto his back with no effort at all, while another person helped to secure it in place. Moments later, the man was hurrying towards the river with my bag of charcoal on his back. I felt like a wimp. A humbled, defeated wimp.

Despite my dejection at having failed yet another task, no one mocked me. They continued to smile and make me feel like a member of their tribe even though I was very sorely lacking in the skills that kept them alive in the sometimes dangerous environment in which they lived. I consoled myself by realizing that I had not ever needed to hoik an eighty pound bag of charcoal on my back at home and I probably never would.

I caught my breath and stood up, continuing to watch the Jivaro moving quickly with their loads down to the river. The native jungle men work at extraordinarily tough physical tasks for long periods of time, so they seem to be made of intricately carved hardwood with beautifully shaped muscles that any bodybuilder would be proud to flex and show off. I have to admit that despite the strict requirements of the *dieta* against having anything that resembled carnal thoughts, I would admire the beauty of these men and wondered what it would be like to have one as a partner.

Much to my surprise, the feeling seemed to be mutual. Earlier on, Jav and Olaff had told me that I always had to watch out or the men might carry me off into the bushes. I must have looked incredulous, because Jav nodded solemnly at Olaff, who tried to match his uncle's pseudo seriousness.

"They will carry you off for sex, Judita! You must be very careful!"

I busted up laughing and couldn't stop. You guys have no idea who you're dealing with here! I was in the music business for years with all that sex and drugs and rock and roll stuff. Heck, I might just carry one of *them* off!

I couldn't explain why I was laughing so hard. Sometimes I had the feeling that they were trying to shock or embarrass me, perhaps to see what I was made of. I may be a klutz when it comes to jungle skills, but I don't embarrass easily.

One of the things I had noticed was that while there seemed to be family units, I didn't see many people in their later teens or early twenties. On voicing my observation to Oscar, who was taking a brief rest in between bag runs, he looked a little sad.

"You are right, Juyushi," he said. "Our young people want the same things as others around the world like money, name brand clothes, fancy electronics and so on. They don't want to stay here because the life is hard and dirty. They don't want a life of poverty and picking produce to carry to the city. Most of my children live in Iquitos now."

"So, if they're in the city, are they also not interested in learning the ways of healing and ceremony?"

Oscar shook his head slowly. This was clearly another topic that caused him some sadness. "No. As you see, it's a hard life. It takes many years to become a *vegetalista*, the path that you are now on. Sometimes they start learning, then decide it will take too long and quit. The young people don't have so much patience nowadays."

"So, foreigners like me come from other cultures and we are helping to preserve their practices," I thought silently. And in that instant I made a vow to myself that for the rest of my life, I would do my best to honor their practices and traditions.

We hung around and socialized for a little while, then I went back to our shelter area for a rest. As I came through the bushes into the small, cleared area, I stopped in astonishment. There was a giant jungle pig slurping all the water out of my *encanto* bucket! The nerve of that porker!

"Oi! Get out of here! That's my *encanto*! Go find your own water source!" I yelled at the large animal. It turned around and looked at me, and for a moment I wondered how much distance I needed to have between myself and this beast. Not having any useful experience with these animals, my mind flew back to the ferocious sheep of Glastonbury Tor that I was sure were going to come charging after the foolish intruder who was invading their fields.

The whole area around Oscar's shelter and ours was full of wandering animals. I'd seen the pig before, as well as several very cute little piglets. I'd even cuddled one and it squealed in delight.

I had to be on my guard around the turkeys, though. They were mean! There were always several of them near Oscar's structure, and whenever I approached it they came after me. I never saw them do this with any of the Jivaro, so they must have sensed that I didn't really belong there. One in particular was a real jerk. I swear that big bird would hide off in the bushes and wait for me to make my appearance, then it would come galomping out, flapping its wings and making a racket. I would then try to show it who was boss, flapping my arms like a windmill and making a lot of racket back at it. This did succeed in making the aggressive *ave* hesitate momentarily, but as soon as I would start to retreat towards that ladder that led up to safety, it renewed its attack. With the Jivaro lined up to enjoy the ridiculous spectacle, I would then leap quickly up the rungs with the brutish bird right behind me flapping and squawking. Despite all its actions, it never actually got close enough to peck me. Jerky bird! It certainly knew who was the boss, didn't it?

Fortunately for me, not everything in the jungle was aggressive. All around me flitted hundreds of the most beautiful butterflies I had ever seen. There were the well-known Blue Morphos, those very large, almost hand-sized butterflies with iridescent blue inner wings. The outer side of the wings was dun colored, a sort of dull greyish brown, so that when the creature had its wings standing straight up it tended to blend in more with its surroundings. But once it opened those large wings—wow! The sunlight reflecting off the bright blue made them seem otherworldly, as if they'd just flown through an inter-dimensional portal.

Many other butterflies had wings with incredible, intricate patterns and colors. I think they knew I loved them because they'd linger long enough for me to approach slowly so I could get a good look at those amazing wings that were not designed by human hands.

I've been interested in insects ever since I was a child. One of my neighbors ran our neighborhood bug club, of which I was a proud senior member at the grand old age of eight or nine. Now, here I was surrounded by all of these unusual specimens. I'd never seen a real centipede before, or even a millipede, yet there they were, strolling along and going about their business. Giant bugs, colorful bugs, strange looking bugs; they were all here. I was like a little kid, stopping to admire them, or if I was fast enough, snap a photo. As long as they weren't trying to drill into my skin for a blood snack, I was a fan!

For me, no discussion of jungle insects is complete without mentioning the *grillos,* or crickets. In California we generally see one type, a pale brown specimen that hides under rocks and chirps at night. Here, there seemed to be hundreds of different kinds of crickets. They ranged in size from about three-quarters of an inch to nearly twice that. While some are that common, dull brown color, others look as if they'd been painted by an artist who was under the influence of some psychedelic substance. All of them sing together in the night along with the other denizens of the green deep like toads and frogs. The sound is like nothing else on Earth, but it made me happy to know there were still so many of them in a habitat that hadn't been overdeveloped like my own city back home.

Most apprenticeships into magical traditions involve some kind of initiations. I had started mine on the first day with Javier, Oscar, and Augustin, when they had asked me the same questions that had been put to other apprentices for generations before me. Now it was time for me to be baptized into the jungle. This is so a healer can have a stronger connection to the spirits of the jungle, who then can be called on to aid in the spiritual tasks. Learning the jungle traditions involves much more than just doing ayahuasca ceremonies.

Javier led me to a grove of banana trees with a nearby stream. We had to first clear the ground with our machetes, which was one of my favorite tasks. I'd love to say I was quite good at this, but at this early stage I was still a bit clumsy with the big cutting tool. I had to be shown several times how to angle the blade to allow it to do its work most efficiently.

Once this was done, I had to strip off completely and bathe in the stream so I could start fresh. I was like a baby who had newly come into the world, naked and vulnerable. It did feel a bit funny to be starkers in front of my male teacher, but the jungle people don't seem to have the body hangups we Westerners do. He went about his work in the ritual as if I were fully clothed, and this helped the odd sensation I had to settle down and vanish. I must admit I was more concerned about suddenly exposing a lot more of my delicious flesh to the swarms of flies and mosquitos that were just waiting for such a golden opportunity to pounce.

We stripped bark from a banana tree and drank the liquid that seeped out. I then had to rub this bark all over my body to take on the essence of the jungle around me. A succession of different plants was handed to me, each chosen for its correspondence in the body, such as to veins or bones. I was instructed to do the same as I had with the banana bark. As I was doing this, my teacher was preparing the ground for me to lie on by cutting huge leaves and placing them on the area we'd cleared earlier.

Once the leaves were in place, I sat down and slowly ate some grape-like snake berries. I had to focus only on the *selva*, the precious jungle around me, feeling the connection between us until there was no separation. This union would aid in my complete rebirth. Then lying back, Javier covered me with leaves and branches while singing an icaro, then still singing, he sprinkled water on me as if it were rain. I would have liked to have watched the ritual from a nearby tree, but I was buried beneath mounds of jungle plants so I kept my eyes shut.

After remaining buried for about fifteen or twenty minutes, he removed each leaf and branch, one by one, until at last he declared that I had been baptized by the plants. Another trip to the stream to rinse off felt invigorating. There was something about the water in these streams. It seemed to have a tangible aliveness and energy. Sitting in the stream, it was more than just cooling off from the incessant heat and humidity. Was I feeling some kind of transformation? I wanted to tell Javier how I felt but he held up his hand.

"Don't talk now, Judita. Later. We will walk back in silence to allow the experience to settle."

Back at base, our trusty side man, Olaff, had lunch all prepared for us when we walked back to the chief's *albergue*. Dried fish, rice, and yucca. Dried fish again. Yuck! While I knew there wouldn't be any dinner because of ceremony, I just could not eat that tough, funny tasting river leather. I'd been told that I'd be eating a freshly caught, toothless river fish, the *bocachica*, but so far this hadn't happened. When I'd queried this, Javier looked at me as if I were a child.

"You will have fresh fish when we are nearer to the river. Olaff will fish for us." He shrugged as if this should have been obvious. I nodded in understanding. Fish didn't grow on trees, did they?

It seems that wherever man settles, man's best friend is not far away. This is also true in the jungle. Skeletal dogs of indeterminate breeds run wild, sometimes singly, sometimes in packs. Constantly on the move, they search for scraps of any food they can find. While they are not domesticated as pets, some of them seek out humans and are content to hang around for a while before moving on.

I nibbled at my yucca and rice while thinking about what to do with the fish that I couldn't swallow. When I was a child sitting at the dinner table with my parents, I came up with what I thought was a masterful way of ditching food that I didn't like. I'd gaze earnestly at something on the stove or counter and ask, "what's that?" When my parents turned to look, I'd quickly shovel the offending food items off my plate and drop them under the table to where the family dog was inevitably waiting. When my folks would turn back around, I'd pretend to have a mouthful of food to ward off their inevitable question about what I'd seen.

Of course, I then had to cover up the sound of the dog's noisy masticating. This could be accomplished with a few loud coughs or fake sneezes. It appeared at the time that my clever ruse had worked, but years later my dad told me he knew what I was doing all along. The dead giveaway was the dog always sitting at my feet.

There were several dogs in the camp that would manage to climb up the short ladder to join us as we sat on the floor, especially at mealtimes. They were occasionally shooed away, but every now and then they got lucky. This was one such a time. A medium-sized, pregnant female dog with prominent ribs approached me and wagged her tail hopefully. I pulled off a small piece and waited for Javier to turn his head, then quickly handed the bite over.

There was one problem that I hadn't considered: she wasn't alone. As soon as the three other dogs realized that one of their number was eating, they all came over to see what was on offer. Javier was still engaged with Oscar, so I pinched off a few more pieces of the horrible old fish and threw it surreptitiously to the waiting canines.

Like my family dog, the sound of their eager chomping was hard to cover. I saw Oscar look over and say something to Javier, who then turned to look at me. I held up a piece of the fish and put it in my mouth so he could see that I was eating. It didn't work.

"Judita, that food is for you. If you give the dogs your food you are giving away your energy.

I just smiled and nodded. I was busted. What else could I do?

Gagging on the rest of the fish, I saw a man climb up the ladder and greet the group. He looked to be about fifty, very slender, and with the full head of beautiful thick hair that the jungle Indians have. His eyes widened as he saw me, and he turned to the Jivaro chief with a questioning look. I saw Oscar's eyes twinkle as he indicated to Javier that he give the newcomer an explanation.

"This is Judita. She is my apprentice and I am teaching her the ways of the jungle."

I greeted the man who came over and extended his right hand towards me.

"I am Raul. *Mucho gusto.* Pleased to meet you."

Without thinking, I extended the hand I'd been eating with and shook his, passing to him the essence of what I'd had for lunch.

Raul turned back to Javier as I finished the last of my food. I tried to pretend I didn't notice they were talking about me, but they soon turned in my direction.

"Raul has invited us to his house in a few days. He has a sort of zoo where he takes care of jungle animals. You might like to see it."

"Yes, I would. Thank you!"

"If there is anything you need while you are in the jungle, you must call on me."

I was really touched. Here was a man who had just met me, knowing nothing about me except that I was Javier's bumbling apprentice, yet he offered help if it was ever needed.

Thanking him again and saying we'd see him soon, I excused myself to walk back to our tambo for an afternoon siesta. Javier indicated for me to wait for him so we could walk back together.

I felt you wanted to explain to me how you felt after your baptism, ya?"

"Yes. I definitely felt some kind of energetic shift. I--"

He nodded as he continued, holding up his hand again to interrupt me." Many students feel like they always have to talk about what they felt or experienced, to analyze it and perhaps try to find a way to replicate it again. Yes, it's good to notice how you feel, but talking about it, particularly right afterwards, can weaken the energy."

He went on to use an analogy of a balloon, illustrating the movements with his hands. "This empty balloon is you, the student. And now, you are learning many new things, so the balloon is expanding, filling up. When you talk too much right away, it creates a leak so the new energy can't take hold permanently. It drains away. Learn to just experience instead of talking. Ya?"

"Ya, Javi," I smiled. "I also just wanted to say how nice the people are here. Like Raul, he'd never met me before, but he said if I ever needed anything to call on him."

"This is how we are; we look after each other. You are now part of my family, so they recognize this. This is something the *ciudadanos*, the city people, don't understand. They look down on us *indígenas* and say that we're just dumb savages. Sometimes when I go to Belen people laugh and ask me where my arrows and darts are. And when I went to

Lima, people poked me and touched me when they found out I was a shaman, like I'm some kind of curiosity."

I'd told him that perhaps like those who touched Jesus's robe hoping to be cured, maybe the Limeños were hoping to receive some magic.

If it wasn't for my meticulous journal keeping, I would have lost track of time. The general order of my days went something like this: get up at dawn and haul the bucket of cold water holding my *encanto* to the stream to bathe with it. After breakfast, there might be plant walks or other teachings on jungle culture. Selected nights were for ceremonial work. We didn't usually have any activities planned for the afternoons, so Javier would tell me to go back to the casita while he attended to other tasks. At first, I was a bit miffed at this, because I'd felt that he could be teaching me more and making better use of the limited time I had with him. But I eventually came to realize that he needed a break from being a teacher. Overseeing someone's progress in a fairly new subject, along with keeping them safe is a great responsibility.

Determined to be a good student, I took advantage of these large gaps to refine my icaros. I would spend hours walking around a small clearing, singing the songs over and over to commit them to memory. During our nightly ceremonies, Javier would give me the songs as they were presented to him from the plant spirits since I couldn't hear them yet. He taught them to me in the traditional manner: he sang them and I had to repeat them. I was more able to remember the Spanish songs, but the ones in the indigenous dialects didn't seem to stick as easily.

While it wasn't forbidden to write them down, Jav wouldn't allow me to do this as he was giving them to me. I would have to wait until after the ceremony to quickly jot down what I could remember regardless of whether it was correct. All I could do was write phonetically since I didn't know what the words meant. Heck, I didn't even know where one word ended and the next one started!

As I circled the clearing day after day, I was grateful for my musical background. I was able to recall the melodies more easily than the words, so sometimes I would just hum or use that well known icaro filler, the *hai nai nai*. Many times, I would find that as I would work with the melody, suddenly a rush of lyrics would download, so I'd frantically write down what I received before it slipped away again.

During each ceremony, I would be given more information or new steps to add in, but Javier would also test me. As the number of my icaros increased, he demanded that I sing them in a particular order. We would start from the beginning and go through the lot, and I was not allowed to make even one mistake. If we were at song number nine of ten, and I fluffed even one word, it was back to the beginning. Over and over and over. Javier was relentless, and sometimes I just wanted to scream and strangle him, but I was determined to learn these sacred songs.

There were times I would just get really frustrated with Javier. He would tell me we were definitely going to be doing one thing, and I'd take him at his word, then everything would change.

"But I thought you said we'd collect *cortezas* to make medicine today," I would protest after having been told the day before that we'd be cutting sections of tree bark to work with.

"No, no, Judita! Not today!" Jav would vigorously shake his head from side to side.

"But you told me we'd start ceremony at nine!" I'd protest on another evening as I tried to rouse my teacher from slumber.

"No, Judita. 10 o' clock." He'd return to his snoozing.

This drove me bonkers! I'd be told one thing, so I tended to expect that we'd be doing what my teacher said we'd be doing, but then he'd deny even saying it. He might tell me that I'd made some error in a ceremony, yet I knew without a doubt that said procedure had never been discussed before. If I protested that I didn't know about whatever it was that I was being criticized for, Javier would stubbornly shake his head and that was that. End of story. You cannot argue with a jungle shaman. You will not win. You will go crazy. You will learn to let go of your expectations, or you will continue to circle around on the hamster wheel of your mind. And therein lies one of the greatest teachings for life. If we can truly let go of our expectations of how we think things should be, we will be able to live our lives in the true flow of the universe. The now is all that matters.

CHAPTER 13

You Have Husband?

What does it really mean to live in the moment? What does it feel like? And is it even possible for humans to let go of their expectations?

I contemplated these questions one hot afternoon as I was writing in my journal. I continued to feel frustrated with what I perceived to be unnecessary delays in my training, yet I also had to acknowledge that I had no prior experience with this path except for a few medicine ceremonies earlier in the year. What if everything was just perfect exactly the way it was.?

As I put my pen down and stared off into the luscious greenery around me, I heard the voice of my inner guidance filter into my consciousness.

"Why do you struggle so much with this issue of how you think things should be?"

"I dunno, maybe it's just habit. It seems to be a part of the Western mindset to fret about what was or what might be coming in the future."

"Or perhaps it's just you trying to retain control of how you think things should be. Look at what you're doing to yourself. When Javier doesn't do what you think he should do, you get all mad and stomp around like a cranky toddler, don't you? It's really a tremendous waste of your personal power."

"I know, but I guess it's because I don't live here, and I'm just aware that time is ticking on. I just want to be able to get as much learning in as I can before I have to go home."

"All right. But what can you do to change this so that you stop wasting your precious energy?"

"Honestly, I don't seem to be able to do anything about it, because I can't make the training fit with the schedule that I have in my head."

"Exactly! So, what if you just accepted things as they are? Can you allow that everything happens in its own time?"

"Well, I'm going to have to, aren't I? It's either that or continue to battle with myself, and I can see that this is a big waste of time and energy because nothing changes."

"Right. But think about what you and the others are doing here. Everything seems to get done despite what you perceive to be delays, doesn't it?"

"Yeah. You're right, "I admitted.

"So now you know what to do!"

I felt my guide fade away and jotted down some notes about this exchange. As I wrote, I recognized that I'm from a culture where having a serious overload of work is considered desirable, with people studying for years and then working long hours with no breaks until their blood pressure skyrockets, forcing them to take medication or alcohol and other substances to help them combat the stress. The jungle people are not so foolish. While I chafed at what I considered to be others slacking off or delays in my training, I had to acknowledge that the only one who seemed to be unsettled was me.

Putting away my notebook and pen, I decided to head back over to where everyone was socializing in Oscar's *albergue*.

"There you are, Judita! Come and join us! You're missing out on a good batch of your favorite beverage," Javier called out joyfully.

I climbed up the ladder and found everyone enjoying yet another batch of masato. A large bowl was passed to me, and I downed it Jivaro style accompanied by a lot of hooting and cheering.

I think this delicious yucca brew tends to give people wind, because during these sessions there is a lot of farting and belching. I noticed that no one apologized or looked sheepish for their normal bodily functions. Everyone went about their business in a completely natural way, completely unconcerned about what we in the West take great pains to cover up.

But it wasn't just masato that affected the digestion in this way. During one particularly windy ayahuasca ceremony, I'd had to stop singing at times to belch loudly. I just couldn't help it.

"You must learn to have more grace, Judita. You cannot belch so much when you are curing patients," Javier admonished me.

While I agreed, I thought I could see a mischievous twinkle in his eyes. Ayahuasca ceremonies are not for those who worry about their bodily functions. Belching, farting, and purging in many forms is all part of the work. I find it rather liberating myself!

During the course of our training, Javier told me several times that so far, none of the people he'd brought into the jungle for training had lasted more than a few days.

"Even locals from Iquitos?" I asked in surprise.

Javier nodded. "Ya, Judita. Everyone wants to be a shaman but very few are actually willing to put in the time and hard work that results in transformation. They have this picture in their heads that we live this glamorous life as spiritual leaders, but the reality is very different as you've already seen. I bring them to the jungle and they complain about the food and the bugs until finally *whoosh!*" He made a sweeping motion with his hand.

As I thought about this, I decided it wasn't just because the training itself was difficult, but it was more that the environment in which the work was taking place could be very uncomfortable for a city dweller. It was hot and humid, and the bug bites were torturous. I often felt exhausted from the heat and the burning intensity of the hundreds of bites all over me. It became a case of having a strong will to succeed. I simply refused to be one of those who wimped out after a few days. I was going to make it, even if it killed me!

Another thing I found to be a bit trying at times was the lack of enough private time to rest and assimilate everything that I was experiencing. It felt like the proverbial drinking water through a fire hose. If I can have even an hour to myself to sit quietly without having to engage in anything, I can then recoup enough energy to take on the next step of the training, but I wasn't always able to have this simple luxury.

Having grown up in a culture that doesn't seem to prioritize developing deep meaningful relationships, I was noticing how the opposite seemed to be true with the jungle people I'd met so far. Their interpersonal relationships took center stage rather than just being something to do when they had a bit of free time. Anyone can come to visit without prior notice and be warmly invited in. Socializing is deemed to be an important way to stay healthy, and I rarely saw individuals on their own like I do in my own country. In this manner, the Jivaro had accepted me into their extended group, therefore it was considered bad manners to leave me alone unless I indicated I needed to work on my icaros, take a bath, or just collapse in a heap under my mosquito net for a while. Even during some of those times I would find someone coming along the path to visit and I certainly did not want to be rude.

While our night training so far had only involved me and Javier, he suddenly decided to have Olaff join us one evening without telling me. While I adored Olaff immensely, suddenly having a witness seemed to throw me off and make me feel very self-conscious even though he simply sat quietly on a nearby log. I totally messed up the order of the songs, forgot the words or certain procedures, and generally made a huge mess of the ceremony. I went to bed that night feeling yet again like a huge failure. It didn't help that the next morning when I was presented with two of the stale white bread rolls for my breakfast. I looked up at Olaff, who smiled sweetly.

"Our supplies are getting low. We will have to restock."

Fortunately, we found some additional food on yet another plant walk after we'd finished the meager breakfast. This time it was a macambo fruit, which is closely related to cacao. I'd seen the small skewers of the grilled lima bean-sized seeds on offer in the markets and found them to be utterly delicious. The fruit itself was somewhat strange looking, like some extraterrestrial's idea of an American football, only a little smaller, yellow, and veiny looking. The outer skin was thick and tough, so Olaff gave it a quick smack with his machete to crack it open. He handed me one half, and I could barely see the outlines of the seeds embedded in the soft pulpy flesh.

"The seeds don't come out easily, so it takes some work to get them prepared for grilling or frying," he told me. "They have a thin protective skin around them and are tricky to handle because they're slippery. You have to use your hands and pinch out a section of the pulpy inside, then you nibble at it until you find the hidden seeds."

I questioned this nibbling part, so my jungle friends showed me how to remove the skin with the teeth rather than trying to peel it off with the fingers. I tried both methods and the first one was definitely more effective.

Since the Jivaro placed so much emphasis on relationships it wasn't surprising that everything was shared. They considered it to be bad form to hoard food without offering any to others no matter how hungry someone was. Hunters hunted for the group. Whether it was meat or fruit, everything that was collected came back to be shared. When I pointed out to Javier that I had noticed this, he nodded solemnly.

"It is this way because jungle life is hard and unpredictable. One day I will share my food with you, and on another day when I am hungry you will share what you have with me. In this manner, there is not so much inequality.

There are many who take advantage of the natives' generosity without giving anything back. People come into a *curandero's* camp and want a ceremony or a healing, and then they go away without giving anything in return. Even a small amount of cash or food makes a big difference here as you can see."

I digested this and filed it away for the future as my teacher continued.

"The goal should be to always walk in balance. There must be some kind of energy exchange. Most of those who come to me have very little, but they somehow manage to give me something for the work I do for them. Even if all they can give is a piece of fruit from their garden, I can share it with my family. If you have more, it's good to give more. This helps to keep things in balance."

This made me feel really glad he'd told me about bringing gifts to the Jivaro. Had I truly understood the situation I would have insisted on bringing a lot more, or at least as much as we could carry.

Javier continued talking about other indigenous groups that were more well off than they let on. "They put on things that make them look like savages for the tourists, maybe do a dance or ritual and let you take photos, but they're really just money merchants. If you were allowed to walk through their village you would find generators, refrigerators, and televisions. But they will not allow outsiders to see these things because it would ruin the illusion of their being poor jungle Indians." He followed this up with a ridiculous impression of one group's tourist dance routine and we all laughed so hard we nearly rolled off the platform.

"I'm going stay here at Oscar's for a while. You go back and practice your icaros now!"

I wandered over to the small clearing I used as my practice area. It wasn't large, but it gave me enough space to walk around in circles as I reviewed the tricky lyrics and melodies of my ever growing repertoire of medicine songs. I found the repetitive action of circling put me into a light trance state, and this somehow helped me to remember things more easily.

After some time had passed I realized I was hungry. Needing a break, I decided to head back over to Oscar's to see what was going on. I arrived at the large house just as Olaff was setting out our lunch. All the guys seemed to think this was really funny because they had just been talking about calling me in when I showed up. Someone made a joke about "she must be a shaman already," which caused a few guffaws. I made a mysterious movement with my hands for emphasis but knew deep down it was going to take a lot more than coincidentally showing up for a meal for me to really earn that title.

Lunch was wonderfully filling. We ate the last of the too salty, rubber fish accompanied by mounds of rice, boiled *plátanos* and fried macambo seeds. I silently wondered when I was going to be able to enjoy some fresh fish. As if reading my thoughts, Javier said.

"You will have more fish in the next place because we will be closer to the river. Olaff can fish every day and we won't have to eat this preserved fish."

Oh, glory hallelujah!

After we finished eating and visiting, Jav and I went for another stroll through the jungle. I carried my trusty notebook with me to make notes, but I doubted I would ever be able to learn even a fraction of the knowledge my hosts had. I just found these times very precious. Although I was still in the early stages of my training, I greatly appreciated being able to actually learn as my teacher would have, by being a part of the jungle and learning from the inside out, rather than the other way around.

On the way back, I returned to my tambo to find the giant pig once again slurping up the water in my *encanto* bucket. This was the third time today that it was invading my space and I couldn't make it go away. It was really annoying to have that huge porker constantly chomping, grunting, and farting only a few feet away from me while I was trying to write up my notes.

This was going to be another work night, meaning there would be no dinner, so I remained where I was, reviewing songs and ceremony practices. As it got dark, the woods became aglow with fireflies. I'd never seen a real firefly before and suddenly I was surrounded by many little twinkling lights. It was so magical. I felt that the jungle was letting me know everything was just fine. What a beautiful gift!

As I sat in the dark, listening to the incredible night song all around me, I had the sense that while I was Javier's student, I would have to make this work my own. It is necessary to have a human teacher during the earlier stages, but as the student progresses it's all about their relationship with their own spirit guides. There was a strong feeling that the jungle itself was teaching me through Javier, and I expressed my gratitude.

I also felt grateful that I'd found a teacher who was right for me at this stage in my learning process. I felt safe and well taken care of, and I realized this is a key element in the student-teacher relationship. There were certainly times when I needed the human intervention. For example, during one of the training nights I was having trouble with a certain melody. I just couldn't seem to get it dialed in and I was getting frustrated. Jav got up and told me to open my mouth. He blew smoke from his ever-present mapacho into my mouth three times, and astonishingly the blockage vanished!

Even though I was determined to be the first of Javier's students to complete the training, I was aware that the more I started to feel somewhat relaxed, the more the jungle challenged me to prove my worthiness. Sure, it was hot and humid and at times physically tiring, but the biting bugs had to be the hardest element of all. We were not in some screened in jungle lodge with Wi-Fi and running water: we were completely outside twenty-four hours a day, every day.

Rather than developing a tolerance to the intense pulsing and itching, the bites seemed to multiply and spread. Every now and then it was as if someone flipped a switch and they would all start itching at once. This seemed to happen at certain hours of the day, following some mysterious bodily rhythm.

One of the nights that we worked only with the *agua florida* was the worst. I must admit that at first, I was reluctant to drink a cologne made of artificial ingredients, but if Javier did it, then so would I. But there was something in it that seemed to trigger all the bites, and I went into a frenzied itching that was so bad that I couldn't concentrate. I kept making mistakes, and this in turn had the knock on effect of prolonging the ceremony, as Javier repeatedly made me go back to the beginning and start over. I wanted to scream at him and pound him with my fists, but I knew this wouldn't be a great idea, and it certainly wouldn't solve anything.

Successful magical work requires that the student have a very strong sense of self-discipline, so my apprenticeship served to not only learn different healing methods and run the ceremonies, but also to work on my self-discipline and ego. These are probably two of the hardest things for any shamanic student to work with, especially in the beginning. Jav had been right when he told me that he could stay in the jungle for weeks or months without coming back to the city, but I could not, at least not at this early stage. Part of me wanted to stay here forever with these lovely, welcoming people, but another part was starting to long for a bed and some different food.

"Do you want to go to see Raul's zoo today?" Jav asked me the next morning.

"Sure! Let's do it!"

"It's not a big zoo like you might be thinking. It's just a small area where he takes care of jungle animals, but you'll get to see some of them up close and maybe even hold them!" I saw his mischievous eyes twinkle and wonder if I was about to be tricked again.

I enjoyed the fairly easy stroll between the little settlements. There were designated paths that were fairly level, and every now and then we'd come upon someone's house. Unlike my own culture where we spend much of our days inside houses and buildings or our cars, the jungle people mostly remained outside. If they weren't attending to some task around the base of their structures, they might be sitting on the raised floor watching to see who would come by. Everyone would wave and greet each other. I really liked that.

Javier's friend, Raul, was also a medicine man. He greeted us graciously and invited us in to sit down. I asked him about the kind of healing work he did, and he told me that he doesn't work with ayahuasca or do ceremonies. His specialty was helping women with conditions around pregnancy and childbirth. He also knew a lot about the medicinal properties of plants.

Curious about the fact that he'd created a zoo in the middle of the jungle, I wanted to ask him about this and see some of his charges.

Yes, it might seem like a strange thing to do," Raul admitted, "but I wanted to create a small sanctuary so I could breed rare local animals and bring them back from the edge of extinction. Come! I'll show you."

His small facility had añujes, which looked like giant guinea pigs; capybaras, very large rodents that also resembled guinea pigs but could get as large as a medium-sized dog; peccaries, a funny-looking animal that looked like a bristly boar mixed with several other animals; cute tree sloths; anacondas; turtles and more.

Judita wants to hold the anaconda!" Javier sang out as Raul looked to me for confirmation.

"Uh, I guess so. I've never held a snake before. What do I do?"

Before either man could answer my question, my teacher had picked up the five-foot long serpent and placed it over the back of my neck so that its tail and head ends draped down in front of me. It felt cool and quite heavy.

Now I know how feather boas got their name," I muttered as the snake shifted.

"Try holding it behind its head and about a foot in front of the tail," Raul suggested.

I could really feel the power of the snake's muscles rippling as I held onto its two ends with my hands. "These things don't bite, do they?" I asked.

"No, Judita, but you must be very careful with a boa. They will wrap themselves around you and squeeze you death!" Javier wrapped his arms around his upper body, bugged his eyes out and pretended to be suffocating. I should've known I'd get a dramatic response from my teacher.

"He doesn't smell very good," I remarked, hoping I'd be able to get the stink out of my shirt.

"You don't have to be too concerned with this one as she's still pretty small for an anaconda," Raul told me. "They can grow up to thirty feet and weigh hundreds of pounds. You wouldn't even be able to lift a big one." The snake had started squirming more, so he came behind me and lifted it from my neck and shoulders.

"Well, that was interesting. I've never held a snake before," I declared, secretly hoping this was the first and last time. I don't dislike snakes; I have a great respect for them and just prefer to let them go their own way.

"Have you seen a tree sloth before?" Raul asked me as he pointed to a sleepy adult hanging from a nearby branch.

"Not a live one up close like this," I replied as I studied the languid animal's face. "It's odd, but it kind of reminds of a little human; there's something about the eyes and the way it looks at us."

"You can hold her too if you'd like. She's a lot less squirmy than the boa," Raul told me.

"Sure, why not?"

"Hold out your arms as if you're reaching for something."

I followed Raul's instruction as he disengaged the sloth from its branch. He stepped forward and arranged it so that I was cuddling its body with both of its arms wrapped loosely around the base of my neck. I felt like I was holding a toddler. About a minute later, the sloth seemed to feel heavier. I looked at my companions for an explanation.

"She fell asleep, Judita. Now you'll have to hold her until she wakes up," Javier laughed.

Laughing at his friend's silliness, Raul offered to take the sloth back, guiding it gently back to the branch it'd been hanging from.

As we visited, I had the sense that Raul was sizing me up. Several times he mentioned that he was only a few years older than I.

"You have husband?"

"No."

"Boyfriend? Someone special?"

"Er, no. Not right now."

He smiled and extended his hand as if that settled everything. "I am looking for a wife. How many children have you borne?"

"Um, none."

Raul looked shocked, then turned to Javier, who shrugged.

"Why do you not have any children?" He just could not believe this.

I didn't want to go into the long and complicated reasons for my lack of offspring. The only thing that mattered was that I did not have any.

"Well, I would want to have children. We love children and have as many as we can! Maybe you could consider it." He looked at me hopefully.

I couldn't believe this was happening again here so soon. I'd never experienced anything like this before, and I wasn't quite sure how to behave. In a different kind of situation, I very likely might have pursued this farther as I did find him rather handsome. I decided to tell him that my body would no longer allow me to have children, that I was past childbearing age.

"Oh, we can change that! We have many plants here in the jungle to *recalentar los ovarios*." Warm up the ovaries, eh?

I looked at Javier for confirmation that this was possible, and he nodded vigorously. I let this sink in for a moment, thinking of my own culture with its complicated medical procedures and injections. Raul continued to look hopeful that I would consent to be his wife and bear him many children.

I think I was beginning to understand how the jungle people paired up. The indigenous men and women had fairly delineated roles in their societies. The men would travel around looking for work, usually temporary bouts of the very physical labor that gave them those muscles of steel. The women took the domestic side, rearing the children, washing the clothes by hand, cooking, and cleaning. To me, both sides lived hard lives.

While the idea of being a Jivaro medicine man's wife did intrigue me, it's not something that I could jump into on short notice. Being with this tribe for only a few weeks and having to focus on my training didn't give me the chance to really feel how life would be like here on a long term basis. Even if I'd have agreed to stay, I'm not sure how long I would have lasted for various reasons.

I'd been raised in a very different society where women can fly planes and take on roles that used to only be filled by men. I thought of all the things I'd done so far in my life—even being able to have this great adventure—and I loved being able to freely do what I wanted. I knew I'd be expected to take on a traditional female role here were I to pair up with this attractive medicine man.

I also had spent time watching the jungle women do the laundry. The combination of large families and a dirty environment meant laundry had to be done almost every day. While we were travelling in the jungle, I would have to wash my own clothing by hand in the *quebradas*, but I knew at some point I would be going home to a nice washing machine.

Even more than domestic duties, the single biggest thing that concerned me was that I hadn't developed the resistance to bug bites that the locals had. Only a few days in and my entire body was covered in the most insanely itchy bites I had ever experienced. The darned things would crawl up under my clothes and I'm sure there were some under my skin as well. In contrast, I watched mosquitoes and flies land on the bare shoulders of my companions, then buzz off without biting. I know I'm repeating myself, but I just cannot emphasize how much I suffered from those bites! And because these tiny things were such a huge factor for me, my mind immediately flew to them when considering extended stays in this land of eternal greenery.

Before we headed back to headquarters, I thanked Raul for his hospitality and his offer. "Right now, I live far away in another country and I look after my aging parents. My work is there. I know I'll be back one day, but it would really be hard for me to live here and suffer so much."

I showed him various areas on my body where the skin looked like red cottage cheese. He bent in closely and conferred with Javier. I couldn't quite understand all of their conversation, but it seemed that they were discussing what might be attacking me and what plant might help. The problem was that there was such a large, affected area and more than one type of bite so it was hard to say for sure which insect was the guilty party.

"I did bring some medicine with me but I can't use it during *dieta* periods." This time it was my turn to look hopeful.

Raul wasn't able to suggest anything without more time, and Javier was getting impatient to go, so we said our good byes and headed back down the path towards Oscar's. The walk should have lasted about an hour, but the strange rumbling in my guts had been growing over the hours and now I had to make an emergency run into the bushes. Then, one of my biggest nightmares came true: I ran out of toilet paper!

"Javier! Do you have any tissues with you?" I asked frantically. "I need some toilet paper!"

He looked at my head peeking over the tops of some bushes. "Use leaves. Then you will be a real jungle woman."

"Oh, gawd! Which ones? I don't know which ones to use!" Seriously, I didn't want to use any!

He pointed to a bush which was fortunately within my reach considering that my pants were slung down around my lower legs and I couldn't walk far. I had no choice. I used leaves for toilet paper for the first time, and it didn't kill me. Funny that, huh?

We were coming to the end of our stay with the Jivaro after nearly a month. As much as I would have liked to have stayed even longer, I knew we would need to go back to Iquitos to restock our supplies for the next leg of my training, which would be carried out in his ancestral village much farther away.

Javier decided that we would have one more night ceremony so we could review everything I'd learned so far. We went over the purpose of each item used in the work before running through all my icaros.

Fortunately, nothing threw me off my game and I was able to get through the series without having to go back and start over.

My teacher told me how happy he was that I had been able to take in everything he'd given me, including all the songs. "I've had a few pupils who could maybe learn three icaros in one month, but they couldn't retain anything. He made a motion of sweeping his hand from in front of his chin over his head.

"But I don't feel any different! I feel the same as when we got here!" I moaned. "And I didn't see any spirits!"

He gave me one of his face splitting grains that showed all his teeth. "Have patience, Judita. If I gave you enough ayahuasca right now so you could see *los doctorcitos,* the little doctors, you would not be able to stay in control of the ceremony because the practices have not been ingrained deeply enough in you yet. Remember that night in Sacha Wasi when you stayed in the back room because you couldn't move?"

As I nodded I suddenly had the thought that what we were doing was laying the foundations. It was similar to the way an athlete practices a skill over and over so the movements come without thought. I was learning the practical things first so as we went in deeper, the more subtle things would have a framework to build on. I had a brief vision of building a house and then filling it with furniture and personal items. If there is no house, there is nowhere to put all of those things. I looked at my teacher and saw him nod. He knew.

PART FOUR

Río Napo

CHAPTER 14

Coming Out of the Closet

We left Oscar's camp early the next morning. The Jivaro chief had seemed genuinely sad for our departure and said he'd love to join us for our next adventure. I too had felt a bit downcast at having to leave these lovely people but knew we had to get back to prepare for the second phase of my training.

The recent rains had caused a considerable rise in the river's water level. We didn't have to pole the boat over sandbars this time, so we were able to make it back to the Bellavista port at a good speed. The cool river breezes felt wonderful on my burning skin and I wished we could've stayed on the water for many more hours. We were on our way back to Iquitos, and I wasn't looking forward to it. While the jungle had its own sounds, there was a strong natural energy to those sounds that I found calming, despite all my bug bites There was nothing about Iquitos that I found natural or calming.

First up on arrival back at the house was a bucket shower with soap and shampoo. After changing into city clothes, I spent some time cleaning and organizing my gear, making sure it was ready for the next part of my training adventure. Javier had told me that we'd be going out some time in the afternoon to restock our supplies and gear up for the next leg of the journey, so I went to look for him. Julieta's mother told me that both he and her daughter had gone out, and she didn't know when they'd be back.

I decided that I didn't feel like just hanging around for what might be hours, so I walked into the city center to catch up on my email. Finding an internet facility with fast speeds just off the plaza, I settled in behind a computer. I found several emails from my sister, Bobbi, telling me about a blowup at home that involved me even though I was thousands of miles away. Maybe this hadn't been such a great idea after all.

She told me that the wonderful organic gardener that my parents had employed had decided to retire in order to spend more time with her daughter, so they'd hired a new gardener to replace her.

"They found someone through a flier. You know, those ones that are thrown onto every driveway or left on the front step," my sister explained. "Well, I took him around your yard and told him which plants not to touch: all the ones that you especially planted and took care of. He got all weird when I showed him your daturas and said they were weeds. After I left he cut them all down."

I felt my heart sink because I'd worked so hard to nurture those plants and now they were gone thanks to one of those mow, blow and away we go yard yahoos. I sat back in my chair and allowed my mind to wander back to around two years ago.

I'd been a member of a group that was learning about certain indigenous practices. During one evening meeting, we'd passed around a ceremonial pipe that contained a small amount of datura, a potentially deadly plant, in the smoking mixture. I had always found these plants attractive and wondered about their effects but wasn't foolish enough to try them without expert guidance. The group's leader, an Apache woman, had been taught about the correct usage of healing and ceremonial plants from her elders, so I felt safe and was keen to participate.

While I didn't notice any particular effects after smoking, I did have a remarkable experience about an hour later once I was back home. I was lying in bed, in that dozy state before sleep takes you away, when suddenly the spirit of datura appeared to me. She looked stunningly beautiful as if there were hundreds of tiny lights intertwined through her leaves and flowers. I knew this spirit could be quite dark and pull people into her world if they weren't ready to receive her, but this felt as if she was trying to make herself attractive to me, to show me that she wasn't always so dark when approached in the right way.

I laid there in awe as she told me she wanted to ally herself with me, and that I needed to get some plants for my yard. While you can't buy datura plants in your local nursery, they do grow wild all over many areas of Southern California, Mexico, and throughout Central and South America. I had been able to find a few specimens in a remote location that allowed me to dig them up and bring them home. I'd carefully replanted them in large pots and tended to them with love, and they'd grown into large, beautiful plants with many of the fragrant white flowers that I adored sticking my nose into. I loved them and was so happy to see them in my yard. And now they were gone!

"Anyway, that's not the end of it," my sister continued. He told Mom and Dad that there were poisonous, hallucinogenic plants growing in their yard and they had a fit. But he told them everything was fine now because he'd killed them. Just letting you know because you'll probably hear about it when you eventually get home."

Idiot! Those plants were purely ornamental and not only that, but they were also in pots! *Pots!* Who plants weeds in pots? They weren't just growing in some random corner of the yard; they were carefully situated under a tree towards the rear part of the yard where there were not harming a soul. Weeds or not, they were *my* plants!

Letting out a long exhale, I finished my computer session and decided to wander over to Ari's Burger, where I ordered my usual guarana infused Infiel drink and a salad with freshly shaved palm hearts called *chonta*. The usual ambient noise of this now familiar place somehow made me feel a bit better.

By the time I was done it was too hot to walk the long distance back to Javier's house, so I flagged down a motocab. I found everyone waiting for me when we pulled up. I explained that I didn't know where they'd gone or for how long, so I'd decided to go out to check my email and get some lunch. I didn't tell them that if they couldn't be bothered to let me know they were leaving for a few hours, why should I?

"Next time, please do leave us a note or something. We were a little worried about you," Julieta said.

I nodded and went to my little hut at the back of their house to rest in the fierce afternoon heat. My mind kept going back to my destroyed daturas and I couldn't shake the sadness. I heard some children squealing in the main house and hoped they'd stay there for a while until my malaise passed. But my wishes were for naught. Three cute little girls, related to the household in some way, came charging into my house and all started talking at the same time. They started picking up my things and running around, and I had a hard time understanding them. I really wanted to tell them to go away but I also didn't want to be rude. The purpose for their visit soon became clear when they asked me to buy them presents.

"Lots of beautiful gifts for us!" chirped one little girl.

"Yes! Lots of presents for us! You give us many things?" another one asked hopefully.

I let out a long sigh and told them to go back into the house. I just wanted to be left alone in my hut for a while. I was hot and tired and not feeling sociable. I began to notice that the noise from the street kept increasing, so I thought I'd better go see what was happening. I found everyone gathered around the front door, excitedly looking out into the street.

"What's going on?" I wanted to know.

"It's a party!" yelled Jav as he pointed to a large sound stage that had been erected just a few doors down.

"What for?"

"For the anniversary of our street!"

In response to my puzzled look, he explained that the street's neighborhood association was organizing the event to celebrate the creation of their street, an uneven, unpaved road. The music was already loud, but I was told the real fiesta would be starting around sunset.

Thinking this was a rather odd thing to observe, I turned once more to my teacher. "Um, Jav, why do you celebrate the anniversary of your street?"

He gave me one of those looks that I interpreted as being something I should have already known.

"It's just another reason to celebrate life!"

I looked at my teacher, uncomprehending, after he explained the custom and desperately wished I was back in Oscar's camp. There were no big sound stages with ear-deafening loud music where the Jivaro lived.

Around sunset, my bug bites were starting to flare up again so I took a couple of antihistamines, hoping they'd knock me out so I could sleep off my misery. While waiting for them to start working, I hung around and socialized for a bit, then retreated back to my little house. My dreams of a peaceful night were not to be. Even though my quarters were behind the main house and muffled some of the street sound, the sheer volume was enough to rattle the cinderblocks and *caluminas* that the houses were constructed from.

The noise went on all night long at an excruciating volume and I wanted to cry in frustration. I was dead tired, sad, and my body was so itchy from the bites that I half expected them to break open and emit some kind of worms or crawling bugs that had been munching on me from the inside. Nothing worked to alleviate the extreme itchiness of whatever was affecting me.

I eventually did pass out, but the sleep was not refreshing. The high dosage of antihistamines I'd taken left me feeling disoriented and groggy as the morning light arrived. I laid in bed listening to the sounds of the day increase in volume. Motos raced up and down the street and stereos blasted their deafening *cumbia*. I eventually hauled myself up, desperately wishing for a good hot cup of coffee. That would have put the world to rights at once!

I still felt sad about the loss of my plants, and Javier was annoyed that I couldn't snap out of it.

"What is done is done and you can't change it, so why do you let it affect you so much? You must let it go and move on. Today we need to go buy everything for Rio Napo," I was told as he eyed me, assessing my mood.

"Can you give me an idea of how much we'll need? I want to make sure I have enough money," I replied. I might as well have asked the good citizens of this jungle town to turn down their radios and TVs. The impression seemed to be that I could just conjure up the soles as needed; no trips to the ATM were required.

"We don't need much. We're taking a *lancha*, so there is a crew fee for all three of us, but we don't have to pay for the boat gasoline this time. That's it."

"Really? Just the *lancha* costs? No food or gifts? No supplies or anything else? At no point we're going to have to buy anything else like food?" With my recent experiences now behind me, let's just say I was a bit suspicious.

"Oh, ya ya. Maybe rice and a chicken." Rice and a chicken, huh? Well, that'll keep us going for, hmm, let's see, maybe one meal?

The temperature continued to rise in the afternoon and I was just wilted. I needed another bottle of aguardiente to keep my camalonga refilled. The previous one I'd bought had somehow evaporated—in other words, someone drank it, and it wasn't me. We made a quick trip an aguardiente seller's house but didn't continue on to the market as I thought we were planning to do, instead returning to the house where I plopped wearily into a chair. Javier followed behind me and turned on some really loud music and suggested I stay there to keep cool. My head was pounding as the music seared its way inside and threatened to blow my skull open if I didn't escape. I wondered how it was that the people here weren't deaf. I took my bottle of sugar cane liquor and retreated to my little house in the back.

Mealtimes here were very irregular, sometimes even nonexistent. My issue was that no one ever said anything about whether there would be a meal or not. So when my stomach started to rumble, I padded into the kitchen to see if I could help with any preparation, but no one was there. My esteemed teacher had vanished once again despite his declaration that we needed to gear up for the next excursion. I helped myself to some leftover limeade and took a big glass back to my *casita*. I looked at my aguardiente bottle sitting on the shelf and suddenly it seemed like a great idea to add a dash to the lime drink. It really lifted my mood, so by the time Jav reappeared to collect the boat money and my hammock I felt better.

By now, I realized that Javier wasn't always good at communicating with me. I didn't need to know every detail of every move, and indeed in shamanic work we have to learn to trust the process. But still, just giving me a bit of information about when we'd be leaving or if he had to go out for errands would have made a big difference to my peace of mind. He told me he'd gone to one of the ports to arrange our passage to Rio Napo early tomorrow morning, and I felt disappointed to have missed out on this jaunt. I would have liked to have gone with him to learn more about how to book passage on a boat here because there were several ports that served the city.

Since we were planning to be away for several more weeks, I thought I'd make another run into the center to check my email. I found another message that my sister had sent telling me about more madness and mayhem at home. My mother was still fuming about the dangerous narcotics I'd been growing in our yard but now there was something else.

Bobbi told me that she'd been giving our folks an edited version of the emails I'd sent to her about my adventures because she felt it would be easier for them to digest. She'd mentioned our staying with the Jivaro, but not about any of the training details. Armed with this one word, my dad, who was quite computer literate, decided to Google "Jivaro". And what was the first thing that came up? Their old, notorious, head-shrinking practices. My mother had another fit, and Bobbi told her that this is exactly why I didn't give them all the details and confide in them.

The universe works in its mysterious ways, and while we often suffer through challenging situations, whining "why me?" somewhere down the road we will be given the answer to that question. This latest situation became an important turning point for me. For years, I'd hidden who I was from my parents because of their criticism and judgment. I know they wanted the best for me and that they knew nothing about shamanism, but I couldn't be someone I was not. It was time to come out of the closet.

Sitting back in the chair, I closed my eyes and thought about what I wanted to say. I was far away and wouldn't be back for some time, so any fallout from my words wouldn't hit me in the face, at least not for a while.

"Dear Mom and Dad," I began. "Bobbi told me that you were concerned about the indigenous tribe I'd been staying with. Please rest assured that I do still have my head and am safely all in one piece. Although it would be better if we were all sitting down together to have this conversation, I realize that there is never an ideal time so I'm going to present to you a few things for your consideration.

"We are all adults, and I dearly wish I could communicate more openly with you. I feel that so many times in the past when I have shared my activities and interests with you, I've been shot down and criticized. Remember when I told you about the animal communication course I'd done a few years ago? All I got was derision and snide comments for nearly an entire year about that. 'Ha ha! Judy talks to animals! What's next? Trees?'

"Honestly, I don't try to be unconventional or contrary on purpose or to annoy you. I just wish you could accept me as I am instead of trying to shove my round peg into your square hole and then getting mad at me when I don't fit.

"Now be honest, guys. How would you have reacted if I had told you that I am a shaman's apprentice? This is not something new that I'm doing to have fun in the moment; this is a calling from way back.

"You might as well know this is not going to be a solitary trip. I'm at the beginning of my training and plan to come back once or twice a year and work in between to finance it all." I sat back and reread what I'd written, trying to imagine their reactions.

Realizing my dad might then decide to Google the word shaman and read about all sorts of weird things which might totally freak them out, I thought I'd better explain a bit more. I told them that a shaman is a healer who works with the energy of the Creator, perhaps being a sort of cross between a doctor and a priest.

"I am telling you all this because I would love to have your acceptance. But even if this is too much to ask, I will continue to walk my road without it."

My sister had also added some new information about the daturas that made me feel a little better. "You know how Dad always likes to look out the back windows at what's going on in the yard? Well, apparently he saw Pedro cutting down your plants and rushed outside to try to stop him, but by the time he got downstairs and out in the yard it was too late."

So I shifted the subject of my email to this and told him I appreciated him trying to help save my plants and how sad I'd been at their destruction.

"I know they can be misused, but I am not intending on using them for ingestion. I am merely in a sort of guardian role, and I think they are beautiful plants."

After rereading my message several times, I took a deep breath and hit the send key. I'd sent a blank carbon copy to my sister so she'd know what I'd presented to them in case there were more questions. I had no idea of how my words would be received, but I felt this needed to come out. I needed to be me and hoped they would agree that since I'm an adult now it would be far more pleasant to be able to keep the lines of communication open.

That done, I returned to the house, and I suddenly decided it was cerveza time. Javier and Olaff were waiting with another friend who'd come around, and they all backed me up enthusiastically, so we made a beer run. Javier thought it might help to speed my recovery if we played my favorite Maná CDs. The other guy, who'd I'd never met before, left briefly, and returned with a gift for me. It was Maná's *Acceso Total* DVD, a compilation from their live shows. I was so thrilled! I downed a few beers and danced around like a fool but it did the trick. I think I just needed to blow my cork to release all the pressure I'd been holding in.

After a while, the talk turned to religion. For some time, I had been curious about the long white plastic rosary that Javier often wore around his neck. He told me that he was Catholic, and this really surprised me. In the Catholic world I'd been raised in, things like magic and shamanic ceremonial healing were not looked at in a positive light. I wanted to know how he could be both a shaman and a Catholic.

Javier suddenly became very animated, and he dragged me into their bedroom to show me their altar. "For us, Jesus is the Master

Shaman. In his teachings he tells us to do as he did, such as healing the sick. We don't just drink ayahuasca and sing icaros; we also use prayer in our healings."

He took another rosary off the altar and placed it around my neck, telling me that wearing this indicates that one has been trained in the use of prayer or *oraciones*. "I will teach you about this too. It is good that you already have your Catholic background because it will help you to understand more."

I wanted to ask more questions but he held up his hand. *"Más tarde.* Later."

So, the crazy day ended on a higher note than it had begun. Tomorrow we'd be headed up the Napo River to the pueblo of Nuevo Progreso on a *lancha,* whatever that was.

CHAPTER 15

Nuevo Progreso

It was now a little over one month since I'd returned to Peru for my shamanic instruction. There were still two more training phases of similar length to complete for this first phase of my apprenticeship. The ayahuasquero's apprenticeship lasts between four to five years depending on the tradition, so I still had a long way to go. I didn't live in Iquitos, so I'd have to make trips down once or twice a year to put my time in. We were now on our way to our second location, the village where Javier was born and raised: Nuevo Progreso on the Napo River.

After puttering around on the river in different versions of oversized canoes, I found the *lancha* experience to be at the opposite end of the spectrum. While I'm a fairly intrepid traveler, I might have been a bit hesitant to book a journey on one of these Amazonian riverboats by myself until I'd done it a few times with someone who knew how to work the system because I found it to be a little tricky.

There were no organized travel agents to help book the passage, and there were definitely no online reservations. The first step was to find out which port served the desired destination. You'd then have to go to that port to not only find a boat that was going where you wanted to go, but also when it would be leaving. There might be one leaving right away, or not for a few days.

For our journey up the Rio Napo, we had to leave from Puerto Masusa, which serves locations along the Amazon River. To me, the port looked like something out of an old 1940s movie set and not a very salubrious one at that. There was a mild undercurrent of danger lurking below the surface for the unwary, even during this late morning hour. Vendors hawked food and drinks and anything else you might need for your journey. The scene was loud, colorful, and chaotic, and I was glad to have Javier and Olaff with me. I'd been told to always keep an eye on my belongings and never leave anything, even for a moment, even if it looked like everyone around us was asleep once we were settled aboard.

Our craft, the *Rey de San Pedro*, was not one of the largest in the lineup at Puerto Masusa. The motley assortment of waiting *lanchas* made me briefly think of Mississippi steamboats, but without their paddlewheels. To add to my slight sense of unease, not even one of these riverboats looked new or attractive. Some appeared to be way past their service prime and threatened to disintegrate at the slightest hint of rain or wind. Ours looked like a bunch of old boards nailed together in haphazard, boxy form to which a diluted coat of white wash was slapped on. But ugly or not, these water taxis were the workhorses of the rivers, cramming people, animals and almost anything else you can imagine into their multi-level, cavernous spaces.

Since many of the journeys made by *lancha* were longer distances, those in the know would string up a hammock to snooze away the hours on an upper deck. This is why Olaff had come down to the port early: he had claimed a good spot down at the far end near the viewing platform and set up our three hammocks for us.

The journey to Nuevo Progreso, where Javier had been born and raised, took about nine hours from the Iquitos port. I alternated between lying in my hammock and standing out on the rear viewing platform watching the river slide away behind us.

Sometimes Javier would come out and join me and introduce me to people he'd just started talking to. I was beginning to see how he enjoyed weaving tales and sucking people in as far as possible, all the while nodding vehemently for emphasis when someone would question the veracity of what they were being told. I must admit I became his willing sidekick for many of these incredible fables, much like when Geraldo had assured the Bora Indians that I was his wife.

Despite the cattle car like conditions, my initial concerns melted away and I found myself enjoying the ride very much. People shared the space with small market animals like chickens, and sometimes it seemed as if we were on a piece of the Belen market that had broken off and floated down the river.

One of the things that I felt a bit uncertain about was knowing where to get off. I knew I didn't have to worry about this since I was traveling with Jav and Olaff, but I wanted to learn how to work the river travel system myself. *Lanchas* are like slow city buses that pull over at every single stop, taking ages to reach their destinations. Some stops were more obvious, having a small dock or dedicated landing area, while others were just drop off points along the bank.

It was late and dark when the *Rey de San Pedro* angled toward one of those nondescript banks.

"This is where we get off," Javier announced.

"Be ready to grab up your stuff and get off fast," advised Olaff. "The boat driver will want to move off quickly, and people don't want to wait any longer than they have to."

Again, I was grateful for my two companions who'd done this many times before, so I just followed their lead. We got all of our supplies off the boat within a few minutes, and the *lancha* started pulling away before we even made it up the bank. An older man came towards us, and Javier introduced his Uncle Alfredo. Like Augustin back at Oscar's camp, he was in his seventies but was still able to hoist a large load onto his back and move quickly up the steep incline. The house he shared with his wife, Imelda, was close by and enclosed on all sides, unlike the open structures we'd stayed in with the Jivaro.

After chatting about our plans regarding my instruction and just visiting for a while, we cleared away a section of the bare wood floor to use as our sleeping area. Our mosquito nets were hung in a neat row just as they had been in the *Casa del Shaman* and our gear stowed in a corner. During the day, the nets would be rolled up and the sleeping pads stowed so the space could be used for other activities. I felt cold and was grateful for the new blanket I'd just purchased. It had never occurred to me that it could be cold in the jungle, so I'd spent a few nights in the previous location curled up under a sheet with my clothing piled on top of me in attempts to trap some warmth next to my body.

After a good night's sleep, we spent the morning wandering around the small pueblo of Nuevo Progreso to meet many of my teacher's relatives. This was mostly for my benefit, so that I could become familiar with the surroundings, and the other residents would know that I was there as a guest of one of their resident families. This is a fairly standard protocol when visiting an indigenous settlement because if you are not a recognized member or resident, you need to ask for permission to be there. I soon found myself to be something of a curiosity, particularly among the children. Several quickly attached themselves to me, poking my arms and clothing, even pulling up my long sleeves to examine my watch. I looked at Javier for an explanation.

"They have never seen a *gringa* before," he explained.

Despite this village being quite remote, I found it hard to believe that I could possibly be a pioneer any place in the world, a world that had been explored through the centuries by brave adventurers. Jav vigorously nodded when I expressed this but knowing that he was prone to stretching the truth out of stories at times until it was thinner than a wire, I couldn't be sure until Olaff nodded his assent.

"I have never been here either, but I'm really glad to be a part of this. There will be new biological specimens for me to check out for my studies because we are so far away from home. There's no reason for tourists to come here. It's just a small pueblo on a big river."

Whatever the truth was, it did appear that the children had never seen a person with such pale skin and funny clothes before. These lovely little souls were dressed in rags and didn't even have the ubiquitous rubber flip flops that the good people of the jungle were so fond of. One of them, a boy named Jhony, had epilepsy and could not speak clearly, so I had some difficulty in understanding him. He was about seven years old, dressed in dirty, torn clothing, but to me he had the air of pure innocence that exuded something of a heavenly light.

From the moment he laid eyes on me, Jhony did his best to be at my side, which often meant being physically attached to me in some way. While I adored the sweet jungle children, I found it somewhat challenging to be followed around and poked constantly, especially when I was tired. Sometimes I'd retreat to the house, only to find them at the windows and doors, staring in at me. While we were at Alfredo's house, they were a constant presence.

"Why don't you buy some candy to give them?" Jav suggested with a smirk, knowing this would seal my fate.

"I suppose they don't get many treats here, do they?" I asked, somewhat sadly.

Jav shook his head for emphasis. I felt a bit guilty for wanting a little time to myself or to just not be the object of such intense fascination.

"Is there anywhere to buy candy here?" I asked him doubtfully.

"Ya, Judita. Come! I'll show you the store."

The store proved to be another of those small jungle *tiendas* that don't really have much to offer. These little shops usually have no electricity, so they tend to be a bit dark and dingy. No electricity means no ice or refrigerated goods. There are the usual warm sodas and stale white rolls, and a few other items like canned goods and sad looking yucca roots. Yet right there in the middle of a dusty back shelf, I was surprised to see what looked to be new bags of *caramelos*, the local individually wrapped candies that seem to be commonly found wherever we went.

I bought two bags of the candies while Jav and Olaff chatted to the owner. It seemed that they were being offered a large, freshly caught river fish, and were discussing the possibility of it being suitable for our meals. The eleven pound *zungaro* was a type of catfish, and it would serve to feed us until Olaff could do some fishing. My two companions closely examined the fish before pronouncing it acceptable, and I handed over more money for its purchase.

Next, Javier wanted to show me the village school. The small, neat building was old, but the villagers had kept it in good condition, painting it with happy hues. Colorful children's drawings adorned the walls, much like the schools in my own country.

We waited in the doorway while the teacher spoke to the class, then she turned to us. Jav explained the reason for our visit and that he was showing me around the pueblo.

The young female teacher shared this information with her students and then told us, "they want to sing you a song."

She led the children in a sweet song about all of the Americas, and I found myself getting choked up. I had to turn my head to try to hide my sniffles, and I just wanted to gather the entire group up and hug them all.

I was not about to be let off lightly as the teacher then requested that I make a speech to the class. I felt like an emotional mess, being such a stranger in this small village, but at the same time being accepted so easily already. I managed to croak out a few lines about how happy I was to be there and what a nice school they had, then I held up the bags of candy. I looked at the teacher for approval and she smiled and nodded. Going through the few rows where children of varies ages waited in anticipation for their treats, I had to really control myself not to break down in tears. It was just so sweet that I felt deeply touched. I wanted to give each child their own bag of *caramelos!*

As we continued along on our tour, I noticed that there were no facilities, unlike in the Jivaro village. Giving this pueblo a name that translated to mean *new progress* seemed rather optimistic for such a very poor place. While Oscar and his people seemed very hale and hearty to me, many of these folks appeared to be frailer and more sickly.

As we returned to Uncle Alfredo's house, Jhony ran up and wrapped himself around me. I desperately wished a healing power could run through me and into him, curing him of his affliction. As if he had sensed my thoughts, he looked up at me with such a loving look that I swear he could have been an angel. That little boy was pure love, no doubt about it!

A few neighbors stopped by to chat, and then once again, my single status came up for discussion. As I tried to explain that I was training to follow in my teacher's footsteps and thus could not really pursue any kind of romance, the jungle people would smile at me and laugh.

You are here, away from your home. This means you are single and you can pick any man," one of Alfredo's neighbors informed me.

Looking at Javier with a question on my face, I saw Olaff trying to hide a smile.

"It's true, Judita. We have one partner in the home, but when we travel, we can be single if we want."

I didn't know whether to believe him or not. "Seriously, Jav. Is this the custom here or something?"

Again, the vigorous nod. "Ya, Judita. You can have sex with anyone you want when you are away from home. Is custom here."

Oh dear.

For some reason, wherever I went with Javier I would be unceasingly questioned not only about whether or not I had a partner, but also if I was having sex with anyone. As I said, I'm not a prude, but I thought this was quite nosy!

Our plan was to use Uncle Alfredo's house as a base between deeper jungle forays. We would trek farther into the forest and build our own shelter where I would be receiving more teachings out in the wild. I was becoming more desperate to do this because I felt a bit like a zoo exhibit when I was in the house. Unlike in Oscar's camp, where Olaff and Javier would hang out with the Jivaro while I had some badly needed time and space to myself, there was no such luxury here. The house only had two rooms, so there was nowhere to escape to. And every door and window opening was filled with children staring in intently, watching my every move. Some of the bolder ones would edge in until Imelda shooed them out.

Bathroom breaks had to be planned with the deviousness of a secret agent. While Imelda and Javier kept the house from becoming filled with curious onlookers for my sake, there was no way to carry these boundaries outside the house. I had been shown the designated toileting area, so whenever I had to go to the bathroom, I'd have to try to sneak out through the back door and quickly find a secluded spot to do my business. Because I was being watched so closely, as soon as the children realized I was no longer within the safe confines of the house someone would be on my tail. More often than not, I'd barely have time to pull up my pants and start back towards the house before several kids would come running down the path and fling themselves at me.

So while I loved the people, I was beginning to feel somewhat claustrophobic in the house. A heavy rain had come in, and this held up our plans to move out to our own camp. Javier seemed to be in no hurry to get back to the work of training me, and I could see he was enjoying just hanging out with his extended family members and spinning his wild stories.

Sheltering during yet another downpour, the three of us sat with Alfredo and Imelda. Javier told them how much I had enjoyed masato. Alfredo told me they have many words for this yucca beer.

"Here, we call it *ponayado*, and we make it very strong!" he puffed his chest out proudly.

"And freshly made is called *jujupiana*," added Imelda.

Whatever they wanted to call it, I sure would've enjoyed a big bowl of the fermented jungle beverage right about then.

Our hosts spoke Kichwa, a regional variant of Quechua, as their first language, and I was furiously trying to write down some of these new terms. Being older adults of a mostly unwritten language, they weren't always sure of the spelling of many words, so I would write them down phonetically and ask Olaff about them later. I was very grateful to have a scholar who studied the local customs with us.

"Dinner is ready!" he announced, carrying in a large pot. He'd been cooking outside over a fire underneath a makeshift roof that kept away the rain.

The zungaro fish had been cut into several pieces, with each of us receiving one part in our bowls. I looked down at a fish mouth floating in my bowl and cast my mind back to a day many years ago in the past. My ex-husband and I had loved exploring all the culinary delights that London had to offer. One day, after imbibing a lot of some forgotten alcohol, we found ourselves in London's Chinatown.

"Whoa! Look at what's on the menu! Fish lips!" I'd read in amusement.

"Fish lips? Do fish have lips? Seriously?" Anthony had asked.

Sometimes when you're just in that sweet spot of inebriation, you get a jolt of courage to do things you probably wouldn't consider doing while sober.

"Let's get 'em! I want to try fish lips!" I decided.

So we ate fish lips. They weren't much to write home about. For one thing, there wasn't much to them. For another, they were a bit chewy. Still, it made for great anecdotes. I never thought I'd see them again as a food choice, but here they were again, a big set of fish lips right in my soup bowl, many miles and years away from Chinatown in the heart of London.

"Get that down your *tongoro!*" Alfredo instructed with a smile, as he pointed to his throat.

The soup was delicious and the mood shifted towards that favored jungle topic: sex.

Javier and his aunt and uncle fired off words which had different rude connotations. There was one phrase that apparently involved dogs, but I didn't quite catch the entire meaning, and maybe it's just as well that I didn't.

By morning, the rain had finally stopped and we decided it was time to move out and build our camp. Just as I was wondering what was for breakfast, a small boy brought around a basin full of *huani de yucca* treats. These consisted of cooked, mashed yucca mixed with various spices and cilantro leaves. Somewhat similar to the *juane*, it was wrapped in a *bijao* leaf and steamed. As I was enjoying the freshly made food, Javier gave me one of his face-splitting grins.

"Our being here, or rather your being here, is giving the people ideas on how to make money. Ha ha, Judita, you are going to be fat and they are going to be rich!" he doubled over laughing, and what else could I do but join in?

If I thought I was a klutz in the previous camp, I was now the official Klutz Queen of Rio Napo. We were building our own shelter alongside a small lagoon. Javier assured me that this area, like the *Casa del Shaman*, had been used by shamans-in-training for many years. It was wild, stunningly beautiful, very densely planted, and teeming with bugs.

Olaff and Javier immediately set to work cutting down small trees for the shelter poles and setting them in particular places. I wanted to help so Olaff showed me how to choose a tree that rose into a Y-shaped set of branches, then trim it so that it was just a pole with a V-shape at the top. Cross poles could then be set into the groove to construct the roof.

I shuffled off through the bushes in search of a small tree that I could prepare as Olaff had instructed. It couldn't be that hard, could it? I spotted a likely volunteer and set to work at its base with my trusty blade. I'd seen my two companions do this and was certain I would be just as successful. I didn't realize I was making one crucial mistake, so I continued to whack away at the poor tree until I was able to detach it from the remaining strands that held it to its base. Proudly, I dragged the poor thing over to where the boys were building the shelter.

"I brought another tree to use as a pole!" I announced.

Javier and Olaff looked at each other and came over to examine my offering.

"We can't use this. It has big split! Too much force." My teacher abruptly walked back to his task.

I looked at Olaff, who was trying to be kind and soften his uncle's sharp retort.

"How did you cut this down?" he asked, making various motions with an invisible machete using his hand.

I pantomimed how I'd hacked at the tree with the blade straight on, thinking that this would give the strongest force. Understanding rose in Olaff's eyes.

"A machete is not an ax. It's best to angle the blade like this and aim the force down. This reduces the stress that causes splits like this."

As he ran his finger down the long split I hadn't even noticed, I felt like an idiot. I'd completely forgotten that I'd been shown this technique before. How could I not have seen that?

"When you do an angle cut around the trunk, you end up with more of a point, which makes it easier to push into the ground. Also, look at the Y. It's uneven. You want the two branches that angle off to be at the same level so the cross pole will sit correctly in it."

Now it seemed so obvious. Okay, so I made a mess of my first shelter pole. Fine! I'll try again.

Thanking him for his helpful feedback, I trundled back into the woods, looking for another victim. This time, when I did find one, I applied my lessons and managed to sever the tree from its base without causing any more damage. I quickly trimmed off the branches that grew out from the two that formed the V-shape and brought the pole back to the shelter.

"We don't need it now. We're done," Javier snapped as he examined my pole. "You must learn to work faster."

I must have looked somewhat crushed, so he told me I could make the roof.

"Follow me. I will show you which leaves to use."

Jav took off through the bushes at his usual fast pace. Within seconds, the leaves had obscured his disappearing form and I charged after him so I wouldn't lose sight of him. I saw him standing at the side of the path, looking up. On seeing me, he pointed at the huge leaves overhead.

"Banana leaves. They are good for the top because they are waterproof. See? You can bend them easily."

Javier quickly chopped down a leaf to demonstrate the technique. "Ya, Judita?"

"Ya. How many should I get?"

My teacher looked at me as if I'd asked how many legs a chair should have. While I thought this had been a reasonable question, he obviously did not.

"How many? Enough to cover the roof!"

He quickly took off back through the bushes, leaving me on my own in front of the group of banana trees. I had the funny feeling that if they'd had tongues, they'd all be sticking out at me.

"Okay, I got this!" I set to work and managed to successfully cut a number of the large leaves without damaging them. Once I had as many as I could carry, I brought them back to the shelter frame, where I was shown how to layer them over the cross poles. At this point, I could see how simple this shelter was to construct, yet I knew if I'd had to do it on my own it wouldn't look anything like this. I'd end up buried beneath a big pile of banana leaves.

I noticed Olaff was working down by the water's edge and asked Javier what he was doing.

"Olaff is making us a bathing platform. You don't want to stand in the mud to shower, do you?"

Again, something like this hadn't even occurred to me. Perhaps I was still traumatized by that guy in the Tracker camp telling me it was time to lose some wood when I hardly knew how to whittle. I sighed, realizing that I was still way out of my element and wondered if I'd ever be a competent jungle woman.

We spent the rest of the day transferring our gear to the shelter and settling in. Despite the heat and the swarms of crazed mosquitoes, I was glad to be making the trek back and forth to the house because it enabled me to memorize the trail. While some jungle trails are well travelled and easy to see, others, like this one, are rarely used and overgrown. Even a few new leaves across the path can alter its appearance and create doubt in the mind, leading one to veer off the trail and get lost.

I had a special reason to be concerned about this, and an old memory began to bubble up to the surface of my consciousness.

As I'd previously mentioned, back in the early 90s I decided to work on getting my private pilot's licence. As I was studying for my undergraduate degree in electrical engineering, I was thinking about specializing in aircraft electrical systems. I sent away for a catalog from a school which offered some really interesting master's degree programs in avionics and spent many hours reading course descriptions and planning my studies.

"All very well to read about lift and drag," I told myself, "but far better to experience it and know how it feels in the body."

And that is how I ended up in a Cessna 152, crisscrossing back and forth across the English countryside. The movie, *Top Gun*, was very popular at the time, so I pretended my little Cessna was an F-14. Wearing my leather bomber jacket and David Clark headphones, I imagined tearing across the sky in a real jet.

One windy day as I was returning to base, the tower informed me that the runways had been changed and I was now to use the alternate landing strip approach which was ninety degrees to the south of the main paved runway. This meant landing on the grass at an angle, kind of like the way some crabs scuttle along.

In full *Top Gun* mode, I came in faster than I was supposed to in those conditions, sliding on the wet grass. But there, in the little cockpit, I was a Top Gun flying master, and I brought my 152 to a perfect stop in excellent form. Immediately, the grumpy woman who worked in the small air traffic control tower started berating me, which I suppose was deserved.

My flying instructor, on the other hand, who was an ex-Air Force pilot, smiled broadly and gave me two thumbs up. "Brilliant landing!

Don't let that old trout in the tower bring you down. Jolly good one, that!"

But my jolly good luck was about to run out. Working my way up to my final exams, I plotted my three-airport course for my solo navigation exam. I'd done this once before with my instructor sitting silently beside me, and I'd executed perfect maneuvers, returning back to base without incident.

I was on my way back to our little school, checking my map and lines of sight. I knew there was a small lake I needed to pass on my right, and this landmark would tell me I was nearly home.

One of the problems I had learning to fly in England was that the long stretches of green countryside were often featureless, or at least it seemed that way to me. Flying by sight means you ideally are looking for permanent features such as a motorway or a railway line, rather than something that might be moved like a tractor or a hay bale. From two or three thousand feet up, many of the features blended together, which could cause the novice flyer to become confused and lost.

Looking out of the plane's windows I saw the body of water off in the distance. I knew it should have been closer on my right than I was seeing, so I figured I'd tracked too far to the left and adjusted my course to the right. There is no need to do this if you are sure of your heading and follow it as you should, but that day I was sure that I was too far west and my compass must be off.

As I flew along, I suddenly felt a cold fear come over me as I realized I was flying over Windsor Castle, which was definitely forbidden airspace. A few moments later, I looked down and saw that I was over a very large runway and there was a jumbo jet waiting to take off. Oh dear. Heathrow Airport, one of the world's busiest airports. I was now costing them quite a lot of money in delayed take offs while my Cessna 152 putted overhead in very forbidden airspace.

I knew what I was supposed to do when I got lost: I was supposed to radio in, identify myself and let the controller know that I was aware of where I was so that they knew what to do and how to help. They could talk me back to safety and get me out of the jumbo's path.

But did I do this? No, I did not. Somehow I just knew I could get back to the airfield on my own. I still should have radioed in and talked to the control tower. I can't explain what came over me, but like the super jet landing in the wet grass, something took over me and I was determined to find my way back to the school on my own.

The gods of the skies were with me that day and I arrived back, making a perfect landing and then steering my little plane to the parking area. I got out and looked around, feeling smug. I did it! I had gotten away with it! My flying instructor came over and congratulated me for a successful return. The backslapping did not last long.

My name was being called from the small building that served as the flying school and office, and I saw the Chief Flying Instructor heading my way looking very angry.

"What's the matter with him?" asked my instructor, Scott.

"Um, gee, well, I guess we'll see." I must've looked horribly guilty because Scott's look changed from exultant to puzzled.

I was being motioned to come into the Chief's private office and I knew the game was up.

"What on earth were you doing out there? I have the Civil Aviation Authority on the phone and they want to have words with you."

"I, um, violated forbidden airspace and didn't radio in."

"What? Why? You knew what to do, didn't you? Where were you anyway?"

"Windsor Castle and Heathrow."

The Chief Instructor's eyes bugged out. "Here, speak to them."

The man from the CAA was quite firm and I was in trouble. I groveled and told him how I had become disoriented during my navigation exercise and found myself too far east, with my instinct being to get the hell out of there as fast as possible.

"How did you get back if you were lost?" the officer wanted to know.

"I can't explain it. I just followed my instinct and kept adjusting my course."

Long story short, I was let off the hook because I was still a student pilot. Had I already gained my license, I would've been in bigger trouble, possibly having the license suspended or taken away. Once the Chief Instructor realized that he was also not going to get in trouble, he relaxed a bit and asked me to tell him about my various flight segments.

"We knew you were doing well because we were getting reports from the other airports you landed at. And then you ended up back here as if nothing had gone wrong."

"Yeah, well, I know. But tell me something. How did they know where I'd landed? How did they track me back here?"

"They were tracking you on radar."

Really? Little old me? This'll make a great story someday. Someday.

Like that movie effect where people go back and forth in time and you see blurred waves as they vanish, I was once again standing on the overgrown trail, deep in the Peruvian Amazon jungle.

"Judita? Are you all right?" Javier was peering at me closely.

I laughed. "*Sí*, Jav. I'm just fine! I am really fine." I slapped a branch lovingly and made a vow to myself to hone my awareness skills so that I would always be able to find myself on the right path. Heathrow airspace was one thing, but being lost in a jungle this dense could be deadly.

CHAPTER 16

The Lord of the Forest

I loved our quiet camp far from the pueblo. The children were instructed not to go anywhere near the area and to leave me alone while I was there. As before, Jav and his nephew would leave me on my own for hours and this suited me just fine. I could wander around wearing nothing but my rubber boots, confident that I wasn't giving anyone an eyeful. Or maybe I was, but I no longer cared. The jungle was seeping into my being.

One day when the bites on my lower body were driving me insane I decided to sit on our bathing platform and put my legs in the water to cool them down. I was dressed and still wearing my boots, because I just couldn't be sure of what else was in that lagoon besides my itchy gams. I'd heard tales about worms or something equally icky that could burrow into the skin and lay eggs, and I'd already had enough of that kind of torture.

The water did a great job of cooling the rubber boots, which in turn soothed my legs. I was happy to just sit there and gaze around the lagoon at nothing in particular. I saw Olaff approaching from the direction of the house where he'd been for some time helping with various chores.

"That's not a good idea to be sitting there like that," he said seriously as he stood over me.

"Why not?"

"Because there are things in that water that can bite off your feet or legs."

My lassitude vanished instantly and I pulled my legs out of the water. "What? Like giant piranhas? I'm wearing thick rubber boots after all!"

"*No importa.* Doesn't matter. There are small crocodiles and things like that. They would look at your moving legs and think they were fish or something else good to eat. It really is not a good idea to dangle any body parts in water when you can't see the bottom."

Now that he mentioned it, I realized how murky the water was. Because of the near complete canopy there was a lot of shade in this area. Vegetation grew around the perimeters and greenery floated on the surface. Anything could be hiding down there.

"Thanks, Olaff. You came along at the right time."

As he walked back to adjust something on the shelter, I wondered if he and his uncle thought I was an idiot.

We continued with my ceremonial instruction work at night, picking up where we'd left off in Rio Momon. Sitting outside on a log, Jav drilled perfection into me as I added more songs and elements to the ceremony. The trees became my ceremonial participants and I would go around doing my *pasos* and *coreografía* with them as if they were people. I would stop at each one and sing and rattle as the beautiful fireflies illuminated our work.

Pasos is when the shaman walks around during the ceremony and sings to each participant. This usually involves some kind of energetic cleansing or healing with the shacapa depending on what the shaman sees in the person. The leaf rattle can be used to draw off negative energies around a person and then to bestow blessings.

Coreografía is usually reserved for special cases such as when the participant is very ill or lying on a bed during a healing ceremony and can't sit up. This particular procedure includes prayer along with shamanic healing. The shaman will kneel next to the person and raise his or her arms up to the heavens to implore the divine helping spirits, whether with prayer or a healing icaro, to come down to heal the unfortunate sufferer. Javier's path and tradition included both of these practices, but they are not part of every shaman's ceremonial toolbox.

We would often go back to the house for our meals since it was easier to cook there and store the food. It was also easier for Olaff to fish in the Napo River and prepare the meals on the back porch. During these times, I would get lessons in jungle lore and practices, something that made the entire apprenticeship very rich. I'd already experienced things such as learning how to make masato and taking part in a shared community task known as the *minga,* so I was always interested to learn more about day to day life for those who lived away from the conveniences of the city. What did they eat? Where did their food come from? What were their challenges? There were, of course, the ongoing discussions about sex that seemed to pop up at every opportunity. I considered these kinds of things to be the more mundane and practical side of jungle life.

Then, there were what we in the West might think of as only myths and legends, or perhaps just products of creative imaginations. But for the people who live here far away from the bustling practicalities of city life, there was truth to these stories. There are many who scoff at the need for the apprenticeship nowadays, but they are missing the fine pieces of the puzzle that make for incredibly deep work attended by the helping spirits we called the *doctorcitos*, or little doctors. There are other magical beings that can become part of a traditional ceremony, too. If you honor their ways and invite them in properly, they will come.

One morning at breakfast, the talk turned to Javier's grandfather, who had been a *banco* shaman. *Banco* means bench in Spanish, and this term referred to someone who had reached the pinnacle of their profession so as to be where the spirits could sit on him, or in other words, powerfully working though him. A *banco* was supposed to be capable of transcending the limits of the physical body in order to learn from the jungle spirits. My rational Western mind found some of these tales a little hard to believe, yet in a land where everyone believed in magic, who's to say what is possible or not? If many people believe in a magical being, for example, there is a good chance that there will be many sightings of that being and even interactions with it.

"*Abuelo* went into the river with the *yakuruna* to learn their medicine, and he didn't come out for eight days," Javier told me as he widened his eyes for emphasis.

"Wait. Who or what is a *yakuruna*?" I wanted to know.

"*Yaku* is Quechua for water. *Runa*, people. The *yakuruna* are the people who live in the river. They are magical beings who can teach you how to heal, but if you are not worthy, you will drown."

"Yeah, but how could your grandfather live in the river for so long?"

Javier looked at me as if he had to explain something very basic to a child, a look I was by now getting used to. "He was a *banco*. He had the power."

Okay, okay. No further questioning.

And then there was the *chullachaki* issue. The *chullachaki* was well known in the jungle as being the lord of the forest, a trickster and a teacher. Depending on who you spoke to, he was a shapeshifter who either had one deformed foot or one foot that was turned backwards thanks to an unfortunate incident in his own childhood. I was told that despite his amazing transformational abilities, his mismatched feet always gave him away.

"He can lure you far into the jungle, where you will get lost and never come out again!" Javier intoned dramatically.

I looked to Olaff for confirmation and he nodded. "Always look at the feet. If you see me or Javier out there, motioning you forward, make sure you look at the feet."

Okay, I could take this on board. "I sure hope he appears! I want to meet him," I declared.

Javier looked at me, then at his uncle, and replied, "Some advanced shamans may look for him because he can teach them many healing techniques, but otherwise it's not a good idea. You don't know what you're saying."

"Maybe, but isn't that why I'm here? I want to experience what the jungle has to offer."

"Well, the *chullachaki* usually appears on Saturday nights, and all day on Sundays, so we'll have to make sure we're safe here in the house then," Jav declared.

I'd also heard this when we were at the Jivaro camp, but it just seemed odd to me. I looked from Olaff to Javier to Uncle Alfredo and Aunt Imelda. All of them nodded solemnly. I just couldn't shake the feeling that they were all in on some grand joke at my expense.

"Yes, you will have to tear down your camp every Saturday afternoon, move back into the house until it's safe, then you can set up back out there again on Monday," Alfredo said.

This did not make any sense to me at all. Why would the lord of the forest suddenly show up according to a modern calendar created by lowly humans? And why weekends? I began to be suspicious, thinking it must have to do with an excuse to quit work and come back into the village for a rest or something.

"Well, what if I stay out there by myself? I'm not afraid of him!" I retorted.

"He will lure you out in the jungle to have sex with you!" Javier responded with great flourish.

"Oh, brother!" I thought to myself as I tried not to roll my eyes. If I wasn't in constant danger from blood sucking insects and hungry jungle animals, I now had to be on the lookout for a mythical being who wanted to carry me off into the bushes for a bit of nookie. I decided to let the matter drop until I could do more research on the subject.

And then of course, the conversation turned once more to everyone's favorite subject: sex. Those who live in closeness with this very virile force that is the Amazon jungle tend to reflect its energy through expressing this most basic human need as often as possible. Men father children with as many partners as they can, and it is considered good to have many children and to spread one's seed far and wide.

Javier's grandfather, at eighty-nine years old, was apparently a big hit with many of the young women of the village for his incredible virility. I asked Jav how it was possible that someone of that age could still be servicing healthy young girls without the usual age-related issues.

"*Cortezas*. We have many plants here that are like your Viagra."

Now my being from a very youth-centered culture, I had trouble imagining why these cute fifteen-year olds would want to have sex with someone who could be their great grandfather. I'd already seen that huge age differences were not an issue between partners in the jungle, but there were plenty of very handsome young men around to choose from. Why would the girls go for the geezers?

I voiced this question out loud and my four companions were happy to elaborate further.

"As you're starting to notice, Judita, the men and women of the jungle have very traditional roles. The men are generally the main wage earners, and as they age they accrue things like houses and goods and are usually seen as more well off than younger men," Javier started off.

Imelda continued. "Our girls tend to become pregnant at a very early age so they seek someone who can support them and their children. Since there are fewer money-making opportunities for women in the jungle, young girls seek out the older men who have the resources they are looking for. In turn, because these young women are very fertile and can produce a lot of children, this gives the man more esteem in the village."

I looked around as everyone nodded in agreement. It was such a different culture than the one I'd been raised in, so I was grateful for the opportunity to learn first-hand from those I was sharing space with. It helped me understand the world that the plant spirit medicines had come from and I felt that I was richer for it.

Neighbors came by to gossip, and more children came by to stare at me. My little shadow, Jhony, was there with one of his friends who seemed transfixed with me and the various things I wore. He was constantly rolling up my sleeve and touching my watch, then he'd poke me in various places as if to see if I felt any different than anyone else. I tried to be patient, but in the humid heat with my flaring bug bites, sometimes it was just not possible. "Go away!" I wished silently. "Please go away and leave me alone for a little while."

Javier knew I was getting a little frustrated with all the attention, so he called everyone outside. The children followed as he sauntered off with some of the women to help them with an errand, and I sank onto the floor with Olaff to take an after-breakfast nap. Olaff was suffering from a cold, so was taking some badly needed down time to rest. I just felt lazy and soon fell into one of those dreamy dozes where you're not sure if you're awake or asleep.

Although I was lying on the floor in Alberto's house, another part of me was also somewhere out in the jungle. I heard my name being called, and recognized the voice as belonging to someone I knew, yet in the dreamlike haze I was in I couldn't tell exactly who it was.

"Where are you?" I called.

"Here! Over here! Just behind the tree."

And when I reached the tree, there was no one there. My invisible friend would call my name again and again, and I would find myself going farther into the dense greenery. I was getting tired, so when I found myself in a small clearing, I sat down to rest. I realized I was lost and hoped I could find my way back. As I stood up to go, I heard laughter ring out around me. It seemed to be coming from all directions at once. It sounded like someone was coming through the bushes towards me. I tried to run but my feet felt like they were encased in concrete. I couldn't think anymore; it was as if I'd been drugged.

The bushes parted and an unfamiliar being appeared before me.

"Hello, Judy. I've been waiting for you."

The feet! Oh, my God! *The feet!*

Olaff was looking at me with a very concerned look on his face. "Are you all right? You were screaming about feet or something like that."

I sat up quickly and looked around. "I guess I was dreaming. I was in the jungle and I think the *chullachaki* was drawing me further and further in. I couldn't get away!"

Olaff looked at me curiously. "How did you know it was the *chullachaki*?"

"I saw his feet! One of them was pointing backwards! Thank goodness it was just a dream!"

Or was it? I was here in the Peruvian Amazon jungle, a place where the people believe in such magical beings that can shapeshift and live under water. I had declared out loud that I wanted to meet one of them. Perhaps I just had.

When Javier came back from his errand, Olaff reported what had happened. I shrugged it off, but my teacher peered at me closely, looking me up and down and shaking his head.

"That was not a dream. You asked him to come and he came to you. Now he knows where to find you! Come. I have to take you down to the river to break the spell."

Although I insisted I was fine, I still felt like I was caught in a dream.

"You see how you must be careful with what you say here? He tried to take you into his world. Now, come with me!" He grabbed me by the upper arm and dragged me out of the house, pushing me along quickly in front of him down to the river. Once at the bank he told me to take off my shoes but leave everything else on. He kicked off his flip flops and waded in with me.

"You weren't wearing your shoes while you were sleeping, but the rest of your clothing is bewitched. In you go!"

The water was cold, with a swift current. Javier indicated that I needed to submerge myself quickly as he held onto my hand. As I hesitated, he pushed me in. I came up spluttering, and he pushed me down several more times. I heard him uttering incantations, but with all the splashing and submerging I couldn't tell what he was saying. Finally, he pulled me to my feet and looked closely at me again.

"You are now free of the *chullachaki's* spell!" he informed me. "Come, you can change your clothes first, but then we must smoke *mapachos*."

With there being no mirrors, I could only imagine what I looked like. Several people passing by stared as we headed back to Uncle Alfredo's house where the others were waiting anxiously for our return.

"Judita is fine. She must learn to be more careful and not be so foolish again." He looked at me pointedly.

"One question, Jav. Why did you have to submerge me in the river like that? To free me from the spell?"

"Water is a pure element that is known for its cleansing properties. It's kind of like a baptism where the water makes one new again. We can use it the same way to help break spells and many other things you will learn about in time. It's important to act fast and with great vigor in order to overcome the enchantment."

As I peeled off my wet clothing, I wondered if I was still dreaming. One minute we were talking about how a powerful, mysterious being only shows up at weekends, then suddenly I'm being dunked in the river. With all my previous magical experiences, I'd never encountered something like this before. I wasn't afraid, but I was determined to learn more and be more careful from that moment on. And it wasn't even a weekend!

Javier and I continued with our nighttime training sessions. As in the Rio Momon camp, our ceremonial area was situated a few yards away from our sleeping quarters. We sat side-by-side on a large fallen tree trunk which I'd covered with a rain poncho for extra padding.

Ayahuasca can be very strong at times, yet so far in my training ceremonies I hadn't experienced any of the *mareaciones*--the dizziness and nausea which often precedes the vomiting and visions. I know we were using smaller doses than for the ceremonies at Sacha Wasi, but here we were working with a very different intent. These journeys were not so much for inner self exploration as those were, but rather for me to connect to my helping spirits and learn the elements of the ceremonies. I needed to be able to keep a clear head and be very present in order to receive the teachings and be able to remember them. However, if I closed my eyes, even with the small dose I would enter into beautiful gardens filled with flowers and plants outlined with light. When I'd reopen them, I'd see the fabulous fireflies flitting around our little area. As with my enchanted dream, sometimes it was hard to know what was real.

Javier made it clear that we weren't drinking the medicine for its visionary properties. We sought the wisdom that came from the plant spirit herself, the one we called Madre, or Mother.

"Visions are usually a distraction," Javier told me early on. "They can be fun and maybe sometimes tell you things, but it's not what we seek because there is so much more. When you are able to hear the voice of Madre, this is when your life will change."

Our use of this sacred plant concoction was for me to receive teachings directly from Madre. While I was Javier's student, he pointed out that I was really a student of the plant spirit herself.

"As long as you continue to walk in a good way, she will teach you, because there will come a time when you won't need me anymore."

I must've looked alarmed because he continued, "Ya, Judita. It is the goal of every teacher that their students be able to fly without them one day. Don't worry," he patted my shoulder, "it won't be for a long time. You have much to learn."

While the idea of no longer needing my teacher seemed sad even at this early stage, I realized he was right. I had to develop my own relationship with the spirits, just as he had. So while my physical body certainly suffered many discomforts, I acknowledged how lucky I was to be here, and how precious this experience was.

Javier had told me that my graduation for this first phase of my training would occur sometime while we were here in his pueblo. He told me my exam would be in the form of a ceremony where I had no input from my him at all.

As the days passed, Javier added more elements to the work, which were now mostly about refining each part of the ceremonial protocol. As I became more proficient, he began to take on more of an observer's role. There were nights when he appeared to have fallen asleep on me, yet the very second I messed up even one small part of the ceremony, he was right on me. There's no deceiving a jungle shaman!

"Your wedding to Madre Naturaleza is also coming soon. You will need to make your wedding garments yourself."

"What do I make them from? We didn't buy any material or anything."

Again, that look. "Plants. When you marry Madre Naturaleza you wear things from her, from the earth."

"How do I make clothes out of plants, Javier?"

"I don't know. You will have to figure that out for yourself," came his reply as he walked away.

"Like heck you don't know!" I spluttered under my breath. "You know. You're just being difficult. Fine for you; you know how to do these things. I've never made clothing out of plants before. Oh gawd. How am I supposed to do this?"

What also didn't help was that, as back in the Jivaro camp, there still was never any certainty about anything. If one night he would announce we'd start ceremony at a particular time, he'd suddenly show up hours earlier and ask me if I was ready right then. Other nights he would tell me we'd sing together only to roll over and feign sleep during the ceremony.

In many of the Native North American traditions, Coyote is said to be the trickster. I'd never fully understood this, but now I believed I was starting to get the gist of what this meant. My teacher was proving to be a coyote teacher because that is what I needed in order to get yanked out of my logical thoughts of how things should be. As soon as I was sure I'd figured something out he'd pull the rug out from underneath me again to throw me off balance. When I confronted him with this once he said,

"You must go out of balance at times in order to swing into balance. Do you understand this, Judita?"

"I think so. It makes sense."

"No, it does not make sense!" he said with some asperity. "You must stop trying to make sense here! There is no sense in shamanism because it is outside the boundaries of logic and how we think things should be. This is what keeps you trapped in the physical world."

Nodding, I decided not to worry about this. I knew I had a scientist's mind that looked for patterns and numbers that added up. None of that was valid here.

Although we were much farther from the markets of Iquitos than we had been with the Jivaro, I must admit that I enjoyed the food here in Rio Napo far more than at our previous camp. That horrible, preserved fish was nowhere in sight! Olaff was able to provide us with fresh fish from the river and cook it over a little grill improvised with bricks and iron rods.

I also learned a valuable lesson about the *víveres* that we'd brought with us.

"Of course we must keep some for our own use, but we don't give the rest away all at once," Jav said. "They are great tools for bartering. You will see."

I had noticed that he kept a stock of bulk items like sugar and rice hidden from view and had meant to ask him about this. I now took this opportunity.

"I just figured you were hiding the food we brought so it wouldn't get stolen."

"Yes, that is true. These things are like money here. Sometimes we get to trade the dried goods for fresh food. This is important when you are far away from the markets."

Javier's explanation played out shortly afterwards, when a neighbor offered us a fresh chicken in exchange for some sugar and rice. The bird's extraordinary size—about that of a large turkey--fascinated me.

"This is a chicken? It's huge! I've never seen a chicken this size before!"

"Is camoungo." Makes sound like ca-MOONG-go, ca-MOONG-go," Javier demonstrated as Olaff tried to stifle yet another smile.

"It's not really a chicken," Olaff added, then shrugged. "We just call it jungle chicken sometimes."

Giant or not, the fresh poultry was also a welcome change. I'd had the good fortune to enjoy game meat while I lived in Europe and had developed a fondness for birds such as pheasant and grouse. I found the camoungo to be similar to grouse, which can be somewhat gamey for many people. Grilled over the open fire, and served along with rice and yucca, it was a delicious jungle feast.

Chewing the remnants of meat from one of the legs, Javier eyed my empty plate. "It looks like you enjoyed that."

"I did. I can see now see what you meant about bartering. But I have a question--"

My teacher let out an audible groan. "Not another one!"

Ignoring his comment, I continued. "How did they know we had sugar and rice though?"

"Oh they know. We all know, because we all carry *víveres* in some form when we go to the jungle. They may not know specifically what you have, but they know you'll have something that they need. Watch and see what the locals do when we go to the next place. They'll all gather around and try to see what you have that might interest them.

They might ask questions, but you don't tell them anything. Sometimes they even compete with each other, and it can get kind of fierce."

Olaff chimed in. "Yes, so it's a good idea to keep your things out of sight. Even when you do trade, it's best to be discrete. It gives you more bartering power. You don't want to give your whole bag of rice away to the first hunter who comes along with meat."

I let that sink in, trying to imagine a scenario that I hadn't experienced until now. I'd never had to barter for any kind of food before, not even in grade school. My mom had packed good lunches for my sister and me, and I liked pretty much everything that I was given. In a culture where food was provided by my parents or a nearby, well-stocked grocery store, I never knew that this wasn't how everyone around the world lived. Once again, I felt humbled to be sharing this unique experience.

The next day being a Saturday, Javier announced that we would pull up our little camp for the weekend in case the *chullachaki* decided to come back for his foolish apprentice. Despite my recent dream or whatever it was, I was fine with remaining out in the jungle away from the house. It was just quieter and more peaceful, a place where I didn't feel like a zoo exhibit.

But knowing I'd never win any arguments with Jav, I reluctantly packed up whatever of my gear I'd need for the next day or two. I knew that even spiritual teachers needed a break from their students at times, and Javier had already dedicated a lot of his days to my training. Olaff also worked very hard providing us with our meals and tending to the handyman chores when he wasn't out scouting for unusual specimens for his biology studies. Begrudgingly, I admitted to myself that my two caretakers deserved a nice break even if I felt I could keep going.

Jav had warned me that the bug situation would be much worse here, and he wasn't kidding! If I had thought I was suffering in Rio Momon, that had been a fiesta compared to here in Rio Napo. I knew I shouldn't scratch my tortured skin, but at times I just couldn't stop myself. The worst times were when I'd pull off my rubber boots. Inside the boots my legs would sweat and this seemed to greatly aggravate the discomfort. Both lower legs and forearms would just start to throb insanely at the same time along with other areas like my back and abdomen. I wondered if this was what it felt like to be electrocuted. I was so obviously uncomfortable that Javier conferred with his uncle and they soon came up with a local remedy—a grapefruit! I must have looked doubtful as Jav handed me the two cut halves.

"Squeeze a little of the juice on the itchy areas and then rub the flesh over your skin. This should help dry things out and you won't be so itchy."

Still doubtful since none of my commercial remedies had worked, I dutifully followed his instructions. Since I'd been clawing at my poor burning skin, it was especially sensitive to the acidic juice. I hopped around the living space as I waited for the burning sensation to subside, much to the amusement of those present.

On top of this, I seemed to have picked up Olaff's cold, so my entire head was all stuffed up. Yes, I was miserable. Had I been able to rest in peace I might have felt happier, but as soon as the kids realized we were back in the house, they again descended on us en masse. I saw Jav speak briefly to Uncle Alfredo, and then he turned to me.

"Tío says you can go sleep in his room by yourself for a while. Tía Imelda has gone to another village to visit her sister so she won't be back for a while," Javier relayed, using the Spanish terms for uncle and aunt.

Alfredo's room was really more like a small storeroom. The house floor plan consisted of the one main living space, which served as a dining area, bedroom and living room, depending on the time of day. The smaller room was formed by two interior walls set at a ninety-degree angle with a small opening for a door. Large bags of dried food and clothing lined the walls, while other bags dangled from crossbeams in the ceiling. In fact, there was so much stuff in there that there was barely enough space on the floor for my mat. It was small space, but for the next few hours it was my space, and this is exactly what I needed.

Uncle Alfredo shooed everyone out of the house, and the three men went down to the river. Jav and Olaff washed out some clothing, then the latter and Alfredo stayed to fish for a while. I huddled under my blanket and prayed no one would come in and poke their head around the door. I got my wish to recharge my batteries with a long nap, so by the time the three of them arrived back I was in a much better mood.

Alfredo and Olaff had a lot of luck at the river, bringing back three types of fish with names unfamiliar to me: *sherui, karachama*, a type of catfish, and *shuyo*, a predatory wolf fish. None of them looked very attractive! Alfredo and Javier took off on some errand, leaving Olaff to set up the grill and get lunch going for us. I wandered out behind the house where he was watching over the small wood fire and sat down.

"Are you enjoying our journeys?" he asked.

"Yes, this is quite an adventure. But sometimes I feel so out of place. I see how easily you guys move here and I feel like a klutz. Thank you for taking care of me. I'm not used to it."

While Javier was my teacher and general caretaker, Olaff tended to be the one to pass along practical tips for jungle survival that I dutifully filed away both in my mind and field notebook. He was the one who patiently taught me how to tie the ends of a hammock so that the rope would not slip. He was also the one to tell me to make sure I shook out my shoes and boots every morning before putting them on.

"It's best if you can store them upside down before you retire for the night. If you have socks you can stuff them inside too. That will keep out the spiders and other bugs that are looking for a safe place to hide."

In all my years of camping, I had somehow never heard this, nor had I ever found anything hiding in my shoes.

"But surely when you go to put your boots on they'll get squished?" I asked naively.

"Maybe, but you really don't want to put your foot inside if there's a big tarantula or scorpion in there, do you?"

I must have looked horrified, but the young man just smiled. In contrast to his exuberant and larger than life uncle, Olaff was fairly quiet and serious. Intelligent and studious, Olaff loved South American football and was himself a keen player. He was always looking for opportunities to help him provide for his family, but he wanted to work for it; he never asked for anything like a handout. I was so glad he was with us rather than jungle gigolo Geraldo.

Jav and his uncle returned from their errand just in time for lunch. Since I love cooking and trying new foods, I helped Olaff cook the *sherui* and the *shuyo* fishes. They were so unlike the usual salmon and halibut I frequently ate at home, yet they were every bit as tasty to me despite their looks. I always joked that I would likely eat just about anything that was grilled over a flame or coals.

"You want to go meet my grandmother after lunch?" Jav asked me between bites of the delicious fish.

"Sure! I'm ready to get out and about for a bit."

"Olaff and Tío are going back to the river to get more fish."

"Why don't you go fishing too, Javier?" I asked with a mischievous look in my eyes. While I knew my teacher was well capable of jungle survival skills and feeding himself, I saw that he was also quite happy to turn these kinds of tasks over to others while he enjoyed jawboning and spinning tales.

"No, I am very busy today and must see many people. Let's go!"

I turned to exchange a smile with Olaff. We both knew that had been a really feeble excuse.

As soon as we left the house, several children came barreling towards us enthusiastically. Jhony ran up and attached himself to me, looking up with adoring eyes. He was carrying an empty two-liter bottle of Coca Cola in one hand and grabbed onto me with his free hand. Despite how I felt about being constantly poked and examined, I really loved these sweet jungle children. Very few of them had foot coverings of any kind, and most were wearing clothes that in my country would have long ago been relegated to the rag pile.

One little boy who was hovering at the edge of the group seemed to be in pain. I'd seen him at the house before, but now it appeared as if he had stepped on something sharp and was having difficulty walking. Noticing that he seemed to be favoring his left foot, I nudged Javier and asked him to find out what the problem was. After speaking to the boy, whose name was Julito, Jav turned to me.

"He has a cut in his big toe that is infected, so it is causing him a lot of pain. Do you have anything that might help?"

"Let me run back to the house and see."

Rummaging in my bags, I grabbed some acetaminophen and individually packaged wet towelettes. It wasn't much, but it was a start. We stopped in at Julito's house, where we found his mother and some neighbors making farina. Although the women were far younger than I was, they already looked old and defeated. Javier introduced me and explained why we'd come. I gave his mother the meager items.

"The towelettes should be used to clean the wound, and the pills are for the infection and pain," I instructed. "It's really important to keep that area clean."

Secretly, I wondered if we could do more for little Julito. Although I am not a medically trained professional, I thought it seemed like the wound was full of pus because it was red, swollen, and quite warm. I thought of the times as a child when I had things like this, my mother, who was an emergency room nurse, would clean the affected area well, then lance it gently to drain out the pus, clean it well again and apply some kind of cream before bandaging it up. This usually took care of the issue within a day, two at the most. Would something like this work here?

Again, I was being confronted by the odd dichotomy that while I was here to learn how to heal with plants, the people would ask for the Western medicines I carried with me rather than seeking out the medicinal plants from the large pharmacy that surrounded them. I remembered being told back at the Jivaro camp that making plant medicines can take a long time from start to finish, and so if a quicker alternative is available, this is what most folks preferred. I can't say I blamed them!

We continued on to Javier's grandmother's house. Abuelita was ninety-two years old, short, and rail thin. Her white hair, pulled back into a bun, still bore traces of the youthful black coloring she'd had many years ago. Wearing a white blouse and a blue print skirt with an uneven hem, she also was barefoot like so many of her neighbors.

As the boys followed us into the house, I noticed there were no girls around, and voiced this to Jav. He put the question to his relative, who did not speak Spanish, then turned back to me, eyes twinkling in delight.

"All the girls are in the kitchen helping their mother make masato. Maybe you should go help them and pick up some tips."

"Ooh, don't tempt me!"

Javier gave his grandmother a quick synopsis of my love for the intoxicating yucca beverage and she turned to me and smiled.

"She is offering you some *miel de abeja*," Javier told me. "Special jungle honey. It's good for making medicine. If you want some, I can tell her and we'll have to come back for it in a day or two."

"Absolutely! I would love some of that honey!"

Truth be told, I was dying for something sweet. I missed my occasional treats and the delicious ice creams in Iquitos made from local fruits. A little honey certainly would be welcome.

We bid Abuela *adiós* and started down the stairs leading to the ground. I heard something clank against the wood behind me and turned to see Jhony's empty plastic soda bottle bounce down the stairs. He had started to follow us, when he suddenly fell backwards on the landing and began shaking and thrashing wildly. I remembered Javier telling me he had rather severe epilepsy, so I realized he was now having a bad seizure.

Throwing down my bag, I knelt next to the boy and managed to get him onto his side so he wouldn't swallow or bite his tongue. I held him in a protective embrace that allowed him to move but not be injured as his arms and legs flailed out from his body. Eventually, the seizure stopped and he flopped exhausted on the wooden porch. He looked up at me with a sad face full of shame, as if his affliction made him a bad boy. I tried to reassure him that it was okay, but he ran off crying down the path. I felt like joining him.

Looking sadly at Javier, I told him that it felt weird for me to be the pseudo nurse in the village. There was no dispensary or medical professional in Nuevo Progreso, although there were shamans like Javier who could provide limited care when they were available. When I'd first started learning about shamanism, I'd read that there were places on our planet that didn't have even simple facilities for basic medical care. Was it really possible that areas existed where the only care was given by someone who could see spirits and make up plant-based medicines? Yes, it was possible, and I was right in the middle of one, using the commercial medications that I'd brought with me. I shook my head in disbelief at the contradiction and kept on walking.

CHAPTER 17

Mermaid Tales and Other Body Parts

We continued back on the path towards Uncle Alfredo's house. While the people who lived in the pueblos have unquestionably hard and busy lives, they also made sure they took time out to socialize. Unless one was truly in a hurry, I didn't see anyone just going directly from point A to point B. As one walked along, doors would open, people would greet each other, conversations began, and plans might even change. I watched my teacher flourish in his element. This was his village and he seemed to know everyone.

A group of three or four men was coming our way along a narrow path. They were carrying what looked to be small monkeys hanging upside down from the sticks they were tied to. These men were hunters, and the monkeys were dead and ready to be sold for food.

The men greeted Javier heartily and he introduced me. A fast-paced conversation ensued, and I recognized enough of the words to know they were trying to get Javier to buy one of their unfortunate primate catches. He turned and gave me a questioning look.

"They are offering us *mono* in exchange for some of our *viveres*. Would you eat monkey meat? It's been smoked."

I had never eaten monkey meat, and quite frankly, had never planned to. While I didn't have much experience with our distant relatives, I considered them to be like dogs and cats with regard to eating them. It just didn't feel right. But that was in Southern California. I was now far away in a remote Peruvian jungle village where the laws and customs were different. People had to eat, and they ate whatever they were able to catch. This was not the time for me to give a lecture to native hunters about how incorrect it was to eat sweet little monkeys.

I nodded.

The hunters followed us back to the house and Jav brought out the agreed upon exchange. I tried to see how much sugar and rice he'd given them in exchange for one of the smoked monkeys because I had no idea of what I'd do in that situation. I was absolutely certain, however, that he'd driven a hard bargain and that they didn't get one more grain of rice than agreed on.

"So, Jav, how do you know how much to trade? I'm guessing you'd give them more for the monkey than say, for a small fish, huh?"

"Ya, Judita. You just learn what's a fair exchange over time. Now you can really see why it is important to bring such things into the jungle with you, can't you?"

Yep. I totally understood this now.

Olaff and Uncle Alfredo arrived back shortly after we did, carrying a number of river fish. They were delighted at the smoked meat and like Javier, looked in askance at me.

"She said she'd eat *mono*!" Jav declared.

"Really?" Olaff seemed surprised.

"Look, guys, I'm here with you to learn your culture. Not just to learn it, but to live it while I'm here. Now, I admit this isn't something I'd go looking for, but if you eat it, then I'll join you."

"I think we should save it for breakfast and cook the fish while it's fresh," Alfredo suggested.

Given the lack of electricity or any means to keep meat cold, we agreed to follow his suggestion. Olaff and Alfredo dealt with wrapping up the poor primate for the night, then turned their focus to dinner.

This being another off night as far as my training went, we were invited to visit with one of Javier's cousins who was also named Alfredo. To avoid confusing him with his father who was also present, we referred to him as just Al. Al brought out a *preparado* presented in an old two-liter bottle that looked as if it would spring a leak at any moment. Knowing that these concoctions were made up for specific purposes, I asked him what this one was for. He suddenly looked embarrassed and looked down at the ground while the others shuffled uncomfortably. I knew immediately that this meant it had to be one of the aphrodisiac potions. I wanted to giggle, but instead just smiled and held up my hand to let Al know he didn't have to answer.

The five of us sat outside on plastic chairs and passed the bottle around. A couple of other local men wandered by and joined us for a visit. Looking around, I wondered where all the women were, and queried this out loud.

"Oh, they're all in the house tending to the chores and the children. See?" Al turned around and pointed to his wife who was waving happily at us out of a window.

Once again, I considered the fate of the local women who seemed to get stuck with all the domestic chores, while their partners sat around with a bottle of booze and spun stories.

Javier peered at me after he'd taken a swig from the *preparado* and passed it to Olaff. "Do you feel unsafe sitting here with just men and no women around?"

I shook my head. "No, I'm used to it, actually," I replied without explaining as I stretched my arm out to receive the bottle and take a small sip before passing it to Uncle Alfredo. I briefly thought of my professional musician days when I'd party right along with all my bandmates and sound crew who were all men. If they gave me any nonsense I'd just give right back to them!

While I could put away a decent amount of beer, wine or certain spirits, aguardiente didn't always agree with me, and I was being cautious about how much I was imbibing. For me, it was one of those drinks where I don't feel the drunk crash coming like I can with other alcohol. One sip too many and suddenly I could be on the ground. I also didn't know what all the infused ingredients were as there was no label on the bottle. It was definitely a homemade job, so I was going to err on the side of caution.

A full moon rose into the dark jungle night, bathing everything with an ethereal silver glow. I felt comfortable with these men, who were getting more animated with each round. Talk turned to local lore, something that I was very interested in. Because the *sirena*—mermaid— makes many appearances in the Peruvian Amazon tales, and since many of these men were fishermen who spent a lot of time on the river, I decided to ask if any of them had seen one. Several heads nodded vigorously in response.

"I saw one once. She was very beautiful!" Al told us.

"Really?" I was fascinated.

"Oh, yes. It's true!" he affirmed.

I leaned in. "Please tell me about it."

"Well, one day I was out on the river fishing in my canoe as usual. I saw a beautiful blonde woman half submerged in the water. I couldn't see her lower body so I thought maybe she was a *turista* or something. Since she was so gorgeous I just sat and watched her. Then, when she saw me she dove into the water. Suddenly, a whirlpool formed near me. It was very powerful and I knew I was in danger. I quickly rowed towards the bank and grabbed onto an overhanging tree branch where

I hung on for my life. I tell you; I prayed to God to help me. I was so scared!"

"Wow! What happened next?"

"As soon as I said *Dios*, the whirlpool stopped and I was able to get out of the water. But that night, when I was asleep, she appeared In my dreams and told me that had I not uttered the name of God I would have been doomed! I would have been taken down to the underwater world to live with her as her husband."

Several of the others who had joined us nodded in unison as they also reported seeing mermaids while they were out fishing. I checked in with my gut instinct for any signs of what my dad used to quaintly refer to as horse hockey, but it didn't feel as if they were trying to reel me in with a tall tale.

"I've seen a *sirena*, too," Javier chimed in. " It was during the early days of my own apprenticeship. I was by a lake in the jungle and I saw this stunning woman on the other side, on the far banks. I was instantly filled with lust for her because I hadn't had a woman in two years because of all the plant diets. When she saw me looking at her, she vanished!" He snapped his fingers with a "poof!" for emphasis.

"Was that it?" I wanted to know.

"No. I could not get her out of my mind. I tell you; I was obsessed with her! Even in the night she would come into my dreams. My teachers started to notice how distracted I was , so I told them about the woman by the lake. They knew right then that she had enchanted me, so they had to use their magic to remove her spell."

I thought again about how a strong enough group belief can result in true miracles and magic. Our whole human history is filled with myths and legends, and each culture has their own versions. While some of these tales may seem rather incredible, how can we be really certain that they did not exist in some form? I rather wanted to believe in a little bit of magic myself.

I decided to press on and see if there had been any sightings of other beings such as the *yakuruna* or the *chullachaki*. The aguardiente-based drink and the silvery landscape were leading us into another world, a world where one of these beings could slip out of the shadows at any moment.

"I've seen the *chullachaki!*" Javier declared, then added with a laugh, "and so has Judita!"

All eyes focused on me and I shifted uncomfortably. I still wasn't convinced that I'd had a real encounter with the lord of the forest himself, despite my teacher's efforts to break the spell by dunking me in the river.

Al took another swig of the mystery *preparado* and turned to me. "Now it's your turn to tell us about it!"

I looked at Javier who indicated I should go ahead and speak. "Well, I'm not exactly sure I did really see him. I was taking a nap and I dreamt that someone was calling me farther into the jungle. But I did see his feet, and one was turned backwards."

Al settled back and the others straightened up.

"It was not just a dream!" Javier retorted with emphasis. "My student here called him in because she said she wanted to meet him. 'No, I'm not afraid of him,' she said. 'I'll sit out in the jungle alone so I can meet him,' she said."

A few of the men gasped and the bottle went back around quickly. I was beginning to wonder exactly how foolish I'd been.

"No one wants to meet the *chullachaki* unless they are a *banco*," declared Uncle Alfredo. "He's dangerous!"

I reached my hand out again for the now near empty bottle. "Okay, I hear you guys. This is all new to me and I sure have a lot to learn." Six heads nodded in unison.

"Judita is a good student," Javier declared. "She is always writing, writing, writing in her notebooks."

Olaff smiled at me. He was also a student, so he had told me that it was a good thing that I was taking such extensive field notes. In fact, I had been carrying around not one, but two thick notebooks. One was strictly for the teachings such as the icaros and medicine recipes. The other was for personal thoughts.

Somehow, this led into a talk about writing articles about jungle explorations for magazines such as *National Geographic*. The men emphasized that no one has covered this area because it was so remote. Olaff, the future scientist and jungle explorer, became very animated about this topic.

"It's always Brazil, never the Peruvian Amazon. And always the same areas in Peru like the Sacred Valley."

By now, it was obvious that the alcohol was taking effect. All the heads nodded vehemently yet again.

"Ya, there are no roads, so those crews want to take the easy routes," declared a man named Ignacio. "I've seen more than many of those so-called explorers, but they never come here."

I had no doubt this was true for those who lived here. As the moon continued to rise and the aguardiente took a firmer hold, I began to wonder if I could actually lead a team of explorers into this remote area in order to write for *National Geographic*. After all, I already had knowledgeable guides in place and I spoke the language. Yes, I could see the article now. Judy Lemon, Explorer in Residence. I'd have to put in a lot of time to become the area expert, of course, but I was going to be here for a while over the years as I trained to be a *vegetalista*. Hmm, who knows? Anything is possible if you can dream it.

After visiting for another hour, everyone stood up to head back to their houses. It was Saturday night, so we had to be on the lookout for the shapeshifting trickster who might suddenly appear and try to lure us to our doom, or at least a bit of jungle nookie. Between the otherworldly moonlight and the alcohol, I had the distinct sensation that there was indeed someone, or something out there waiting for us. Fortunately, we made it back to Alfredo's without being accosted, although I secretly felt a little disappointed. I knew I was in good company with these capable jungle men, so I would have been open to something amazing happening.

Upon entering the house, we heard strange noises coming from the small room that I had used as a private napping space. Without hesitation, Alfredo plunged in, and we heard a lot of banging and crashing before he emerged holding a now motionless rat by the tail.

"He was eating my papayas! Now something can eat him!" Alfredo marched firmly to the back door and flung the unfortunate rodent out into the night.

The next morning was another day of rest in Nuevo Progreso. We were all supposed to go out to help Olaff fish, but Javier didn't feel like it, so I didn't get to go either because he had other tasks for me to do. I thought back to when I was a child, my dad would take my sister and me on day long fishing trips. He had an old, low power outboard motor that he would attach to small rental boats. We would spend hours on this or that lake or bay, but not once did I ever feel so much as a tug on my line! I had never caught a fish and would've liked to catch my first one in the Napo River.

"Come, Judita! We're going to Abuela's house to get your honey!" Jav announced as he took me by the arm and headed down the path we'd taken the previous day.

We hadn't gone far when Jhony appeared and immediately grabbed my left hand. I was relieved to see that he'd seemed to have forgotten about his seizure the day before.

Javier's grandmother seemed a bit surprised to see us again so soon. Apparently when she offered me the honey, it meant that she or someone else had to go out and get it, so we hadn't given her enough time. I suspected the visit was really more of an excuse to get out of fishing than anything else. She said she'd send word when it was available.

We found Olaff had already returned with a few fish by the time we got back. "We're having fish and monkey meat for breakfast!" he declared proudly as he held up both items.

The smoked *mono* was quite dark and very rich. Even for someone who enjoyed strong game meat, I found it hard to eat a large quantity of the chewy flesh. The meats were accompanied by several of Alfredo's papayas, which helped offset the intense flavor. I enjoyed the food, but I had begun to think I'd kill for a salad. While fruits were plentiful, I didn't see many vegetables on my journeys away from the city. Occasionally you might see the odd, sad looking carrot or tomato, but the leafy greens like spinach that I loved so much were just not to be found.

While most of the jungle people were very generally hearty and well adapted to their environment, I could also see evidence of vitamin deficiencies, particularly in their teeth. With no leafy greens or dairy products, they wouldn't be getting the bone-building calcium they needed to ensure good teeth, never mind the lack of dental care.

After cleaning up the breakfast dishes, Olaff and Javier disappeared for the rest of the day. I wandered back to our camp area, treasuring the solitude and peace. Sitting on the wooden platform that Olaff had constructed for our bathing, I became aware that this area was not as isolated as I'd originally thought. Every now and then I would see people trekking through the distant trees. I wondered if any of them had seen me when I'd been hanging out clad only in my rubber boots.

I felt unsettled. I'd come to the jungle to learn a specific path, yet here I was, wasting time on my own while my teacher was out socializing yet again. I began to feel a little resentful. Was I being used to pay for a recreational excursion? I pushed the negative thoughts from my mind and looked around at the stunning beauty of where I was. So what if I wasn't learning anything at the moment; look where I was! I was in the middle of a precious experience that not many people get to have.

The tall trees seemed to beckon me to look upwards towards the sky. Because of their canopy, patches of blue were only able to be seen here and there through small openings. I allowed my mind to go blank and heard a quiet voice telling me to fly above the trees and look at the big picture. Once again, I was able to appreciate my two companions. They were dedicated to my training and looking after me, and I knew I was being well taken care of. Yeah, so I came all the way down here for a certain amount of time. Was it realistic to expect that I'd be training twenty four hours a day? No, it wasn't. My time here was limited and it was too precious to spend it being negative.

Thanking the jungle spirits for shifting my view, I got up and walked back to the house. I found Uncle Alfredo there on his own and asked where Jav and Olaff were.

"I think they've gone back to Al's," he said with a wink, miming lifting a glass to his lips.

I shuddered, thinking of all the alcohol we'd put away the night before.

"You don't want to go with them?" he asked with a curious look on his face.

"No, it's okay," I replied. "They should have time to be with the boys. We'll be back to work tomorrow."

I decided to take another nap. Part of me said I should also be out socializing, but the extreme heat and humidity tended to zap my energy. I also valued having an extended amount of time to organize my notes. Because of the unpredictability of our schedule, many times I'd had to write quickly during a brief opening, knowing I couldn't possibly get down every little detail. Better to do it now while it was fresh before things vanished into obscurity.

Restless again after my siesta, I changed my mind and decided to wander over to where we'd been last night to see what was going on. Apart from myself and Uncle Alfredo, it was as if the guys had remained in the same places they'd been in the previous night. They had already polished off one bottle filled with *cortezas* like we'd had the night before and were just about to open another *preparado* with an unusual ingredient lying in the bottom. It did not look attractive at all.

"What's that in the bottle?" I asked Olaff. He turned red and looked a bit embarrassed.

"It's an achuni penis!" Javier sang out. "Achuni ullo!"

"Gee, I'm glad I asked. Now what is an achuni?"

Back on safe ground, Olaff described the furry animal that had a long tail with alternating dark and light colored rings and extended nose.

But I wanted to know more. I was guessing that this was some kind of aphrodisiac. I'd already found that the jungle people were not shy when it came to the topic of sex, so I figured I might as well ask since they were obviously having a good time.

"Okay, so why this animal? What's so special about the achuni?"

"*El hueso del pene siempre para,*" explained a man I hadn't seen before.

Apparently, the male of this particular animal species appeared to have his equipment always ready for action. More explanations flowed, and I was able to get the gist of why the achuni was chosen to donate his sex organ for this aphrodisiac preparation. The penis had a piece of cartilage inside that allowed it to remain erect at all times, the symbolism of which was pretty obvious for a drink to promote endurance. I tried to suppress a giggle. Suddenly I felt like we were all twelve or thirteen years old, sneaking into someone's parents' liquor stash and looking at naughty magazines.

Al hesitantly passed me the bottle. *Don't look inside, don't look inside,* I told myself. I took a few swigs and then informed Jav that lunch was ready. He said he wanted to finish up here and would join us in a bit. I waved goodbye to my sozzled group of wonderful friends and trotted back down the path back to the house.

My talkative teacher and his nephew never showed up, so Uncle Alberto and I ate together. It was really hot after lunch so I decided to crawl back under the net and lie motionless to preserve my energy.

Some hours later, I thought I'd go down to the river to cool off and shave my legs. As I floated, I held up my legs and thought I'd never seen them looking the so awful: really hairy and heavily scarred by bug bites. A couple of days earlier, I had ruefully showed Javier and Olaff my legs, saying that they were so ugly they looked like someone else's legs, that I didn't even recognize them. Both of them looked at me as if I'd lost a few marbles, and I realized that in their world minor body things such as hairy legs or stringy hair were non-issues. I reflected on how the natural human body was seen as already perfect and beautiful here. The women didn't wear makeup or use tools to dry or style their hair with. There is no point in using cosmetics in the jungle because the heat and humidity will have it running down your face within a few minutes. Same thing with styling the hair. Here, you just rinse it out in the river and tie it back or up. I thought I was pretty raw looking, but it didn't really bother me. If I had to be honest, I actually found it to be quite liberating.

Enjoying the refreshing river water, I recalled one day when Javier and I and a few other men were sitting around talking about what they found attractive in the opposite sex. I told them about how cosmetic surgery was so popular in my country, and they just couldn't understand it. I thought I'd use the illustration of breast augmentation to help them get a better picture of the procedure. Javier's eyes bugged out.

"*Globos*! Balloons! Ha ha ha!" he'd shouted, slapping his thighs.

This took me by surprise as I had assumed that most men, especially those who knocked back aphrodisiacs containing questionable animal parts, might appreciate a well-endowed female. Instead, they roared with laughter at the very thought of a woman having balloons put into her chest to make her look better.

"So, you wouldn't be interested in going after a woman with a boob job?" I asked the assembled bunch.

All heads shook firmly. I just couldn't believe it, but it was yet another lesson in how different cultures view the world and their conception of beauty. I was filled with appreciation for my experience, regardless of my hairy legs or strawlike hair.

I also thought of the times that I had been propositioned here when I looked like I'd just crawled out of a tent that had slid down the side of a mountain in an avalanche. I was so used to being ignored in Southern California because I was over thirty, and thus over the hill as far as the women in my part of the country were considered. But here, I was a goddess! Yeah! Time to shave those legs!

Uncle Alfredo and I hung out for the rest of the day and enjoyed exchanging stories about our lives. He told me that while he was used to the long separations when Imelda visited relatives or went back to

Iquitos to sell their produce, he was still feeling a little lonely and just glad to have someone to talk to.

At seventy-eight years old, his daily routine might make a much younger city person keel over with fatigue. He starts his morning early as most jungle people do. Those who live without electricity tend to follow the rhythms of the land and the seasons, so they rise with the sun, if not before, and retire after dinner by eight o'clock at the latest.

Around the earth's mid-section, the hours of light and dark are pretty equal. In my experience, it seemed to get dark around five-thirty or six in the evening, and then the first light of dawn might appear at these same hours in the morning. It was like living with a permanent equinox.

Alfredo's first task of the day was usually to chop firewood for the kitchen. In the homes and dwellings I'd been in so far, I'd noticed that there were large piles of wood stacked in the cooking area. There were usually three different kinds of this natural fuel, each in its own neat stockpile. There were wisps and flakes that were used as fire starters, followed by kindling, then the larger pieces for cooking. This practice ensured that there was always a supply of clean, dry wood when it was needed.

I briefly smiled to myself as I recalled many days around impromptu fire rings at the beach, scrambling around in the cool air trying to come up with enough fuel to keep the feeble flames lit, and then feeling victorious upon finding a large, damp piece of wood, only to have it sizzle on the dying fire. Not for the last time, I wondered what my chances for survival would be if I found myself alone in the wilderness.

After Alfredo cut and stacked the wood, he would then head down to the river for a fishing session. He told me he preferred to use a net because it's a faster way to catch the fish. "As you've seen, the Napo has a strong current. I can spread out my net and catch fish flowing with the current by using the water to help sweep them in where I can collect them more easily. Using poles takes much longer and you don't catch as many."

Several hours of garden labor were next on the day's agenda. Many households had their own *chacra*. This was also referred to as a *huerto*, one's own plot for cultivating things to eat and sell at the market. It was this garden that supplied the produce that Imelda took to Iquitos to sell on occasion.

"Well, it's time to turn in for the night. Tomorrow's another busy day. *Buenas noches*," said Uncle Alfredo as he rose from where we were sitting on the floor. Then, "Oh!"

Looking at what he was pointing to on the wall, I saw a huge brown spider. It was about the size of my hand with all my fingers spread out, but it was not a tarantula.

"Maybe we'd better get it outside since we'll be sleeping on the floor in here," I suggested. Net or not, that was one big spider!

"Too much trouble." Alfredo too off one of his flip flops and whacked the hapless arachnid until it fell to the floor. He then used the edge of the shoe to flick the remains out into the night.

It was now eight o'clock, and there was still no sign of Jav and Olaff. I was happy to let my jungle brothers have their fun with the aguardiente potions, knowing I wouldn't be the one to have the dreaded sugar cane hangover tomorrow morning.

Before retiring for the night, I had to visit the bushes. It's one thing to relieve oneself in the jungle during the day when you can clearly see what else might be in the greenery with you, but it's quite another at night. I slid my headlamp onto my forehead, grabbed some toilet paper and made my way to the spot that Alfredo had cleared behind the house. Ducking behind a tree, I looked up to see what looked to be a pair of luminescent green eyes staring at me in the dark. I froze in order to assess the situation. Several times, other sets of eyes would appear, then they'd vanish. Was I being accosted by another of the jungle's magical beings? Well, yes, I was, but this time they were solid and physical. It was only when one pair suddenly flew across my field of vision that I realized the eyes belonged to fireflies.

We don't have fireflies in Southern California, and I just thought they were the most beautiful things I had ever seen. But up until this point, I had only seen them flying, not stationary. The eyes were not eyes at all: they were simply two spots on either side of the beetle's abdomen that gave off a greenish glow.

"Probably yet another jungle boy looking for a mate," I thought as I finished my business. I paused one last time before leaving the clearing and turned back around. The eyes were still gazing out into the dark, then suddenly they rose up into the trees.

"Goodnight, Mr. *Luciérnaga*. I sure hope you get lucky tonight!"

Tucking myself in under the net, I fell into a peaceful sleep, then started dreaming of my cats. They were running all around, making a lot of noise, and then they morphed into a herd of stampeding elephants. The elephants were trumpeting and making a fierce racket as they crashed along their path. Suddenly, one of them charged at me! As I quickly dashed aside, I could feel its trunk make contact with my body.

"Judita! Are you awake? We're back!" bellowed one of the elephants.

I was jolted out of my sleep in time to see my two *hermanos* stumbling through the front door. One of them started to fall into my net, then caught himself.

"Oh, sure. Wide awake now. Gee, thanks. Did you have fun?"

Two very slurred and emphatic *si's* responded.

"Oh boy, are you guys going to feel wonderful in the morning," I muttered, hoping that my own sleep would not be disrupted.

"*Buenas noches, muchachos.*"

"*Buenas noches, Judita.*"

Hic!

We moved back to our little campsite by the lagoon after breakfast, but there were still chores to be done at the house.

"We're going to help Tío haul *plátanos* from his *chacra*," Javier informed me once the basic items had been reset in place and the roof inspected for potential leaks. You can stay here and practice your icaros for tonight. Ya?"

"Ya, Javito."

Sometimes I would get confused with all the things that looked like bananas but were not. I think I can say that while you could easily eat a raw banana, a raw *plátano*—or plantain-- was a different story. I found them to be starchier, hence the necessity of cooking them. Boiled *plátano* was quite popular here, and sometimes it was cooked alongside other items like small fish. Of course, like the yucca root, it was even more tasty when sautéed or fried.

I spent several pleasant hours rehearsing my songs and ceremony routine for the night's upcoming work, then I crawled under the net for a siesta. I wasn't tired, but it was very hot and humid and I had used up all my energy. As I was lying there, I thought I felt a presence of some kind. There was a faint rustling of something large moving slowly through the leaves near the lagoon. I couldn't see anything at first, only the movements of the plants as they were pushed aside. Finally, something emerged that looked like it had come out of *Jurassic Park*. Was it a crocodile? I giant lizard? A dinosaur that had come through a time portal? I couldn't tell.

I decided it might be a good idea to remain alert in case it caught my scent and considered searching out its next snack. Feeling for my trusty machete, my hand found its handle and I felt reassured. I was ready! But it either didn't sense me, or it had something else in mind because it continued along its path. I never did get to see it completely enough in the open to be able to identify it.

Javier and Olaff appeared a little while later and I told them about the creature from the lagoon. Olaff got very excited and asked me all sorts of questions about it. I'm afraid I wasn't able to give him the clear answers he was hoping for, but apparently, whatever it was had been something he himself was hoping to see. He told me the name of it, but it went in one ear and out the other.

"Did you happen to take a picture of it?" he asked hopefully.

"No, I should have. I didn't know if it was dangerous, and since it didn't seem to sense I was here I preferred to keep it that way." I thought of the day I was dangling my lower legs in that lagoon and Olaff's warning. He had been correct!

Jav changed the subject. "Your honey is ready to be picked up. Are you ready to go? We'll be returning here to work tonight. I hope you're ready for your mock exam in preparation for your graduation."

I nodded. Inwardly, of course I still felt nervous. I had invested so much into this trip that I wanted a happy ending. But as with all magical practices, you do your work, then you let go of needing to know the outcome.

Making our way back to Javier's grandmother's place, we passed Julito's house. He was sitting outside forlornly, not running around like the normal jungle boys did. I put my hand on Javier's arm to indicate I wanted him to stop so we could see how Julito's infected toe was doing.

"*Hola,* Julito. How is your toe?" I asked the boy.

"It still hurts."

My teacher and I both asked to see the digit. It was swollen and hot, indicating the infection was still present. I made a decision.

"Jav, what do you think about lancing that toe to drain it? I have soap and alcohol and bandages. We'll need his mother to boil up some water so we can wash the foot first. I think just a small poke with a needle would do it. I also have some with me."

Javier gave me a searching look and then nodded.

"Julito, would you like us to try to make your toe feel better?" I asked the sweet little boy.

He nodded, still looking sad.

"I'm going back to get what we need," I told Javier. "Please go talk to his mother and see if she's on board with this. If she is, start a pot of water boiling. We'll need it for sterilizing the needle and washing his foot."

I returned to Alfredo's house and made my way down the back steps onto the path that led to our camp. Moving quickly, I smiled to myself that at that moment I felt like a real jungle dweller, moving with purpose, and no longer a klutz.

Fishing around in my backpack, I found my first aid kit and checked that I had everything we'd need. I always travel with a small sewing repair kit, so I chose a needle that I thought would be suitable for the job. Returning to Julito's house, I found Javier had taken charge and had a large pot of hot water ready to use.

"Is there a clean towel or cloth we can use?" I asked Julito's mother.

Nodding once with a serious expression, she produced a soft cloth that had been recently washed in the river. It would have to do.

"The water should be safe to use now, so let me first sterilize this needle. Then we'll need it to cool slightly so it doesn't burn Julito's foot." Turning to Jav I asked him if he had explained to the woman what we were intending to do. He nodded.

"First, I'll need to wash my own hands with the soap. Is there a small basin I can use?"

"*Hay balde,*" said Julito's mother, producing a clean bucket.

I poured a small amount of the water into the bucket and tested the temperature. It was still very hot, so I swished it around with a little cold water to make it tolerable so that I could wash my hands. I then dipped the needle into the pot of hot water and held it there until the metal heated up. After tossing my hand-washing water from the bucket I asked Jav to refill it with more from the pot.

"Swirl it around with a just enough of the cooler water so it won't burn the skin. Have Julito sit comfortably with his leg extended on this bench here," I instructed.

I explained to the small gathering of curious onlookers what I intended to do and everyone moved in a little closer.

"Julito, do you want your foot to feel better so you can run with your friends?"

"*Sí*, Miss."

"Okay. We're going to try to release the pressure so it won't hurt anymore. To do this, I have to make a small hole with this." I held up the needle. As his eyes widened slightly, I nodded. "Yes, it will hurt at first, but it will be over very fast. Ready?"

I had his mother wash his foot with the now sterilized water and soap until it was clean and pink, then wipe the infected toe with a corner of the clean cloth that had been dipped in alcohol. Holding my breath and praying for Julito's healing, I poked the pus-filled toe with the needle as Julito flinched in pain. Instantly, a large amount of fluid was emitted from the small opening and everyone gasped. It was not a pretty sight!

Taking the clean cloth, I pressed very gently on the skin around the opening to help as much of the fluid emerge as possible. We washed the foot again, dried it, and then I applied more rubbing alcohol. Taking a closer look at the toe, I could see that the swelling was gone, although the toe was still a little red.

"How does that feel, Julito?" I asked the boy.

"Better. It does not hurt so much now."

"Okay, I've got to put on some antibiotic cream and then we need to bandage this up. It's absolutely important that it be kept clean until the wound heals."

To Javier I said, "What do you think? Ideally, he needs to stay off this foot for a good solid day or two. And it must be kept absolutely clean!"

Javier turned to Julito's mother and spoke to her quickly. I saw her look at me and nod solemnly.

I applied some of the antibiotic cream I'd brought and bandaged the toe up completely. I think I probably overdid it somewhat, but since we were definitely not in a sterile environment and Julito did not wear shoes, I wasn't worried about this.

"Now we wait."

After picking up the small container of special jungle honey, Javier and I returned to our camp site. Olaff had remained at the house to work on the fish he'd caught while we were on our errands. I sure was glad that I didn't have to hunt for my own food like the native apprentices did. Were I a skilled hunter and perhaps had done more advanced wilderness survival training, this might be a different story. Not having to worry about feeding myself allowed me to focus on my singing and healing practices. I'm sure being concerned about starving to death would have been a major distraction for me!

But there are other things that can throw off one's game. Olaff had been instructed to bring lunch out to us as had been done on several other occasions. After we had eaten, Javier announced that they would both be leaving me on my own yet again until the evening.

I ran through the ceremony several times, feeling confident that it was now embedded in my memory. Everything was going to be just fine tonight!

As the day wore on, my nose began to feel quite stuffed up to the point where I had to breathe through my mouth. My skin seemed to itch even more than it had been, and I wondered if there was something nearby that was causing an allergic reaction. Since we would be drinking ayahuasca later that night I was not able to take any of the antihistamines I'd brought with me because the two medicines can react badly together.

As my physical discomfort continued to grow, my chattering monkey mind seemed to shift into overdrive. I began to feel very sorry for myself, being left all alone yet again, unable to breathe and my entire body twitching like mad from all the bug bite reactions.

"Well, this is just fine!" I fumed. "I paid all this money to come here and I keep getting left on my own. What are they doing? They'd better not be into the aguardiente again! Great, what am I supposed to do for all this time on my own?"

I crawled out from under the mosquito net and stomped around, allowing myself to have a big hissy fit. I wanted to let out a really loud, long scream but worried that it might be taken the wrong way. No, it wouldn't have been a good idea to scream and bring everyone running, only to find me having a childish tantrum.

Spying my machete, I snatched it up by its orange plastic handle and decided to take out my frustration on some fallen trees. The action of raising the blade and bringing it down forcefully over and over helped release all the pent up energy. Finally, spent and exhausted, I returned to my enclosed sleeping area and had a good cry. This did nothing for my stuffed up nose, but there was nothing else to do. Some warrior I was!

"Well, Machete Woman, you're doing just fine, aren't you?" I said to myself since there was no one else anywhere within earshot. "Come on, you sniveling weenie! Get your act together! Do you want them to find you like this?" I wondered if any of the indigenous apprentices had ever felt like this.

Javier and Olaff appeared around dusk. I had managed to clean myself up by then, but my teacher peered at me in curiosity.

"Are you alright, Judita?"

"Yes, Jav," I lied. "Just fine." In truth, I think I wanted to strangle him and throw him in the lagoon where the giant lizard-thing could have him for a snack even though he'd certainly not done anything wrong.

Despite my hollow reassurances, Javier knew I was in a snit, so he and Olaff decided to ignore me. I had tried to reason with myself that it wasn't fair to be mad at them and that it was just my ego having a field day. I had to really battle with myself to stuff my negativity down so that it wouldn't affect the night's practice exam. But sometimes, you must lose the battle in order to win the war.

CHAPTER 18

Mother Nature's Bride

The moon was rising above the dark silhouettes of the trees when Javier indicated it was time to start the night's activities. Tonight's ceremony would be a complete run-through of everything I'd learned so far to see how I would do without any input from him. I had managed to fall into a peaceful sleep after the earlier energy-draining bout with my ego. The two-odd hours of not having to claw at my skin or breathe through my mouth helped smooth out the ruffles, and I felt refreshed and ready to get to work.

It was not a good night. Despite my rest and knowing that this was only a practice exam, I just couldn't get into the groove. I started off well doing the usual space clearing with tobacco smoke and singing into the medicine bottle to bless the ayahuasca. My nose was still stopped up, so I was continuing to have to breathe through my mouth, which made singing somewhat difficult. Because I was focusing on my physical discomfort instead of the ceremony, I made mistakes in two of my most solid icaros, and completely messed up a newer third one. I knew the song, but I couldn't even remember how it started!

Knowing how strict Javier was about getting things right, this put me into a mild panic, which then made my skin itching flare with a vengeance. I was back where I'd been hours earlier, concentrating on my suffering and how miserable I felt. And by doing this, I lost all my concentration and committed error after error.

I suddenly recalled that Javier had once told me about apprentices who had to be let go because they couldn't learn the sacred songs that are an important part of the jungle shaman's repertoire, and I wondered if I'd soon be one of them.

"We don't just sing in ayahuasca ceremonies," he'd told me at that time. "You already know that we sing over our plant medicines as we make them to put prayers in, as well as when we work on people. Our icaros join us to our allies. They are our tools. If we can't sing, we can't have that meaningful connection with the little doctors who are the ones that really do the work. We are just conduits for the spirits."

To make matters worse, I tripped over a large tree root as I was doing my *pasos*. I managed to catch myself by grabbing onto the tree, but this rattled me even more. It was all I could do to not turn around and stomp off into the night like a petulant two-year old.

Taking a deep breath, I picked up my leaf rattle and continued as best I could. Normally quite sensitive to the effects of the ayahuasca even with these smaller working doses, I couldn't even feel the *mareaciones*, the seasickness like dizziness that often accompanies the experience. It felt like Madre and all her plant spirits had abandoned me.

Javier said nothing as I blundered and botched my way through the ceremony. He sat in silence, smoking *mapachos* until I closed and sat down next to him on the log, feeling very depressed.

"So, what do you think happened tonight?" he finally asked me.

"I don't know. I just fell to pieces. I'd been suffering all day with my itching and stuffed-up nose and I think it all just distracted me."

"It was not your nose or your skin that caused the problems tonight; it was your mind."

"My mind? How can that be? But I was really suffering!" I protested.

Handing me a *mapacho*, he continued. "You allow your thoughts to create false realities. And then you give them power by getting all emotional and stomping around here like a child. You tried to blame your feelings on Olaff and me, when in fact we did nothing to you. Isn't this right, Judita?"

Ouch! Javier could be blunt, but he was spot on. How could he have known not only that I'd been taking out my frustration on the poor plants earlier on, but that I'd been blaming my rage on him? He'd been nowhere near me! As if reading my mind, he continued,

"And no, I wasn't spying on you either. Olaff and I were busy helping out at the school all day. An important part of becoming a shaman is letting go of the need to have your teacher around for everything, even for company. You must find the strength within yourself and from your own spirit allies. And besides, I have far more important things to do than hiding in the bushes to spy on you."

I felt horrible. Taking a big drag on the cigarette, I let it out slowly while I gathered my thoughts. I should have known he could read my mind or use remote vision to check up on me.

"Oh, Javier, I'm sorry! Sometimes I just feel like I'm so out of my element. I didn't even feel the medicine tonight at all. I was worried that Madre had disowned me for doing something wrong."

"The only thing you did wrong was to allow your thoughts to create a situation that did not exist. This is one of your big problems that you must learn to master.

And don't worry about not feeling the medicine so much right now. Remember, as in Rio Momon this phase of your training is not for that. We are giving you the structure and tools for you to build your own ceremonies and practices, and you can't do that very well if you're heavily under the influence of the medicine. That is coming, Judita. Very soon!"

I looked at my teacher and saw that he was grinning at me with one of his wide, face-splitting smiles.

"Ya, Judita. Our next place will be for working with spirit visions so you will have to drink a lot of ayahuasca. There will be a lot of puking and purging." He then made humorous imitations of someone vomiting all over the ground, complete with accompanying noises.

As I laughed, he continued. "For me, it was a good night. My spirits told me that you were sad, but they also said that you are doing a good job. You are a good student. Don't worry about tonight. Let it go and move forward. Come on! Let's get some sleep."

The following day, we continued with other aspects of the tradition such as learning more about medicinal plants. I was still overwhelmed by the herculean task of trying to learn about so many aspects of plant medicine. This one only wants the flowers, that one requires the leaves, and that other one has its medicine in its roots. Adding to this was that none of the plants that I was learning about here grew in Southern California. Why learn all about these Amazonian plants when I wouldn't be using them when I got home? I voiced this query to my teacher.

"Ya, Judita, you will not see these plants where you live. But what I'm teaching you here can apply to those other plants. I'm showing you how to find a plant that fits your needs and how you learn about its properties and preparation. These methods can then be applied to plants anywhere in the world," Jav replied.

We were about to continue our conversation when Olaff appeared on the path from the house. He seemed very happy about something and leaned over to whisper in his uncle's ear. I saw Javier respond with another of his big grins.

"Come, Judita! We need to go to the house right now!"

Wondering what was going on now, I dutifully trotted behind my teacher as Olaff brought up the rear. It couldn't be a bad thing because both of them had seemed so happy. I was soon to join them.

Waiting in the house were Julito and his mother. The boy was wearing oversized, mismatched flip flops. I noticed that the bandages I had put on his foot were no longer there, and that he was standing on both feet without favoring the one that had been hurting him. Julito's mother said something to him, and he sat down on a small stool and lifted up his foot. Removing the flip flop, we could see that there was no longer any sign of the swelling, and apart from a small dot that marked the needle puncture site, the foot looked as healthy as his other unaffected one.

"No pain! I can walk now without the pain!" he said proudly.

"We want to thank you for your help," said his mother. "As you see, there is no medicine or hospital here. We have no money, but I brought you a gift."

Shyly, she unwrapped a cloth that had been covering a large plastic bottle and handed it to me.

"It's masato. I made it myself. Javier told me you were fond of it."

My eyes filled with tears at the gift of the yucca beer, and my teacher put his arm around me.

"Judita is going to be a great healer, maybe one day even better than me!"

We all laughed and I accepted the bottle, feeling very humbled. All I'd done was imitate my mother, who'd been an emergency room nurse. Despite our challenging relationship, both she and my dad managed to get through what she constantly referred to as my thick skull. I couldn't wait to share this small victory with her when I eventually returned home, and I hoped she'd be proud of me.

At that moment, I also decided to leave whatever I had in my medicine bag that could be replaced in Iquitos. We'd be heading back there soon, and I knew that many of the items such as the alcohol and acetaminophen could easily be replaced there, yet here in this remote village they were non-existent. I told Javier of my plan and he nodded in approval.

"If I leave what I can with Alfredo, he can let people know what is here in case they need help. Of course, this is only a small amount," I said as my voice trailed off.

"Ya but look at what a small amount has already done," Javier said as he ruffled my hair.

Olaff announced lunch, so we settled down to more freshly grilled river fish and root vegetables. While the diet here had been somewhat monotonous for the most part, if it's freshly grilled I'll never get tired of it. When we go into a *dieta*, we accept that we're going to be eating a restricted amount of food which very likely is not going to include a great variety of items, and certainly no treats.

"Did you know Tío had fifteen children?" Javier asked between bites of boiled yucca root.

"Really? Do they all live here in Nuevo Progreso?" I asked him.

"Well, no. We lost five of them many years ago. As you see, there are no medical facilities here, and we are far away from the cities. Some of my children are here, but others have moved to nearby pueblos to be with their partners and families."

"Do you know why the jungle people have so many children?" asked Javier with a smile.

I sensed we were about to head once more into their favorite topic, so I feigned innocence.

"No, Javier. Tell me. Why do the jungle people have so many children? I guess because there's a lot of work to be done, huh?"

Jav and his nephew exchanged glances, confirming I was about to once again be led up the garden path. My teacher leaned closer to me as if about to share a secret.

"Because there is no electricity, so they don't have TVs to watch!" Wink, wink.

We all burst out laughing at the obviousness of the answer.

"Of course. Silly me!" I clapped a palm to my forehead.

In the early days after my return to Iquitos to work with Javier, I had been told that even thinking about sex was supposed to be frowned upon during the apprenticeship. It wasn't that sex was bad, but rather that it was a way to master physical desires and weaknesses. I realized that what we had been doing so far was really just talking about local customs, so I figured I wasn't breaking any rules, especially with my teacher right there with me.

"A *banco* is one who can ignore his strongest desires and work without distraction," Javier had told me.

"Sounds like a woman," I replied slyly, but I think my inference went over their heads.

At various times during our stay here in Rio Napo, my companions had presented me with small capinori branches while we were out wandering around in the forest. When these pieces break from the tree, they bear a strong resemblance to the male organ. I recalled how Harold had proudly worn a small one around his neck, its purpose being to broadcast his virility to suitable females who might be in the area. I kept the collection of the phallic objects and thought I'd have fun passing them out to my friends at home.

After we'd finished lunch, Javier and I started talking about my upcoming marriage to Mother Nature. The purpose of this special ceremony was to create a deeper connection to the spirits of the natural world, so I could have a good working relationship with them. I would then be able to call upon these forces to aid me in my work.

"It's time for you to prepare for your wedding to Madre Naturaleza tonight," Javier told me. "For this, you must make your wedding clothes. But first, I need to show you the special arbor where the wedding will take place. Come!"

My teacher indicated that I should follow him along a path that only he seemed to be able to see. Eventually, he paused and pointed to an area that almost looked as if it had been constructed from human hands.

"This is black ayahuasca. Not so good for visions. It makes you more like…" He rolled his eyes up and jiggled his body all over. "It makes your nerves shake a lot."

The ayahuasca vines were very old and had climbed up the arbor's trees and other tall bushes, where they intertwined and formed a sort of structure. Jav pointed to an opening like a door and told me to go through it. As I did, I had the feeling that I was entering an ancient church. There was an atmosphere of deep reverence, and suddenly it didn't feel appropriate to speak at our normal volume.

"This is where your wedding will take place later. I just wanted to show it to you now."

I felt choked up and emotional. When my teacher had first told me I was going to marry Mother Nature, I thought he was joking and laughed. But there was something about the energy of this place that told me this ceremony would be very serious and important to my transformation.

Back at our camp, I set to work. I'd had some time to think about my plant-based clothing and now at least had some ideas. The same large banana leaves that we'd used to make a roof for our shelter could also be employed as skirt panels. I could make a belt with a *soga*—a strip of thin bark that is often used as rope--and use smaller pieces to tie the leaf stems to the belt. This was the easy part.

The top needed smaller components. I decided to make a short poncho and found some smaller leaves with long stems that I could tie together. I had learned to sew when I was twelve years old, and I'd taught myself to knit and crochet to a relatively competent level. But working with yarns and fabrics was nothing like working with living plants that didn't want to bend and twist so easily. I found myself getting frustrated when leaves would tear or stems would break, but I consoled myself with the fact that at least there seemed to be an unending supply of material to use.

"Well, I'll never win any fashion awards for this outfit, but I think it'll do," I told myself as I inspected the finished pieces.

Javier came over to see how I was getting along so I showed him my handiwork, lifting the pieces gently. I had the feeling that with too much handling, they'd easily return to the jungle floor for recycling.

"*Muy bien,*" he approved.

Javier had told me that we'd also have another rehearsal ceremony for my eventual final exam that would lead to my graduation, so that I wouldn't be nervous about making mistakes under pressure. I think he knew that despite all my idiocies, I was a good student who was making a supreme effort to learn what I was being shown. Since I had already made so many mistakes during that ceremony, it was as if the ice had been broken. It didn't matter anymore. Something had been set free.

This being a ceremony night, there was no dinner. I'd been told that the wedding would take place within the ceremony, but as usual Javier changed the format at the last minute to keep my logical scientist's brain from trying to figure out the exact order of what was going to happen.

"You want to know everything in advance, to figure things out so you know what's coming," my teacher had shaken his head vigorously. "You can't do that in the spirit world. You must let go of your expectations of how you think things should be. When you can do this, you will see the real magic."

I could feel in my body that he was speaking the truth, and mentally added it to the growing list of things I had to work on. I also knew that this topic was related to my unrealistic expectations of how I thought things should be.

As if reading my mind once again, I could see Javier giving me one of his deep, piercing looks.

"If you want to be a powerful shaman, Judita, you must flow with the universe and not try to dictate how everything should be according to what's in your comfort zone. Those of us who live here in the jungle live most of our lives outside of our comfort zones. You already have experienced the heat, humidity, and other things that are a part of our daily lives. There is no electricity, and sometimes there is not even any food. This may not be what we wish for, but it is what is, and you don't see us stomping around angrily when things don't go our way, do you?"

I considered this for a moment before replying. "Well, I can't say I have a lot of experience with this, Jav, but I think you're right. What I've seen from the people here so far is that they just get on with their days and try to make the best of things as they arise. And I'll tell you what; you all seem a lot happier than most of my countrymen who have a lot more creature comforts and supposed riches. I'm working on it, Jav. I'm working on it."

"Ya, Judita."

Figuring that we'd be starting around our usual nine o'clock, I had crawled under the net to while away the time with a nice nap. An insistent hand batting me through the thin fabric roused me from my snooze. I quickly peeked at my watch: 6:00 pm.

"Get up! We're going to the arbor right now. Get your leaf clothing. No talking!"

Shaking the sleep from my brain, I gathered up my already wilting leaf clothing and tucked in behind Jav. We made our way back along the almost obscured path that we'd taken earlier in the day. I was grateful that there was still some light in the sky, but started wondering if it would be dark before we could make it back to camp. As my mind spun yet another of its imaginary stories, I wished it would just shut up. If Javier was not worried about being out in the jungle in the dark, then I should not be worried either.

As we approached the amazing black ayahuasca vine arbor, I could feel a thick silence around us. It was as if the jungle itself was waiting for the ceremony to begin. To me, felt very much like when people gather for a highly anticipated special event, such as a wedding or perhaps a concert, and there is an air of buzzy anticipation that builds to a crescendo.

Donning my wedding clothes, I walked into the arbor. I was told to remain there, meditating on uniting with Mother Earth until I felt a shift. There was something about the ambience inside this natural woven vine structure that made me lose all my fears about being there in the dark, and I wondered what it'd be like to spend the night in this special place.

After some time had passed, Javier entered behind me and performed a short ritual, as if he were taking the part of the minister. Finally, with a solemn tone, he announced, "It is done. Now remove the wedding dress and lay it down here. This is where it will remain. Let's return to camp."

I carefully removed the two parts to my gown of green and laid them reverently on the floor of the arbor. Javier flicked on a small flashlight and led the way back to our familiar camp location. I now had a second chance to show my teacher and the jungle spirits that I had mastered what I'd been learning for the past two months.

Taking our places on the trusty log that had been serving as a comfortable seat, I went through the now familiar ritual. Olaff had joined us, and I realized that I no longer felt self-conscious about having someone else present like I had back in the Jivaro camp. He chose to drink a small dose of camalonga instead of ayahuasca. While they both have very different purposes, Olaff had confessed that he was a little fearful of ayahuasca and had only done it a few times. This had really surprised me as up until then I'd thought everyone in the jungle drank this famous tea all the time. When I questioned him and Javier about this, they told me that more Westerners drink ayahuasca on a regular basis than the jungle folks do. I made a mental note to ask more about this at another time.

With my teacher by my side, everything felt good. I first sang seated and then got up to demonstrate my proficiency with the *pasos* and *coreografía*. I was actually glad to have Olaff as a participant so I could have a real person to work on instead of just trees for a change. When I had finished those three rounds, I returned to the log and lowered myself slowly, savoring the feeling of what I had considered to be a perfect ceremony.

We sat in silence for a short while. While I couldn't be completely sure, I had the feeling that my teacher was engaged in a conversation with an unseen presence that only he could hear. We were seated right next to each other, but it was so dark that I could only see his outline. Sometimes in shamanism, the lines between what we believe to be solid reality and the spiritual world can blur, leaving us to wonder which existence is the true one. It could have been Javier, my human teacher next to me, or it could have been a jungle spirit. Or both.

I felt, rather than saw, the quick nod that seemed to indicate he'd come to a decision. Javier had been wearing a small headpiece made of woven leaves, which was supposed to be a regular part of our ceremonial regalia. I had removed mine after the *pasos* round because it kept slipping off my head. His crown had been made by much more experienced hands and had remained more firmly in place.

He now lifted the leaf corona from his head and placed it on mine. I knew something big was happening, and for once just allowed myself to be, to feel, and not ask questions. Javier lit a mapacho and used his shacapa to sweep the fragrant tobacco smoke down from the top of my head to my feet. He then began to sing a new icaro that I hadn't heard before. It was very upbeat and expressed gratitude.

"Let's work on this icaro. It's for your graduation."

The melody was a bit tricky because it had a lot of changes, but I followed along as he sang. It usually takes me an average of three days to fully learn a song to the point where I no longer need to look at the written lyrics, and this then helps nail down the melody much faster. Despite its complexity, I knew I would eventually commit it to memory as I had with my other icaros, but my mind kept intruding with its usual inane chatter, making the memorization process more difficult. What just happened here? Did I just graduate or something? Is this a trick? Blah blah blah. It just didn't feel right to ask, but dang! I was really confused! Happy, but confused.

I'm sure that Javier knew what was going through my mind and decided to let me stew for a while longer. I felt really good, and that was the only thing that mattered right now. My habit of wanting to know everything would have to wait for now.

The special evening wound down to a close and the three of us retired to our respective cozy spaces under the nets that had been hung closely together in a line: Olaff on the left, me in the middle, and Javier on the right. My guardians, my brothers.

The following morning, we trooped back to the house so Olaff could get breakfast going. As we walked along the now well-worn path, I thought this might be a good opportunity to ask them to clarify their declaration about foreigners drinking more ayahuasca than the jungle people.

"A lot of people here are afraid of ayahuasca and the spirits. We only drink it when we need to be in a healing ceremony," Olaff admitted.

"Ya, we are not like the *pasajeros* who come to the jungle to drink ayahuasca every night so they can have crazy visions," Jav added. "All the foreigners who come here bring a lot of money, but this is not always good. It's made many people here greedy and instead of doing traditional healing ceremonies, the bad shamans do what we call performance ceremonies. They just take the gringos' money and go through the motions like an actor. It's sad, because then you guys go home and think you've taken part in a genuine jungle ceremony," he said with some asperity.

I wanted to ask him how someone could tell the difference between a real and a performance ceremony but I didn't dare. But as he had so many times before, he seemed to read my mind and responded without rebuke.

"You will feel this more as you go on, Judita. Those with vision can not only see all the *doctorcitos*, but we can sense the energy and intent of the one who is leading the ceremony. An ayahuasca ceremony should bring healing and blessings to everyone present. You've experienced a very strong ceremony, ya?"

Remembering my third night in Sacha Wasi, I nodded as he continued,

"Madre can be very strong, but if you are in a proper ceremony you will never feel anything evil. We only work with divine beings who come when we walk in a good way. A performance ceremony is like when you watch something on television. You can see what is happening, but it's all for show; there is no magic behind it all. You come in with nothing and you leave with nothing. You wait, Judita, you will see this one day."

Now back at the house, Olaff set up his makeshift grill and began preparing our breakfast.

"We will soon be going back to Iquitos," Javier announced. "Olaff has to register for his next semester at university."

I tried not to grimace at the prospect of returning to all that noise and sensory overload.

He continued, "It is very special that you are here. I have not brought anyone from the outside here before."

"I am very glad to be here too, Jav. It's precious to me, and I will never forget it. I will carry your pueblo with me for the rest of my life."

"Yes, you will. We will soon be doing a special ceremony to bring you into my lineage, the *curanderos* of Rio Napo. We will become family through my bloodline."

Nodding, I had finally worked up the courage to ask what was still rattling around in my head. "So, um, I guess I passed the test, huh? I graduated?"

I saw a sparkle in Olaff's eyes as his uncle replied.

"Yes, Judita. Believe it or not, you graduated. When I placed my leaf corona on your head, that was it. This is called coronation, and it marks a rite of passage in our tradition. You still have many more years of study and practice, but coronation marks the successful completion of this early phase. I can hardly believe it myself!"

We all got a good laugh out of that last comment. But the truth is, the extreme discomfort I experienced on a daily basis had seemed to cast doubt on my ability to persevere in these conditions that I wasn't used to. How many times did I think, "I've had enough! I am so outta here!" while my teacher waited for me to ask for help in returning to the city as he'd told me so many of his other potential students had done.

But failure was not an option for me. I knew that my divine guidance had led me to this point and I was not about to throw it away for something that could be cleared up in due course. Javier didn't know that my determination had been set in stone at the moment when he'd told me about how most of his new students had fled in horror after a few days of living in the jungle. They may have been weenies, but I was not. I was going to show Jav that I was made of sterner stuff, and that all the work that not only he and Olaff, but our various hosts did on my behalf, would not go in vain. *Ando en fuerza de la medicina.* I walk in the strength of the medicine.

Now that I had passed the crucial coronation stage in my apprenticeship, Javier declared that we would become blood brothers, and thus I would be a part of his lineage. The next morning, I was instructed to bathe and change into fresh clothing, and he did the same. He directed me to sit once more on our favorite log while he looked for a particular thorn.

When I had first been told about the blood ceremony, I pictured what I had seen in the movies: two people making a quick slash on an inside wrist or palm and then quickly joining one to the other so that the freshly flowing blood would mix. This one was not so dramatic. There were two protector symbols that he would be cutting into my skin: one on my left hand and the other on my right inner forearm.

Javier scouted around the nearby area, lifting leaves and peering under fallen tree branches.

"What are you looking for?" I wanted to know.

"The disinfectant. There should be some around here."

After my recent experience with Julito, I was surprised to not have thought about disinfecting my own body before it was cut into with a tree thorn.

"What do you use out here? I have some alcohol wipes."

For a moment, there was no answer as my teacher continued his search. Suddenly, he pounced on something and brought up a mass of a slimy, white substance. "Snail eggs! We must use something more natural in this ceremony."

In my mind, I heard an "Oh gawd, Judy. You're going to allow that man to rub that stuff on your body?" My mother's voice was overlaid with my own.

"Oh, shut up!" I told myself. "Just shut up. Yes, if Javier wants to smear me with large, slimy snail eggs, I'm all for it."

Once again, I got that knowing look from my teacher. I knew he could see my inner battles and bullshit, but he also knew that I was fierce.

"This is going to hurt a bit, Judita," he warned as he began to trace the first design on my left hand.

But it didn't hurt at all. After all the extreme suffering I had gone through with the mosquitos, flies, and fire ants, I found being stabbed and scraped with the sharp thorn to actually feel great. Yes, Javito, your student is a little bit of a weirdo.

After carving the two symbols into my flesh, he then drew blood from the same areas on his body and anointed particular areas of my body. Several other rituals followed which drew our blood ties closer and closer. I was inducted into his lineage of the *curanderos* of Rio Napo which had come down through his paternal bloodline. We were now *hermana y hermano*, sister and brother.

We had one final ceremony at our precious camp near the lagoon. As before, I was left on my own for many hours while my teacher and his nephew attended to tasks in the pueblo. I took the opportunity to not only practice my icaros, but to also belt out songs from my rock god influences such as Ronnie James Dio and Ann Wilson of Heart. My creative mind started to play with words and a new word formed in my brain: *icarock*. I was an unrequited rock star who was now moving onto a different stage. I could combine the power of a rock performance with the power of a jungle ceremony. I would make people rock out with my icaros. This didn't mean I'd be turning future ceremonies into concerts; it was more about power and transcendence. Icarock, indeed!

Our final ceremony went off without any major errors. I was still having trouble with the tricky melodic changes in the "Shaman's Graduation" song, but I had the lyrics down pat.

"What is important in the sacred icaros is not so much the melody, but the words," Javier told me. "The words have power; the melody is just how you deliver them."

I wanted to protest, remembering how exacting he had been in the Jivaro camp. Every note and word had to be spot on. Bringing this to his attention, he responded,

"Yes, at that time you were in the beginning stages so we were working on perfection. You are in a different place now, so different rules apply."

I felt many questions start to take form with this revelation and started to open my mouth, but Javier held up his hand to stop me in mid-flow.

"You don't need to ask about any of this because one day you will see and experience it for yourself."

After I had closed the ceremony, we remained seated on the log and watched the fireflies dance through the trees.

"Do you want to hear the spirits? To speak to them and know they hear you?"

"Well, of course, Jav. You can't do this work without being able to do this."

"Start by speaking out loud to them. You don't have to do this all the time, but when you are in doubt it can help you to focus. Then be quiet and listen." He gave me one of his piercing looks and repeated, "Be quiet and listen. Ya?"

Ya, Javier.

Since this phase of my training had now come to a close, we pulled up camp for the last time and returned to Uncle Alfredo's house. While I knew this would mean being watched and stared at again, for some reason it no longer bothered me.

The end of my training had somehow miraculously coincided with the anniversary festivities of Nuevo Progreso. During many of the recent days that I had been left alone, my two *hermanos* had been helping the committee that planned the festivities. I thought back to the recent celebrations of Javier's street and cringed a bit. Yet this was different for some reason. Maybe it was the fact that there was no electricity, so there'd be no excessively loud music to ruin the ambience.

People had strung up cheap paper decorations for the pueblo's forty-third anniversary. The villagers took advantage of the special gathering by bringing containers of homemade goods to sell, some even setting up small cooking grills. I saw the woman with the *huani de yuca* that I'd had before still offering her tasty goods. I bought some churros from a young girl who told me she needed the money to buy a notebook for school.

Every now and then I could see groups of men carrying objects and quickly hiding them out of sight behind a large tree. I started to pay more attention and noticed there was a constant flow of surreptitious traffic to the site. They seemed to be trying hard to make it appear that nothing unusual was happening. As men ducked off the main path, they would look around to see if anyone was watching. Yeah, I was.

I jabbed Javier in the ribs and pointed to an area behind a large tree where I thought some men were acting suspiciously. "What's going on over there?" I wanted to know, and I had a pretty good idea that he did.

"*¿Dónde?* Where?"

I pointed again towards the men behind the tree.

"*Nada.* Nothing. Just some men talking."

"I don't think so. There most definitely is something going on. Cervezas, perhaps?"

My patient teacher looked at me, and in that moment I had my answer. He most certainly did know what was going on behind that tree!

"So what's the big secret? I'll bet they're not even cold, are they?"

Javier looked around, somewhat guiltily. "It costs a lot of money to bring the beers from the city. No one here can afford to buy them on their own, but when they save enough and pool their money, they can send someone to Iquitos to bring back a certain quantity for a festival like this. But they can't just offer them to everyone. All those men you see have already paid for their cervezas. That's why they're sneaking through the bushes like that."

For some reason, this made me smile. It made total sense to me, and I didn't blame them at all. It did make me hark back to my under-twenty one days when we'd stand in front of a liquor store and wheedle alcohol from sympathetic adults going into the store, usually men. Later, my friend and I got fake IDs and enjoyed the thrill of successfully passing through the ID check done by the door bouncers at our local bars. Once we turned twenty-one, it wasn't as much fun anymore.

The highlight of the day's festival had to be the glutton contest. Each contestant had to consume a bowl of *chapo*, which was a bowl of masato made with plantains instead of yucca. Following this filling introduction was the rapid consumption of four of those hideous, tasteless white jungle bread rolls. Next came three cigarettes to be smoked, followed by a pile of cooked yucca.

I can't remember what the prize being offered was, but only the young men competed. Perhaps it was for a filled stomach, but they all seemed to heartily enjoy the challenge. For a village mired in poverty, this particular contest seemed a bit strange to me. But I was there in their land, so I just joined in with all the hooting and hollering.

The next day, as we gathered our things from Uncle Alfredo's house, I saw Jhony and Julito at the open doorway. Their glances followed my every move as if I would suddenly vanish into thin air right before their eyes. I smiled at those two young boys, wondering if I'd ever see them again. I know that at times when I was exhausted, the constant, intense presence of the children would get on my nerves. Yet

I also knew that they were pure spirits, and my wish was to be able to return to help make their lives a little better if I could.

I took out all the medications from my pack that I knew I could replace in Iquitos. Handing them to Alfredo, I told him to hold onto them until he knew of someone who needed them. I wished I'd brought larger bottles, but sometimes a little of something is better than nothing at all.

A group of children followed us down to where the big riverboat would pick us up. Jhony and Julito, normally all smiles and energy, seemed particularly downcast. When it came time to say our final goodbyes, their eyes were not the only ones to have tears in them.

We had to wait for the *lancha* that was due to arrive around three o'clock in the afternoon. Out in this remote pueblo, *lancha* times are approximate; you can't be sure they'll arrive exactly at a certain hour.

"The given time is generally when it's due," explained Olaff. "It's only approximate depending on loads. If someone upriver is loading a ton of bananas, the *lancha* will be late." His shoulder shrug told me that that's just the way it was.

From my excessively punctual Western mind, this made complete sense, but it also made me twitchy. How long would we have to wait?

With this afternoon departure, we'd be arriving back in Iquitos around midnight if everything went to schedule, later if there were delays. This was a dangerous time to be in the ports, so we wanted to make sure we stuck together.

This part of our journey had brought my Ribereño teacher and I closer together. During the return trip on the *lancha*, Javier revealed more of his life before we'd met. At the age of sixteen he'd joined the military as was required of all Peruvian men of that age.

"If I didn't join the military, I wouldn't have received my DNI." Javier talked about their *Documento de Nacional Identidad*, which was somewhat similar to our identification cards or driver's license. "You have to apply for this before you turn eighteen here.

"I first came to Iquitos at the age of fourteen in order to learn Spanish. I only spoke my native language, Kichwa. Indigenous languages aren't allowed in the military because they can't be understood."

I thought of my Native American Studies classes where I had learned of this same thing happening in my country. On one hand, children were taken away from their parents, put into boarding schools and forbidden to speak anything but English. On the other hand, there were the Navajo Code Talkers who successfully used their native Diné language skills during WWII to outwit the Japanese cryptographers who had been able to decipher English language codes and thwart American battle plans.

Looking at my stockily built native teacher, it was hard to picture him in a crisp white uniform, sent to help guard the Ecuadorian border. The more I got to know him, the more I had been amazed at his various experiences. I thought of how he'd told me that people in the cities often mocked those who lived in the jungle. What a mistake to simply judge someone by their appearance, missing out on the richness of character that these incredible people carry with them.

PART FIVE

Padrecocha

CHAPTER 19

Make Mine Masato

For just a brief time, I felt content to be back in Iquitos, if only to have a break from all of the bugs. Part of me felt some sense of achievement from having my efforts recognized with the rites of passage, but I knew there was still a long road ahead. I was far from finished, but there was no hurry. The only thing that mattered was that I was on that road.

A sweet little cat had appeared and moved into my *casita*, and I was happy to have her company when she decided to take a break from her roaming. On one of her lengthier visits, I was lying on my straw bed and looking up at the ceiling, lost in thought while giving her a tickle at the same time. Suddenly, a large rat ran down a pipe in one of the far corners of the room. The kitty spotted it and sprang into action as only a cat can. Bad timing for the rat, but I was just glad to have one less rodent to worry about.

Javier had decided it was time for me to make my own pot of masato. While this was not part of my core shamanic training, I felt it was important to learn about the culture that ayahuasca came from. It seemed to give me more of a complete picture of the rich tradition of which this sacred medicine was only a part. We did a run to Belen to pick up food for the house and stopped at a stall that was selling large yucca roots.

"How many roots do you usually need?" I asked.

"It's customary to make large pots because it's a lot of work. You don't want to go to all that trouble for only a liter or two. We'll get ten. That should be good for the pot we have," he replied. "We should also pick up some firewood while we're out, as well as some lighter fuel to help get the flames started."

The pot he was referring to was the one in which I'd made my first pot of ayahuasca, so I knew it would need to be scrubbed out well. That was the easy part.

"We'll get this set up before anything else because it's going to take a long time for the water to boil," Jav instructed.

I could have used their kitchen for this project, but I wanted to make it in the traditional way—outside over an open fire. Jav hauled two large breeze blocks over and set the pot on them, measuring the distance between them so that an opening large enough for the fuel was formed.

"You want enough of the bottom of the pot to be supported on both sides, but if you put the bricks too close together you limit the size of the fire space below. Since you're heating up a lot of water, you want as much space as possible, but you definitely don't want one side of the pot to fall in!"

Once he was satisfied with the brick set up, he then filled the pot halfway with water. "We may need to add more water once you've got all those ready. You want about this much water over the tops of all the roots," he said, holding up three fingers together. "The roots first need to be prepped, which starts with cutting off the ends."

I duly wrote down each step in one of my notebooks. "Grab your trusty machete and whack off both ends with the sharp blade," I noted, then comically added, "If you're preparing this at home in California, take a heavy sharp knife and neatly top and tail both ends." Yes, in a way I thought of my notebooks as cookbooks. I might just want to recreate this at home one day.

I struggled with peeling the root until Jav showed me a much faster way to do this by making a long incision down one side. If done correctly, you are then able to slide your knife around the root to loosen the tough outer skin, and it should then slip right off. I guessed that my teacher was able to make this look easy because he'd been doing it for years. It was probably going to take me some time to become as deft at yucca stripping as he was.

One of the key ingredients I felt was missing was the camaraderie. Making something like a pot of masato had seemed to be a communal activity. I thought of sitting with the Jivaro women doing the pre-cooking prep work on the roots while everyone shared tasks and gossiped. Once Javier had showed me how to skin the roots, he took off again, leaving me alone with the large task ahead. It didn't feel so fun this time.

Julieta's sister, Carla, who lived next door, dropped by for a visit. Looking down the long hall and through the open kitchen door, she saw me sitting on the ground as I worked on the yucca. Javier, who'd now stationed himself at the front door to see if any friends passed by, answered her incredulous query as to what I was doing.

"She's making a pot of masato all by herself?"

On hearing the affirmative, she made her way to the back yard where I was still attempting to emulate my teacher's technique of peeling the thick outer layer off the yucca roots.

"Have you made masato before?" Carla asked me, although taking one look at the mess, she needn't have waited for me to answer.

"I helped prepare the roots, but that was it. I'm a pretty good cook so I just need to master the art of preparing these things more quickly and neatly."

"Well, I've made a lot of masato and I'd be happy to help you if you'd like some company."

I quickly accepted and said a silent thank you to whatever angel had overheard me. Carla very likely saved me a lot of time and energy, and she was able to offer a lot of useful tips as we went along.

At last, we came to the part that masato is probably most well-known for: spitting the cooked, chewed root balls back into the pot. After you've pureed the cooked yucca, you drain the pot and preserve the cooking liquid for a later stage. Carla showed me how to grab a golf-ball sized mass and chew it until it liquefies.

I knew you weren't supposed to eat the root puree, but I couldn't help swallowing some of it. Okay, probably more than some. By this time, Javier had trotted back to the yard to see how the process was going.

"You're not supposed to eat it, Judita! If you keep up like that we won't have anything to drink!"

Cramming another ball of the cooked starch into my mouth, I made a face at him. I was starting to get to the point where I'd had enough of the laborious process and somewhat deflated at the thought of how much there was still left to do.

"No, you don't do this to the entire pot. You just need to do enough to start the fermentation. Let's go with ten balls and see how that works," Carla suggested.

The last step was to add in a small quantity of sugar and stir the contents of the pot well to mix everything thoroughly. I asked Carla how long the process took until it was ready.

"It depends. If you want fresh *masato*, which we call *dulce*, sweet, it should be ready by this afternoon or tomorrow at the latest. But if you want the stronger, alcoholic *ponayardo*, you have to give it about three days. You'll be able to try it through all of its stages so you'll learn how to recognize where it's at."

"We want the alcoholic kind," Javier informed us a little too quickly.

I smiled at him. Of course we did!

After thanking Carla profusely for her help, and then tidying things up, I decided to go into town to check my email. I was becoming more confident of roaming around on my own in the city. I found a note from my sister saying that Dad had accepted the explanation that I'd sent to them before leaving for Napo of why I was here and where I believed I was going.

"But Mom doesn't get it. She said, 'Well, I still think she should look for a real job with good benefits, maybe at the post office like I suggested.'"

I smiled as I logged off, thinking about what a real job was. Wasn't being a shaman or healer a real job? I decided to celebrate by going to Ari's and ordering a large green salad, followed by some aguaje ice cream. Simple pleasures are the best, aren't they?

When I returned back to the house, I found my teacher was still at his front door outpost, but he was no longer alone. Two of his friends, Lalo and Ricardo, had joined him, bringing along a few beers. While all three men were clearly inebriated, Lalo obviously had had a good head start over his two companions. As I climbed out of the moto and paid the driver, Lalo's mouth dropped open and all he could do was stare at me.

"Not again!" I said to myself. "Do I have some kind of Martian antennas or something that only they can see?"

Ricardo was actually rather cute. Showing off his well-built torso in a white muscle shirt, he decided his strategy would be flattery.

"What beautiful eyes you have! And your smile! You have a face like an angel!"

I didn't know whether to fall on the ground in a fit of giggles or roll my eyes. No one had ever compared me to an angel before! I found Ricardo to be quite charming, but I'd have to see what he was like sober to really be able to assess his character.

Lalo, however, was on the other end of the manners scale. He leaned in and tried to whisper a question to Javier, but being so drunk it came out at full volume so we were all able to hear it.

"So what's she like, you know, *el sexo*?"

Why he was asking my teacher this, I have no idea, but it was so incredibly ridiculous that I burst out laughing. It sort of reminded me of the Monte Python sketch where Eric Idle is asking Terry Jones if his wife was a goer.

Leaving the men to their adolescent antics, I retreated back to my *casita* and inspected the masato. It looked a bit like bread dough now, just at the phase where it was starting to rise. I took a small taste and it could only be described as green. I settled into my hammock to update my field notes.

So, while I at least had my masato project, I found myself falling into the same annoyances as before. No, I wasn't expecting to be entertained or catered to by any means, but Jav and Juli had a tendency to suddenly vanish without a word. Because I didn't know where they'd gone or when they'd be back, I wasn't sure what to do with myself. All it would have taken was for one of them to let me know they'd be gone all day and not return until some approximate time. That would have freed me up to perhaps take off on a short expedition, or maybe even plan another night away somewhere close by. I then wondered if my annoyances were part of what Javier had told pointed out: my constant need to know what was going on, to have everything all figured out.

I walked into the lounge to find Olaff plopped in front of the television.

"Everything good at home?" I asked him.

"Yes. I was able to get all the classes I wanted for next semester. That was important because it's my last semester at university." He smiled and added, "I can't wait to take off again soon though."

"Me either. I hate sitting around here not knowing what's going on. No one's around and I don't know when they'll be back. I'm thinking of going back into the center and hanging out. Wanna join me?"

"Sure. The big game is on at six so Javier will be back by then."

"Game?"

"The World Cup. Peru versus Costa Rica."

"So I expect I'll get a beer request then," I said to myself.

My jungle guardian and I took a moto back to the city center. Our day alternated between rounds of Pilsen Callao and hanging out along the malecon, the boardwalk that overlooks the River Itaya. While I was wearing sturdy hiking sandals, my young companion sported an old pair of flip flops, which were common footwear in this city. As we wandered along, one of the upper thong parts decided to separate permanently from the rubber sole, and Olaff briefly staggered as the shoe came off his foot. I knew he didn't have the money to buy a new pair, so I told him I'd replace them. I liked Olaff a lot, and if there was anything I could do to make his life a bit easier, I'd be glad to help him out.

Even after we'd returned several hours later, Jav and Juli were still not back. After checking my masato, I checked in with myself. Yes, I was still irritated, so I decided to walk over to the Plaza 28 de Julio, where a group of children was performing old Inca dances. As I sat and watched, I realized I was hearing different voices inside my head now. They weren't the indignant stirrers of my ego; they were more tranquil. They had a different feeling.

"Are you paying attention to how you feel?" came one.

"Well, yeah. I'm pissed off. We come back to the city and my teacher just dumps me and goes off the whole time without even checking in to see if I'm still alive! I get that he's not my babysitter, but would it be so time consuming to walk a few feet to tell me he'll be gone all day so I can make my own plans? One little sentence! Would that be so difficult? Grrr."

"Good point. Now, without adding in all the emotion and animal noises, what does this tell you?"

"What does this tell me? I feel like after all we've been through that all I am is a walking wallet. Give me money for this! Give me money for that! Pay this bill! Give us beautiful gifts." I almost said grrr again but stopped myself.

"So pay attention to how you feel, but go in much farther, past the anger. This is where the real story lies. Don't always trust your eyes and ears. The truth can always be found inside of you."

I was so engrossed in my inner dialog that it never occurred to me to ask who was speaking. It definitively was not the voice of my ego.

"Go back to your first few days in this country on the north coast. Do you remember what the group leader told you about emotions?"

"Yes, he talked about how anger blocks messages from our spirit guides. Something like that. Not just anger, but all strong emotion. Like dark clouds blotting out the sun."

"Uh huh. You got it. For the rest of your training here, we want you to listen to what your body is telling you. If someone tells you something, or you see something, check right in and see if your gut feelings match what you're being presented with."

"Okay, I think I get what you're telling me. But how will I know for sure?"

I'm sure if spirits had eyes, the ones who were speaking to me surely would have been rolling theirs at that moment.

"Pay attention to your gut. It will not feel settled, tight, clenching, like a fist hammering on you to notice what is really happening. You've had this ability all your life and used it without realizing it. Now it's time to polish up that valuable tool and start using it intentionally. We are always with you. We will be helping you."

"Thank you. I appreciate what you've told me."

The ensuing silence let me know that the transmission had ended. The asinine voice of my ego then took the opportunity to chime in once again.

"Well, what a load of nonsense that was! Let's stomp back to the house and give that jungle shaman a piece of our mind! You don't have to take this crap!"

"No, I really don't. So shut up!"

Good thing we humans have the gift of thought. If anyone had been able to hear me chatting with disembodied beings and then telling my own ego to shut up, they may have backed slowly away before running off in the opposite direction.

But no one was backing away, quite the opposite in fact. Two young men in their early twenties had inched up to the concrete step just above the one on which I was sitting.

"Hi, Miss! Hi!" greeted the one nearest me.

I turned to look at the handsome boys, who were giddy and grinning like Cheshire Cats. Deep within, the voice floated back into my consciousness.

"Here we go. Tune in to your intuition right now. You're going to get a chance to practice what we were just talking about. Listen to their words, then feel how your body reacts."

I smiled back. "*Hola, chicos.* Wassup?"

"Where you from? What's your name? Speak English?"

I decided to have a little fun with these guys since they didn't feel dangerous to me. "I'm Julie from California. You?"

"I'm Beto!" said the one closest to me. Beto had his hair styled in a very modern cut and gelled to keep it in place. He wore a light blue button-down shirt and jeans and newish, name brand sneakers.

"And I'm Charlie! My English is better than Beto's so you can talk more to me."

Charlie was very skinny, but taller than his friend. A thick lock of hair kept falling down into his eyes so he'd have to push it away frequently. He wore a baggy white T-shirt with faded black writing on the front, and light-blue jeans. He also sported a nice pair of sneakers.

"So you both speak English, huh?" I asked them.

"Yes! Can we practice our English with you?" Charlie asked eagerly.

A mild sensation appeared in my midsection. I recognized it as one I'd had before, but probably dismissed as nerves or indigestion. I was being cued to pay attention.

Seeing that I wasn't going to tell them to get lost, both Beto and Charlie scooted down to sit on the step next to me.

"Okay," I decided to let out a little more line as the gut feeling persisted.

"They want more from you than to improve their language skills," I heard inside.

"Of course they do," I replied internally. I wanted to roll my eyes but Beto and Charlie were unaware that they weren't the only ones I was talking to.

"You have boyfriend in California?" Charlie asked.

"You really pretty! We glad you are speaking to us," Beto added.

"Gee, thanks. So what did you want to talk about?"

"Remember; it's all about the money. Learn to follow the energy back to the source," I was instructed inside.

"Come on! I'm just getting the hang of this instinct thing, and now you want me to follow energy. How can I do that?"

"Just feel it and don't ask questions."

"No husband in United States?" Charlie persisted.

"Why do you want to know that?" I was winding them up a bit.

"Because you so pretty but sitting alone," Beto said.

"Here it comes."

"Beto's father is a great shaman, you know? You want do ayahuasca?"

Oh boy, just like lambs to the slaughter.

"What's that aya stuff? I don't know what a shaman is. What are you talking about?"

Both boys looked at each other in alarm. They hadn't expected me to not know what shamans were, or what ayahuasca was. That's what most people came to Iquitos for, wasn't it?

"We show you. You come to our jungle lodge? It's not far," Beto said.

"Uh, I don't think I want to go to the jungle. I'd be afraid of all those bugs," I lied, hoping they wouldn't notice all the bites on my arms and legs.

"Is okay. We have nets. You come?" Charlie asked.

After a bit of probing, it seemed that the nearby lodge—if there indeed was one—was quite a long boat ride from Iquitos.

"So you must have a boat then?" I tried to look serious.

"No, but we know someone with a boat. You will rent it for us. We take you there now! Yes?" Beto urged.

"Oh, I will, huh? And just how much does it cost to rent your friend's boat?"

Once again, Beto and Charlie looked at each other in a panic. They hadn't anticipated this question so there was no smooth, prepared answer.

"Never mind, guys. But tell me, what do you do at a jungle lodge?"

Thinking they still had a chance, they both started talking at once about men who go into altered reality and sing while people drink this aya stuff and they have visions and everybody is happy.

"Sounds crazy, *hombres*. So how much does it cost to stay at a jungle lodge?"

"My father gives good price! For you, maybe $200 for one night. Is really cheap," Beto informed me.

"$200 a night? You know this is a scam, don't you?" My inner voice almost sounded amused.

"It's almost funny. They have no idea who I am or what I do." Then I added as an afterthought, "Or what I've already been through."

"But ceremony extra. Maybe $100 for you," Charlie piped in.

"I see. So I get to pay for the boat to a lodge far away, and then I pay for the lodge and the ceremony? Gee, this is getting kind of expensive."

I looked at my watch. It was almost six o'clock and the big footie game was about to start. I figured it was about time to head back.

"Where you going?" Beto asked with some alarm.

"Home to watch the World Cup."

The two would-be scammers looked at each other. "Home?" they nearly asked on unison.

"Well, yes. I may be from California, but I live here." I let this sink in. It was kind of true in a vague sort of way.

"You have TV? Can we come with you?"

"I'm afraid not. My husband wouldn't like it very much."

"Husband? You said you no have husband in United States," Beto objected.

"I never said I did or didn't. Besides, he's not in the United States; he's here in Iquitos!" I gave them a sweet smile as I stood up and stretched.

"Have a nice evening, guys. It's been fun talking to you." I started to walk away and heard one of the yell behind me.

"Wait!"

I paused.

"You can give us money for a moto?"

"Sorry, I spent all my money. I'm flat broke. *Nos vemos*. See ya!"

I could just imagine the two of them looking at each other and asking, "what just happened here?" as I giggled all the way back to Javier's house.

The party seemed to have already started by the time I arrived back at the house. My teacher seemed briefly annoyed that I'd gone out again, but I reminded him that he'd gone out without any word himself, and I was not about to sit in the lounge all day and watch stupid TV shows.

There was no time to continue with this topic as it soon got very animated in the little concrete lounge. I like watching soccer myself, so I stayed to watch Costa Rica trounce Peru. No one seemed surprised.

"We don't have a good team," commiserated Olaff.

I'd decided not to say anything to Javier about what I found so annoying. He and Juli were just doing what they always did. I think he and I shared the same taste for being out and about, and not being stuck in the house with domestic duties where everyone wanted something from you all the time. I did mention that good communication was important to me and would go a long way towards preventing bad feelings before they arose. I think my words went in one ear and out the other. Male jungle shamans are used to being in charge, and they don't take instructions from women.

The next morning, we began preparing to make our way to our last training location in nearby Padrecocha, where Javier apparently had more relatives we'd be staying with. As he'd alluded in his village, during this phase we were going to drink much larger quantities of ayahuasca so we could commune with the spirits.

Padrecocha was only a twenty minute boat ride away from the Bellavista port, so we'd planned to stock up on fresh supplies before heading out. As we shopped for the usual items, it struck me that we'd eaten far better out in the jungle than we did in the city. I knew money was issue, but I never saw anyone eat anything substantial here. Liters of full sugar soda and refined carbohydrates like cookies seemed to be a frequent snack. It was as if meals didn't exist, but people can't live on sugary junk foods alone.

In addition to our usual supplies, my four liter bucket of maturing masato would be making the journey with us. Julieta's father had a car, something that was not very common in Iquitos. In addition to the many mototaxis, people rode scooters and motorcycles. Occasionally you'd see a few cars, but they were the exception rather than the rule.

The only advantage of having the car was that we were able to fit everything in one go. It was a small sedan that had seen better days. Okay, to be honest, it had seen better years. I sat in the backseat, jammed between Olaff and our packs, the masato and my encanto in its bucket. I prayed we would all get to the river port safely.

There was a nice surprise waiting at Bellavista. Not only did we have the same boat as when we'd gone up Rio Momon, but the dour-faced Jivaro shaman, Augustin, was to be our driver! Although he still would not look me in the eyes, for some reason I was just delighted to see him. Somehow, his taking us on to our next adventure connected everything for me. I felt more like a local instead of someone whose exit stage left was on the not too distant horizon.

CHAPTER 20

The Stream of Love

We were once again on the river, and I heaved a sigh of a relief. Our little group was now headed towards Padrecocha, which was to be our final destination for this trip. Although I was glad to get away from the bugs for a few days, I was still finding it difficult to take these brief breaks in my training. I would have much preferred to just keep going for months without needing to return to the chaos in the city. As the delicious breeze stirred my hair, I realized that while what I wanted was my ideal alone, there were real-life issues that had to be attended to, even for magical jungle shamans. I knew Javier loved being out in the wild even more than I did, but he had a family and domestic issues to tend to on our breaks. And of course, we needed to replenish our supplies.

Olaff jumped off the *Rey de los Reyes* first and pulled it up onto the sand. I hopped off next and was surprised to find myself on a very nice beach. Javier then stepped off the little craft, and I saw him confer briefly with his nephew before turning to me.

He pointed off in the distance saying, "We have a long walk to get to the camp. See that ridge? We have to make our way over it with all the equipment, then the path is up and down, up and down." He mimicked the motion with his hand.

As I waited for him to get to the point, a group of young men suddenly came running over the ridge in our direction. It looked like a race, and in some ways it was. My companions seemed to be expecting them, and Javier turned to me again as the lead man skidded to a stop in front of us, spraying sand into the air with a flourish.

"These *muchachos* are *cargueros*," he explained. "For a small fee they can carry all our equipment for us." His raised eyebrows signified the decision was mine since I would be the one paying the small fee.

I checked in with my gut. This was my training, my expedition, and therefore it was up to me to handle its financing and all the costs associated with it. However, I was getting a little fed up with being nickel-and-dimed at every turn. Whenever I tried to get some idea of our expenses so I could figure out my budget, I would be assured that this was it; we only needed these items and nothing else. Yet inevitably, it wouldn't be long before more requests for money or items would be forthcoming, even for things that had nothing remotely to do with the overall journey. It had gotten to the point that when we were in the city and I'd see certain people approaching, I'd start to cringe because I knew that some new urgent situation had arisen that required cash. My cash.

"So how much is this small fee?" I wanted to know.

Javier put my query to the winner of the race. "Five soles. Each man!" came his reply.

I leaned over to Olaff and asked him if this was a fair price. I trusted him and knew he wouldn't try to bamboozle me with bullshit.

"Yes, it's okay. Like Uncle said, it really is a long walk and the path is hard with all this heavy stuff." He looked around and added, "And it's also really hot!"

That it was. While Olaff had been our handyman, food supplier and chef, he also had had to carry a lot of the heavy items for us. I suspected he was hoping I'd go for the deal to give him a break.

"And just how many *cargueros* do we need?" I asked Jav.

He and Olaff did a quick estimate and turned back to me. By now the entire group of eager young men was standing in front of us, anticipating who might be the lucky ones chosen to make a few soles.

"It depends on how much you want to carry yourself. If we each take a bag I think four will do."

Four men times five soles. Twenty soles translated to about six dollars. Yes, sometimes one must splurge on a few luxuries. I agreed and let Jav deal with the negotiations.

It turned out to be very worthwhile to hire the porters. While the trail was not as treacherous as the one from Rio Momon to the Jivaro camp, it was steep in places, and with the intense Amazonian sun beating down on us, I was grateful to be carrying just a small load this time.

Our hike took us through the pueblo, which seemed to be well maintained. Despite the size of our group and the number of things we all carried, the inhabitants of Padrecocha didn't seem to be too interested in us. I mentioned this to my companions because it was such a contrast to what I'd experienced in Nuevo Progreso.

"We're close to Iquitos so they do get *turistas* here," Olaff told me.

"Oh good. Maybe I'll be able to blend in with the locals, eh?" I joked.

In reply, Olaff just gave me one of his sweet smiles.

Passing the small town, we continued onto a narrower path for quite some time. We finally arrived at the crest of a small hill, where we paused briefly. I could see a lovely stream below us, but no signs of people or a camp.

Javier suddenly called out a loud "Hoooo!" and waited for a reply.

"Why does he do that?" I asked Olaff.

"When you're in the jungle and approaching an area like this where you can't be seen from far off, you announce your presence with a sound like hoooo. This lets the people know you are not an enemy. We also use it to find people who are lost in the jungle sometimes, like the children. Remember this in case you ever go wandering and can't find your way back."

This seemed like sound advice to me. I recalled the blowgun I'd used in the Jivaro camp and decided I wouldn't want to be on the receiving end of a surprised dart.

Someone out of sight responded with another hoooo. Javier and the unseen man exchanged this sound several times as we approached, allowing me to see how it could be used as a homing beacon.

We made our way down the hill and crossed the wooden bridge that spanned the *quebrada*. Javier held up his hand, indicating that we pause for a moment.

"This is called the *Quebrada de Amor*," he informed me. The Stream of Love.

Did I dare ask why it was called this? Yes, I dared. Of course I did.

"You will soon see, Judita!"

As we continued along the path, we saw an older man coming towards us. Like Uncle Alfredo, Tío Abuelo Juan was in his late seventies. I was becoming more confused with all these relations of my teacher and wondered if they really were related to him in the way I thought of family ties. Olaff explained to me that the title of *tío abuelo* referred to the brother of someone's grandfather. I quickly tried to figure this one out with what I already knew about Javier's family. I knew that one of my teacher's grandfathers had been a *banco* shaman in Rio Napo, but he hadn't mentioned anything about the other one. I decided all these relationship titles would drive me crazy if I tried to figure them out, so I would just take them at face value. If Juan was Javier's uncle-grandfather, that was good enough for me!

Juan's camp was neatly manicured and he showed us where we'd be staying. As with Oscar's *Casa del Shaman*, there was a small tambo set towards the rear of the camp where the three of us would once again hang our mosquito nets side by side.

I was really wilted from the long walk in the heat, so Olaff offered to string up my hammock for me. I gratefully accepted and climbed in for a brief battery recharge. Although I am used to the Southern California heat, it is much drier and it doesn't seem to take so much out of me as the much more humid jungle heat does.

Once I'd cooled down a little, Jav suggested I take a dip in the stream, which wound its way through the camp. The *Quebrada de Amor* was deep enough to submerge oneself in, which was a real delight. The water was clear and clean and I knew I'd be spending a lot of time in this Stream of Love.

"There don't seem to be as many bugs here," I commented to Olaff as I toweled off.

"Right. The family takes care of this place and grooms it, cutting away the plants near to the camp, which helps to reduce not only the mosquitos, but also other things like snakes. They rake all the leaves that fall and burn them, and the smoke keeps the bugs away."

Javier strolled over and showed me the communal outdoor kitchen area with benches and tables.

"People come here from the city to relax. They pay money to Juan to use the facilities like the stream, and they can make a *parrillada* and eat in a nice area."

I recalled this term from the event I'd attended with Geraldo at his mother's house earlier in the year where I'd been one of the barbecue chefs. So much had happened in one year, and it wasn't over yet.

I could sense that Jav was back in his visitor's form, happy to be away from domestic cares and ready to have some fun. He was once again in his element, and I don't think my sociable teacher stopped talking long enough to take a breath.

Once we'd settled in, Javier announced he was going for a swim and asked me to come along. Although my bathing suit was still wet from the previous dip, I just loved that water and was happy to get back into it.

It was around sunset, and I saw the planet Venus in the sky, so I pointed this out to him. I should have known that this would lead to chatting about love goddesses and aphrodisiacs and how this lovely stream got its name.

"You watch, Judita. You will see the old men bringing their young girls here to have sex."

"But why come all the way out here?" I dared to ask the foolish question.

"You have seen that many family members live in a small space," he explained. "There is no place for intimacy because there is always someone in the home. So we have to go to other places like this."

I noticed he'd said *we* instead of *they*. I wasn't about to ask if the old men were cheating on the partners they had left back in the city. Yes, this was going to be a different location altogether for this phase of my training!

It was hard to imagine that this was supposed to be the most difficult part of the three phases Jav had planned for me. He'd told me that he felt sad for all the suffering that was to come for me, but I couldn't really imagine the form it might take.

"Is it going to be worse than that night in Sacha Wasi where I was rolling all over the floor?" I asked him. That night had been so insanely strong, with such violent purging for many hours. How could anything be worse than that? I had observed that he'd brought the *completo*-sized pates this time instead of the smaller *poco* ones. We'd used both of these hollowed out gourd cups at the Sacha Wasi retreat, working our way up from the smaller *poco* to the avocado-sized *completo*.

"You will see, Judita. *Vas a ver.*"

The next morning Olaff announced that we had to make a bread run to pick up some *panes*. *Panes* were the tasteless white bread rolls that I'd come to loathe. I even created a nickname for them: *penas de la selva* or just *penas* for short. Sorrowful bread products, they were indeed!

A nice-looking man strolled over to where the three of us were chatting about the day's plans.

"This is Rider. He lives in the village but spends a lot of time here helping out," Javier told me.

Rider, pronounced as Reader, was in his early fifties. His handsome features were similar to those of most of the other jungle men I'd met so far. Rider was slender and well-muscled, with thick black hair cut just above his collar. Like Ricardo back at Jav's house, he seemed to light up when he saw me. I was just so unused to this enthusiastic male attention. I have to admit that there were a few times when I kind of wished I was here for different reasons besides a shamanic apprenticeship with all its rules and restrictions.

Rider, Javier, and I made our way back to the pueblo, while Olaff attended to other camp tasks. I was given a tour of the small village in between picking up the few items we needed. The sun was already beating down mercilessly, and even at this early hour it was debilitating. As we walked along, I noticed with some amusement that there were two nightclubs and pointed this out to my companions.

"We will resume your training in a couple of days, so tonight we will have some fun!" Javier told us with relish. I was beginning to suspect my teacher was quite a party animal and wondered if this would affect my training in any way. I knew we couldn't be serious all the time, and that this first three-month period of our training together was not for mastering the entire path. It was solely to lay the foundations of this ancient jungle healing tradition. Refinement and deepening would come later on.

Scoring the hideous squares of cotton wool disguised as white rolls was the easy part of the errand. Once we'd completed the purchase of the rolls, it was time to be led into what I now refer to as The Incredible Fainting Chicken Caper.

"We are looking to buy a couple of chickens to bring back to camp," Javier told me.

"How do you find them in order to buy them?" I asked.

"Look for a sign that says 'Hay pollo,' which tells you that the vendor has chickens to sell."

Coming from a country where it's common to buy meat that's already been processed and ready to cook, I was learning that such conveniences were non-existent in a small jungle village even if there was electricity. We were now looking for live chickens that we'd have to process ourselves.

The three of us walked up the main street without seeing such a sign, so we started to meander back off the path towards where the inhabitants had built their houses. I don't know why I expected to find a lot of households selling chickens, but once again my expectations proved to be false. Just as we were about to call it quits, we stumbled upon a property advertising chickens for sale.

Having found the sign was one thing, but actually trying to buy the birds was quite another. The doors and windows of the ramshackle property were open, so it appeared that someone was home. Javier was in his element as he pounded on the door and yelled into the house for the seller to come out.

The reason for the delay soon became apparent: the chicken vendor was completely wasted on aguardiente. Scurrilous and nearly incomprehensible, he demanded to know why we were on his property.

"What are you doing here? Who is she?" he glared at me suspiciously.

Javier pointed to the sign advertising chickens for sale and told the man we wanted to buy some and that we had cash. Here in the jungle, that phrase was usually enough to open seemingly closed doors.

"I don't have any chickens today! Go away! Go away!"

Rider stepped in and backed up Javier's mention of the sign. At that moment, a rooster suddenly let out a loud cock-a-doodle-doo. All eyes turned to the left where an overgrowth of bushes and greenery hid a previously unnoticed fenced-in area. Javier and Rider strode firmly over to where we'd heard the bird noise and peered through the fence to see quite a number of chickens and one noisy rooster. With all of us focused on the birds, the hens began to cluck and chase each other around.

Javier, Rider, and I turned back around to see the man coming down the steps towards us in a huff. I suddenly had the feeling that we'd interrupted a nap. It was still early, yet he must've been at the bottle for quite some time to have gotten himself into this state already. With the addition of the heat, he had probably been settling in for his first snooze of the day when we appeared.

Realizing that his chickens had given him away, he begrudging began negotiating with us. I was happy to let Javier and Rider deal with the extremely inebriated chicken vendor, and wished I could have filmed the entire interaction because it was so ludicrous. The man would seem to focus on the sale, then he would start rambling on about something completely different and talking to people who were definitely not part of our little group!

Prices for two birds were finally agreed on and once again I opened my purse. Rider held his arms out to indicate that he would carry the unfortunate fowl back to our camp. I was glad for this because it was a long walk, it was hot, and most of all, I'd never carried live chickens around before.

"Let's stop for a cold soda!" suggested Jav when we were once again on the main street.

"But what about the chickens?" I wanted to know.

"What about them? Maybe they'd like a drink too!"

I should have known better than to ask such a logical question.

I normally don't drink sodas but here in the sweltering jungle I agreed, but only on one condition: they had to be cold. While we in more developed areas take things like electricity and refrigeration for granted, not everyone else in the world has these amenities. We enquired in various establishments if their sodas were cold only to see heads shaking at each request.

About to give up, we started to pass by one establishment and looked inside. The affable proprietor waved us in and urged us to sit down and cool off with a couple of warm colas.

"We may as well. We have a long, hot walk back to the camp," I said with a sigh.

Rider tied the chickens to a chair and we sat at a table. The cloying sweetness of the drink didn't sit well with me, and I wished for a cold glass of plain water.

We were the only customers in the place, so the owner invited himself to join us while he fished around for my marital status. He addressed his queries to Javier as if I were a child, while I sat there trying to keep a straight face. By now, I was getting used to the high level of interest and all the questions about my romantic availability.

Since it seemed that no subject was off limits, Javier and I had devised a few responses in order to quell their curiosity. Unfortunately, he didn't always want to stick to the scripts.

"Yes, it is rather unfortunate that a woman of her age does not have a man," Javier told the nosy shopkeeper as if letting him in on a secret. "It makes her very sad."

It was all I could do to not pour my thick warm cola onto his head.

"She is looking for husband?" he asked hopefully.

"Yah! Judita is available and looking for husband!" chirped Javier as Rider momentarily choked on his soda.

"I am not!" I protested, giving my teacher the stink eye. It did not faze him one bit, and I realized how much he enjoyed putting me on the spot and seeing how I would react.

The shop owner's eyes grew large and he leaned in closer. "Maybe you are looking for Peruvian man? I am looking for a wife."

"I can't consider anything like that right now because I'm studying with Javier here."

Javier, being the master jive talker, wound the man up even further by declaring that while I may be his student, at night we slept next to each other. While this was true, he failed to clarify that each of us had our own separate sleeping mats and mosquito nets. The shopkeeper's eyebrows shot up and he paused for a moment to see if any more juicy details would be forthcoming. Since they were not, he excused himself to tidy something behind the counter. But before he moved away from our table he slapped Javier on the back as we walked out and sold us a few more of the warm sodas to take with us.

"You are a troublemaker, Javito!" I glared at him.

"Ha ha ha, Judita! You must not be so self-important! You must learn to laugh at yourself. Besides, many men here would like to be with you. Maybe when you are finished with me you can look for a husband. Maybe even Rider!"

At this surprise twist, Rider straightened up and smiled.

"Well, this is all my own doing," I thought, fuming. I was the one who wanted more of his attention, didn't I? And now I was right in his crosshairs and couldn't escape.

"Rider's other name is Monkey. You know why we call him that?"

"No idea, Jav. Why do you call Rider Monkey?"

Eyes wide and in full flow, Javier replied, "Because he's a man who is very popular with the ladies. He's always after them, aren't you, Monkey?"

Instead of grabbing Javier by his collar and giving him a flying lesson like I might have, Rider just smiled and continued walking. Now it was Javier's turn to slap Rider on the shoulder, and the two of them laughed like they had a secret between them. I had no doubt that they did. Men! I rolled my eyes.

We continued on the long hike back to our newest camp. Rider carried the two chickens upside down, tethered together by a long cord. They squawked and flapped their wings as we walked, making their carriage a bit challenging. After a while, I realized that the chickens had gone quiet, so I asked the guys to stop to check on them. It appeared that the birds had passed out from being carried upside down in the heat.

On arrival back at camp, Rider handed the two birds to Olaff, who tied them to a shady table leg while he continued his lunch preparations. Able to cool off, the birds started to come back to life. But one was not to be long for this world. Olaff saw me watching and grinned.

"You want to do the honors?"

"I've never done it before. It'd be better to see how you do it than to cause the poor thing any unnecessary suffering." The thought of killing an animal with my bare hands didn't sit well with me, and once again I pondered my solo survival chances out in the wild.

Olaff had only intended to dispatch one of the birds, but the second bird, on seeing her companion's neck wrung right in front of her, promptly keeled over and died from fright!

Since the next phase of my training was due to begin in a couple of days, we decided it was time to see how my first batch of masato had turned out. There was a final stage to the preparation before serving where a quantity of water was added to the bucket. Rolling up my sleeves, I was instructed to reach into the deep bucket and squeeze the yucca solids, removing the hard and thready pieces.

"When the masato is served, you will get some pieces of the yucca in your cup. For this reason, you must ensure that all the solids are small and chewable," Javier instructed.

Once all this had been done, I had to follow the proper traditional way of serving. The entailed serving everyone in the camp first, including the children, and myself last.

"It is the custom here that whoever makes the masato is served last," Rider explained. I made sure to jot this down in my ever-present field notes.

I waited anxiously for the verdict. As I looked around at the circle of faces, I heard Javier call out, "Judita wants to know how it is. This is her first time making masato."

Olaff started the ball rolling by smiling and giving me thumbs up. Rider was next, and indicated he was already up for a refill. If I had any remaining doubts, they were quickly dispelled by the number of cups being held out for refills.

"*Muy bien*, Judita. Your first pot of masato is a success." Javier and I briefly clinked our gourd cups together.

I have always loved anything to do with food, including the shopping and preparation for a meal. I've spent days grinding and cooking individual spices and ingredients for complex dishes with the aim to always present as authentic a dish as possible, and this included my masato. I was thrilled that I'd succeeded!

The night's entertainment turned out to be a trip to one of the pueblo's two discos. Because I'd spent countless hours in bars and nightclubs as a professional musician, I was no longer keen to visit places with overpriced drinks and music that was too loud. But I was curious to see what the village disco was like. It was just too great of an opportunity to pass up.

The boys bathed in the stream and slapped on cologne for our night out. I think they were sweeter smelling than I was. I didn't see any point in dousing myself with one of the artificial scents that were so popular here. We had that long walk into town, so I would be wearing another, more natural scent by the time we arrived at our destination.

We chose the older, more established disco called Maria's. Most dance clubs open at a late hour, but some will allow you to enter early if you're going to drink. Maria's was one of these.

We scored a table that overlooked the dance floor, not noticing that it was on the same level as the club's sound system loudspeakers. The music level was tolerable for a few hours, so we all enjoyed the refreshing Peruvian beers and danced. Olaff, normally so serious and reserved, would use the table as a set of bongos. He knew all the songs, and played along with them as if he were a session percussionist. He was really very good, much to everyone's amusement.

Once the club opened, a DJ hopped behind the mixing desk and kept shouting into his microphone in between the songs. By now, I was pretty hot and wilted, and the volume of the music kept increasing to deafening levels. The novelty of visiting a jungle disco had worn off, and I found myself wishing I'd stayed in camp to have a more peaceful night.

But tonight we were in for a special treat: the Miss Primavera contest! It was currently the spring season in Peru, hence the name of the event. This was supposed to be a beauty contest to show off the local girls who lived in Padrecocha. Two of the eight contestants actually came from Iquitos, and this really got Javier going. With several cervezas under his belt, he became quite vocal about the so-called intruders. And when one of these interlopers, a very skinny girl with buck teeth won, he was on his feet yelling that the contest had been fixed. Could this be the same solicitous shaman that had led us through a ceremony of light to rid us of our negativity back in Sacha Wasi? Yes, it certainly could be!

By now, my head was pounding and I desperately wanted to get back to camp. I wasn't completely sure if I could find the way on my own in the dark yet, so I had to wait for my ever-more sozzled brothers to finish their rounds of beers, and they were in no hurry. Earlier, Jav had told me that he and his nephew had talked a lot about how great our team was and how they were enjoying all the adventures as much as I was. I could feel that he really meant it, and it touched my heart. Enjoy your beers, *hermanos*.

When the sensory input went into overload I would escape outside for a break. There was a concrete block to the right of the door that was a perfect, if hard, seat. During one of these breaks, I heard someone call my name, and I looked around for Javier.

It turned out to be Rider. He lived in the house next door to the disco, and he and his wife, Lucilla, were leaning out of a window trying to get my attention. I told him I was waiting for Javier and Olaff to take me back to camp, but they seemed to have forgotten about me.

"Wait for me. I'll be right there!" Right then, two stools were passed through the front door and we were able to sit and chat.

I was trying not to be annoyed again, but after financing all the rounds, I felt that the least they could do was to poke their heads out every now and then to make sure no one had carried me off into the bushes or something. It was now well after midnight and there were a lot of drunks stumbling around. No one was threatening or belligerent, but I didn't want to have to deal with any unwanted attention on my own.

Rider offered to walk me back to the camp in exchange for a pack of cigarettes. That seemed like a fair deal to me, so I went in to inform my now quite oblivious caretakers that Rider was escorting me, so they could stay until the sun came up if they wanted. For some reason, this really spurred them into action. Jav downed the rest of his beer and the two of them finally emerged from the noisy club. Perhaps it had something to do with the fact that I carried the only flashlight, and there was no moonlight to illuminate the way.

"I thought you'd gone back to camp!" Javier said.

"Um, no. I'm not completely sure of my way yet. I've had a couple of beers and didn't want to get lost." I replied.

Nope, it was not a good idea to be lost in the jungle at night, particularly if one was a bit tipsy. My hands twitched with the thought of strangling my teacher, but once again I resisted.

Juan was there to greet us as we arrived. He and his wife and one of their grandsons had offered to guard our camp while we were away—for a fee, of course. When I had queried this latest request hours earlier, I'd been given a very reasonable explanation.

"This is Saturday night in the pueblo and as you see, most people are in the town drinking. There are thieves who know you are here, so if they found out you were away for hours, they could slip in and steal everything you've got. Lots of houses get broken into on the weekends when people are out drinking. Most of them are riff raff from Iquitos, not here," Juan told me.

Again, I was learning more jungle survival skills. This sort of thing hadn't occurred to me, and it seemed that Jav and his nephew hadn't thought of it either. If a couple of bucks saved our equipment from vanishing, it was well worth it.

Juan and his family owned the land but lived nearby. No one actually lived here full time. It was more like a place of recreation, a park where you could spend a pleasant day grilling meat and swimming in the *Quebrada del Amor*. The downside to this was that it was a day tripper's destination, which I thought was not the most ideal for intense shamanic training. I then considered that perhaps this was yet another of my preconceived notions of how things should be.

Their ubiquitous jungle radio blared me out of sleep in the morning. I'm normally an early riser, but since we'd not laid down until nearly three in the morning, that warranted a few extra hours. The radio may have awakened me, but not the two men who slept on either side of me. They were still dead to the world.

Nature called, so I pulled on my boots and grabbed a roll of toilet paper. I'd purchased a shovel for our group's use, and we'd made a small clearing to use as our latrine. Pulling up my pants, I noticed what looked like a stick riding up with the fabric. I was about to pluck it off when I realized it was a very large stick insect. I loved praying mantises and these insects seemed somewhat similar to them, at least in the head. They would look at you with those weird alien eyes and cock their heads as if they understood what you were saying.

I'd never seen a walking stick this big and knew that it wouldn't hurt me. I slowly slid my hand to the side of the bug so I could estimate its length. It spanned the length from my wrist to the end of my middle finger, roughly about seven inches. I was impressed! It seemed happy to hang onto the fabric of my pants so I wandered back to camp with my little freeloader.

Today was Sunday, so I knew we would not be resuming my training when my companions finally roused themselves from their deep slumber. The jungle people, at least the one that was my current teacher, took the idea of Sunday as a day of rest and play very seriously.

The only thing on the day's agenda was the village football game later in the afternoon. Olaff had begged off, saying he had things to do in camp, so Jav and I headed back on the path into town. Before leaving the area, I had picked up my trusty machete since parts of the forty-five minute walk were rather overgrown and wild. Seeing this, Javier shook his head.

"No one carries a machete in the pueblo. It's an unwritten rule to prevent problems when people drink too much aguardiente."

I considered this and acknowledged that it was a good idea, so I put it down by its familiar orange handle and patted it tenderly. Machete Woman would have to be bladeless for a few hours.

We had passed the local playing field on our hike in from the river, and I'd been told that it was in high demand every Sunday. This certainly was the case today. We watched the game for a while and then went in search of a cold drink.

By some odd twist of fate, Maria's was already open with the music blaring at full volume. Plopping ourselves down at a table nearest to the door, we ordered a round of ice cold sodas. I'm not a big fan of sugary drinks, but in the jungle it seemed like you had a choice between sodas and beers. I opted for bottled water whenever I could get it, but it often seemed that the shop or eating place we were in had just run out—at least that's what we were told. The local shops had a very limited range of products and tended towards those that wouldn't go off quickly in the heat. This meant that canned and bottled products, as well as a small assortment of packaged foods, were usually what was on offer. Occasionally one might see a few vegetables, but they never looked very appealing.

Thinking I wouldn't be able to stomach another soda, I switched to beer and Javier was happy to follow along. Since my teacher seemed to love to talk about sex, I decided to ask him about the local custom of suddenly being single and available once one was away from home.

"So, is it common to have more than one partner here?" I asked him.

"Ya, Judita, but not just one or two. Four or five is customary."

Four or five? I shook my head to clear it. A part of me wanted to laugh for some reason, but I didn't. From what I had seen so far, it seemed like this multiple partner arrangement was the norm here. People talked about it incessantly and considering the number of times I had been chatted up, I knew it wasn't just Javier trying to pull one over on me.

While initially their wide open romantic arrangements seemed a bit surprising to me, I wondered if perhaps they were acting more in accordance with the rhythms of nature than my own supposedly more sophisticated culture did. Here, sex was discussed frequently and with great relish, and so far I hadn't seen anyone blush or take an opposing view.

In contrast, the Western culture that I had grown up in generally aimed for monogamy, but judging by the number of affairs and divorces, I'd begun to wonder if the human animal was truly meant to live for up to a possible fifty years or more with only one partner. There was no one right answer to this.

As I sipped my beer and tried to ignore the thumping music, I suddenly recalled a funny incident from many years ago. I was still living in London at the time but had made a trip back to California to visit my parents. Many Europeans seemed to have a less prudish view of the body than my fellow countrymen, and the Continental people didn't get all overheated at things like topless beaches.

I'd bought a women's magazine to read on the long trans-Atlantic flight, and the feature story was about women's breasts. The well-written article was matter of fact and conversational, and there were several photos of women unclothed from the waist up to illustrate that no one size or shape was the norm. There was nothing at all sexy or titillating about the article.

When I had finished the magazine, I added it to the pile of paper recycling in an open bin that we had put on the street for collection. My dad had a workshop in the garage and spent a lot of time tinkering with many different projects, often working with the door up so he could get some fresh air and better light. I'd come out to talk to him and see what he was working on.

"What did you put in the paper recycling bin?" he asked me.

For a moment I was blank. "Why do you ask?"

"Well, I saw a man walk by and suddenly stop and do a double take. He didn't see me watching him in here, but I was curious as to what he was looking at. He suddenly looked around to see if anyone was watching, then he snatched something up and hurried up the street. I think I saw him go around the corner."

Then I remembered the magazine and burst out laughing. "Oh no! I know what he took! He took my women's magazine with the article on boobs!"

"What kind of magazine were you reading?"

"Just a regular women's magazine that talked about health and body issues."

I told him about the article and said the neighbor had likely seen the word "breasts" in big type on the cover, and thinking it was a girlie magazine he'd snatched it up and hidden it under his arm. We both got a good laugh out of that one.

Javier's voice jolted me out of my amusement. "What are you laughing at, Judita?"

"The differences in our cultures, Javito."

I told him about the man taking the magazine and said that to me, it had illustrated the differences in attitudes between our worldviews regarding a very natural human need.

"We like to think we're really open, but sometimes I think there's a deep, underlying attitude that sex is only acceptable between a married man and woman. Everyone feels the urges but they either try to suppress them or they come out anyway. There's a lot of guilt and shame and judgment. Here, it's completely the opposite. It just seems so much healthier to follow the natural urges of biology."

Jav nodded as he took another sip of his beer and looked thoughtful, then gave me one of his face-splitting grins. "Ya, Judita."

CHAPTER 21

The Night of the Naka Naka

In a small jungle pueblo, where the inhabitants may not always know where their next meal was coming from, a table that is able to order seemingly endless rounds of cold beer in the disco attracts notice. Someone at that table is able to pay for all that good alcohol, and there are others who want in. Lucas was one of those.

Javier and I were still at Maria's disco bar. We were chatting about how much we were enjoying our adventures and travel together despite my many mistakes and misunderstandings. Lucas had been standing by the ordering window, not far from where we were seated, and it didn't take long for him to observe the repeated rounds of cerveza going to the same table. Watching the dynamics, he picked out Javier as the one to zoom in on.

He made his move straight for my teacher.

"Hey, amigo, how are you?"

Javier looked at him through slightly blurry eyes and instantly became suspicious. He returned the basic greeting, then turned back to me, hoping to discourage Lucas from any further attempts at conversation.

It didn't work.

"Is it okay if I dance with her?" he asked Javier.

Jav looked at me, indicating that if I wanted to dance with this stranger, it was fine by him. I was feeling a bit more energetic than on our previous foray to this bar, so I thought a few passes around the dance floor might do nicely.

Unfortunately for me, my new partner's idea of dancing was far from what I was used to. Lucas grabbed my hand and continued to spin and fling me around wildly, which kept me off balance. I didn't recognize the steps he was leading me into so I just tried not to crash into him or anyone else. I felt like I was on a ride called the Octopus, which was a standard attraction at fairgrounds when I was a child. Lucas seemed to be all arms and legs like a dancing sea creature, while I was the helpless prey caught in his tentacles.

I finally managed to extract myself after a couple of songs and made my way back to the table where I took a deep swig of my beer. Lucas followed me back, beaming happily. He continued to try to get Javier to talk to him, so after a while I wondered if the two had perhaps known each other and had a falling out. Jav was visibly annoyed so I asked him if he knew the new guy.

"No, but I know what he wants." He made a motion of raising an invisible bottle to his mouth.

Lucas, who somehow had been able to get himself under the influence of something, was not exactly picking up the straightforward signals we were sending. He saw the gesture and took it to mean it was time for another round. Still certain that Javier was the one with the *dinero*, he turned to me and declared loudly,

"He is my very good friend!"

"Oh yeah?" I challenged. "What's his name?"

Without answering, he pushed ahead. "Can I join you?"

Without waiting for a reply, he plopped himself onto an empty stool before we could object.

We had been on the verge of ordering another round, so I stood up to make my way to the ordering window. Returning with the new round, Lucas tried his luck. Seeing that I was in fact the one who was buying the beers, he turned his attention to me and began telling me how beautiful and rich I was. Kicking Javier under the table to play along with me, I informed Lucas that Javier was my partner, hoping to discourage any further unwanted attention.

"Wow, he is very lucky! How about a beer? Looks like you two are having a good time!"

Javier glanced at him sideways, visibly annoyed. He grabbed what was left of my previous Pilsen, which was now warm, and whacked it down in front of our new friend. Lucas let out a protest and started to pout. It was ridiculous, and once again I wished I'd brought along a video camera.

Our uninvited guest had been standing with another man, who had seemed content to let his friend make a fool of himself. But now, seeing Lucas seated with us and with a beer in front of him, the friend made a dive for the last empty stool at the table. Javier stood up and angrily told them to get away from our table, then motioned the staff who was watching the scene from behind the serving window. Not wanting to alienate such high-paying customers, a couple of bouncers managed to convince the two moochers to take a walk outside.

We finished up our beers and decided to see if there was anyone hawking food nearby. Since there were no fast food joints in Padrecocha, we looked for someone offering cooked food, usually from a grill in the front of their house. We found a nearby family selling barbecued chicken and boiled rice, along with some tasty salsas. I enjoyed sitting outside with the family and just relaxing when everything suddenly went south.

Lucas the Mooch had spotted us and aimed straight for Javier, plonking himself down in the seat next to my teacher. No longer worried about being escorted out by bar bouncers, he was free to annoy us with requests for some of our dinner.

When the food was not forthcoming, he leaned over and whispered something in Javier's ear. I saw a momentary change of expression on my teacher's face and wondered what was passing between them. It looked like some kind of negotiation, but finally Javier shook his head and the Mooch got up to leave.

"So what was all that about?" I wanted to know.

I shouldn't have asked.

"He was offering me money to have sex with you. He finds you really attractive!"

I nearly choked on my chicken, my eyes bugging out. "You can't be serious!"

"Yes. You told him I was your husband and he believed it, so he asked my permission."

There was that face splitting grin again. With Javier, I never knew if he was telling the truth or not. I knew he liked to lead people up the garden path at times and he could be very convincing.

"So he bugged us to buy him booze and food. Where's he going to get the money to pay for me?" As soon as I asked that, I realized how ridiculous it sounded. I added, "Well, I hope you told him no way!"

"Ya, Judita. I told him I rent out my other wives but not you because you're special. He'd have to pay more anyway!"

What could I do but laugh? This stuff never happened to me at home!

It was late when we left the pueblo, quite a lot jollier than when we'd started out. On the way back to camp, I saw something that will forever remain imprinted in my mind. Here and there, dotted along the path leading from the main street to where most of the houses were, lay men who appeared to have just fallen in their tracks and died. I was concerned that they might need help, but Javier held me back as I started to go towards one who was lying face down in the grass without any sign of movement.

"It's okay, Judita, they've drunk the aguardiente," Javier explained, flashing his wide mouth full of very white teeth.

It seemed that each of these poor men simply had had one too many and had just fallen in his tracks as he tried to get home. I recalled how cautious I'd been with the cane juice in Javier's village. One swig too many and it was lights out! It was just so unusual to see not just one passed-out drunk, but several, all lined up along the path as if a giant invisible bowling bowl had knocked them down. Javier told me that they were safe here; it was not a town like Iquitos where you had to watch your back.

"Don't worry, Judita. Their families will come find them and carry them home. They know where to look for them."

Reluctant to leave them helpless to the jungle night, I allowed Javier to lead me farther down the path, past the small settlement of concrete houses that marked where civilization ended. While I had not been allowed to tote along my trusty machete, I had thought to bring a flashlight. This turned out to be a very good thing. Only too late it occurred to me how foolish we were to be tripping around in the dark without our protective gear, but Javier didn't seem to be too concerned.

My small light illuminated only the area right in front of us. There was something directly up ahead that caught my attention. Curious, I moved in closer, aiming my torch right at the long line of moving color that blocked our path. The light must've made the snake mad, because it suddenly decided to stop crossing the path and come towards the light--straight at us!

"*Naka naka*! Run!" shouted Javier and we ran backwards to try to avoid the venomous snake.

What could we do? Four or five feet of brightly colored, black and red striped snake were blocking our path ahead, but we certainly did not want to venture into the surrounding greenery to try to avoid it, especially without our rubber boots. Goodness knows what else was lurking out there in the tropical darkness. But wait! There *was* something lurking out there! Something big was coming at us through the dense greenery to our right.

Two men emerged from the shadows, both carrying machetes. They were both short and dark like Javier and were obviously very at home in the wild surroundings. The *naka naka*, on seeing these two additional possible threats, stopped to take stock of its situation. The hunters took the scene in quickly, and in a flash one of them had whapped the snake on its head with the upper edge of his machete. The colorful serpent that only moments ago had been racing towards us now lay still at the edge of the path. I felt sad that he had lost his life so easily. Perhaps he too, had only been on his way home for the night.

Javier bent over and peered at him. "We must bring him with us. Olaff might like this for his collection."

"Whaaaat?"

"Didn't you notice how Olaff spent his free time in our other camps, especially in Rio Napo? He collects specimens for the university and for his studies. He has to make a run back to Iquitos tomorrow morning to do something for his courses. We will bring him this *naka naka*," he decided firmly.

There was only one problem: we didn't have anything to put him in. As I was pondering what Olaff would do in the hot and humid jungle with a dead snake, I saw Javier eyeing my mid-section. I only had my daypack with me, which was about the size of a small decorative cushion.

"We will put him in your pack." Javier was already indicating that I remove the dark turquoise bag. I unfastened the belt and opened the main cavity. Luckily there was not much else in there, so the snake could be coiled up and placed inside without damage. I handed the bag to Javier. Despite appearing very dead, he took no chances when picking up the inert reptile. He grabbed it quickly behind the head, coiled it loosely, and stuffed it in. Zipping the bag, he handed it back to me.

"It's your bag; you carry it."

I drew back a few steps. "No! You know how to handle poisonous snakes. You carry it!"

Jav shook his head firmly from side to side and continued holding out the bag. You do not argue with a jungle shaman. You will never win.

I'm sure I saw those white teeth gleam in a wicked smile at my look of horror. Dead or not, I was now hoiking a poisonous jungle snake in my bag, and we still had a long way back to camp. Our two saviors also smiled and bid us goodnight. When I turned around again, the Amazon night had already swallowed them up.

The camp's resident dogs barked an alarm as we entered the area. Both in Iquitos and in the jungle, there is a large population of very sorry-looking dogs. Most families didn't keep them as pets, but some could be partially domesticated to become guard dogs with a little food.

Juan's area hosted a pack of these mangy mutts, none of whom were friendly. Each one was so gaunt that you could see its underlying bones. And it was almost inevitable that the females were pregnant. They tended to bark a lot at night, and I suppose that even without intruders, there is plenty to bark at in the jungle.

The dogs continued to bark even as we got close enough for them to recognize us. This surprised me somewhat as we'd now been there for a few days and I'd kept trying to win them over with a few food scraps when I could spare them. The noise briefly woke Olaff, who had been sound asleep, but on seeing it was us, he closed his eyes again and rolled over. We gladly crawled under our own mosquito nets and joined him.

The next morning we were up early because we'd planned to take a long hike to a magical watering hole after breakfast. I handed my bag to Olaff. He looked at me with a question on his face.

When we told him what his gift was—a dead *naka naka*, he got very excited. He also seemed highly amused that we had carried the snake back in my little daypack, which he referred to as my girlie bag. Olaff was no fool. Excited as he was to see what we'd brought for him from the night's excursion, he wasn't going to take any chances. He prepared a deep hole in the ground and quickly whacked down a few palm fronds to use as a cover. Rider and some of the other men who lived nearby came over to see what was going on. Cautiously opening my bag, he quickly dumped the snake into the pit and stood by with his machete. He looked up at me and smiled, then laughed. Then Javier started laughing and I felt like I'd missed the punch line.

"Ha ha ha, Judita! You carried a deadly snake in your bag and he was only sleeping!" The two of them obviously thought this was hilarious.

"You mean he's not dead after all?" The vision of a pair of annoyed fangs puncturing through the thin fabric of my bag and inserting themselves into my skin must have entered my thoughts, changing the look on my face to one of disbelief.

Amidst gales of full-bellied laughter, my companions pointed at the poor serpent. Although he still seemed stunned, he was very much alive.

"What are you going to do with him?" I asked Olaff.

"Preserve him in some aguardiente until I can get back to Iquitos later. I think we have enough here in camp."

I could hear the men chuckling as I turned away from the pit. I shook my head, also laughing, as I walked off towards the stream for the first bath of the day. You just never know what will come next in the jungle.

What did come next nearly killed me. Olaff went back to the city for the day, taking his snake prize with him. This left Javier and Rider to be my guides on a very long and intense plant identification walk. I grabbed my field notebook to take notes and once again my teacher laughed at me.

Javier nudged Rider. "Judita is always writing in her notebooks. She should have a university degree by now!"

While the areas around jungle establishments are generally cleared and groomed, it is a completely different story as you start moving away from these. I tried not to trip on all the fallen branches and roots as I made sketches of the plants and described them.

Some years earlier, I had completed training to be a trail guide at a local nature reserve, and we had an abbreviation that we always used when referring to many of the park's birds: LBB. Little brown birds. As I described the plants in my notebook I came up with another abbreviation: MGL for medium green leaves.

"Jav, I don't know how I am ever going to remember all these plants. They don't grow where I live, so it's not like I'll see them a lot."

"Don't worry about this right now. What is important is that you make a connection with the plant. Note its characteristics and features, color, and leaf size. Does it have a smell? Then you can carry this back to learn about the plants that grow near you."

A tall mound caught my attention, and this proved to be a giant termite nest. It was made from small pieces of dirt, but when Rider hacked into it I could see it was like a honeycomb, but very papery. In fact, to my surprise there did turn out to be a cache of wild jungle bee honey inside. Some clever bees had moved in and taken over a portion of the mound for their own use.

"This termite nest can also be used as medicine," Rider told me, indicating the papery parts.

"Really? How?"

"You can cook chunks of it in boiling water--termites too--and then let it cool down enough to drink."

"And what would you use it for?"

Jav stepped into the conversation with a tale of a child whose lungs were being eaten away by microbes so he couldn't breathe well. "If you look carefully you can see that the structure of the termite den resembles the structure of the human lung inside. It works on the spiritual level."

I let a melee of images flash around my head. For one thing, the idea of one's lungs being eaten away by anything sounded horrible enough. But then I wondered how my native teacher knew about anatomy and physiology. I decided not to ask this time, fearing it would lead into yet another lecture about the sexual practices of the local people.

The other feature that made me stop in fascination was the *huicungo* tree. If you could imagine a pine tree that had become possessed by evil spirits, you can get the picture of what this looked like. It was full of dark-colored needles, each of which was nearly two inches long.

"This is the witchcraft tree!" Jav announced with a flourish.

"I can see that. I sure wouldn't want to fall into those sharp spikes!"

My teacher proceeded to tell me how the *brujos* used the needles to harm their intended victims and I made sure to take everything down in my notebook. He also gave me a very particular method for dieting the plant which would allow the *virote*, a spirit dart, to enter my essence where it could be used for different things, both good and bad, depending on the intent.

"When you are a shaman you must find out who all your enemies are. You must never eat or drink anything they give you or you will be under their power. And don't drink ayahuasca with them either! If they are after you, they will put some of their evil essence in your drink, and that's it for you!" Javier loved to be dramatic. His voice rose to a crescendo, his eyes became wide, and he used the side of his hand slicing across his neck to indicate that the drinker would definitely not come to a good end.

As the sun rose higher, it became very hot and uncomfortable. The temperature seemed to be hotter here than at either of our previous encampments. I started to feel very drained and had to keep resting. I hadn't brought enough water with me and I felt like I was going to collapse. Rider found some young coconuts and opened them, so we drank fresh coconut water. Here and there, he would whack open some stem and instruct me to drink the clear liquid that flowed out. I felt bad for having to continually stop, but my guides didn't seem to mind. We had no agenda. It was just an everyday stroll through the jungle.

"I don't think we're going to make it to the magical stream after all," Jav declared. "Judita is ready to die on us, and it's a walk of many hours just to get there. Let's head back to camp.

While I felt disappointed at not being able to make it to the planned destination, I knew he was right. Just like trying to hoik the heavy bags of charcoal at the Jivaro *minga*, I had to listen to my body even if I didn't like what it was telling me.

By the time we got back to our camp I felt like I was going to pass out. I was helped to my hammock and told to lie still for a while. One of the children came over and fanned me with a palm fan, and I thought this was sweet. I must've fallen into a doze, but somewhere deep in my sleepiness, I heard something that sounded out of place here.

"Come on, Baby!"

I roused myself from my nap as I heard someone call out again, "Come on, Baby!" Looking around to see who was speaking English here, I saw my teacher in the water, beckoning me in.

"Where on earth did you learn that phrase?" I wanted to know.

"I heard it in a song. What does it mean?"

I thought it was odd that he was asking this since he seemed to be telling me to come on into the water. I explained it as best I could. Both he and Olaff were picking up a few English words and phrases and this just tickled me.

Not needing an excuse to get into the wonderful water, I joined my teacher for what turned out to be a very interesting lesson about the world of the *brujo*, or black magician.

I'd already known that Javier's entry into the shamanic world had been driven by a desire for revenge on the *brujo* that killed his father when he was young. He had told me that while he had started his own training with the intent to kill his father's supposed assassin, after some time had elapsed he realized that it wasn't the way to go.

He went into a long discourse about the good versus evil wars there in the jungle, and I listened with rapt attention. I had been a huge fan of the Harry Potter series, and now here I was listening to tales of real fights between the forces of good and evil. Most of the causes seemed to be based on jealously, such as imagining that your neighbor had more than you did, or lust. No wonder there was such a huge market for those *preparados* with silly names in the market!

"So how did you find the person who taught you that stuff?" I asked. I was tapping into my gut to see if there might be any residual tendency on his part to switch back over to the darker side, but I didn't feel anything.

"He was older than I was, and he could suddenly produce wads of cash and get any girl he wanted. It's what all of us want."

His revelation took me a little by surprise, but I appreciated his honesty. After all, shamans, no matter where they are from, are first and foremost human beings with natural desires and emotions. However, it is their lengthy and difficult training that allows them to master these desires so that they don't interfere with their work.

"So how does one turn down the wrong path anyway?" I asked.

"*Brujos* are basically failed *curanderos*," he replied as we floated into a different area of the stream. "The next part of your apprenticeship will be to make as many connections with plant spirit allies as you can so they can help you in your work. This will involve extreme *dietas* where you'll think you're dying of hunger, and you cannot even think about sex at all. That is probably the hardest requirement, especially for men. If a person cannot master his desires, but still knows how to manipulate energy and cast spells, then he becomes dangerous."

Having begun my path as a ceremonial magician, I was able to understand his point. Magic itself, or let's say, the very energetic base behind it, is a neutral force, neither good nor bad. But it's the intent that one puts into it that makes the difference.

"So tell me how you initially started on that path," I requested.

"Well, I had a lot of spirit communication at that time—not from good spirits—and I was told that in order to become a black shaman I first had to send away my angel of light. She was very sad and didn't want to go, but I knew what I wanted then so I sent her away.

As time went on, the bad spirits would tell me to kill members of my own family, then other innocents. That's about when I started to wake up and realize where I was heading."

"Thank goodness for that!" I interjected with emphasis.

"The harder part was that I had to reverse course and chuck out the demons so I could call back my angel of light."

"How did you do that?"

"I just called her back in. Even if someone sends away their angel of light, the divine being doesn't really go away. Because our helping spirits need our permission in order to interact in our lives, they just stand off to the side and wait, hoping that the one who sent them away will eventually realize that they made a mistake and wants them to come back in after all."

Floating on his back, he gave me a searching look.

"So what do you think of that? Are you afraid now?"

"Not me. I know what you're talking about," I replied as I told him about the magical interests that had ultimately led me to shamanism.

"Even if you are a *curandera*, a good healer, you must still know how the *brujos* work because this will help you to heal those who have had the bad magic cast on them. This is why I told you how to use the *huicungo* tree. You must know what plants they use and how the energy feels. Do you think you can do this, Judita?"

"Yes, I think so." I had a sudden thought and put a question to him.

"How do you consider love magic? Good or bad?"

The face-splitting grin seemed to separate his jaw from his upper facial features. "Very good. Love is always good! Don't you think so?"

"No, I was taught that it was a form of black magic because you are interfering with the will of another person without their consent."

"So you wouldn't want someone to put a love spell on you?" he looked at me curiously.

"No, and anyway it wouldn't work."

"Why not?"

"Because if I was not interested in the man who tried to bewitch me, no amount of hocus pocus is going to make me run into his arms. Same thing in the other direction. If there was a man I wanted, I would not use magic to try and lure him my way. I would prefer that his interest in me came from him, and not from me interfering with his will. Does that make sense?"

Although Jav nodded, I had the feeling that he didn't really agree with my point of view, but that was okay. And since we were already on the slippery slope leading to the favorite jungle topic of sex, I decided to ask him something that had been rattling around in my head.

"Jav, from what I hear from you, it seems like everyone in the jungle is up for it all the time, with just about anyone, regardless of their relationship status or not. Would you say there's some truth to that?"

"Ya, Judita." Again, that face-splitting grin. He submerged himself in the water up to eyes, making himself look a bit like a crocodile ready to strike.

"Okay, so if this is really the case, why are there so many aphrodisiacs? All those potions in the Belen market with rude names. Why do people need those?"

"It's just part of the lifestyle here, part of the jungle customs. All those *preparados* and *pusangas* you see in Belen are not used to start things off, but to add ecstasy and enhancement to the relations."

"Hmm. I'll have to buy a bottle of something when we get back to the city to see if it works on me, but it probably won't."

"Why won't it work? They're very effective."

"Because I think desire is the greatest aphrodisiac. Two people who are really into each other don't need anything else. But I get what you're saying about enhancement."

I secretly believed that no potion from a bottle, nor any incantation to try to seduce me would work if I wasn't interested.

Later in the afternoon, Olaff arrived back from Iquitos. I asked him how the specimen identification had gone. Smiling broadly, he replied "It was a *naka naka*. You're lucky it didn't come back to life in your bag!"

The three of us had a good laugh at this. Lucky indeed!

CHAPTER 22

Facing My Demons

After we'd spent the weekend settling into our camp by the stream with the amorous name, we were ready to resume the last phase of my training for this trip. I was soon about to see why my teacher had expressed sorrow at what I was going to encounter through drinking much larger quantities of ayahuasca at each ceremony so I could learn to deal with the denizens of the other dimensions.

We had chosen a very nice spot under a large tree with a wide canopy. It was part of the daytime picnic area, so the ground underneath the tree had been cleared and logs placed strategically for people to sit on. There were also a few roughly hewn tables and stools, so we set up our altar at one of these tables.

One of the basic tenets of successfully working with shamanism is to let go of your expectations of how you think things should be. It seemed to me that this teacher frequently created situations that would result in my having expectations about certain things. For instance, I was often told quite firmly that ceremonies always began at nine in the evening, and with some exceptions, they had.

Tonight, I was suddenly told to get ready, that we'd be starting soon after it got dark. When I queried the earlier starting time based on Jav's insistence that we always started at nine, I was then told it depended on the location. This sounded like a lot of horse hockey to me, but I came to realize that this was yet another way my teacher was trying to knock my need to know everything out of me. Still, it was kind of annoying.

Although I had already had that epic journey earlier in the year, I realized I was feeling kind of nervous because he'd planted the seed that I'd be vomiting a lot and having big visions.

"Are you afraid, Judita?" Jav asked as he peered at me. So much for my projection of false confidence!

"I think I'm more afraid of violent purging than seeing spirits. I don't know why, after that night in Sacha Wasi."

The broad grin and white teeth extended across his face as he patted me on the shoulder.

"It's okay to be afraid, but you must learn not to be afraid when the spirits come up and touch you!"

While we had been taking small doses of the medicine in the two previous settings, we now moved up to the *completo*. The plan was to trade off singing throughout the night, but by the time I got to my third icaro, the nausea hit me like a powerful wave, and I slid off my seat to hurl in some nearby bushes. When I returned to the table, I found I was unable to sing as planned as the waves of *mareaciones* kept washing over me. As I became dizzier, I also found it impossible to sit on the small stool because it seemed to wobble back and forth as if were made of rubber. I finally gave up and decided to lean against a tree for support.

Visions of insects came in, most with wings of light. I could hear the beautiful night chorus singing in the physical world and see their glowing counterparts in the spirit world. Plants appeared and it felt like I was moving through them like a soft breeze, or at times flying over them.

Sometimes ayahuasca can make a person feel very heavy, as if they can't move. I felt a nudge to lie down on my belly to connect with Mother Earth, no longer caring about what else might be lying on the jungle floor with me.

Little by little, the bugs and plants vanished, and demons appeared to take their places on the screen within my mind. At first, it was like a quick flash. I didn't want to give them any attention, so each time one would appear I would firmly state "no" and open my eyes, but eventually, they became more persistent.

"We know you are one of us, so we invite you to join us!" said one red-faced devil.

I was really irritated with this one because I felt he was ruining my night. Here, I'd planned on singing with my teacher and having lovely visions and I got these guys instead.

With the demon's declaration that I was one of them, the battle was on! It didn't help that I was completely incapacitated, lying face down in the dirt. When I had to vomit, all I could do was raise my head a little and try to shoot it away from me. Nearby, Jav continued to sit at the table and sing, seemingly unaffected by the strong dose.

There was one black devil that appeared to be the ringleader, so he'd keep popping in and out among the others. He had this all-knowing smirk on his face that I just wanted to slap all the way across the jungle had I been able to raise my arm.

"Your parents were demons, so that means you are one too," he laughed. "You might as well stop resisting us and join us. Come, now!"

At this point my language became rather fierce and basically ran along the lines of, "get the eff out of here you effing piece of shit!"

I called on my guides and uttered some prayers and incantations for strength. I connected with people back home who were members of my spiritual community and heard them tell me "we've got your back!"

This ridiculous dialog seemed to go on for a long time, with the demons trying to entice me over to the dark side and my foul-mouthed responses in return. Encased in my deep fog, I heard the resident dogs begin to bark, and the incessant, sharp noise really rattled me. Javier continued to drive the ceremony and I had a sudden realization. While we had been at Sacha Wasi, I'd thought that Javier didn't always sing clearly at times in the ceremonies, that it sounded like he was mumbling. It now sounded like he was doing this again, and I understood that he was indeed feeling the effects of the medicine. He was just as intoxicated as I was, but he had a lot more experience with how to manage the strong power.

I don't know how long this battle went on, but Javier eventually ended the ceremony and came over to see how I was doing. I gave him a brief and slurred synopsis of the stupid, annoying demons that were trying to pull me over to the dark side, and that I was having none of it. But after hours of this, I was exhausted.

Telling me not to move, Jav made several trips back and forth to the stream to collect enough water to pour on my head. He used blowing and sucking techniques to help pull the medicine out of my body, and it sounded like there was a freight train rushing between my ears.

This didn't seem to help subdue the strong *mareaciones* that I was still feeling, nor did it stop the visions. I just wanted to be able to get up off the ground but was finding it difficult to move my body.

"You must get up. I need to take you to the stream to immerse you now."

"I know. But I don't think I have any more legs. I can't move!"

Up until this point, I had seen my teacher as a fun-loving joker who didn't seem to take things too seriously, but now I was seeing yet another side of him. Although I felt that he was also under the influence of the medicine, he bent down and hauled me up by the waist, throwing my right arm over his shoulder. I had become a dead weight so this did not happen in one smooth move.

Eventually, he managed to drag me to the water's edge, which was only a few feet away. The two of us nearly fell in backwards but managed to find a quick sense of balance before this could happen. He forcefully dunked under me several times as he had in Rio Napo, and the cold water helped me to clear the fog in my head. I felt like a huge mess, soaking wet and dirty!

As this was all happening, I heard the dogs coming closer to where we were. They were in a frenzy far greater than just alerting the residents to the presence of intruders. I understood that the negative energy I was feeling was also radiating out and infuriating them. They sensed me as an enemy but completely ignored Javier.

Jav grabbed me around the waist again and half walked, half dragged me across the space to our sleeping quarters. This also seemed to enrage the dogs. At one point, I had him stop and hold me around the waist as I bent double and hurled into another set of bushes. The dogs circled in closer and one lunged at me, biting at my lower leg. Fortunately, he only got a mouthful of loose pant material rather than skin. This seemed to really spur Javier into action and he quite firmly shooed them away.

"It was the white dog that tried to take off my leg. She's the one I always fed, too." I shook my head sadly. "Well, she's had her last scraps from me now." I looked at my teacher.

"How are you feeling, Judita?"

"Very wobbly, but I'll survive. I'm sorry I ruined the ceremony and caused so much trouble."

"No trouble. This is part of your training. Nothing is a problem."

Nothing is a problem. That phrase stuck in my head. Somehow, it helped to explain my teacher's happy-go-lucky attitude. It didn't mean that there weren't trials in life, but it was rather how you labeled those trials. To him, he was just doing his job, even if that meant hauling his student up from a face plant in the dirt and dunking her in cold water while sucking the medicine spirit from the top of her head. All in a day's or night's work for a jungle shaman and his apprentice!

To top off the tumultuous night, a fierce storm came in not long after we'd crawled under our bed nets. I was feeling a bit more balanced and gave thanks to the rain spirits for waiting until after we'd gotten under cover. Unable to fall asleep, I concentrated on the thunder and lightning and the sound of the water hitting the leaves that made up the roof of our shelter.

As I focused on those fierce forces of nature, I felt something release inside of me. Although I was not standing out in the rain, I had a sensation that it was washing away the last traces of negativity around me. In that moment, I also knew that the dogs had not been attacking me, but rather the spirit demons that were around me. I'd seen the dogs in the area during the earlier phases of our ceremony, but they had not been aggressive at that point. It was only once the door to my own demonic inner world opened that they sensed trouble. Perhaps it wasn't me that the white dog had been trying to bite after all.

The next morning, I awoke feeling just as clear as I had after my wild ride at the retreat center. Once we'd finished our breakfast, Javier questioned me about my visions. When I told him I'd been seeing demons and devils he seemed surprised.

"Oh no! That should not have happened."

"Maybe, but it did. Why do you say it shouldn't have happened?"

"Well, the plan was that when you sang, I would concentrate on my visions, and vice versa. We were looking to connect with the good nature spirits of this land so we could get their teachings."

"Those guys were trying their damndest to convince me that since my parents were demons, I must be one too."

My teacher peered at me with concern.

"I mean, that's ridiculous! My parents are human beings!" I declared forcefully.

"Are you sure?"

My eyes bugged out and I looked at Jav as if he'd lost his mind. I was going to splutter "well of course I'm sure," but then I stopped.

"Haven't you told me all about the battles with your mother, the criticism, and constant belittling? Isn't your life hell at home?"

I was speechless. Yes, I had described it as hell, but describing a situation this way is quite different than actually fighting off demons who were trying to convince you that your family was part of theirs.

"Madre gave you those visions and she never lies. You must take some time to think about what this all means."

I nodded as he continued.

"Remember, when you drink ayahuasca, it's not supposed to be a one-way journey like you're sitting there watching a TV show. During the visions, you should constantly be asking questions like why am I seeing this, what does this mean, and so on. It should be an interactive conversation between you and the teacher spirit. Does that make sense?"

"Yes, it does."

We continued to talk about the ceremony during the day. I realized that all the talk had centered around my experience, so I wondered what his had been like.

"Well, I didn't really enjoy it either," he confessed when I asked.

"Why not?"

"We were planning to have a lovely night for one thing. But mostly I found the dogs to be very disturbing much of the time because they kept the spirits we wanted to work with away. There were very many healing and curing spirits who were trying to get in to work with us, but every time they did, those dogs chased them away."

As I was wondering how a physical dog could keep away some non-physical beings but not others, he continued. "I had a lot of difficulty dragging you across the open area at the end. I was also *bien mareado*, and trying to hold you up, move forward, and keep the dogs away all at the same time was really hard."

"Wow. I thought you were Superman. You did a very good job. Thank you."

"*Sí*, Judita. I also felt how much those dogs disturbed you with their constant barking. I am going to talk to Rider and Juan and see what we can do about this. It's essential that we don't have these kinds of distractions."

Nodding, I strolled away slowly, chewing on this strange event. While my home life, particularly with my mother, was anything but peaceful, not once did I see my parents in any of my visions. No, there was something else there just below the surface that I couldn't quite access. Could it be possible that I was the one who was demonizing them? Whatever the message was, I felt it was pretty important and that it would lead to a breakthrough once I was able to understand it.

I also considered that my expectations of how the ceremony was going to be had created a fantasy that turned out to be quite different than what I would actually experience. Perhaps it was a necessary part of my training to have to face these kinds of things and learn how to deal with them.

I couldn't resist wandering over to the area where we'd been the previous night. Yes, there was our altar table and seats looking as firm and practical as ever. I placed my hand on the stool I'd used for such a short time and tried to make it move back and forth.

"What are you doing, Judita?" Javier had followed me to see what I was up to.

"Ayahuasca is so strange, Jav. I tried to sit on this very solid stool last night but I swear it was swaying all over the place like it was made of rubber. That's why I went to sit against the tree. But of course this wood isn't moving at all now."

"No. At least not in this dimension."

"What do you mean?"

"When you are deep in the medicine, you are walking between the worlds. This is how we enter the spirit world and why it's easier to see them during ceremonies. Since everything in the physical world has a counterpart in the spiritual realms, perhaps you tried to sit on a spirit bench without realizing you'd changed worlds. You'll get used to this kind of thing with time."

Several questions arose all at once, but then got stuck in my throat as I stood there with my mouth hanging open. I'd known about the spiritual dimension counterpart of physical things and beings before, but for some reason, Javier's explanation sounded a bit like one of his tall tales. There was absolutely no point in trying to argue with him because I wouldn't win. And what if it was true?

"You will see this. Maybe we can work with being more aware in the next ceremony."

"Yeah, sure. Sounds good."

I wandered over a few feet to where I'd been lying in the dirt. I could see that something had disturbed the dry soil and was able to detect a vague outline of where I'd lain. Just a few inches away was a long stream of carpenter ants going about their business and I wondered if they'd been present in the ceremony too. Javier was still standing with me so I put the questions to him.

"I know many types of ants forage at night. Were these guys here last night when I was lying on the ground?"

My teacher's face spilt into that wide piano key smile of his. He nodded.

"Ya, Judita. They were on you when I took you to the stream." He made a motion with his hand of them being washed off and swimming away."

"But they didn't bite me. I don't have any new bites, which really blows me away."

"That's because we were protected by our guides. Those dogs couldn't keep all the good spirits out."

There was a lot to consider, between rubbery spirit seats and the fact that I'd had large carpenter ants all over me, yet no bites. And then all this back and forth about dogs letting some spirits in and keeping others out. A goofy version of a song I learned as a child, the "Hokey Pokey", suddenly slid into my brain.

"You let the good spirits in; you keep the bad spirits out. You grab your leaf shacapa and you shake it all about. You drink the ayahuasca and you turn yourself around. That's what it's all about. Yeah!"

"I think I'll go float in the *quebrada* for a bit."

Juan joined us for a simple lunch of rice and fish. He told me some local fairy tales, including one about a forest ogre who fattened children up to eat them, which sounded like a jungle variant of stories I'd heard as a child. Unlike the fishermen in Nuevo Progreso, I had a really hard time understanding Juan when he spoke to me. At seventy-eight, he was missing several front teeth which affected his speech, and he tended to mumble when he did speak.

"Did you know that ol' Juan here has three wives, Judita?" Javier asked me suddenly with a mischievous look on his face.

"No, I thought he was married to Abuelita." I used the term for grandmother because that's how she'd been introduced to me. I realized I hadn't even been told what her real name was.

"She's his primary wife. Isn't that right, Juan?"

Old Juan looked at Javier and nodded.

"I have two other wives as well. One of them is going to have my baby and Abuelita is just thrilled. She can't wait!"

"Where do the other two live?" I wanted to know.

Juan made sweeping motions with his arm and tried to respond with a mouthful of fish, so Javier answered for him.

"They live nearby in their own houses. He moves around so he can spend time with each of them."

"And no one gets jealous?" I was imagining a scenario where one wife might think she wasn't getting as much attention as the others.

Both men shrugged. "Human beings have emotions. It can happen, sure, but since everyone knows what's going on, they know what they're getting into beforehand," Jav answered.

"So, I've noticed that the jungle people refer to husbands and wives. Are they really married, or is that just a term they use for their partner?" I asked.

"A few are married, but mostly not. We *indígenas* prefer to be free." Jav answered and Juan nodded his agreement.

I was beginning to wonder if I had actually exited the alternate dimensions of the previous night. There was so much coming at me and I needed time to process it all. I knew my teacher loved telling me outrageous things to see how I'd react, but I couldn't just be suspicious of everything he said. And since Juan himself had confirmed what Javier had told me, I decided to accept it.

"Ha ha ha, Juan doesn't need RC, do you, Juan?"

Juan made some kind of muffled reply and they both laughed. Something stirred at the back of my mind. I'd heard of this before, hadn't I? What was it again?

"What's RC?" I asked.

I knew I was in trouble when Javier's eyes grew wide. That usually signaled that he was about to come out with something shocking. He leaned in as if telling me a secret.

"Rompe Calzones!"

Oh yes, the underwear ripping potion. I recalled having been told about it before.

Not noticing my comprehension, Javier carried on. "Yes, it is a very popular *preparado* here. The couple drinks it and gets so hot that they tear off each other's clothes and rip the underwear apart!"

"Hmm, well it sounds like you're right that Juan certainly doesn't need RC then," I said.

We all laughed, and old Juan looked mighty pleased with himself.

Javier decided that after the crazy ceremonial experience I'd had, it was important to take a short break of a couple of days to let that energy settle before we went in again. Although I chafed at what seemed to be another delay in my training, I had to agree with him, because I now had more understanding of how important it was to allow one ceremony's energetics to finish settling down before embarking on the next one.

Our next night ceremony was completely different, but like its predecessor, it also had some undesirable elements in it. Rider had prepared a nice, thick *palo* for us to sit on, so we had him place it near our special bathing hole, which was only a few yards away from our last location. We'd enjoyed the fallen tree that had served as our bench in Rio Napo so much that we wanted something similar here. It also was a lot closer to the ground for me so I didn't have to worry about wobbly, interdimensional spirit benches. Juan had also taken the dogs out of the area for us, so the night started off with great promise.

Old Juan had decided to join us for some reason, although he didn't drink the medicine. I wondered why he was with us as he didn't seem to have anything to work on, but as with Olaff, I thought it was nice to have an additional person to work with.

We'd planned to resume with what we'd started to do in the previous ceremony: drinking a large amount of the brew and trading off singing. Since I was now serving myself, I was briefly tempted to pour less liquid into the gourd cup in the hope of being able to stay more in control. But I decided to go for it and had a really great example of why ayahuasca should not be referred to as a hallucinogenic drug.

A drug is something that has been formulated to produce the same results each time it's taken. It has to be reliable. Ayahuasca is nothing like this at all. Sometimes she gives visions, and other times, no matter how much you drink, you will not see a thing. Although I'd taken the same full cup, I had no visions and very little nausea. So much for the hallucinogenic part there!

As I started singing, Juan would attempt to sing along with me even though he didn't know the songs. I found this to be distracting and tried to sing over the top of his warbling. Jav and I traded off singing duties successfully and just as I thought things were going smoothly, Juan decided it was time to chat. No sooner had one of us finished a song when Juan would butt in, trying to get Javier's attention. At first, I'd wait briefly, thinking that maybe he needed help, but when it became obvious that he'd only joined us for the social aspect, I got a bit annoyed.

"*Canta, hermana!*" Javier instructed as I looked at him in question during one of Juan's rants.

"How can I sing with him talking so much?"

"Just keep singing! Sing loudly!"

I carried on for a few more songs, but the situation got more and more ridiculous. Instead of barking dogs, tonight we had Juan interrupting us. I turned to my teacher in frustration.

"Jav, I can't go on like this because I can't concentrate. Why is he talking so much? Can't you ask him to leave us in peace?"

"He's drunk on aguardiente. He finished off his own supply earlier on, so he came for your camalonga. Look, he's just grabbed your bottle!"

I watched in disbelief as the wizened old man unscrewed the top of my camalonga and tipped it to his mouth. Taking a deep slug, he smacked his lips and recapped the bottle. Camalonga is meant to fortify the spirit and help guard against negative influences. A medicine for these purposes is going to be pretty strong in its taste and ingredients, which camalonga most certainly was! The times when I'd drunk even a small amount of the alcohol-based *preparado*, the fierce potion would almost feel like I'd been smacked with a giant sea wave while being electrocuted at the same time. Yet Juan didn't even flinch! He'd smacked his lips!

"He came in drunk and you knew? You let him?"

"I thought maybe he would just pass out," Jav responded, his voice trailing off.

Juan was too drunk to be reasoned with, so there was no question of his early departure. Well, if I couldn't get rid of him, I could put my foot down.

"Jav, this is pointless. This whole night has gone down the tubes and I'm really disappointed. I'm going to spread my blanket out over there under the tree and just lie there away from you guys. That way, if you want to chat, I can still try to get something from what's left of this ceremony." I was mad and there was no dissuading me. "And I'm taking my camalonga with me!"

I picked up my things and relocated far enough away where any talking would not disturb me further. Settling down on the ground, I let out a long exhale and tried to put the disaster behind me. Now that I was no longer concentrating on my singing and driving the ceremony, the *mareaciones* crept in slowly and I found myself able to enjoy some lovely visions of plants. They looked like nothing I'd ever seen on earth, glowing with a luminous beauty that made them seem otherworldly.

"Well, of course they're otherworldly, child. These are the plant spirits." It was Madre herself speaking to me now. "Look up into the canopy of the tree you're lying beneath."

The spirit of the great tree presented himself with a head that reminded me of the sea god, Neptune. But instead of carrying a trident, he wore a crown of leaves made from the tree. What really struck me was his sheer joy. I heard him laugh and he made me think of Santa Claus.

Other beings appeared and I realized I was now in the fairy realm. I thanked them for showing up despite all the noise, which was still going on in the background. I was also grateful that the night hadn't been a total waste.

After a while, the beautiful visions faded and a fatigue set in. Jav and Juan were now making no pretense of ceremonial etiquette and were just jawboning back and forth; Jav deep under the influence of ayahuasca, and Juan deep under the influence of aguardiente.

I picked up my things and started to head back to our sleeping quarters, thinking no one would even notice I was gone. I was wrong.

"Where are you going, Judita?" Jav called over.

"To sleep. Finish *ceremonia*, ya?"

Crawling under the bed net, I breathed a sigh of relief. Now freed from any responsibilities and safe under the *mosquitero*, the *mareaciones* returned again and lasted for several more hours. I came to enjoy these secondary ceremonies when they happened. As I've already mentioned, ayahuasca is quite unpredictable. You can drink a cup at the beginning of the night and sit there completely sober until the very end when the leader says finish *ceremonia*, or something to that effect. Then you wobble off to wherever you're sleeping and watch what I call the jungle television for a few hours. The only thing missing is the singing, unless you consider the delightful chorus of crickets, frogs, and night birds.

Unlike other times when I'd taken a large dose and purged, I hadn't felt the need so far. But sure enough, sometime in the early hours I felt the call to visit the bushes. I ignored it for as long as I could, but eventually knew I shouldn't delay any longer. I was too lazy to put on my pants but slipped into my boots and moved away from our little shelter. A nice stereo purge (both ends at once) erupted and I felt all of the night's negativity vanish into the greenery. Once back under the net, I was able to slip into a peaceful sleep. Perhaps it hadn't been such a bad night after all.

The following morning, my teacher asked me about my dreams. Dream work is very important in shamanism because it often reflects how the work in the physical affects the inner spiritual worlds and vice versa. Shamans frequently ask their apprentices about their dreams as this is a good way to monitor progress. I'd felt a bit despondent about using my dreams as an indicator of progress because most of mine were just a bunch of disconnected nonsense.

But this time I did have a dream that was quite unlike my usual mental trash. I was back in my parents' house, but it had shrunk. Then I realized that they had moved into a smaller property while I was away, but they never had mentioned that this was in the cards. I was still dressed in my ceremonial regalia and looking around I'd declared "I can't call this home!" Instead of my leaf crown, I was wearing a tall feather headdress. There was an older man with me, a senior shaman, who was teaching me something, but by the time I had awakened I could not remember any of the lessons.

Javier nodded as I told him about this dream. "It is an indication that you are changing. You must trust in these signs."

I sighed. "But Jav, why does it have to take so long? I've been doing spiritual work on myself for many years now. When will I be able to have the strong vision I need in order to do this work well?"

My teacher peered at me as if he was looking for something. "How do you know you don't already have it? Maybe you should stop looking for something outside of you and look inside for a change."

This kind of reply really annoyed me. I looked inside all the time, but what I was looking for wasn't there, or I either couldn't or didn't see it. Not for the last time, I just wanted to strangle my teacher!

"So what was it like for you in the early days, Javier?" I wanted to know, changing the subject slightly.

"I was very shy when I had to sing in front of people, like what you call stage fright. Madre showed me that I would be going to many different lands and meeting new people, and this has come to pass. Transformation doesn't happen overnight. You must be patient, Judita. And look inside!"

We briefly discussed the night's issues, but since I felt I'd already said what needed to be said, I saw no point in holding onto the negative feelings. Let them go and move on.

"I think it will be a good idea to prepare a plant bath today. Let's go for a walk and gather some fragrant plants," Javier suggested.

Remembering the day where I'd nearly fainted from the heat, we just took it easy. It was still early, but the temperature can rise very quickly. I had no problems this time and hoped that perhaps I was becoming more attuned to the jungle instead of fighting with it.

Plant baths can have different purposes. At the beginning of this trip when I'd made my first pot of ayahuasca, I'd used the solids from the plant material to make a bath. Its purpose was to connect me more to the plant spirit I was learning to work with. Plant baths can be used for purification and cleansing, to fortify the energy bodies, or just simply for the enjoyment of splashing fragrant water all over oneself.

I found I liked making plant baths because the preparation was like a meditation. All stalks and stems are removed, leaving only the soft leaf material. Depending on which plants you choose, this can be quite a laborious task. But as with preparing something for consumption, it's important to monitor one's thoughts when making something that will affect the energy bodies. You want to ensure that you are only putting positive vibes into whatever you make, whether that be a meal or a plant concoction. Once this part is done, I added some of the lovely stream water. Javier sniffed the plants and looked thoughtful.

"We need a dash of Abut," he said with finality.

I had mixed feelings about this cologne. Many of the men wore it to make themselves more attractive to women, but I found it quite overpowering. I would have preferred to add in some agua florida but I stood by as Jav grabbed his own bottle and dumped a good amount into the plastic tub along with the leaf material and water.

"Stir it with your hand now to mix it well."

Once mixed, Jav pronounced the bath ready. We both rinsed off first, then poured the fragrant water all over in a steady shower.

Make sure you get your crown," he instructed as he pointed to the top of his head. "This is very important."

"Can I ask why?" I dared.

"Because this is your connection to the spirit world. A good shaman always keeps their connections clean."

"Okay. Makes sense."

"Stop saying that, Judita!"

"Oops, sorry, Jav."

Whatever residual effects I'd been feeling from the night before disappeared under the fragrant water. I was now clean in all dimensions!

CHAPTER 23

Lucas the Dancing Octopus

Since we were only a short distance from Iquitos, Olaff, our trusty side man, continued to go back and forth from our camp to the city for his classes. He seemed to thrive on the action and being able to bring his studies to life and the jungle life back to the classroom.

I was lazing in a hammock one day when he walked into camp carrying a large bundle of supplies that we'd commissioned him to bring back on his return.

"Would you like some *hierba luisa* tea? I can make us a pot."

"Sure. Hot tea sounds wonderfully refreshing on a hot day," I joked.

I was fascinated with the kinds of classes he was taking. Unlike in the United States, a degree course at his local university didn't require general education classes. It was assumed that general education requirements had already been fulfilled in the basic and higher levels of obligatory schooling that finishes around the age of sixteen.

"So, what classes are you currently taking?" I asked as we waited for the water to boil.

"Aquatic environments, maintaining fish stocks, inundation, and local tribes."

"Inundation? Isn't that flooding?"

"Right. We have to learn which areas will flood when the rivers rise in the rainy season."

"I'd be really interested in the one about local tribes. I'll bet there are many more than most people know of."

"Yes, there are still uncontacted tribes out there, but I worry that one day all of their territory will be taken away for oil and other enterprises. There is one tribe that is quite violent, and they guard their land and resources viciously. They will still kill outsiders if they feel like it. There was one case where a group of medical workers went in to help them out. There was some kind of misunderstanding, and all the medical personnel were slaughtered. Apparently, they're not so bad during the day, but at night they get into the aguardiente. I'm sure you've noticed how popular it is in the jungle."

I nodded, recalling the line of men lying along the path away from the village as if they'd been knocked down by a giant bowling ball.

"And then there's jungle etiquette," he continued. "Each tribe has their own customs, and it can be tricky to know how to deal with them so that you're not shunned."

"Shunned? Really? That sounds a bit extreme. Don't they give any slack for someone who doesn't know their ways?"

"Nope. If you are in their territory, you are expected to know how to greet the chief, what to give him as a gift, and so on."

"Yeah, that's why we need local guides like you, eh?" I poked him in the ribs.

"It's not just about money. It may save your life, or at least create a good relationship. Can you imagine going to visit the Jivaro without the *víveres*? You probably don't really understand how much that allowed you to be in their space."

"There is a lot to learn," I conceded.

"So if you go visit some tribes like the Yaguas, and they offer you something, you have to take it or they will be really offended and no further communications will be possible."

Thinking about the suri grub, I asked, "What kinds of things might they offer you?"

Olaff laughed heartily. "A big bowl of masato, for one! You'd have no problem with that, would you?"

"I'd be their best friend!" I laughed as I slapped my knee.

"So if they served you some great masato and you drained the bowl, you could get more by returning the bowl to them right side up. If you didn't want any more, you'd turn the bowl upside down."

"I'll have to remember that one. Right side up for me!"

I made light of this on the outside, but deep inside I realized how delicate relations with other cultures can be. Even if someone goes in with good intentions, the slightest thing can be taken as a grave offense. I filed this information away and decided that it would be a good idea for me to always hire a local guide from now on.

"Judita! We have to go to town right now to buy candles for tonight. Come on!"

It was Jav, who had suddenly appeared next to us. I'd been so interested in Olaff's tales that I hadn't noticed my teacher coming up to join us.

"What do we need candles for?"

"I had dreams last night that we need to create a certain atmosphere for our work tonight, so we need to buy a bunch of candles."

I sighed. No matter how much I tried to keep the budget under control, Javier would do his best to break it with sudden demands for things that were supposedly vitally important. And typically, the errand would turn out to just be an excuse to get out and jawbone, to see what was going on in the pueblo. Fortunately, the heat of the day was already ramping up as we walked, so this discouraged my sociable teacher from dragging out the errand for any longer than it needed to be. We found the candles that he'd seen in his dream, then came directly back to camp feeling pretty wilted.

"I think I'll cool off in the Love Stream," I informed the guys. "Oh! There's someone in my spot!"

The *quebrada* provided numerous bathing spots as it wound through the camp and into the jungle, and it was deep enough to submerge oneself if you sat on its sandy bottom. I'd staked out a small pool formed by a bend in the banks that was slightly deeper than the rest of the stream. For the most part I'd had this area to myself, so was rather taken aback to see it was now occupied by two people.

At the mention of other people being in our area, Javier perked up quickly. He excitedly grabbed my hand and half-ran me behind some bushes where he had an advantage point to spy on the intruders.

"Look, Judita! Remember what I told you about the couples that come here? Now you can see why it's called the *Quebrada del Amor!*"

I did not want to spy on the amorous couple, but I was rather curious to see if they were as Jav had described to me earlier in our stay here. The girl was quite young, in her late teens or early twenties. She was a typical pretty young jungle girl with long hair and a very slender figure. The man was much older, probably in his sixties.

"See? What did I tell you about the old men who come here to have sex with young girls?"

"Well, you were right. That's for sure!"

I was almost as fascinated by how excited my teacher was that I was able to witness one of his cultural points in action as I was by the couple themselves. I tried to picture something like this back in Southern California and it brought up a question.

"OK, Jav. I don't want to stand here and spy on them. But I am curious to know if they are here as a real couple or if she's a working girl."

"Maybe sort of both. These older men look for the young girls to have sex with so they can create more babies for them. Someone her age is very fit and healthy. They may have made an agreement to make a baby, in which case he will pay for its upbringing, plus a little more for the mother and her family. So yes, technically he is probably paying her, but not in the way that you're thinking. It's more of a business agreement."

"So it sounds like they won't be a couple."

"Right. She will continue to live with her parents so her mother can help her raise the baby. The money he gives them will help out with some bills, so this kind of arrangement is actually welcome here. What do you think about this?"

I must admit I was a bit speechless. The idea of parents accepting a much older man's offer for their daughter to bear and raise his children outside of a relationship was hard to wrap my head around. "Hey, if everyone is happy, then why not? I can't imagine a man of that age back home asking some young girl's father if it's okay that he has sex with her and gets her pregnant, and everyone is thrilled about it. It's just different, that's all."

We slipped back away to the kitchen area where Olaff was preparing a light snack of boiled yucca roots and white rolls for us. As we ate, the happy couple walked by, waved, and said their thanks for the use of the area. I smiled at them and waved back.

Javier turned to his nephew. "I told Judita about how the old men bring young girls here to make love, and now she believes me!"

Olaff looked at me for my reaction.

I shrugged. "I told Jav it was just different from where I come from, that's all."

"Ya, I told her that pretty much anything goes in the jungle," Javier said with a knowing nod and a big smile, while Olaff just continued to look amused.

"Anything?" I asked.

"Well, we draw the line at incest," Jav replied and Olaff nodded. "Those that cross this line are called *runamula*, or horse people. It is said that at midnight on Tuesdays and Wednesdays, they turn into flaming black devil horses and gallop through the pueblos. It's nature's way of saying 'this is not what was intended.' You know, it's not good for the child. They are born with illnesses and disabilities."

I understood the science behind this but had a bit of trouble with the galloping devil horse part. "So, I have to ask this. Why Tuesdays and Wednesdays?"

My teacher shrugged. "That is just the way it is here."

"Hmm, just like the *chullachaki* being out and about only on weekends," I thought to myself. I decided that if I had to come up with one phrase that summed up life in Peru, it would have to be "that's just the way it is here." It would do absolutely no good to voice my doubts or question my companions any further. The jungle is a wild place and there are many mysteries within her green shadows. Better to just believe in the magic.

Wanting to change the subject from the ever-popular topic of local sex practices, I turned to Olaff. "I know you spend a lot of time in the jungle as part of your studies. Have you, yourself, ever had any interesting encounters with spirits?"

"Oh yes. If you are going to go into the jungle you must have great respect for her, as well as her spirits. One of my classes was how to survive in the jungle. It's a very useful class for anyone who goes into the jungle, especially from the city. Those like my uncle here grow up learning the skills."

"So what about the spirits?"

"We just know about them from our parents and people around us. The class teaches us to find food and stay alive, but we learn about other skills more through word of mouth. It's not a good idea to just go wandering aimlessly in the jungle."

"So, what do you do when you go in?"

"Well, before I go in I pray and ask for signs to warn me of any imminent dangers. One day, one of my classmates and I were going in to look for various samples of plants, and we suddenly smelled fresh strawberries. This is not something you'd normally smell in the middle of the *selva*, so we knew it was very odd. We took this as an omen, so we turned around to go back. It turned out that there was a very big cat up ahead of us, lying in wait, and we would have walked right into her path."

"How did you know that if you'd turned around?"

"We ran into some hunters who told us about her. Another thing is that if I hear anything I can't identify, I'm outta there."

"I guess with all your classes and fieldwork you have a sense of what should be there and what shouldn't, so you'd know if something seemed off, huh?"

Olaff nodded and continued. "It's not just the animals you have to watch for. There are all kinds of spirits who live out there like the *tunchis* and *malignos*."

"I haven't heard of them before. What are they like?"

Javier jumped into the conversation. "*Tunchis* are generally not harmful spirits—they're most often spirits of the dead that are still stuck here in the earth plane—but the *malignos*, like their name, are the bad ones." His eyes grew wide as he added the next part. "*Malignos* eat *tunchis!*"

The thought of one spirit eating another seemed a bit far-fetched to me so I looked to Olaff for confirmation.

"*Tunchis* have very high pitched sound like hweee hweee hweee, that sounds like a whistle. *Malignos* have a more nasally haaaw sound."

"So have you actually heard these yourself?" I wanted to know.

"Oh yes! Anyone who spends time in *el monte* will eventually hear them. One time when I was on a class fieldtrip, my tent companion started making fun of the *tunchi* noise, and it was not a smart thing to do."

"Really? What happened?"

"Well, when you make a sound like the spirit, it comes to see who you are. It's like you're shouting out 'Hello! Anybody out there?'"

"Did anything happen to your tent mate?"

"It sure did! Even though the *tunchi* isn't really a harmful spirit, it can still cause temporary insanity. My classmate developed nervous shaking and frothed at the mouth like he had rabies. He went on a trip into another dimension that lasted about three days. We couldn't get him out of it so we had to take him to a shaman to be healed."

Unlike his dramatic uncle, Olaff had a sincere, grounded way of describing things, so I tended not to wonder so much if the strange tales were fact or fiction.

"What did the guy think about what happened? Did he realize what he'd done?"

"No, typically with these kinds of things the victim has no memory of anything, so he refused to believe what we told him. It was kind of dumb because one moment he's with us making funny noises, then suddenly he wakes up and finds himself at a shaman's house, lying on a bed. He still wouldn't believe any of us."

"I guess that might be kind of hard if you had no memory."

"Maybe. But another time a *tunchi* came into my tent. I prayed for it to go away and it left me alone."

I just loved hearing these tales. I had done so much research before coming here, such as reading books written by anthropologists about jungle lore and culture, but now I was hearing it from the locals themselves. I was seeing that many of the things I'd only read about were taken very seriously by those who lived here. Once again, I was very grateful to be in the middle of this often uncomfortable, but truly amazing experience. I had come here to train in a particular shamanic tradition, but I was seeing how the practices and ceremonies were just a part of a greater whole. It was very precious to me.

We set out the candles that had been purchased earlier in the day. We had lit them before the ceremony started, but then Jav declared that we had to blow then out, since it's common practice to work in the dark. He had made such a fuss about them, yet they were only lit for about fifteen minutes, and then never used again.

I went into the night's ceremony feeling as if I had already taken the gourd full of medicine and was starting to feel the nausea. I poured myself a cup that was about three-quarters full and instantly gagged on it when I tried to drink it. For some reason, it tasted worse than it usually did.

Despite this, I never felt the true *mareaciones* nor did I purge in any manner. I fell into a pleasant lassitude and wanted to stop singing so I stretched out beneath the large tree whose spirit I'd seen on a previous night. My teacher did not join in with the singing to start off with, so I sang for a while and then told him I wanted to just lie on the ground and experience whatever came through. Several beautiful butterfly-like spirits appeared, as well as some plant fairies. After all I'd been through, it just seemed so peaceful and exquisite.

Javier finally took over the singing duties in order to allow me to take my journey into the other realms. Eventually, he too joined me on the ground and we both looked up at the stars. I told him about the fairies I'd seen and he seemed surprised. With a thoughtful look he responded,

"Ah, this is because you're a woman. Most apprentices are men, so we tend to see great spirit warriors in all their regalia."

"Oh? So you've never seen a fairy?"

He shook his head and reiterated that men see great warriors, as if the idea of fairies was something silly.

This ceremony ended up being quite different from our previous ones that had followed a certain protocol, since we decided to simply be with the spirits of nature without singing. Or perhaps it wasn't we who had made this decision but Madre herself, as a way of teaching me that the path of ayahuasca was not set in stone. If the spirits want to take the ceremony off in a different direction than originally planned, then just follow along without resistance.

Javier seemed to want to talk, and I reluctantly engaged with some difficulty. While I was not nauseous, I was quite deep under Madre's influence, so it was hard to form words. It was a night where the tables were turned and I was the master healer working for him. He revealed many things to me that he'd been keeping in because he felt he didn't have anyone else with whom he could talk to safely. We then agreed that this would be more of a casual ceremony but with an important twist. Javier told me that what we were doing was more like when I would see patients, rather than just doing ceremony for tourists who wanted to have visions.

"You have to learn how to talk to your clients under the influence of the medicine and be present with them. You're doing just fine talking to me even though the medicine is strong."

I was in mid-nod when a horrible screeching sound suddenly ripped through the night somewhere close to us.

Alarmed, I asked what it could be. I recalled how Olaff said he would turn back if he heard something he couldn't identify. I thought it sounded like some kind of insane bird, but being so deep in the medicine I couldn't really be sure of what I was hearing.

The sound continued to rent the peaceful night so we decided we'd better haul ourselves off the ground to find out what it was. As we moved cautiously towards the kitchen area, we were confronted by a very strange sight. There was a chicken dangling upside down from a tree branch, squawking furiously!

"What the ...?" I couldn't complete my sentence.

A light rope had been tied around a tree branch well out of reach, and the other end was looped around one of the chicken's legs. The poor bird was making a huge fuss, which caused it to swing back and forth over our heads.

"He fell off his perch," was my teacher's assessment.

"Perch? What's with the rope?"

"She belongs to Juan's family. You know. You've seen her around here, haven't you?"

Peering up into the shadows, I tried to see if I recognized the chicken, but it was difficult in my current state.

"I think so, but why is she tied up there?"

"It's how people protect their chickens and keep them away from predators when they don't have a coop. Normally, the birds roost in the trees at night so when they're tied up they can't escape, but nothing can get them from the ground, like the dogs. She must've lost her footing and slipped."

The ridiculous scene was about to get even more so. The two of us had been fine with nothing more to do than lie on the ground and chat quietly. But now we were up and trying to retain our balance in the dark with a madly squawking chicken swinging over our heads on a rope as if it were a poultry pendulum.

"We must do something!" I declared. "We have to save the chicken!" I turned to Jav and saw that he was looking at me as if I'd suddenly morphed into a giant chicken myself.

"What do you propose we do? She's out of our reach and there's nothing to stand on," Jav noted.

"Well, we'll find something! I know! I can climb onto your shoulders! Scootch down!" I ordered.

What followed must have looked like a scene from a comedy movie where the two main characters attempt what should be a simple task, but it ends up degenerating into a farce. Despite my declaration that we had to save the poor bird; I'd disregarded the fact that we were both still quite heavily under the influence of the strong jungle medicine. Just trying to stand up on rubbery legs was hard enough, but as I tried to climb onto Javier's back one or both of us would lose our balance and we'd tumble to the ground. After the fourth fall, we both lay on the ground recovering our breaths.

"This isn't working!" I said petulantly.

"Ya, Judita. Maybe we'll have to leave her up there."

But by now, I was obsessed with the idea of rescuing the upside down squawking chicken who was still swinging back and forth just out of our reach.

"We must find something to stand on! Come on, Jav! Let's look around!"

If my teacher had previously been telling me this ceremony had been for learning how to talk to someone coherently while under the influence of ayahuasca, it now became an exercise in overcoming perceived limitations of the body. The solid ground beneath our feet felt like a trampoline, and spirit beings would suddenly appear in front of us, making us stop suddenly so we wouldn't run into them. I started to laugh.

"What's so funny?" Jav asked.

"This whole night. This is the most ridiculous thing I've ever done, and especially during a ceremony! Think about it, Jav. Here we are, barely able to function in our bodies, yet we're wandering all over trying to find something to stand on so we can rescue a chicken that's dangling upside down from a tree. And I just stopped to avoid running into a tree spirit that isn't even solid anyway. I'm going to remember this night for the rest of my life!"

Javier looked at me and then broke out into one of his great belly laughs. We both laughed ourselves breathless for a few minutes at the realization of what we were trying to do, knowing a night like this would never come again.

Once we were able to catch our breaths, we managed to find a large bucket.

"It looks like this is all we have. Let' see what we can do," said Jav.

Somehow, the added height of the bucket enabled us to reach the chicken and get her back on her perch. She instantly stopped making such a fuss and went quiet. My teacher and I looked at each other and burst out laughing.

"How are you feeling now?" Jav asked me.

"You know, I'd like to go back to where we left off and just gaze up at the sky for a bit before turning in. The ceremony doesn't feel complete yet, even though it wasn't like our usual ceremonies."

"There is no usual with Madre," Javier replied seriously.

We'd gotten up very early the next morning to beat the heat for our latest plant walk. I slipped on my long pants and long-sleeved t-shirt, then pulled on my rubber boots after having checked them for creepy crawlers. Looking up to see Olaff smiling at me. I pointed at the empty boots and he gave me the thumbs up. Yep, always remember to check your shoes and clothes before putting them on in the jungle. Got it!

We paused by a *sangre de grado* tree and my teacher raised his machete. "I want to show you something, so pay close attention. This is an important lesson. Do you remember the day we went to Belen and I was showing you some of the medicines? And do you remember the *sangre de grado* from one of the vendors? "

I nodded.

He made a small cut in the bark and a small trickle of pale, pinkish-red liquid emerged. It looked very similar to the way a cut bleeds on human skin. Javier told me to put some of the sap on my finger and give it a good smell. I noticed a faint ginger-like smell, not at all strong or pungent.

"Now spread that onto your skin like this."

I followed his example of taking a few drops and rubbing them into my skin. As I did that, I saw the color change to an opaque brownish red. It wasn't transparent like water, and this made me think that it would probably blend in with darker skin.

As the fluid dried, it changed color yet again, this time to a milky white, and its texture felt somewhat like soap.

"How does that feel to you?" Jav asked me.

"A bit like I'd taken a piece of soap, put a drop of water on my skin and rubbed the soap in."

"Make sure you make notes of these stages, the changes of color and thickness. "These changes in the *sangre de grado* are unmistakable."

Something was tugging at the back of my mind, an insistent nudge to recall a faint memory.

"So, does this look like the stuff that vendor tried to sell us?" Jav peered at me intently as I tried to recall the details of that day in the market.

"No, it was not like this at all. One thing that really stood out was the smell. It wasn't pleasant like this; it was gross!"

"And do you remember what happened when you put it on your skin?"

"Yes. It was weird. It was like water with red spots in it. It was like something that didn't mix well, like oil and water. And not only that, but it also never turned white like this did."

Seeing my frown, my teacher continued. "Remember that I am always telling you that you have to try all the medicines you prepare so you know how they feel in the body, right? It's just as crucial to learn how to spot fake medicines. Pasaje Paquito is full of these fakes that dishonest vendors will happily charge a lot of money for from someone who doesn't know how to recognize the real thing."

"But surely they also have the authentic medicines?"

"Of course they do! If a person like me who really knows about plants asks for something, those vendors know better than to try to cheat us. Sure, sometimes they'll still try, but when you call them on it they suddenly have just the right thing under the counter."

In the days that followed I noticed a subtle change in myself as I set about my tasks. While Jav still trotted next to me on plant walks, he also left me more on my own when it came to collecting plants and making up medicines. While I'd initially felt it that it was important to follow my teacher's instructions exactly, I now found my own ways of doing things. Maybe it was more of listening to my own inner guidance as well as that of the plant spirits'.

"You are going to be a great shaman one day," Javier declared as he nodded approvingly at the way I was meticulously preparing some cortezas—tree barks—one day. "I think you will be an even better shaman than me!"

I set down my knife and eyed my teacher with suspicion, wondering if was pulling my leg for the hundredth time.

"I think I have a long way to go to catch up with you, Maestro. There is no way that I will ever have the knowledge of all the Amazonian jungle plants that you have."

"Maybe not, but you have great strength. You are already making this path your own. This is what it takes. You can't always call on your teacher or others; you must learn to rely on your own spirit guides and follow their guidance."

I nodded. He was right. I still had a long way to go, but I'd also come a long way even in these few months.

"And speaking of your spirit guides, here's one now!" Javier pointed to something behind me and started laughing.

I heard the clucking before I saw her. The chicken that I had insisted on rescuing during one of our recent ceremonies seemed to have adopted me as its guardian. Everywhere I went in the camp, that silly bird was able to find me. I'd even taken to trying to play hide and seek with her, to see if I could escape from her loving devotion, but she always found me.

"I've never had a chicken follow me around before. It's weird," I mumbled.

Olaff was obviously amused. "You saved her life. She loves you."

I turned to look at the plump white bird, who seemed to cluck more excitedly at being acknowledged. I knew that one day it would end up as someone's dinner, but I'd requested that this not happen while I was there. It was just too ridiculous being pursued by a crazy chicken, yet it would've broken my heart to have her presented to me on a plate.

"Olaff and I have decided that we should celebrate our last night here at Maria's. You in?" Jav looked at me expectantly.

"Of course. I'm the one supplying all the cerveza. What would you do without me?" I laughed.

Juan and his family once again agreed to watch our camp for a few soles so we could enjoy the last blast with no worries. Jav and I had made running jokes about Lucas, the aspiring freeloader, and we had decided to nickname him *El Pulpo*--the Octopus--because of the way he had seemed to be all arms and legs when he'd flung me around on the dance floor.

You know how sometimes you make up something that you know is stupid, yet for some reason it just becomes funnier and funnier? You keep laughing for so long that after a while you're not really sure what you're laughing at anymore. This is what happened with El Pulpo. By the time we arrived at Maria's Disco for the last time, El Pulpo had become almost a legendary character, and Javier and I would collapse into gales of laughter as we created more to his story. Olaff would just look at us, not understanding what was so funny since he hadn't yet met the guy. His luck was about to change.

Somehow, I just knew that he would be there—he had to be there—for our final celebration. Lucas did not disappoint, and by the end of the night Olaff would know exactly what we'd gotten so hysterical about because the object of our mirth acted out everything that we'd embellished.

We took our places at the same table we'd sat at before, which although level with the loudspeakers, afforded a good view of the dancefloor and the rest of the club. By now, the DJ knew who we were and greeted the three of us by name over the sound system. But then he added a fourth person to our party even though he wasn't yet present.

"A warm welcome to Judy, Javier, Olaff, and their very good friend, El Pulpito!"

I couldn't believe what I was hearing and looked to Javier for an explanation. That wide smile split his face and he started giggling. Somehow, he had tipped off the DJ without my notice, and I just lost it. The three of us had only just started on our first beers but we were laughing as if we'd already cleaned out the entire cold storage room. I was about to come up with a logical explanation, such as knowing that we were at the end of a very long, successful journey when I saw our fourth companion enter with some friends. I jabbed Olaff in the ribs and he choked on his beer.

"There he is! It's El Pulpito himself!"

This set off another round of laughing as we watched their small group sit down at a table at the side of the dance floor. Lucas looked around and spotted us, then made his way to our table as if we were old friends. We introduced him to Olaff, who by now was desperately trying to hide a smile behind his beer bottle. Lucas was relatively sober at this point but after greeting us he returned back to his friends, who were drinking aguardiente. We saw him take a big slug out of their bottle, then he suddenly leapt onto the dance floor and set about for some crazy, mad dancing.

I took turns dancing with Javier and Olaff, loudly shrieking every time the DJ would announce our names. After a while we noticed our friend had disappeared and were somewhat disappointed at his mild antics after our previous encounters. We need not have been, as the universe gave us a wonderful grand finale.

Sometime after midnight, Lucas suddenly reappeared. His hair was loose and wild and he was absolutely wasted. He made a beeline for our table and gushed all over us as if we were the greatest friends he'd ever had. He'd alternate between wild bouts of dancing and trying to wheedle drinks from us as he had before. Each time, he was directed away from the table by the club staff.

Jav and I got up to dance and we saw him edge into an empty chair at the table next to us. From there, he plopped himself into Javier's chair and started bothering Olaff. When we returned, Jav asked his nephew what had happened.

"He was asking me to dance with him!" Olaff turned a bit red but we all just laughed, and he finally joined in. "Now I see what you mean about him. He's very strange."

It was a fitting night for a celebration. Weak from laughter, we staggered out of Maria's to make the long hike back to camp. As before, there were quite a few men in various stages of inebriation or passed out along the path. Some had collapsed from too much aguardiente and had lain where they'd fallen. Others were groups of men who were trying to help each other get up from the ground. One would help his companion up to standing, only to have the two of them immediately fall over again. Then the other one would attempt to hoist his friend up and down they'd tumble again. I was fascinated and tried not to laugh.

"This is why I love pueblo life," said Jav as he watched me look around. "It's free and anything goes. If you fall down while you're flying, no one will bother you. Let's get going!"

We slept in as much as the noisy jungle would allow. Unlike in many developed areas with electricity, the good folks of the jungle usually awaken before dawn to start their days. Even if you wanted to sleep in, the sounds and the heat would rouse you from your slumber to remind you to get a move on with the day's chores.

As we began to pack up our things, the younger members of Juan's extended family began to drift over and crowd around us.

"Remember, Judita, back in Napo when I told you to watch out for people coming around to see what they might get from you?"

I nodded as he continued.

"If there is anything you want to leave here you can give it to someone, but you don't have to. You might want to save things for the next trip so you don't have to buy them again."

In truth, I really didn't have anything I wanted to leave because most of what I had was my own personal stuff like clothing. And I certainly wasn't about to leave my trusty machete behind! Nope, that was coming home with me.

Javier shooed everyone away, and we continued packing up our camp. As we prepared everything for carriage back to the river, my teacher stopped what he was doing and called for our attention.

"Olaff and I want you to know how much we've enjoyed all this with you. All these adventures have made us really happy, and we are hoping it won't be too long before you are able to come back and continue. Isn't that right?" he looked at his nephew, who nodded.

"We want to tell you something else too. Not one person, especially me, expected you to stay the course. We thought you'd run away screaming like so many others have. In fact," here he looked at Olaff rather sheepishly, "we even placed bets on when you would leave."

I looked back and forth at my two companions, mouth agape in surprise, but only momentarily. A flood of emotions ran through me, such as indignation, but I quickly checked it.

"Well, I guess you all lost your bets, then, didn't you?" They both nodded, and he continued.

"What really surprised us was not just that you kept going with all the insect bites and very obvious discomfort, but that you joined in with us and shared our culture. You not only liked drinking masato, but you also made it for us, and it was really good!"

"And I wanted to say how much I appreciated all the beers," Olaff added. What he didn't say, but what we could all feel, was," because we don't often get the chance to be treated to drinks like that."

"Aw, guys. I guess this is why I survived. I don't mind a good round or two myself, and it's always fun to share it with great companions."

Javier looked serious. "As you've seen here, alcohol is a big part of life in the jungle. It provides a break from the boredom and backbreaking toils of the day."

"There is a lot of jungle to explore," said Olaff. "We'd love to be able to share it with you."

"And El Pulpo!" Jav shrieked suddenly, throwing his pillow in the air.

Laughing together once again, we finished packing up our camp. Juan and Rider helped us carry our things to the beach to see us off. Javier scanned the river and let out an enthusiastic wave.

"Here comes our ride!

"I peered in the direction he'd indicated but there were quite a few craft on the Nanay and I couldn't tell which one he had waved at. A few moments later, the now familiar lines of the *Rey de los Reyes* angled towards where we stood on the beach.

"And look," Olaff nudged me with one of his sweet smiles, "it's your friend!"

Indeed, old Augustin, the grumpy Jivaro that wouldn't look me in the eye, was once again at the helm. As he climbed out of the boat and came towards us, I had this overwhelming urge to run up to him and give him a big hug and a peck on the cheek just to be devilish. Just the thought of actually doing this made me crack up and they all turned to me with questioning looks.

I put up my hand and shook my head. "It's okay, guys. Nothing to worry about. Really!"

Augustin looked at me suspiciously as if he had seen what was going through my mind, then quickly turned back to Javier. The latter nodded to Juan and Rider, who loaded our gear into the small boat.

We said our goodbyes to the two local men who had been a part of our lives for this last stage in my training for this trip. So much went through my head at lightning speed—the chickens, Juan and his three wives, Maria's disco and El Pulpo, and of course, the ceremonies and other work. Was my jungle training about to come to an end now? I felt like I was just getting started!

"Ready, Judita? We've got to get going now," Jav said.

"Yeah. I guess it's time to go."

As the *Rey de los Reyes* putted back towards Iquitos, I turned to watch the beach disappear. This time, it was I who waved at a distant sight.

CHAPTER 24

The Lost Encanto

I had allowed myself some spare time at the end of the trip to transition back to city life. It was hard enough for me to go from the jungle back to Iquitos even for a day or two, and I just couldn't imagine having to summon the energy required to deal with the four airports I had to pass through. Not unlike the integration that should happen after ceremonial work, I felt it was important to process and decompress a bit before I shifted back to the world out *there*.

I felt that my teacher had planned the training stages very well, going from the somewhat remote Jivaro camp to the very remote family pueblo in Rio Napo, then finishing up nearby in a place that still had one foot in the city. If anyone had asked me which location had been my favorite, it would've been a tie between the first two. I absolutely loved living with the Jivaro who'd treated me as one of their own. Rio Napo was magical, both for its remoteness and abundance of fireflies, but also for its ragamuffin children. If I had to be honest, this last phase was my least favorite because it was so close to the city, although I did rather enjoy the silly parts like the upside-down chicken rescue and of course, our *muy bien amigo*, El Pulpo.

"Are you happy to be back in Iquitos?" Julieta asked me once we'd settled back into their house in that noisy city.

"Mixed feelings. I love being out in the wild and being with the people who live there. It's such a different world. But I can't stay there forever. I know I've got to go back to California and apply what I've learned here, although at this time I have no idea how I'm going to do that."

"Ya, Judita," Jav chimed in as he peeled a banana. "Remember in the beginning when I told you that I have to go into *el monte* at times to recharge, and that one day you would understand this? Do you now?"

"I sure do, Javito! Now having spent so much time in nature I can really feel the difference when we go back and forth."

Chucking the banana peel on the floor, he continued. "And this is important. When I used to work in the jungle lodges, the tourists would come and have a great time and many wouldn't want to go back to their countries and homes. They would say, 'Oh Javier, it's so magical to be in ceremony and be in the jungle. I don't want to go back to my boring job or horrible family.' But this is what we do this work for."

I must have looked a little puzzled so he continued. "We work with the plant spirits and other shamanic healing methods so that we can bring the new energy back into our daily lives. We may have wonderful ceremonies but we can't stay in those ceremonies forever. What we want is to bring the energy of the ceremonies out into the world to carry with us."

"I think I see what you mean. As we change our energies through the work we do on ourselves, we can take this higher vibration with us wherever we go."

"Right! So unless you return to your old, destructive habits, the new energy will remain. This is what your family members and coworkers will feel. We have to come out of retreat in order to share the healing with others who can't come to the jungle or wherever. You've seen the people who come here to this house for help. Many are too sick to make the long journey away from their homes. They can't even get on a boat for a short ride. You will find the same things yourself. You must carry the ceremonies with you, even when you're sitting on the plane going home."

As I considered this, he continued. "I know I keep telling you this, but it's important that you really understand that there's way more to being a shaman or *curandero* than just doing medicine ceremonies. Simply doling out plant medicine and singing icaros does not make anyone a healer or whatever term you want to use. If you haven't done the groundwork and welcomed in your spirit helpers, your offerings will be weak and ineffective.

"Ceremonies are only a small part of a greater whole. Sometimes we have to do extractions or bring back parts of the person's soul that has fled for some reason. You came here to open up your own abilities as a healer. You don't have to serve plant medicine to anyone now if you don't want to. Maybe you will walk a different path. The main thing is to do this work on yourself first so the doors will open for communication with the spirits. If you don't have that, how can you heal?"

I took this in and nodded. Although I knew I had a lot more to learn, I also realized how far I'd come, even in just the past year alone. I'd been so broken, so angry, so directionless. Back in Sacha Wasi,

Harold had told me I was strong. Now I could see more easily what he'd seen in me. I'd endured many hardships and fallen on my face many times. There were occasions when I felt that I just could not go on even one minute more. Yet here I was still alive after having been reborn in the jungle. Once again, I felt very humbled and emotional.

Perhaps it was knowing that I was at the end of my life-changing journey that caused me to not feel so annoyed at being back in Iquitos this time. I also noticed that Javier didn't disappear for long periods as he had on our previous returns, so perhaps he too was feeling the clock ticking. We and Olaff decided to wrap up our time together with some fun excursions. The first one was to attend a dance concert featuring two very popular local bands, Kaliente and Grupo Explosión. The latter had a song about ayahuasca that also included tributes to masato and RC and how these things of the jungle could make you crazy. I'd heard it just about everywhere we went in the city, and now we had our chance to see the band itself who'd created this jungle masterpiece. Of course it was very loud and energetic, this cumbia of the *selva*, but we downed a few beers and danced the night away.

We also took a day trip to a local recreation area not far from the Iquitos airport called Zungarococha with the entire family, including Julieta's mother. This lovely place got its name from the zungaro catfish that lived in the *cocha*, or lake. We brought food to make a picnic on the beach and swam in the refreshing water when the heat of the day got to be too intense.

In between the various activities, Jav, Olaff, and I talked about plans for future expeditions. Since we considered ourselves to be a group of intrepid explorers, we decided to give a nod to Grupo Explosión and call ourselves Grupo de Exploración. I came up with the idea of having matching T-shirts made with not only our names on it, but also that of our wildly flailing friend, Lucas the Dancing Octopus. We'd continued to shriek ourselves breathless about our inebriated friend and his antics, so we wanted to have something with which to commemorate our ridiculous interactions with him. I created a simple design of a large dancing octopus holding several glasses of beer and a full pitcher in his tentacles. On the back of the shirt there was a picture of a *lancha* on the river bordered by green leaves and jungle birds with the words Iquitos, Peru, and Rio Napo underneath this. Each of our names was inscribed at the four corners. I still have mine.

"You are going to bring your encanto back with you, aren't you?" Javier asked me as he walked into my little casita. I had packed up all my clothing and was staring at the large stone sitting in its bucket of water.

"Of course I am! I'm just wondering how to take it with me."

"You can just bring it on the plane with you and set it at your feet."

I looked back and forth between my teacher and the encanto. "What about the water?"

"He has to stay in the water. The bucket has a good lid. Just make sure it's on tightly and you won't have any problems."

Sure, no problems. What could possibly go wrong? If anyone asks questions I'll just tell them it's a sacred object. Everything will be just fine.

For the last time, Olaff pulled his family's motocab up to the front of Javier's rustic house on the backstreets of Iquitos. He briefly revved the engine, then the motor faded into silence.

I'd already brought my things from the casita through the yard and main house and set them neatly in the small living room with the concrete floor. My dark turquoise backpack, bought new for this adventure, rested against a white plastic chair as it awaited the final part of this journey. A blue canvas carry-on sat on the chair, and the encanto bucket stood on the floor next to the backpack. All these things I'd carried over the long months, the clothing and bedding washed in the streams and hung on trees to dry, the little souvenirs like the red and black huayuro seed necklaces, and my field notebooks full of recipes and magic and plant information now radiated with a different energy. They, like their owner, had been changed in some way.

Olaff and Javier and I stood briefly in an awkward silence, knowing we'd reached the end of an amazing journey and unsure of when the next one might be. My plan was to return twice yearly and find some kind of work in between to pay for the jaunts. I knew I'd be catching hell from my folks about the need to go get a regular job, but I figured I'd deal with that when the time came. Then, as usual, Jav quickly snapped to attention and broke the mood.

"Ready, Judita?"

"Ya, Jav. I guess I'm as ready as I'll ever be."

Julieta came forward to give me a hug and express her wish that I'd soon return. Some of the neighborhood kids who'd I'd befriended ran in for their own hugs and then ran back out again. They would only be returning a few steps to their way of life whereas I would be returning to another world that now seemed alien to me.

Jav and I climbed into the back of the moto after he and Olaff strapped my bags onto its rear rack and then tied them securely with rope. The young biologist mounted the driver's seat and revved the engine, then he turned the motocab around on the unpaved street. We were on our way to the small Iquitos International Airport.

I checked my pack through to Lima and showed the ticket agent the *encanto* that I'd planned to bring on the plane with me. He looked at the large stone in the bucket of water for a moment.

"I think it'd be better if we encase this in plastic and put it into a box for the flight. Let me see what we can find."

It didn't take him long to find a small square box that looked like it was just made for the bucket and its special guest. I'd seen the plastic wrapping services in the Lima airport, where they were frequently used to encase suitcases. If you can imagine a typical roll of kitchen cellophane that is pulled out of a rectangular box and cut off to cover food containers, then blow that up on a grand scale and turn it into a machine, you'll have the general idea.

"First we'll seal the bucket in plastic wrap, then we'll put it into the box and wrap that in plastic as well to make it more secure for the journey."

I felt a sense a relief at knowing I would be able to take my precious healing stone with me after all. It was time for me to go. Turning to look at my jungle brothers for the last time, I felt my throat get thick and my eyes tear up. Something unsaid passed between the three of us and we were reluctant to break the spell.

"Okay, Judita. Don't miss your flight. We'll be in touch soon," said Jav as we went for one last round of hugs.

I walked into the security line and paused briefly before going through the door to look back. My companions were already gone. I was now on my own.

It didn't take long for my unusual cargo to attract attention. Although the ticketing agent hadn't seen any problem with my carrying a large rock in a bucket filled with water onto a plane, the crew at the security screening section had other ideas. Once the box had passed through the scanner, one of the female agents cut through all the layers of plastic wrap that I had just paid to have done at the check in counter. She lifted out the bucket and held it up so her fellow agents could examine it. I was still using the same bucket that I'd originally bought for the encanto at the start of my training. It was clear plastic with an orange lid, so the contents could easily be seen through the sides.

"What is this?" she asked.

I explained that it was an *encanto*, a sacred object used for healing, and that my teacher had given it to me as part of my training. Since we were still in the jungle town of Iquitos, the airport employees were all locals and probably were at least somewhat familiar with the area's traditional medicine and some of the tools used by the *curanderos*. After a quick consultation, they decided it was acceptable for me to carry my package on the plane. The first female agent then attempted to use the now cut cellophane to rewrap the bucket and box. Needless to say, what had been a careful and neat job now looked like a complete mess and a good deal more suspicious.

Nevertheless, I made it onto the plane and placed the now ragged box at my feet. I settled into my seat and watched the plane fill with people heading for Lima. Most of the other passengers looked to be Peruvians, and they carried their own versions of funny looking packages. Some were stuffed into overhead bins, while others were wrestled down the aisle and shoved onto floors between seats. Perhaps my *encanto* hadn't been the strangest thing the airport screeners had seen after all.

Flights from Lima to the United States usually leave quite late at night—generally anywhere from around 11:30 pm to 2 am. Since I had a gap in my itinerary of about eight hours before I had to check in for my international flight, I'd arranged to visit some new friends in Lima.

Esteban and Lupe lived in the Miraflores area of Lima and had a small import/export business. Esteban's father, Mario, owned a combination shop and travel agency in my city. I had discovered this small business before my first trip back in January and returned to buy bottles of *chicha morada*, the popular purple corn drink I'd fallen in love with in the Andes. Since these were the days before the internet allowed travelers to easily make their own arrangements, I had booked my airline tickets for this trip from him.

Being a family run business, Mario had encouraged me to contact his son and daughter-in-law if I had spare time in Lima. I figured it'd be more fun to meet some nice people instead of hanging out by myself for many hours, so they arranged to pick me up from the airport. They'd take me back to their house to rest, we could get some lunch, and then they'd return me to the airport for my late flight home. Sounded good to me!

I liked Lupe and Esteban on sight. I found them to be *muy simpático*, very likable. After living in my simple open casita with the straw mattress to sleep on and no hot water, never mind the jungle locations, it was quite nice to have some clean luxury again.

"So, Papa tells us that you are here to be a shaman, is that right?" asked Esteban when we were settled on some very comfortable printed couches in their living room.

I winced at the word shaman, which I wasn't sure I'd ever want to use to describe myself. Javier had used it occasionally, although he made it clear it wasn't a word that came from the jungle. He'd used it in more of a general way at times but not to describe himself. I'd cringed because I felt this term had become overused and abused. Too many people used it in a boastful way, and I'd find myself rolling my eyes when I'd hear yet another person decked out in feathers and crystals proclaim themselves to be a shaman.

"*Curandera*, yes," I replied, hoping to redirect them to the word for healer that was more commonly used in the jungle and that I preferred. I gave them a condensed version of how I'd met my teacher and our ensuing adventures in the jungle.

"You really lived in the jungle? With all those snakes and bugs? Weren't you afraid?" Lupe's eyes were wide.

"Not really. More afraid of being chewed to death from the bugs though. For me, that really was the worst part. I was well taken care of so I knew that I'd be alright."

They were also curious about my now badly wrapped box, so I explained about what the *encanto* was, why I had it, and how to use it.

"So you will use it in your work when you return?" asked Lupe.

"Yes, as appropriate. I've grown quite attached to it after carrying him absolutely everywhere for all these months."

I explained briefly how I'd been shown to use the large stone to take away negative energy by running it down the body so that it would pick up the psychic dross, kind of like a shamanic vacuum cleaner.

I really appreciated being able to talk about these somewhat esoterical things with people who not only were interested in some of their own country's practices, but who also exuded a lot of respect for their fellow countrymen and women who engaged in them. I also explained about the wrapping palaver, so we taped things up as best we could.

The hours passed quickly and soon we were on our way back to the Jorge Chavez airport. I was glad I had had the opportunity to get to know them and share my new passion, and I was now ready to move on.

"*Buena suerte!* Good luck!" they both said as we hugged each other at the entrance to the check in area.

Hey, I'd been lucky so far. What could possibly go wrong on this last part of my journey?

Entering the ground floor of the Lima airport, I headed for the check in desk for my airline. I was glad to hand over the backpack and lighten my load a bit. I indicated the box and carry-on bag to the agent and was relieved that there were no questions. In hindsight, it would have been a lot better if I had been queried about the box's contents.

After receiving my boarding pass I headed upstairs to pass through security before arriving at my departure gate. The Lima airport directs passengers on domestic flights to the right hand screening area, while those for international go through a more stringent inspection on the left side. My purse and carry-on bag passed through the scanning machine without a hitch, but when I put the box containing the *encanto* through, suddenly everyone was on high alert.

A female agent took the box and asked me what was in it. Once again, I explained that it was a sacred healing object.

"We need to look at this!"

"Sure. Of course." Having already passed successfully through the Iquitos airport with my precious package, I felt confident that I'd soon be on my way with it once again.

Where the screener in Iquitos had seemed to handle opening the box more delicately, the one in Lima tore into the wrappings as if she thought it was a bomb that needed to be defused within ten seconds. The transparent bucket containing my large *encanto* stone sitting in its water was set on the counter. Several more screening agents came over to take a look and I had a sudden flashback to my arrival at Heathrow Airport many years before.

One large, intimidating looking man intoned, "You cannot take this on the plane!"

"Why not? I brought it from Iquitos in the cabin."

"It is a dangerous weapon. You will have to leave it here!"

"Absolutely not! This is in no way a weapon! It's used for healing and it has to come home with me. It's one of my tools! I argued.

"You may say this, but it is against international regulations to allow such objects on board that could be used as a weapon. This is a large, heavy stone and could be used to knock someone out!"

I was briefly stunned and thought someone had tried to knock *me* out! Okay, naïve and stunned. It had never occurred to me that a very large rock could be used to conk someone on the head during a flight. It just wasn't in my mindset. You know the phrase where someone talks about seeing their life passing before their eyes? In a flash, I saw Javier present me with the stone, and every step I'd taken with it for the past months. And now it was in danger of being confiscated. I was ready to fight!

"What will happen to it?"

"We will take it out of the bucket and just throw it outside somewhere. It has no value," the male agent said, glowering at me.

My head spun. For my sacred rock to be so dishonored as to be chucked out in some back alley like trash was just not acceptable. I realized that I was not going to be able to take it on the plane with me, so I tried another tack.

"Can I have a receipt for it? I'll get someone to pick it up."

"No. We only issue receipts for items of value. This rock has no value."

At this point, I was beside myself and not caring if they hauled me off for creating a disturbance.

"Who else can I speak to about this?"

"Well, you can ask the folks at your airline departure gate and see if they'll grant you an exception. But we'll have to hold the item here."

"Fine. I'll be back!" I charged through the airport to my boarding gate and once again pleaded my case. Without even seeing the item, the gate agents shook their heads.

"We cannot allow an object that can potentially be used as a weapon on the plane. It's airport policy."

"But what if I gave it to you all sealed to be kept in a secure area? After all, sometimes you do this with items like musical instruments."

"I'm sorry. We have our rules."

Rules, schmules! I ran back to the screening area and waited patiently while the agents finished a round of scanning. They already knew the answer before I told them about the gate agents' refusal.

"Okay, I will have to leave the stone with you. But I demand to have a receipt and some kind of paperwork because I'm going to call someone to come get my package."

By now, the male agent I'd nicknamed Mr. No was sick of me and pointed out his supervisor, who'd been watching the proceedings a short distance away. I stomped over to the man and once again asked for paperwork. He shook his head and reiterated that receipts were not issued for items with no value.

"Well I'm not getting on my flight without one!" I declared firmly with my hands on my hips.

We locked eyes and I realized that I might be very close to being detained, but at this point I didn't care. He rolled his eyes and called over a junior agent. I handed over my rock in the bucket to her, and they insisted on dumping out the water.

"Come with me and I'll write you up a receipt for this, um, thing," she said.

I carefully inspected the paperwork I was given to make sure there were no surprises hidden in the print.

"Where will this be held?" I wanted to know.

"We'll keep it in a secure area. Someone will come for it?" she asked with obvious disbelief. After all, who would waste time driving to the airport to pick up a rock?"

"Yes, I have friends here in Lima. I'm going to contact them and send them a copy of this receipt so they can get it for me."

"Why didn't you pack it in your checked bag?"

"I should have. It just never occurred to me that a sacred healing tool could be used as an act of violence. Believe me, I've learned quite a lesson from this!"

For just a moment I thought I detected a look of pity in her eyes. I knew that the security agents were just doing their job. They probably had to deal with all sorts of situations like this daily, but very likely not one where someone was so attached to a plain looking grey stone.

I thanked the agent and made my way back to the departure gate and plopped down in a chair. I saw the gate attendants eye me, looking for possible signs of trouble. I smiled at them and held up my lone carry on and purse, indicating that I no longer had the object of such disruption.

Although it was late, I tried to call Esteban. It hadn't been that long since they'd dropped me off and I hoped that they might still be up. Despite several tries, no one answered, so I left a message about what had happened, saying that I'd be in touch once I got back home. There was nothing more I could do.

As my flight was called, I duly lined up with the other passengers. Taking one last look down the airport hall, I wondered where my precious *encanto* was. I felt that given my naivety about trying to bring such an object on an international flight, I had done all I could to ensure that we'd be reunited at some point.

I handed my boarding card to the agent and passed onto the jet bridge. It was my final act of faith.

To be continued.

Javier (L), Olaff (R) and me holding a picture of El Pulpo.

GLOSSARY

Agua florida   "Flowery water" is a very popular, commercially made cologne used frequently in Latin American shamanism for clearing negative energies.

Aguardiente   A clear alcoholic beverage made from sugar cane, water, and flavorings such as anise. The alcohol proof is roughly the strength of a brandy at 30%, although this can vary upwards. Each region has its own aguardiente recipes, so the drink I refer to in this book is made locally in the Peruvian Amazon. The name is often translated as fire water. Agua (water) + ardiente (burning)

Artes   A shaman's power objects, most commonly seen in the mesa norteña traditions that work with San Pedro. During the ceremony, these *artes* come to life and can act as portals for the spirits. Artes can include parts of plants, stones, statues, swords or other objects used in the ceremony.

Bien   Good. *Muy bien*, very good

Brujo (male) / Bruja (female)   A person who uses negative energy and black magic to hex people.

Casita   The diminutive form of *casa*, house. A little house.

Concentrado   A strong extract of coffee made by boiling water and ground coffee (and sometimes sugar) and then leaving it on the stove for a day. It is served with hot water so the drinker can dilute it to their own taste.

Contrachisa   A potion made of the outer skin of the San Pedro cactus (Trichocereus pachanoi). It is the first of three medicines consumed in a San Pedro ceremony. Its purpose is to clear out negative spiritual energies so the healing ceremony will be more effective.

Cortezas	Tree barks. A small amount is cut from the tree and made into a medicine by decoction.
Cumbia	An energetic style of music that is very popular in the jungle, although it can be found elsewhere in Peru and Colombia. Most local parties and bars seem to have this music playing loudly so everyone can drink and dance with abandon.
Curandero / Curandera	Usually said to be the opposite of the *brujo*, so a curandero/a works with positive energy and divine spirits to heal.
Cuy	Quechua term for guinea pig, a popular dish in the Andes where they are raised as food.
Dieta	1. A period of cleansing made before an ayahuasca ceremony where the participant removes certain things from their usual diet and lifestyle such as alcohol, red meat, physical stimulation, etc. 2. A much more restricted *dieta* is also undertaken with chosen plants for healing purposes or to gain that plant's spirit as an ally.
Enamorado / enamorada	Lover, beloved
Icarock	This is a term that I made up. It consists of icaro + rock. It refers to the energy present in a rock concert that takes the listener out of space and time. Strong plant medicine ceremonies, especially those with music, can also take the participant into non-ordinary reality. To *icarock* is to be in a ceremony where icaros are being sung and the participant feels a state of bliss and high energy.
Icaros	Sacred songs that direct the energies within a ceremony. These may initially be transmitted from teacher to student, but as the apprentice gains knowledge, they are expected to receive their own icaros from the plant spirits.

Lancha	A large riverboat designed for traveling long distances.
Maloca	An open ceremonial structure, typically round and open on the sides.
Masato	A light beer made by fermenting cooked yucca roots. It is most commonly made by women, and they help to start off the fermentation process by placing small portions of the yucca in their mouths to mix with saliva, then they return the treated mash to the pot.
Monte	*El monte* can have several meanings, such as mountain or hill, but in this book it refers to wild or undeveloped land, such as what one would find in the jungle.
Preparado	*Preparados* are generally made with a base of aguardiente or other white spirit infused with many roots, barks and other ingredients according to their purpose. *Preparados* can be made for a variety of purposes, such as a simple medicine. They are commonly encountered as aphrodisiacs with suggestive names, or as pusangas (see below).
Pucuna/virote	Both terms refer to darts. The pucuna is a physical world dart that is used in hunting, often dipped in some kind of poison. A virote is a spirit dart thrown by someone who wants to hex or kill another.
Pusanga	A special kind of *preparado* which is made to attract a specific thing such as money or a lover. These very fragrant concoctions are meant to be rubbed all over the body while the user concentrates on the desired outcome.
Selva	Jungle
Shacapa	The leaf rattle used by many jungle shamans in ayahuasca ceremonies. Its primary use is as a rhythmic accompaniment to the icaros. It can also be used to cleanse a person's energy field

	and direct energies away from the ceremonial space.
Shaman	A person who goes into alternative realities to confer with their helping spirits for healing purposes.
Singado	A potion made with a base of aguardiente, (see above) a sweetener like honey, and the smushed up leaves of local tobacco. It is then strained and snorted into individual nostrils during a San Pedro ceremony.
Tambo	A simple dieting hut that consists of a wood platform raised several feet off the ground, covered with a roof of woven leaves. A bed with a mosquito net, a hammock, and a small table form the basic furniture. More elaborate structures enclosed with walls are referred to as *casitas* (see above), although it's common to use these two terms interchangeably.

ABOUT THE AUTHOR

Judy Lemon's early fascination with all things otherworldly led her into the multidimensional universes of shamanism. A profound shapeshifting experience convinced her that she'd found her life's work.

Judy has studied and apprenticed with indigenous and other master teachers in Europe, the United States and throughout Latin America for over twenty years. She was initiated into the lineage of the *curanderos* of Rio Napo, Peru through her first jungle teacher. Later apprenticeships with other *maestros* took her deeper into the healer's world of plant spirit shamanism.

Judy is a shamanic practitioner, teacher, writer, musician, and Somatic Experiencing© trauma therapist (SEP) who brings years of comprehensive training and knowledge into her work.

She has contributed stories based on some of her magical experiences to four anthologies published by Sacred Stories Publishing: *Crappy to Happy; Mayhem to Miracles; Animals,* with Dr. Steven Farmer; and *Shamanism,* with Oscar Miro-Quesada.

www.ingramcontent.com/pod-product-compliance
Lightning Source LLC
Chambersburg PA
CBHW060853120626
46553CB00001B/68